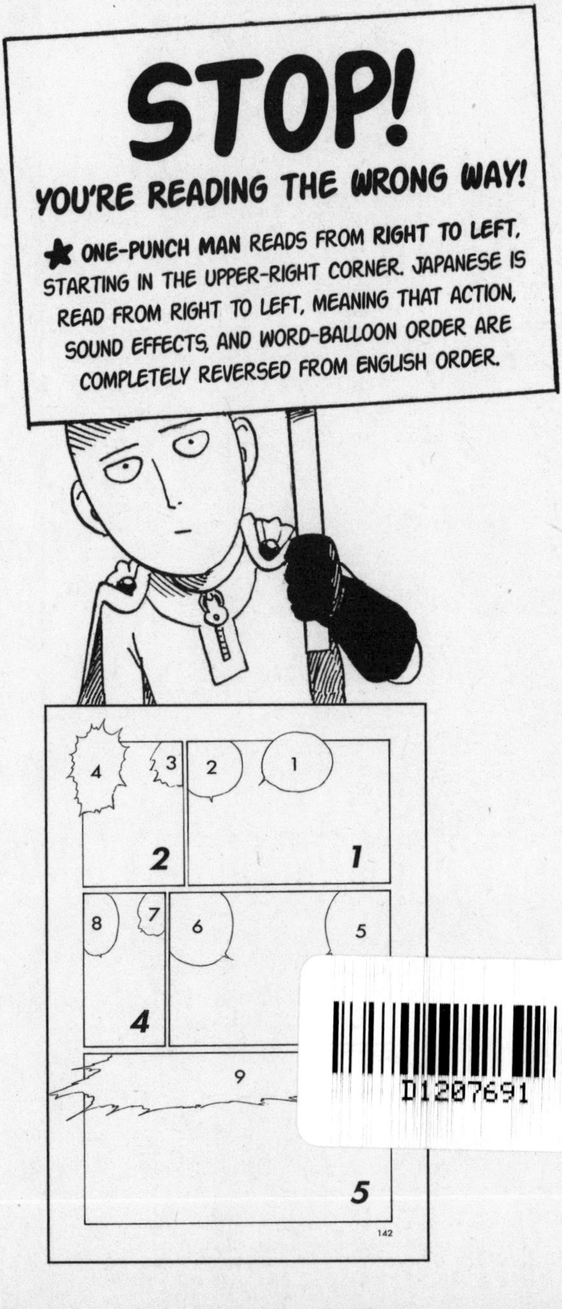
STOP!
YOU'RE READING THE WRONG WAY!
ONE-PUNCH MAN READS FROM RIGHT TO LEFT, STARTING IN THE UPPER-RIGHT CORNER. JAPANESE IS READ FROM RIGHT TO LEFT, MEANING THAT ACTION, SOUND EFFECTS, AND WORD-BALLOON ORDER ARE COMPLETELY REVERSED FROM ENGLISH ORDER.

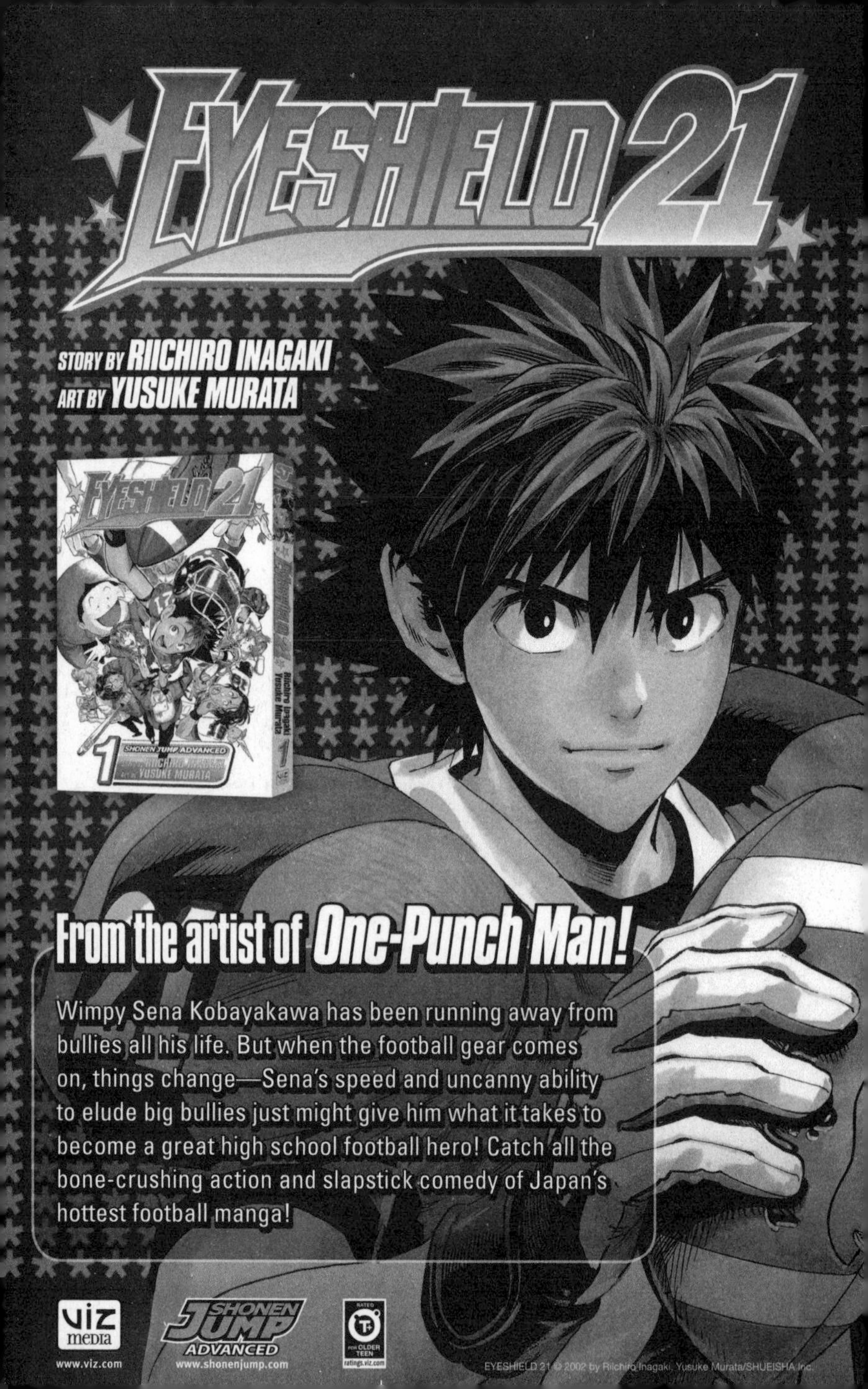
EYESHIELD 21
STORY BY RIICHIRO INAGAKI
ART BY YUSUKE MURATA
From the artist of One-Punch Man!
Wimpy Sena Kobayakawa has been running away from bullies all his life. But when the football gear comes on, things change—Sena's speed and uncanny ability to elude big bullies just might give him what it takes to become a great high school football hero! Catch all the bone-crushing action and slapstick comedy of Japan's hottest football manga!
viz media
www.viz.com
SHONEN JUMP ADVANCED
www.shonenjump.com
RATED T+ FOR OLDER TEEN
ratings.viz.com
EYESHIELD 21 © 2002 by Riichiro Inagaki, Yusuke Murata/SHUEISHA Inc.

ASTRA
LOST IN SPACE

CAN EIGHT TEENAGERS FIND THEIR WAY HOME FROM 5,000 LIGHT-YEARS AWAY?

It's the year 2063, and interstellar space travel has become the norm. Eight students from Caird High School and one child set out on a routine planet camp excursion. While there, the students are mysteriously transported 5,000 light-years away to the middle of nowhere! Will they ever make it back home?!

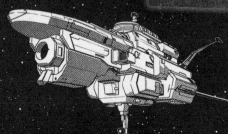

Black ✦ Clover

STORY & ART BY YŪKI TABATA

Asta is a young boy who dreams of becoming the greatest mage in the kingdom. Only one problem—he can't use any magic! Luckily for Asta, he receives the incredibly rare five-leaf clover grimoire that gives him the power of anti-magic. Can someone who can't use magic really become the Wizard King? One thing's for sure—Asta will never give up!

SHONEN JUMP

VIZ media
www.viz.com

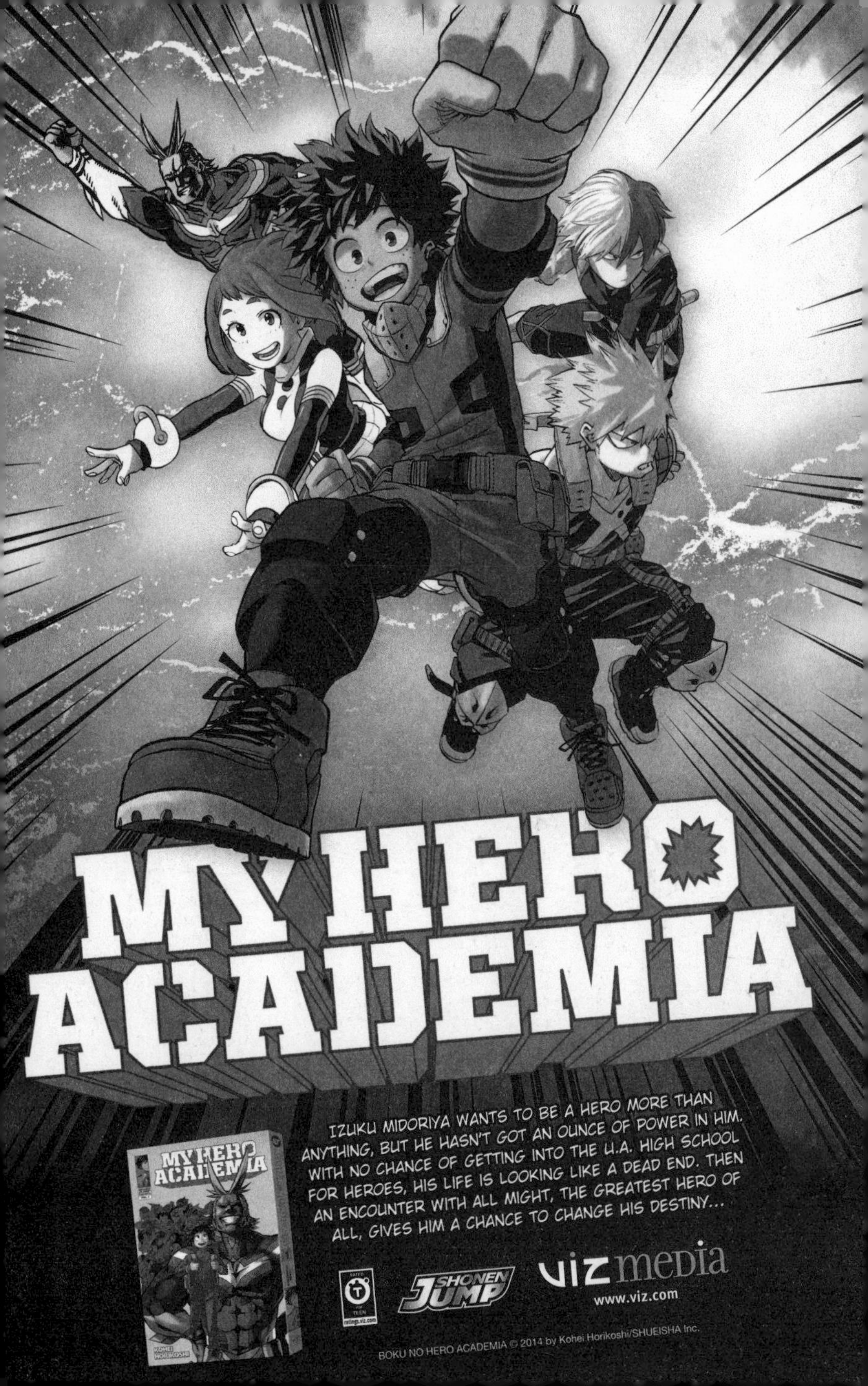
MY HERO ACADEMIA
IZUKU MIDORIYA WANTS TO BE A HERO MORE THAN ANYTHING, BUT HE HASN'T GOT AN OUNCE OF POWER IN HIM. WITH NO CHANCE OF GETTING INTO THE U.A. HIGH SCHOOL FOR HEROES, HIS LIFE IS LOOKING LIKE A DEAD END. THEN AN ENCOUNTER WITH ALL MIGHT, THE GREATEST HERO OF ALL, GIVES HIM A CHANCE TO CHANGE HIS DESTINY...
MY HERO ACADEMIA
KOHEI HORIKOSHI
RATED T TEEN
ratings.viz.com
SHONEN JUMP
viz media
www.viz.com
BOKU NO HERO ACADEMIA © 2014 by Kohei Horikoshi/SHUEISHA Inc.

DEMON SLAYER
KIMETSU NO YAIBA

Story and Art by
KOYOHARU GOTOUGE

In Taisho-era Japan, kindhearted Tanjiro Kamado makes a living selling charcoal. But his peaceful life is shattered when a demon slaughters his entire family. His little sister Nezuko is the only survivor, but she has been transformed into a demon herself! Tanjiro sets out on a dangerous journey to find a way to return his sister to normal and destroy the demon who ruined his life.

VIZ

ONE-PUNCH MAN
VOLUME 17
SHONEN JUMP MANGA EDITION

STORY BY | ONE
ART BY | YUSUKE MURATA

TRANSLATION | JOHN WERRY
TOUCH-UP ART AND LETTERING | JAMES GAUBATZ
DESIGN | SHAWN CARRICO
SHONEN JUMP SERIES EDITOR | JOHN BAE
GRAPHIC NOVEL EDITOR | JENNIFER LEBLANC

ONE-PUNCH MAN © 2012 by ONE, Yusuke Murata
All rights reserved.
First published in Japan in 2012 by SHUEISHA Inc., Tokyo.
English translation rights arranged by SHUEISHA Inc.

Printed in the U.S.A.

Published by VIZ Media, LLC
P.O. Box 77010
San Francisco, CA 94107

10 9 8 7 6 5 4 3 2 1
First printing, August 2019

VIZ MEDIA
viz.com

SHONEN JUMP
shonenjump.com

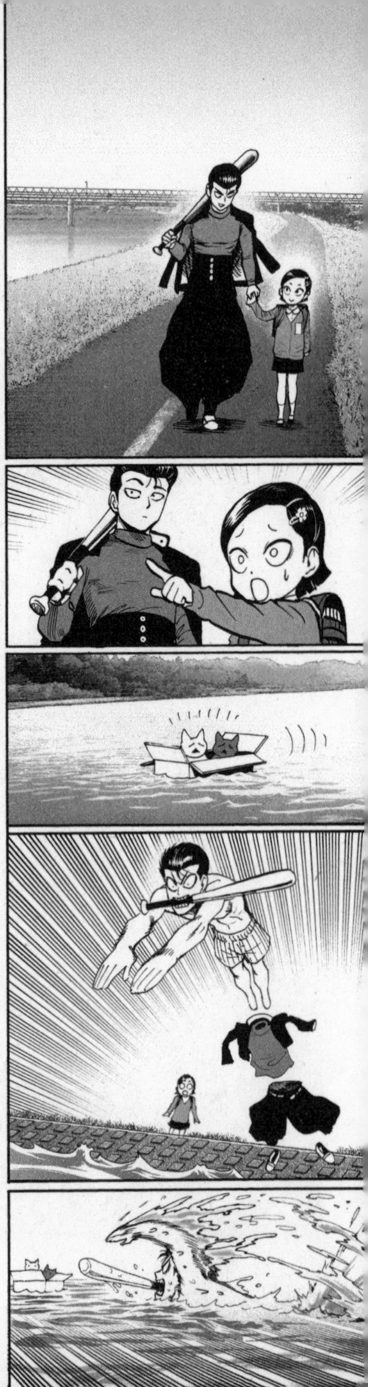

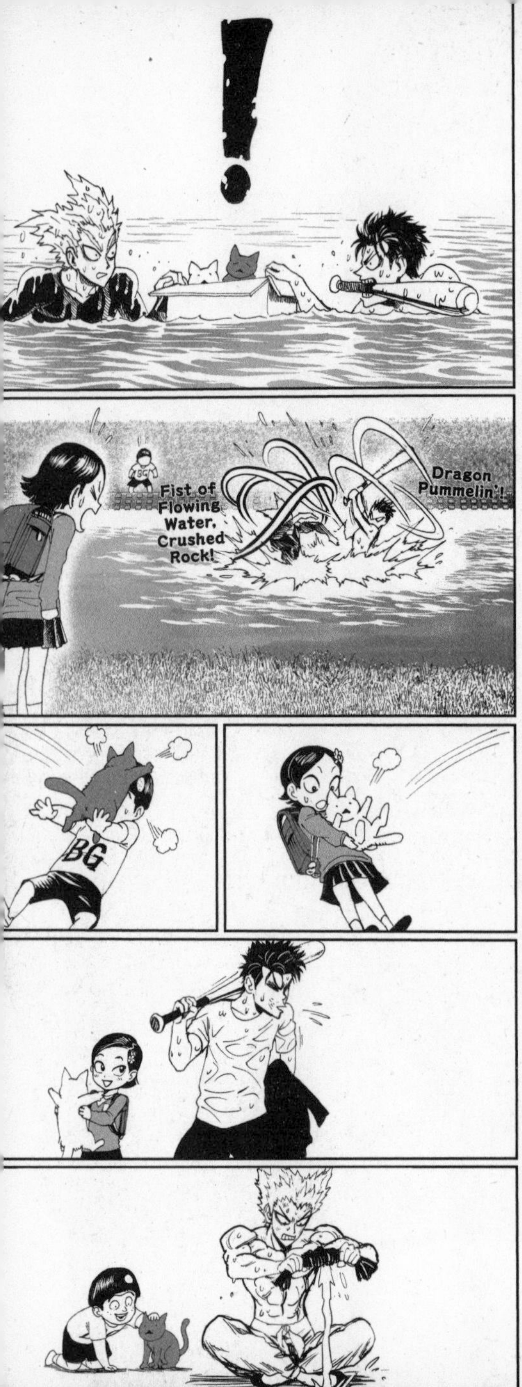
!
Dragon Pummelin'!
Fist of Flowing Water, Crushed Rock!

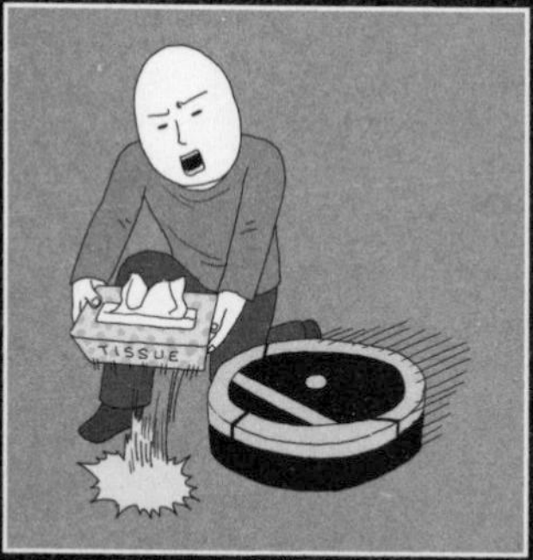
TISSUE

ONE

I bought a vacuum cleaner that moves around cleaning by itself. It's cute. Like a pet.

—ONE

Manga creator ONE began *One-Punch Man* as a webcomic, which quickly went viral, garnering over 10 million hits. In addition to *One-Punch Man*, ONE writes and draws the series *Mob Psycho 100* and *Makai no Ossan*.

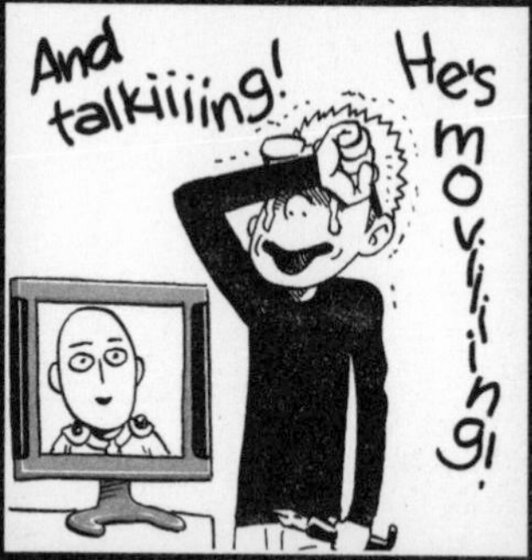
He's moviiiiing!
And talkiiiing!

YUSUKE MURATA

One-Punch Man is becoming a TV anime! I'm thankful to everyone who made it happen and looking forward to seeing it completed. When I watch it, I'm definitely going to weep!

—Yusuke Murata

A highly decorated and skilled artist best known for his work on *Eyeshield 21*, Yusuke Murata won the 122nd Hop Step Award (1995) for *Partner* and placed second in the 51st Akatsuka Award (1998) for *Samui Hanashi*.

ONE-PUNCH MAN 09

ONE + YUSUKE MURATA

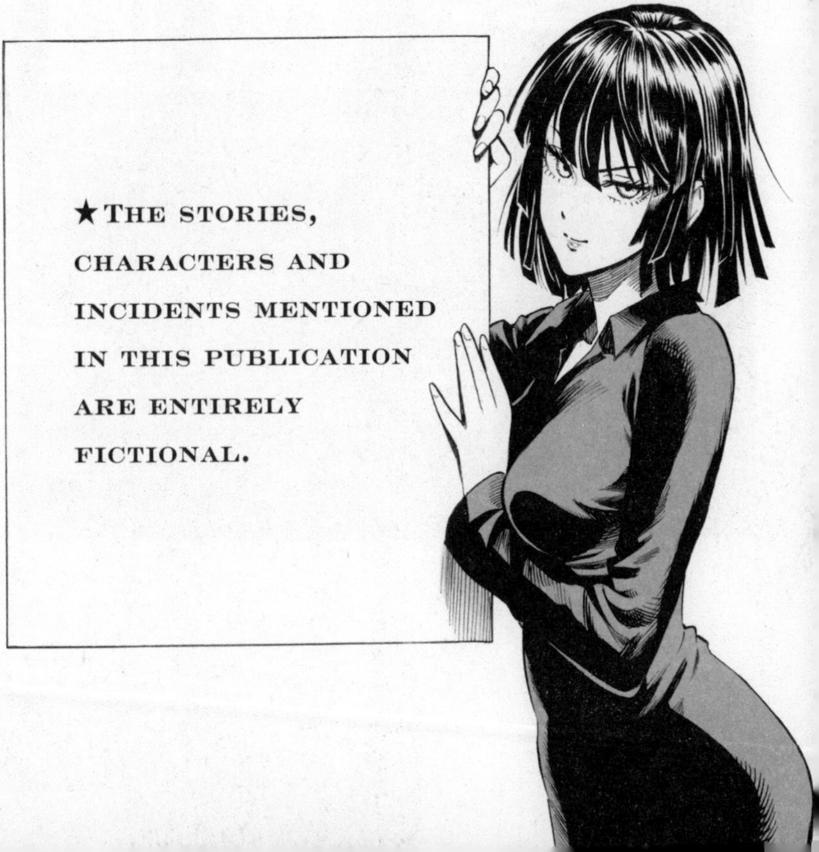
★THE STORIES, CHARACTERS AND INCIDENTS MENTIONED IN THIS PUBLICATION ARE ENTIRELY FICTIONAL.

17 ONE-PUNCH MAN

BECAUSE I'M THE BALD CAPE?

STORY BY
ONE
ART BY
YUSUKE MURATA

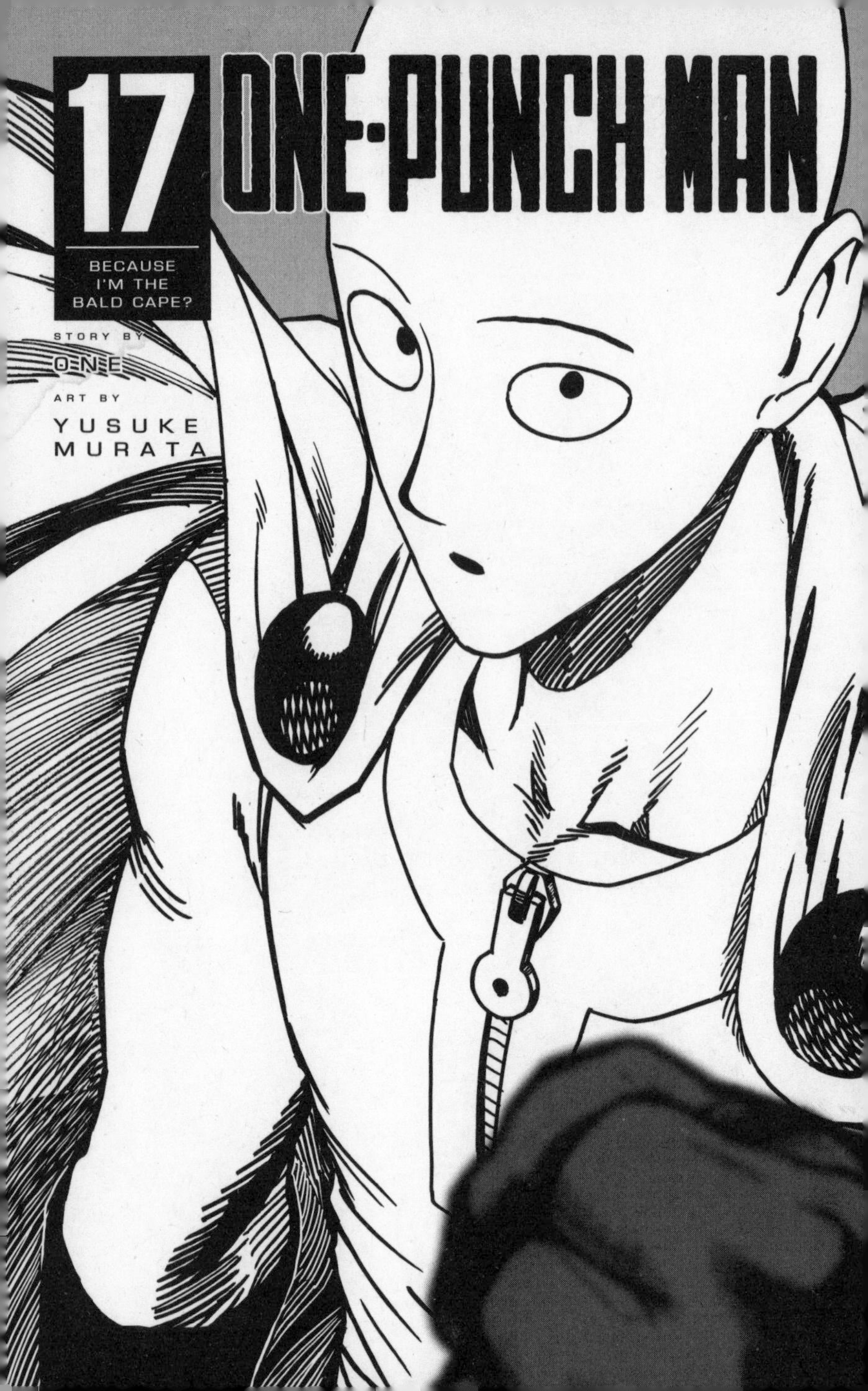

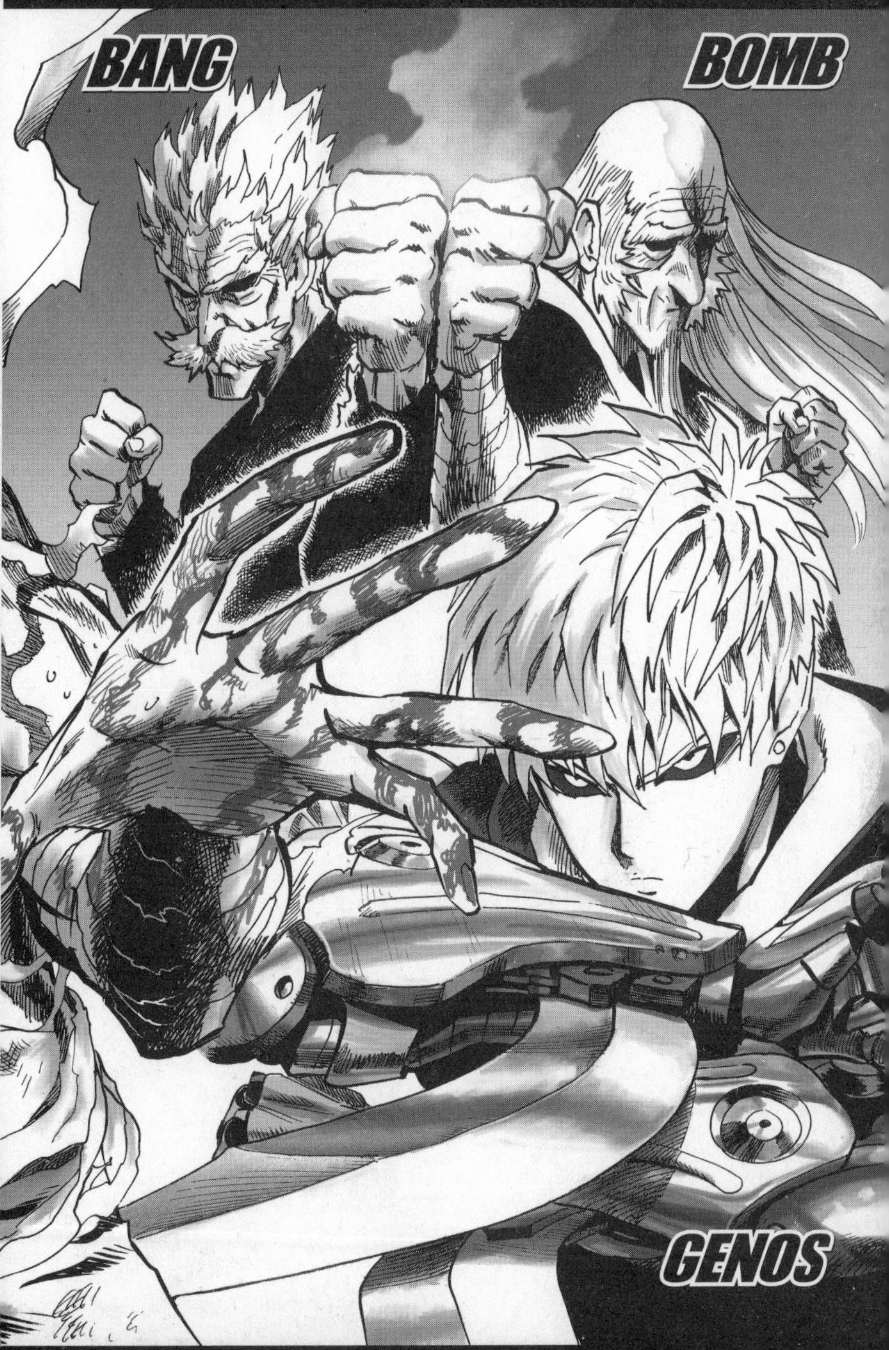
BANG
BOMB
GENOS

CHARACTE[redacted]

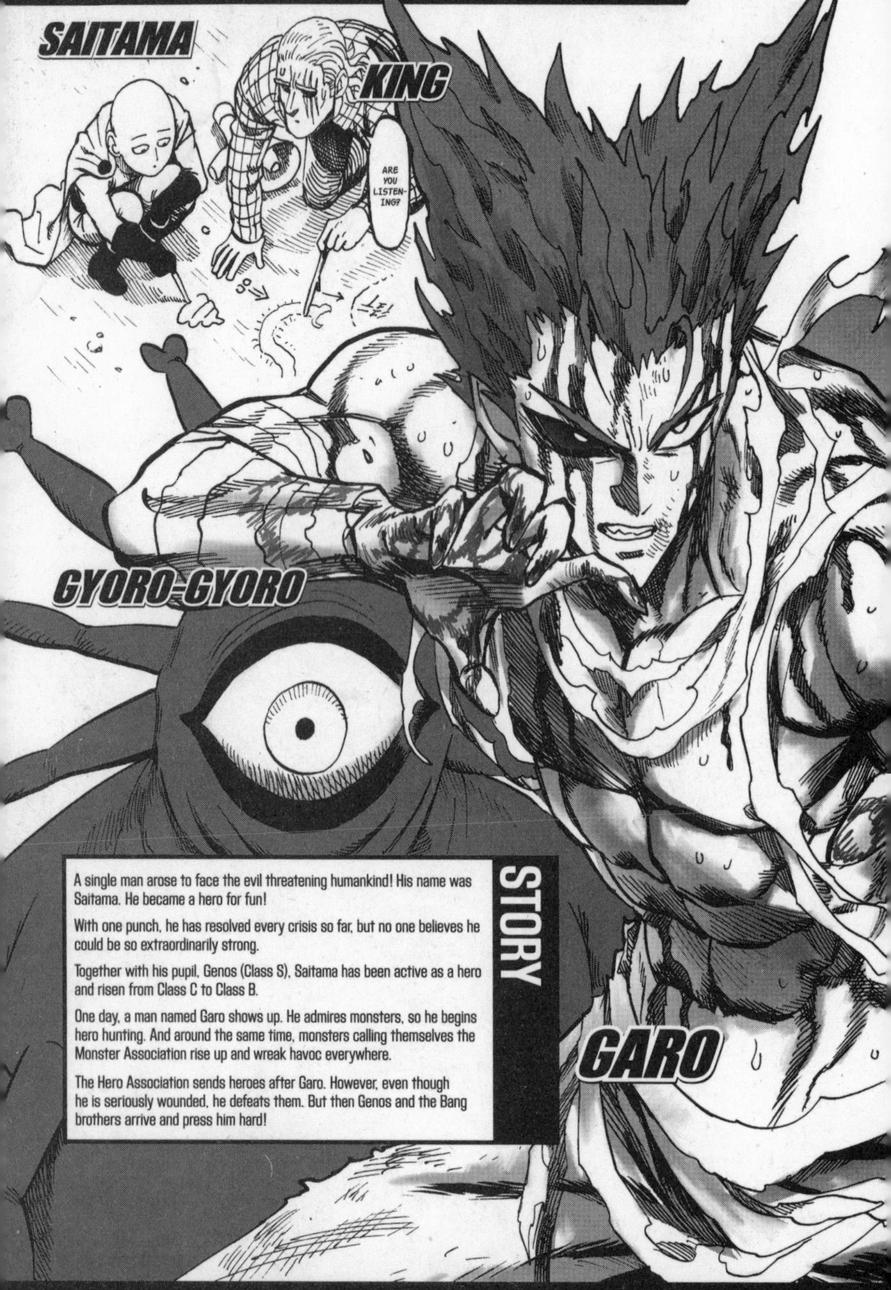
SAITAMA
KING
ARE YOU LISTEN-ING?
GYORO-GYORO
GARO

STORY

A single man arose to face the evil threatening humankind! His name was Saitama. He became a hero for fun!

With one punch, he has resolved every crisis so far, but no one believes he could be so extraordinarily strong.

Together with his pupil, Genos (Class S), Saitama has been active as a hero and risen from Class C to Class B.

One day, a man named Garo shows up. He admires monsters, so he begins hero hunting. And around the same time, monsters calling themselves the Monster Association rise up and wreak havoc everywhere.

The Hero Association sends heroes after Garo. However, even though he is seriously wounded, he defeats them. But then Genos and the Bang brothers arrive and press him hard!

CONTENTS

ONE-PUNCH MAN VOLUME SEVENTEEN

17

ONE-PUNCH M

ONE + YUS

My name is Saitama. I am a h
strong. And that makes me sa
lost my hair. And I lost all feeling of battle. I wo
like to meet an incredibly strong enemy. And I would like to defeat it wi
one blow. That's because I am One-Punch Man.

[BECAUSE I'M THE BALD CAPE?]

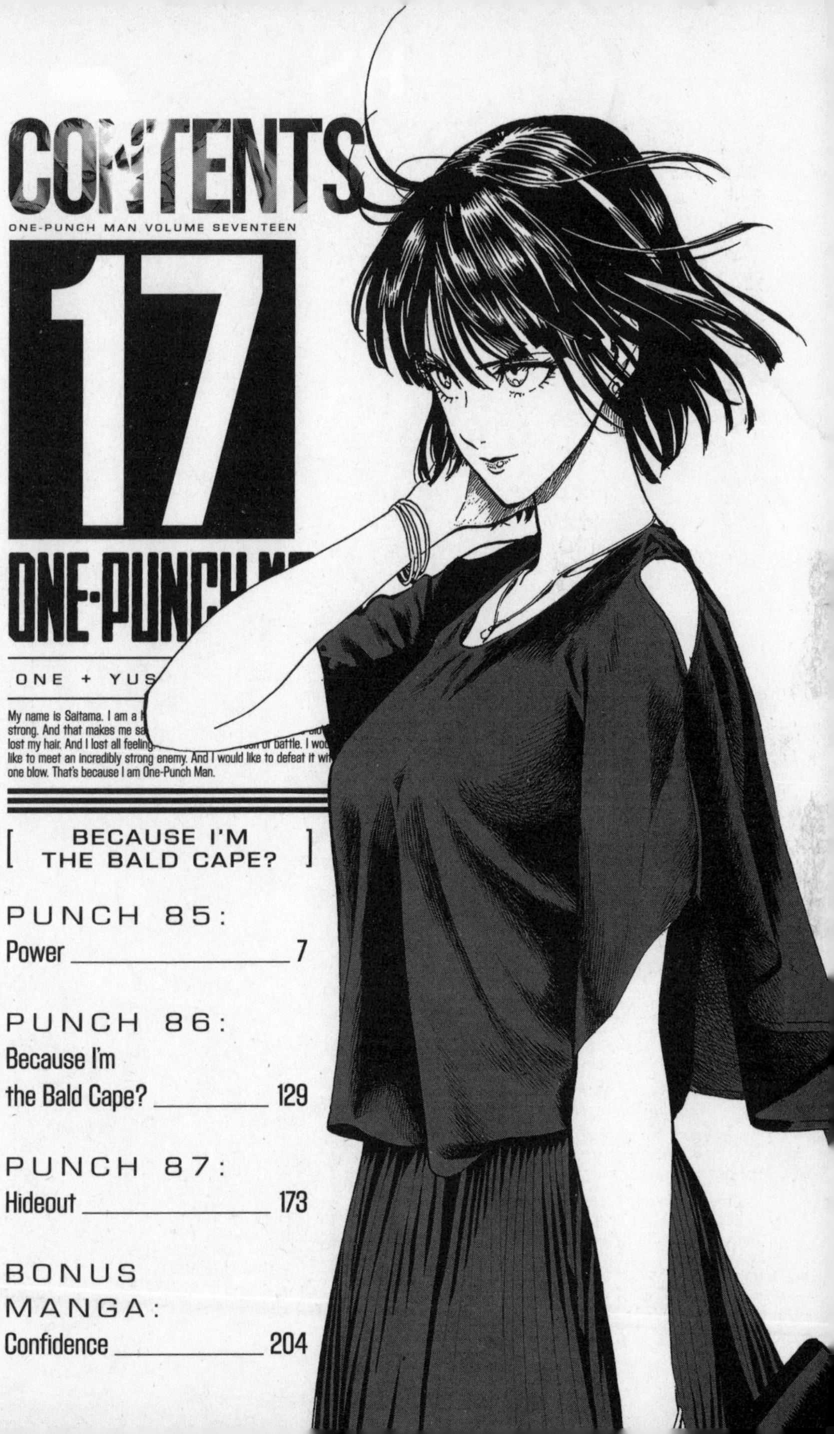

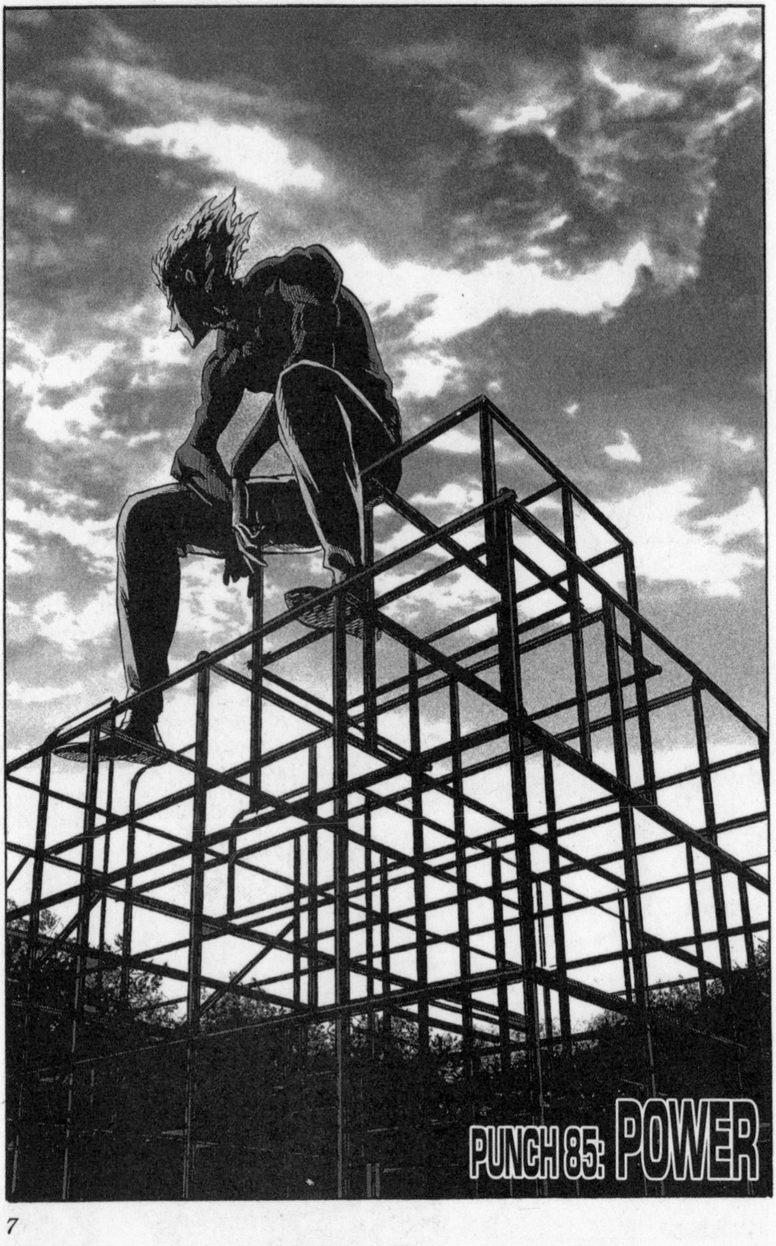
PUNCH 85: POWER

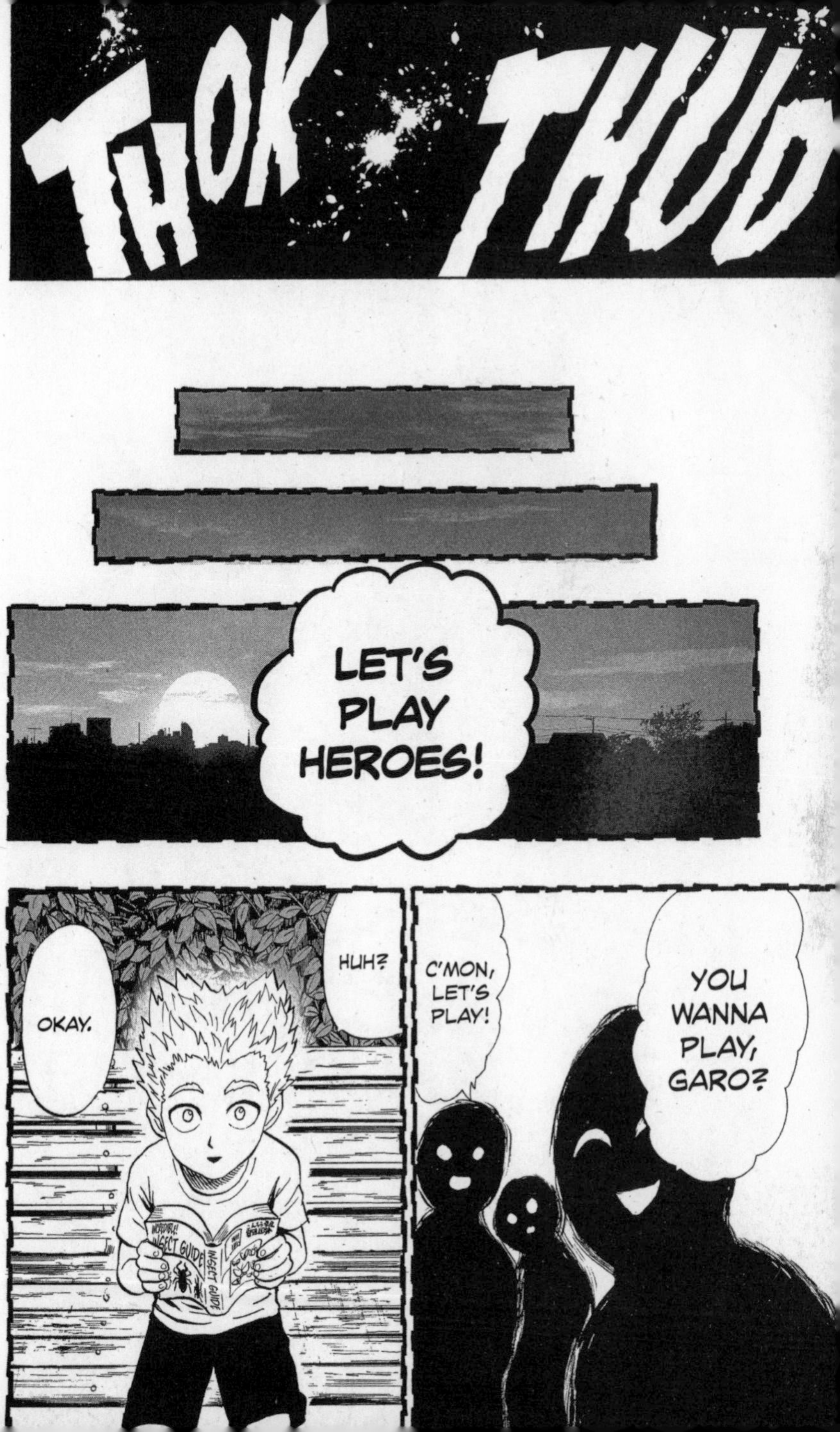
THUD
THOK
LET'S PLAY HEROES!
YOU WANNA PLAY, GARO?
C'MON, LET'S PLAY!
HUH?
OKAY.
INCREDIBLE! INSECT GUIDE

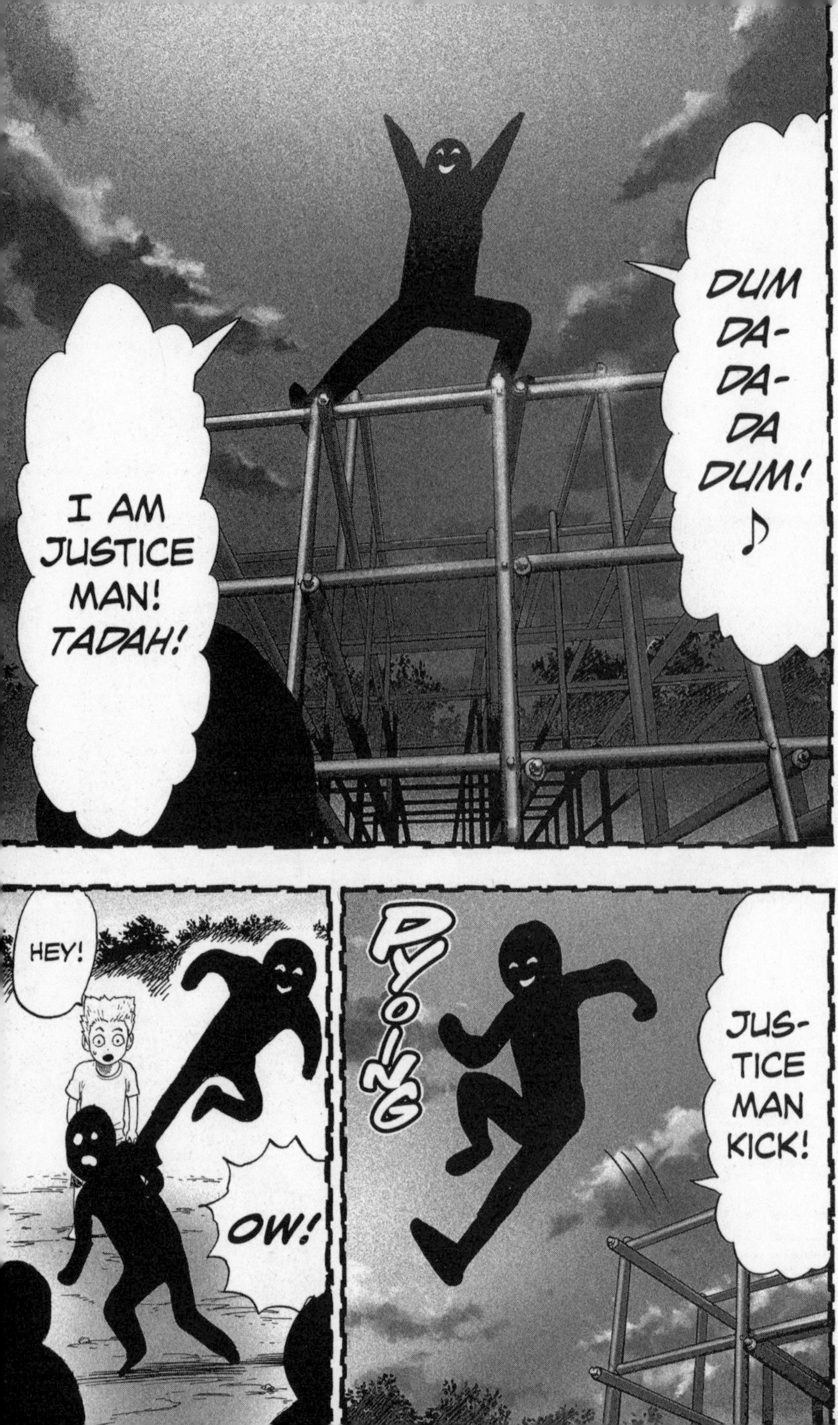
DUM DA-DA-DA DUM! ♪
I AM JUSTICE MAN! TADAH!
JUS-TICE MAN KICK!
PYOING
HEY!
OW!

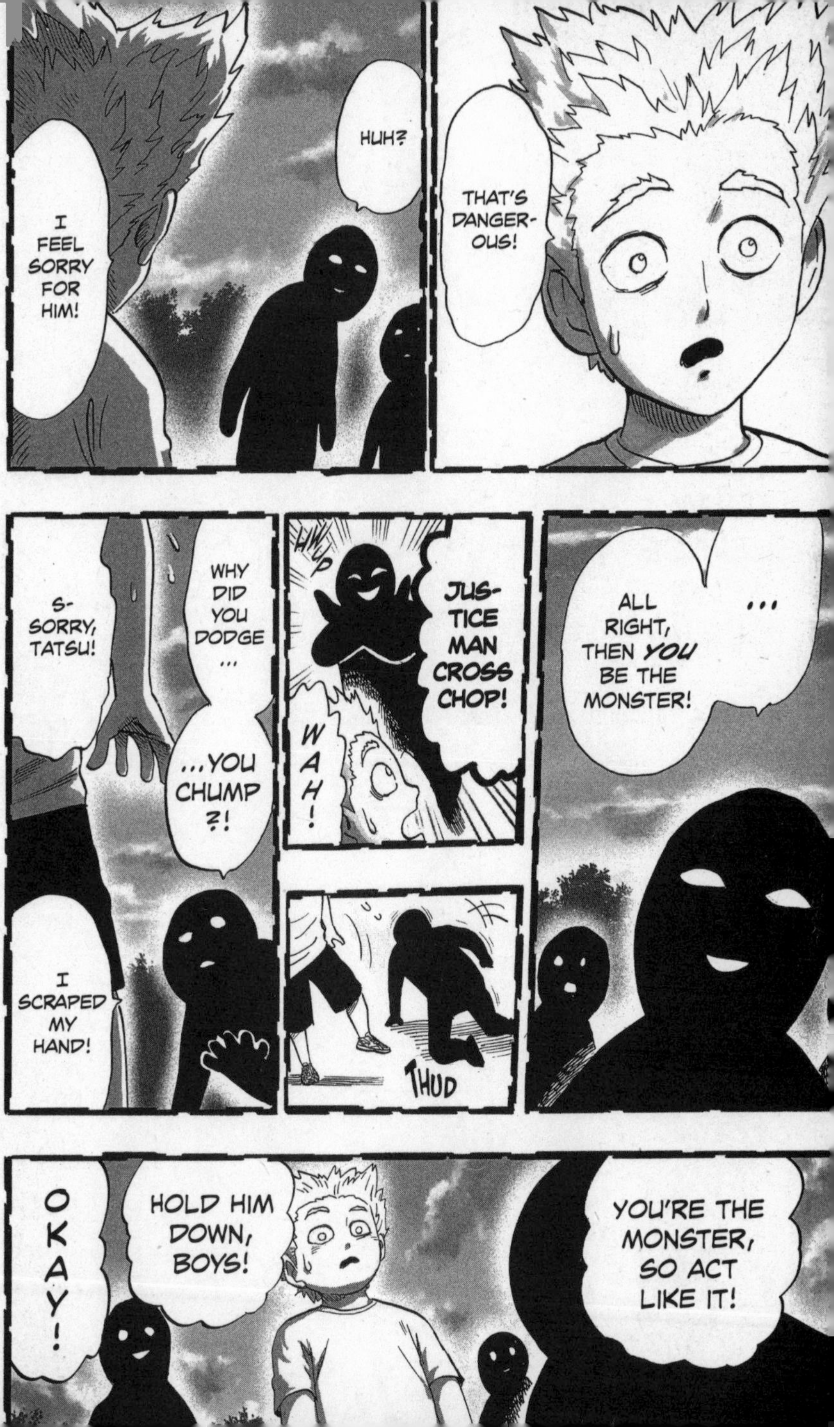
THAT'S DANGER-OUS!
HUH?
I FEEL SORRY FOR HIM!
...
ALL RIGHT, THEN *YOU* BE THE MONSTER!
JUS-TICE MAN CROSS CHOP!
WAH!
THUD
WHY DID YOU DODGE ...
...YOU CHUMP?!
S-SORRY, TATSU!
I SCRAPED MY HAND!
YOU'RE THE MONSTER, SO ACT LIKE IT!
HOLD HIM DOWN, BOYS!
OKAY!

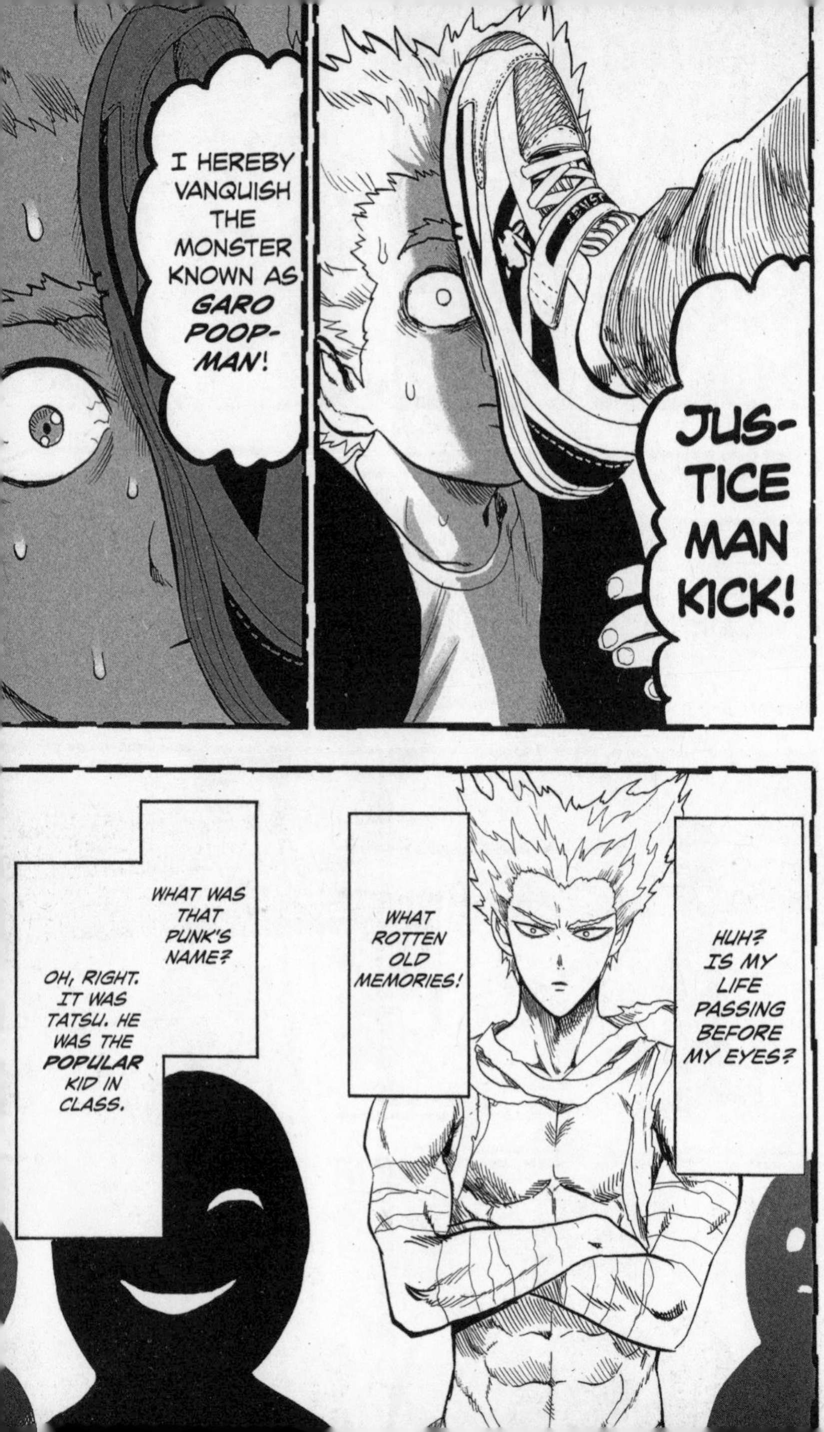
JUS-TICE MAN KICK!
I HEREBY VANQUISH THE MONSTER KNOWN AS *GARO POOP-MAN*!
HUH? IS MY LIFE PASSING BEFORE MY EYES?
WHAT ROTTEN OLD MEMORIES!
WHAT WAS THAT PUNK'S NAME?
*OH, RIGHT. IT WAS TATSU. HE WAS THE **POPULAR** KID IN CLASS.*

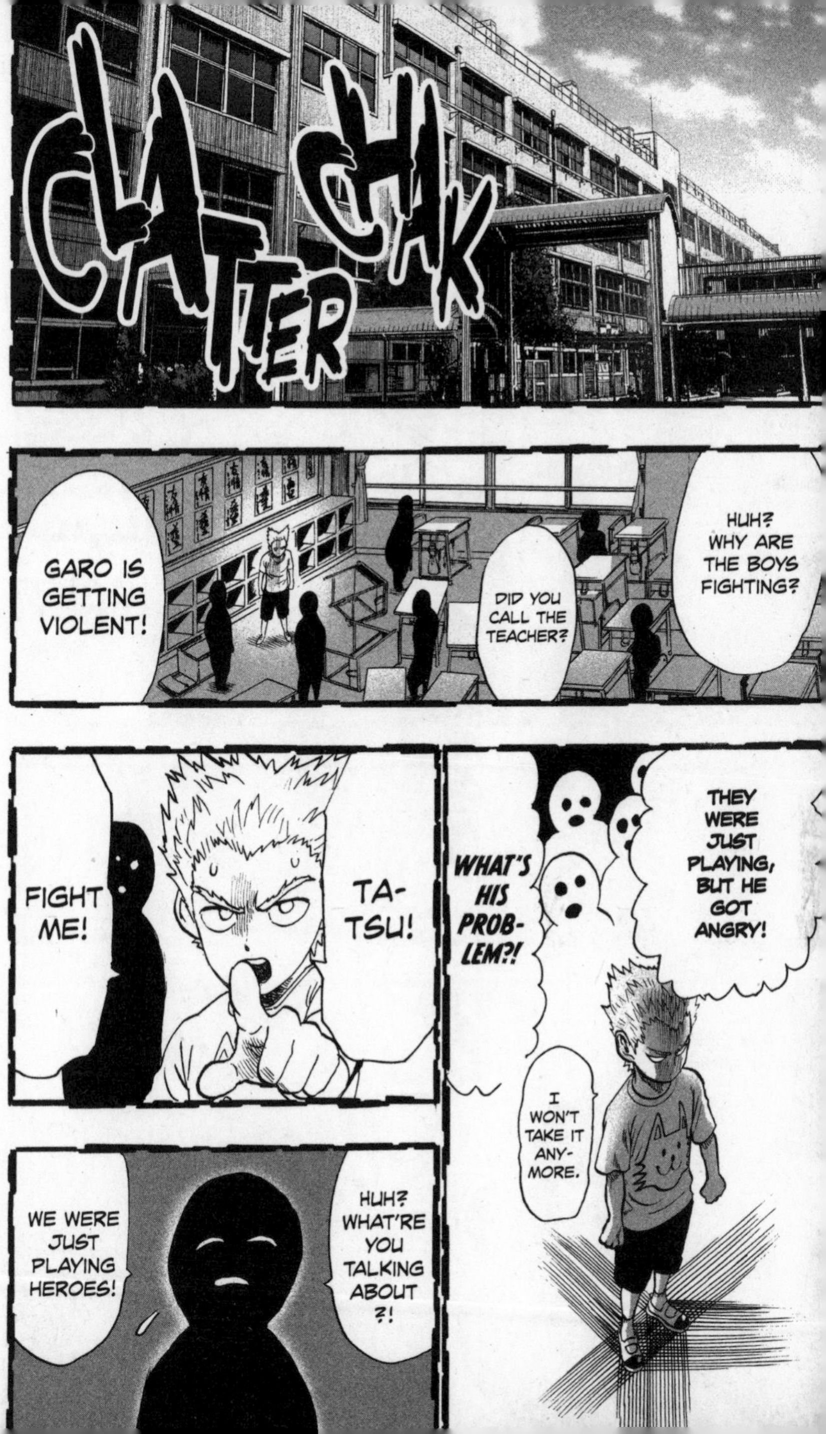
CLATTER
CHAK
HUH? WHY ARE THE BOYS FIGHTING?
DID YOU CALL THE TEACHER?
GARO IS GETTING VIOLENT!
THEY WERE JUST PLAYING, BUT HE GOT ANGRY!
WHAT'S HIS PROBLEM?!
I WON'T TAKE IT ANYMORE.
TA-TSU!
FIGHT ME!
HUH? WHAT'RE YOU TALKING ABOUT?!
WE WERE JUST PLAYING HEROES!

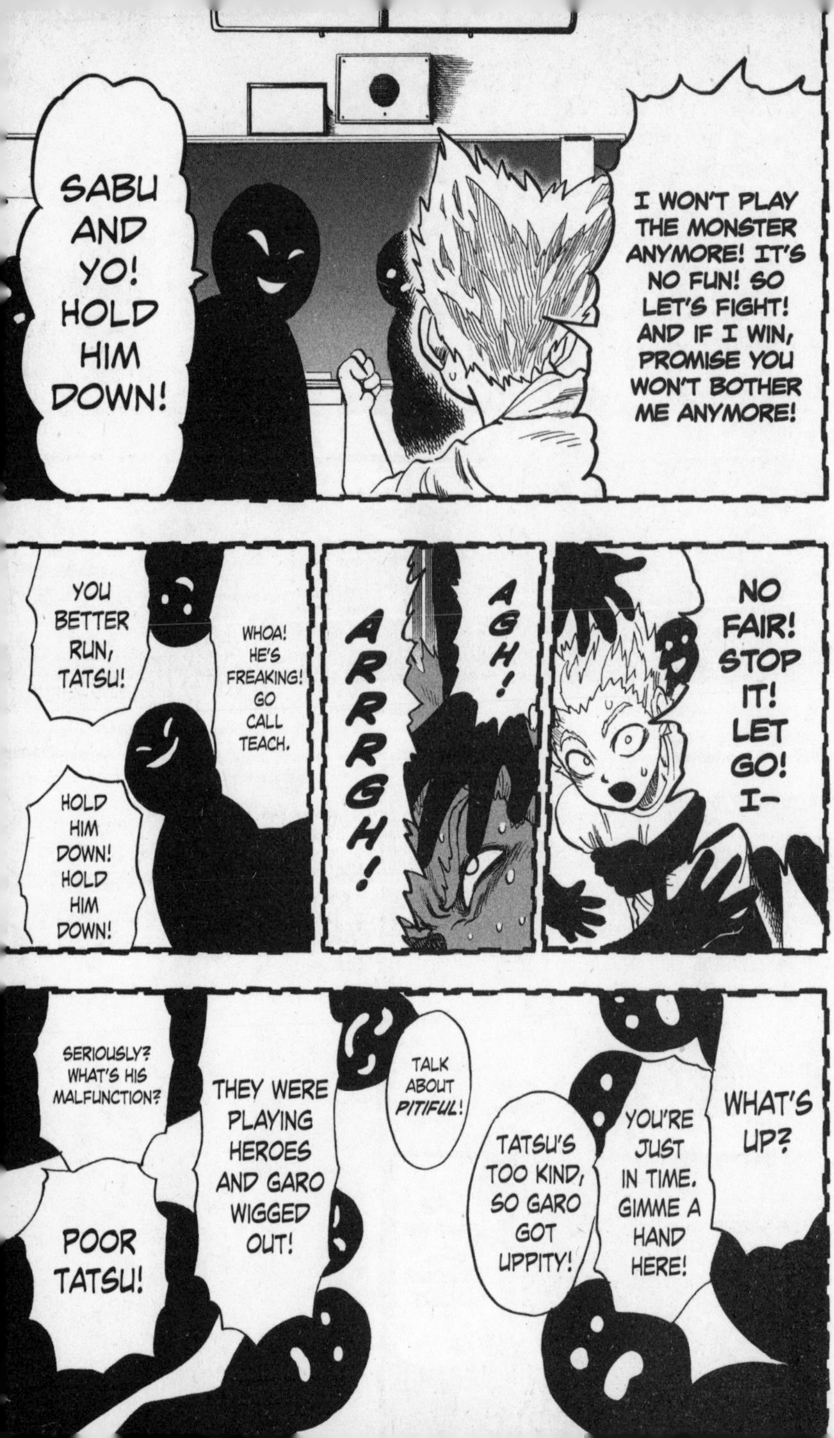
I WON'T PLAY THE MONSTER ANYMORE! IT'S NO FUN! SO LET'S FIGHT! AND IF I WIN, PROMISE YOU WON'T BOTHER ME ANYMORE!
SABU AND YO! HOLD HIM DOWN!
NO FAIR! STOP IT! LET GO! I—
AGH!
ARRRGH!
YOU BETTER RUN, TATSU!
WHOA! HE'S FREAKING! GO CALL TEACH.
HOLD HIM DOWN! HOLD HIM DOWN!
WHAT'S UP?
YOU'RE JUST IN TIME. GIMME A HAND HERE!
TATSU'S TOO KIND, SO GARO GOT UPPITY!
TALK ABOUT *PITIFUL*!
THEY WERE PLAYING HEROES AND GARO WIGGED OUT!
SERIOUSLY? WHAT'S HIS MALFUNCTION?
POOR TATSU!

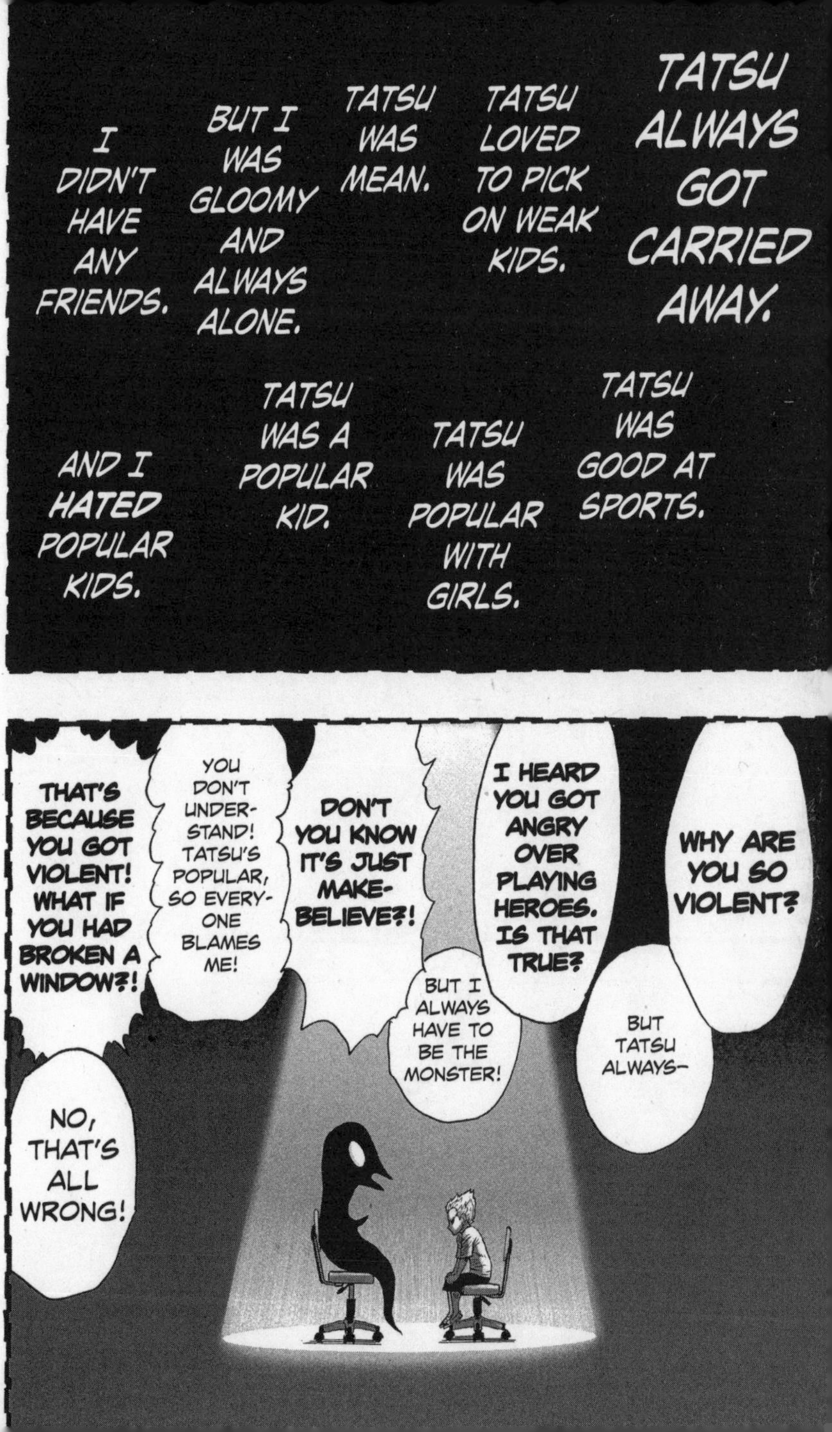
TATSU ALWAYS GOT CARRIED AWAY.
TATSU LOVED TO PICK ON WEAK KIDS.
TATSU WAS MEAN.
BUT I WAS GLOOMY AND ALWAYS ALONE.
I DIDN'T HAVE ANY FRIENDS.
TATSU WAS GOOD AT SPORTS.
TATSU WAS POPULAR WITH GIRLS.
TATSU WAS A POPULAR KID.
AND I HATED POPULAR KIDS.
WHY ARE YOU SO VIOLENT?
I HEARD YOU GOT ANGRY OVER PLAYING HEROES. IS THAT TRUE?
DON'T YOU KNOW IT'S JUST MAKE-BELIEVE?!
YOU DON'T UNDER-STAND! TATSU'S POPULAR, SO EVERY-ONE BLAMES ME!
THAT'S BECAUSE YOU GOT VIOLENT! WHAT IF YOU HAD BROKEN A WINDOW?!
BUT TATSU ALWAYS—
BUT I ALWAYS HAVE TO BE THE MONSTER!
NO, THAT'S ALL WRONG!

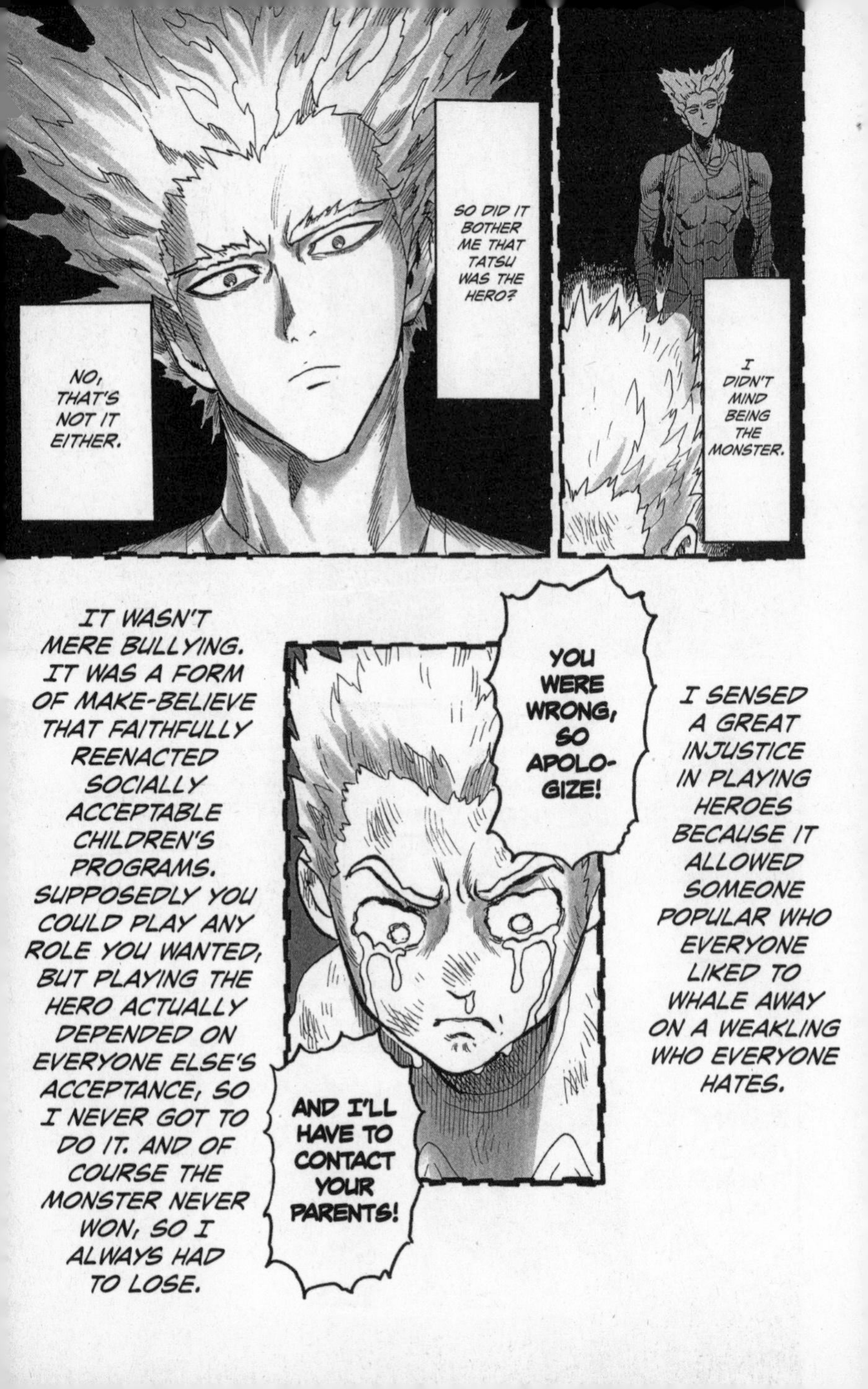
I DIDN'T MIND BEING THE MONSTER.
SO DID IT BOTHER ME THAT TATSU WAS THE HERO?
NO, THAT'S NOT IT EITHER.
I SENSED A GREAT INJUSTICE IN PLAYING HEROES BECAUSE IT ALLOWED SOMEONE POPULAR WHO EVERYONE LIKED TO WHALE AWAY ON A WEAKLING WHO EVERYONE HATES.
YOU WERE WRONG, SO APOLO-GIZE!
AND I'LL HAVE TO CONTACT YOUR PARENTS!
IT WASN'T MERE BULLYING. IT WAS A FORM OF MAKE-BELIEVE THAT FAITHFULLY REENACTED SOCIALLY ACCEPTABLE CHILDREN'S PROGRAMS. SUPPOSEDLY YOU COULD PLAY ANY ROLE YOU WANTED, BUT PLAYING THE HERO ACTUALLY DEPENDED ON EVERYONE ELSE'S ACCEPTANCE, SO I NEVER GOT TO DO IT. AND OF COURSE THE MONSTER NEVER WON, SO I ALWAYS HAD TO LOSE.

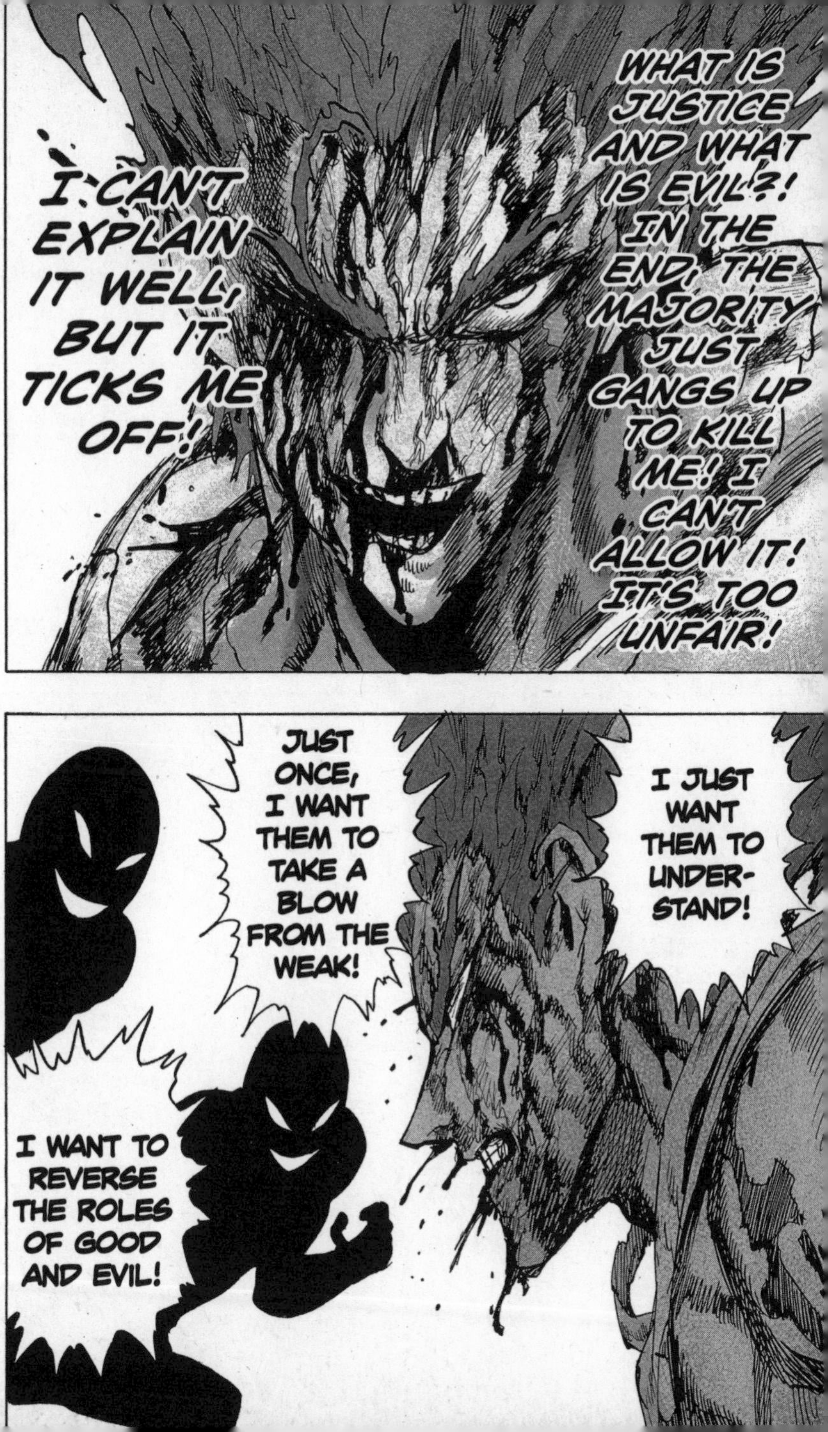
WHAT IS JUSTICE AND WHAT IS EVIL?! IN THE END, THE MAJORITY JUST GANGS UP TO KILL ME! I CAN'T ALLOW IT! IT'S TOO UNFAIR!
I CAN'T EXPLAIN IT WELL, BUT IT TICKS ME OFF!
I JUST WANT THEM TO UNDER-STAND!
JUST ONCE, I WANT THEM TO TAKE A BLOW FROM THE WEAK!
I WANT TO REVERSE THE ROLES OF GOOD AND EVIL!

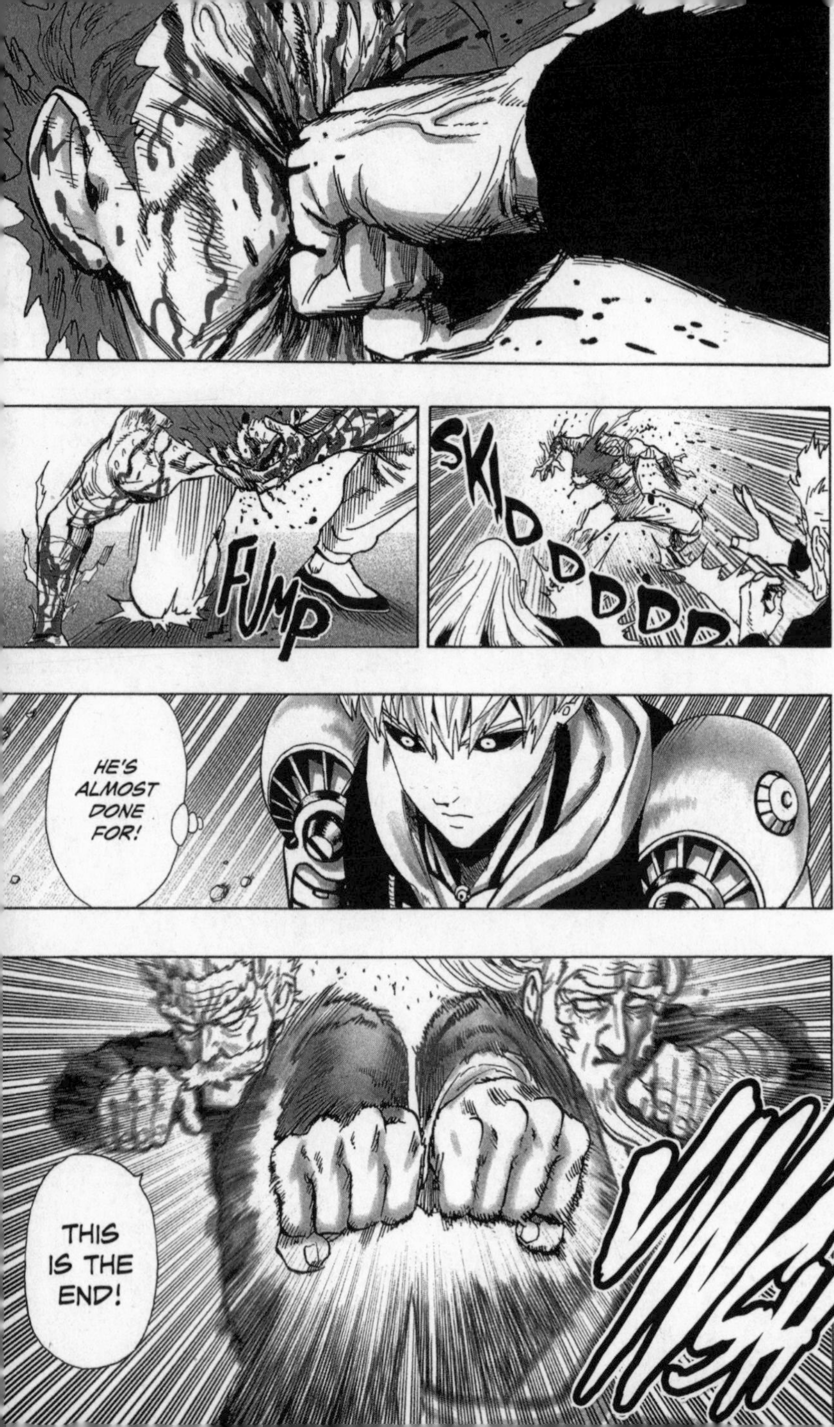
SKIDDDDDD
FUMP
HE'S ALMOST DONE FOR!
THIS IS THE END!

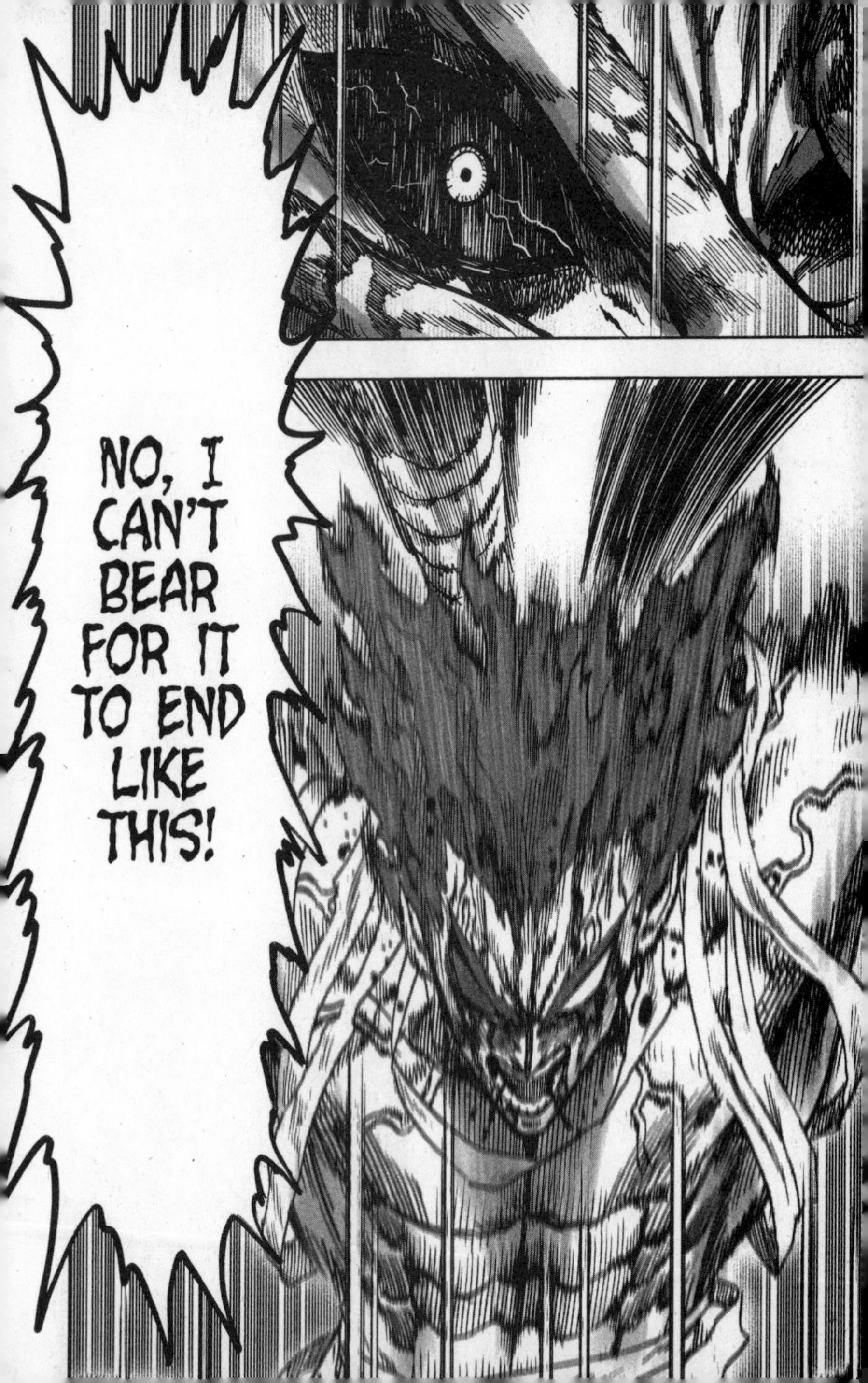
NO, I CAN'T BEAR FOR IT TO END LIKE THIS!

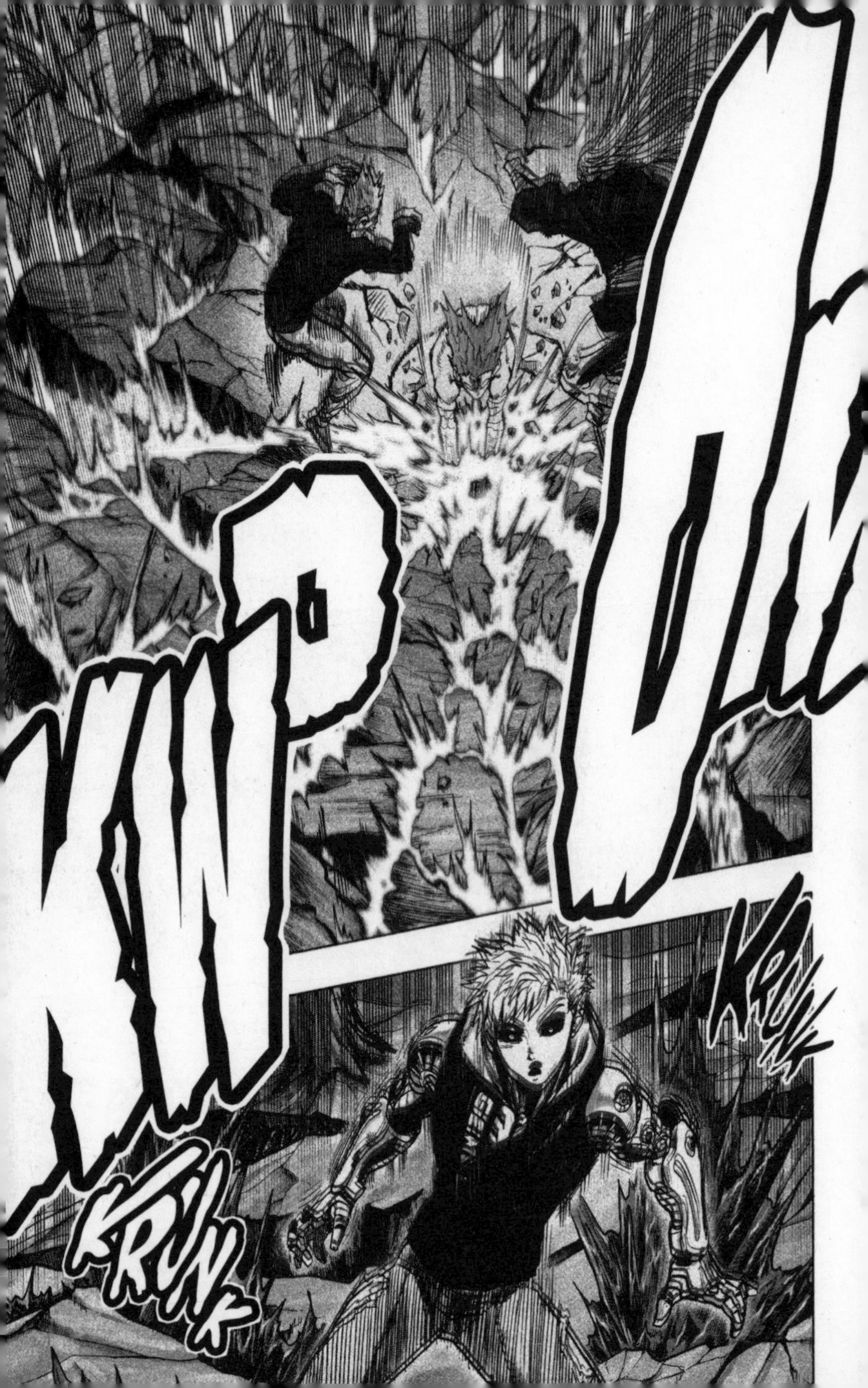
KRUNK
KRUNK

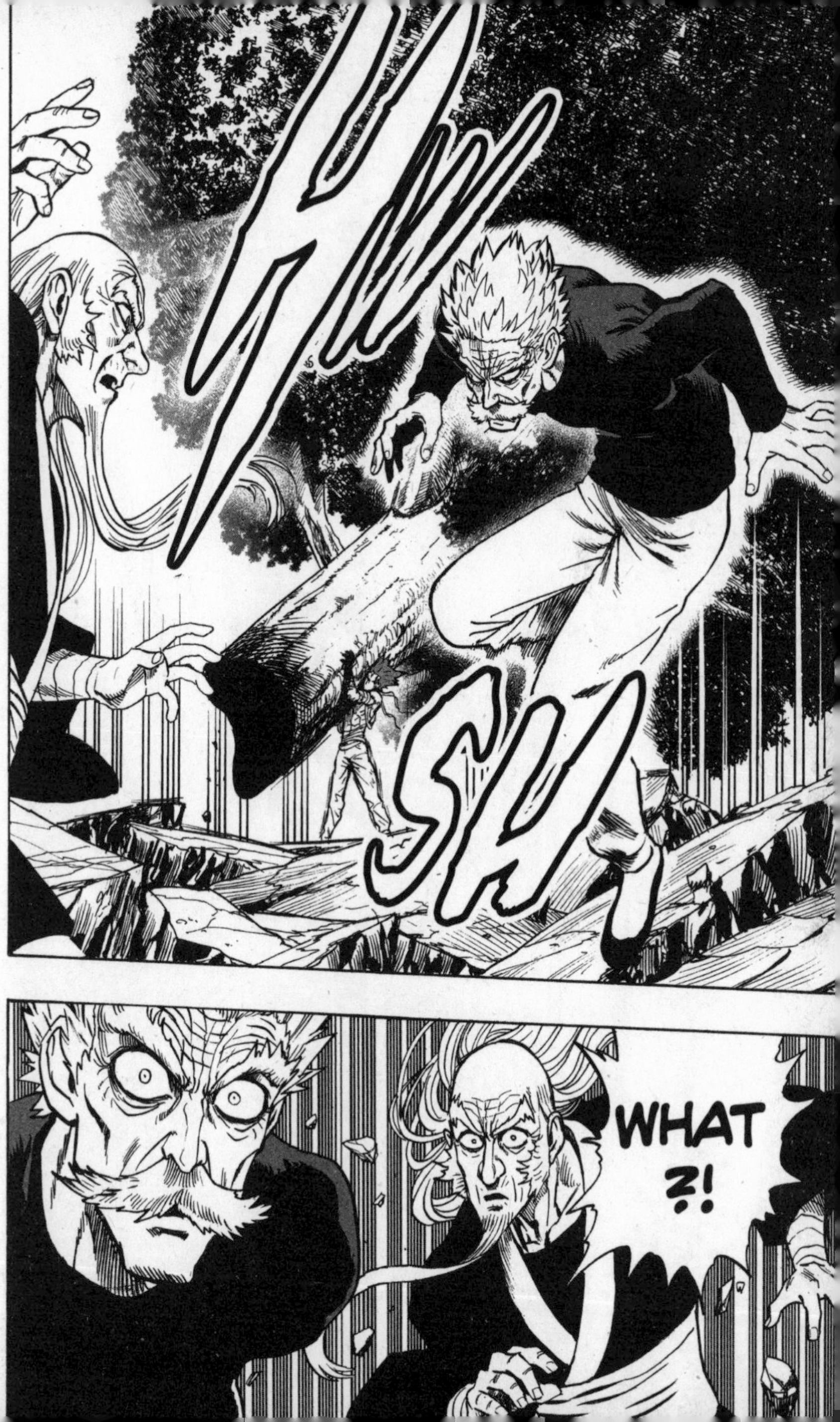
SHH
WHAT ?!

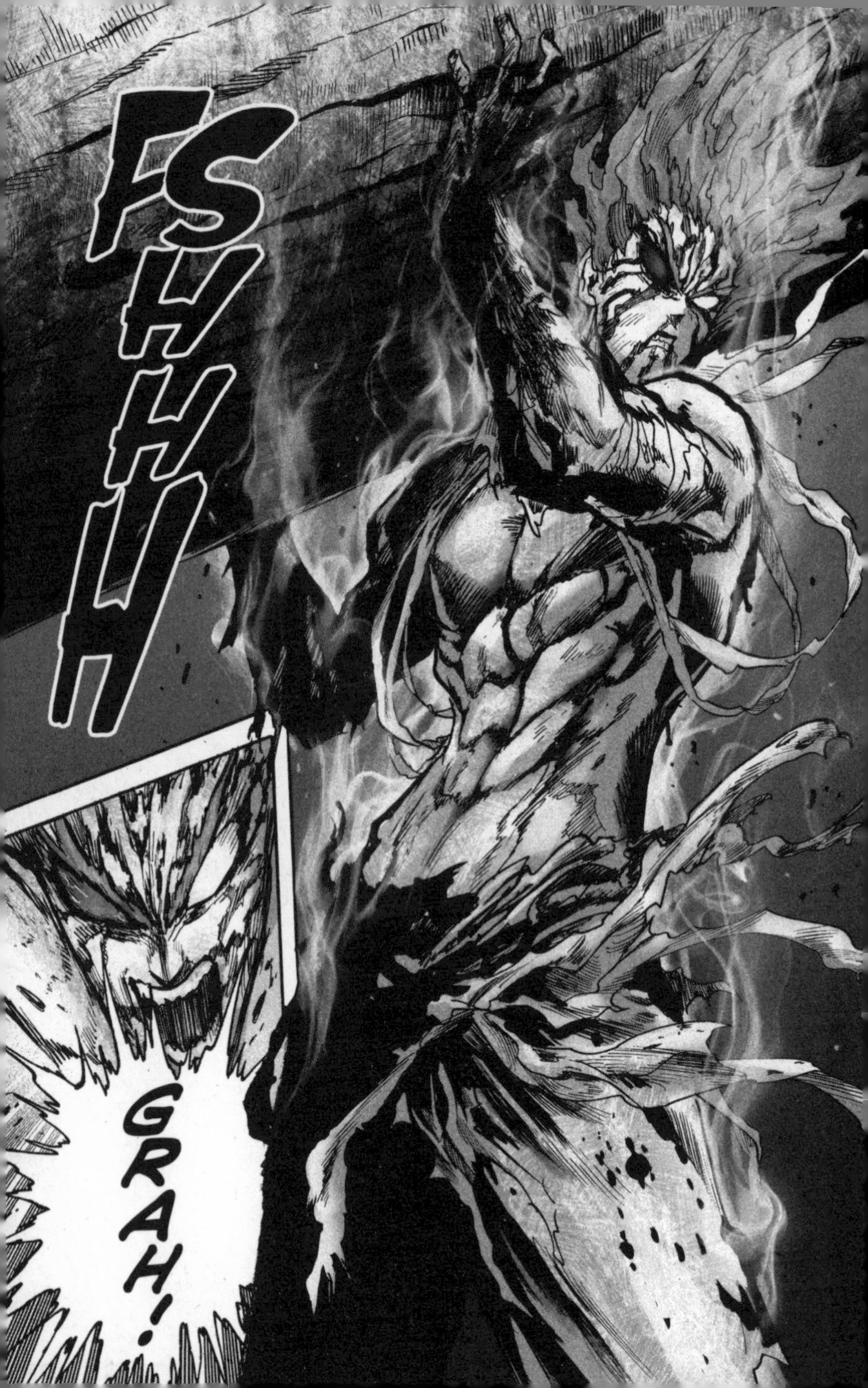
FSHHHH
GRAH!

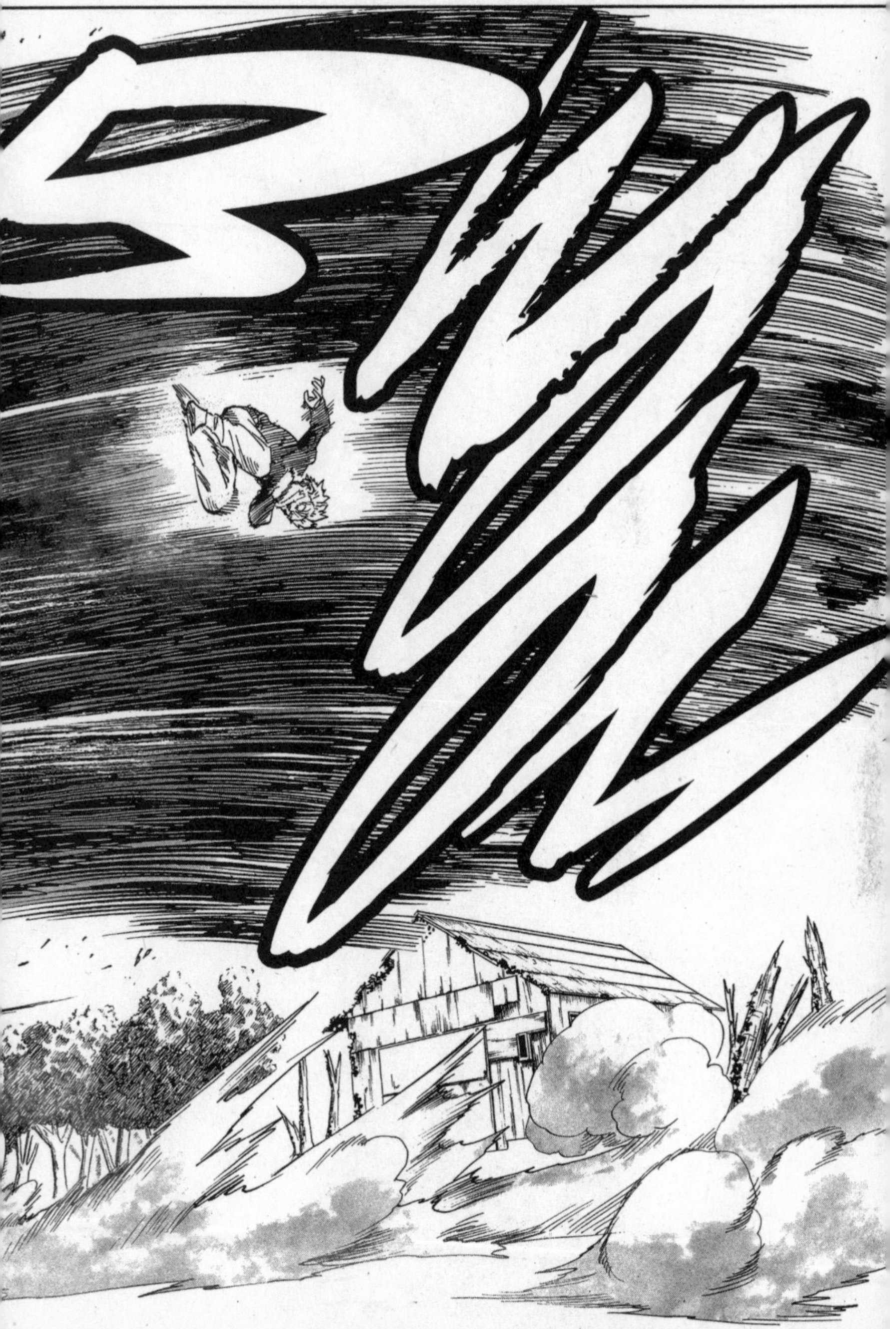

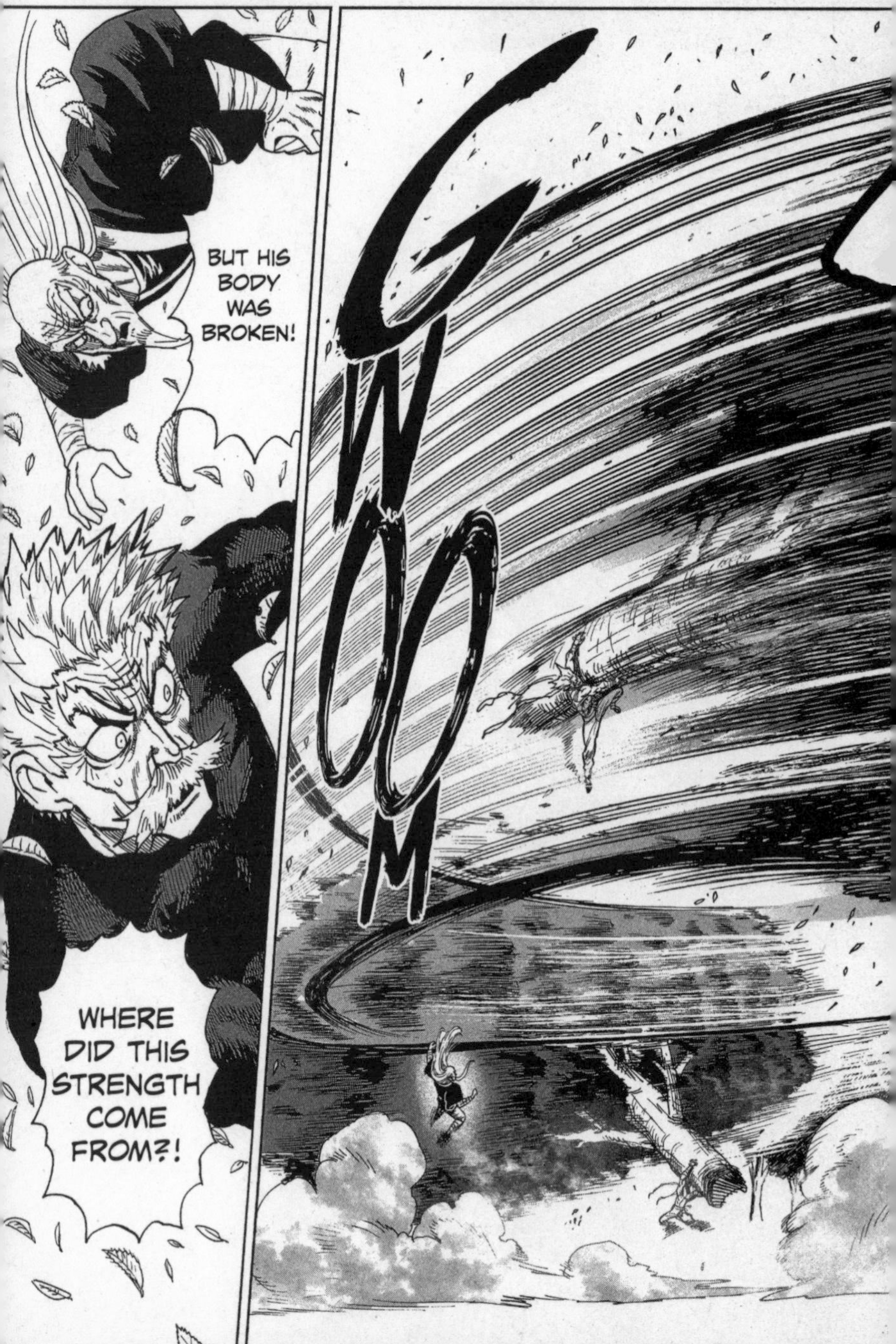
GWOOM
BUT HIS BODY WAS BROKEN!
WHERE DID THIS STRENGTH COME FROM?!

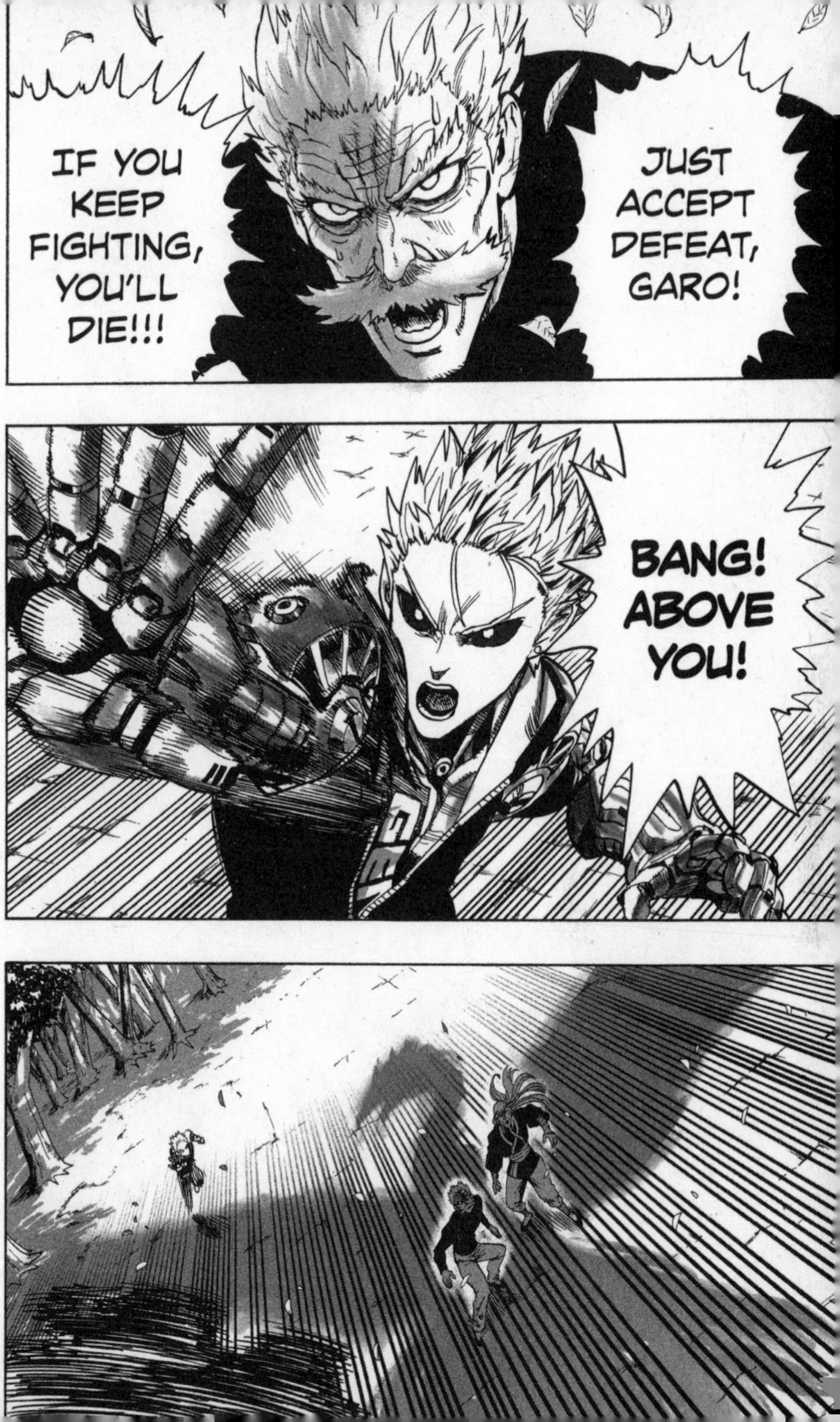
JUST ACCEPT DEFEAT, GARO!
IF YOU KEEP FIGHTING, YOU'LL DIE!!!
BANG! ABOVE YOU!

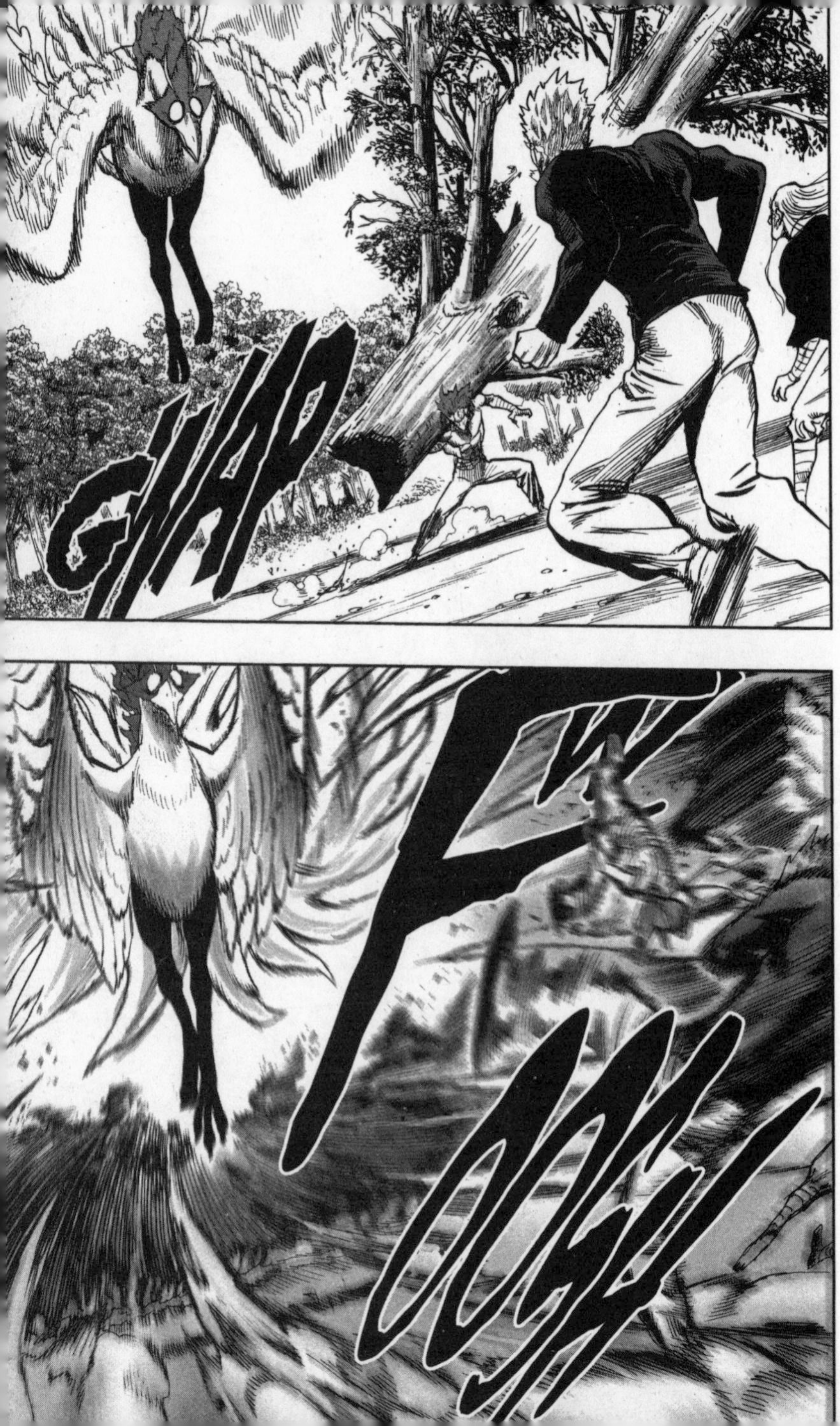

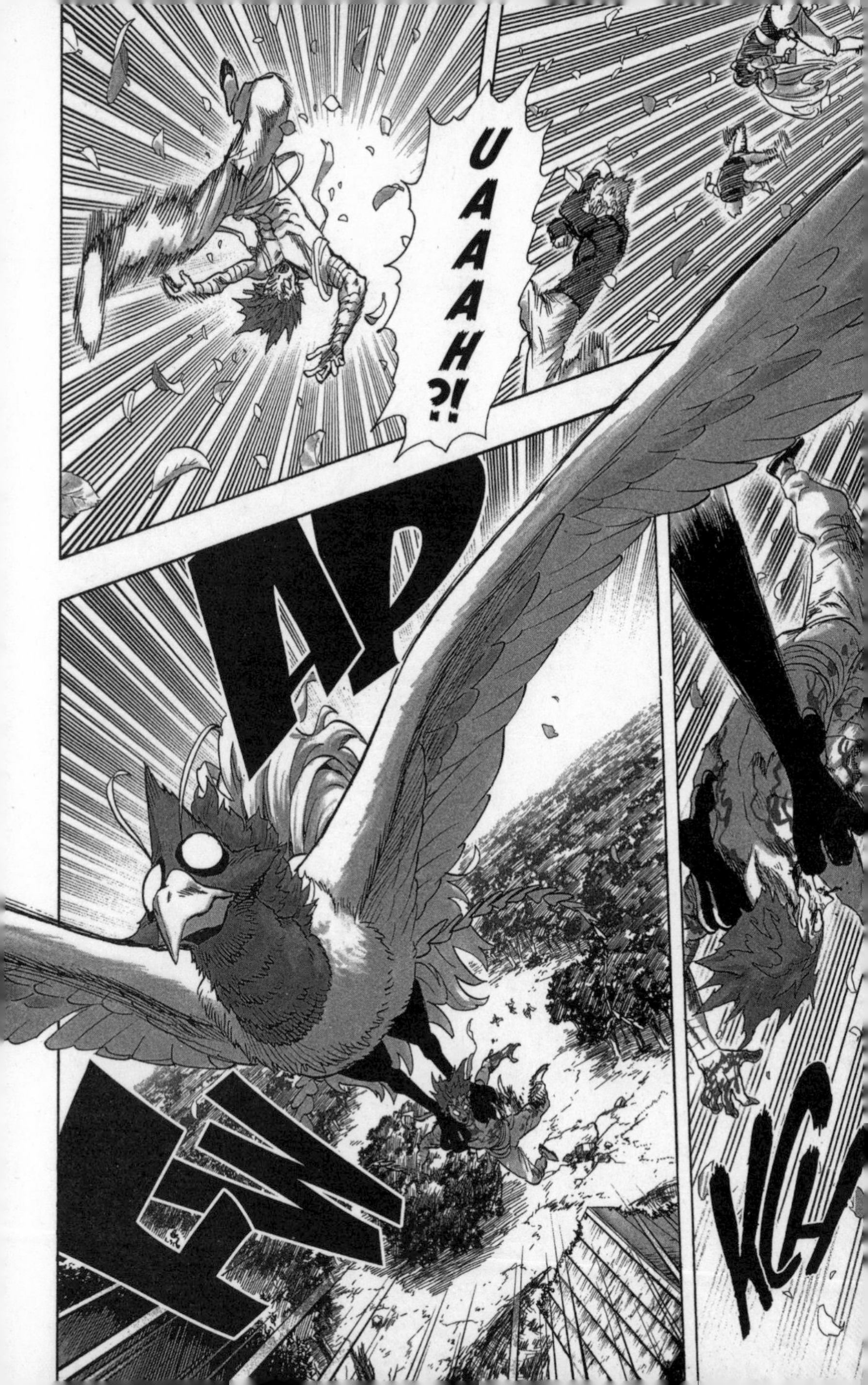
UAAAAH?!

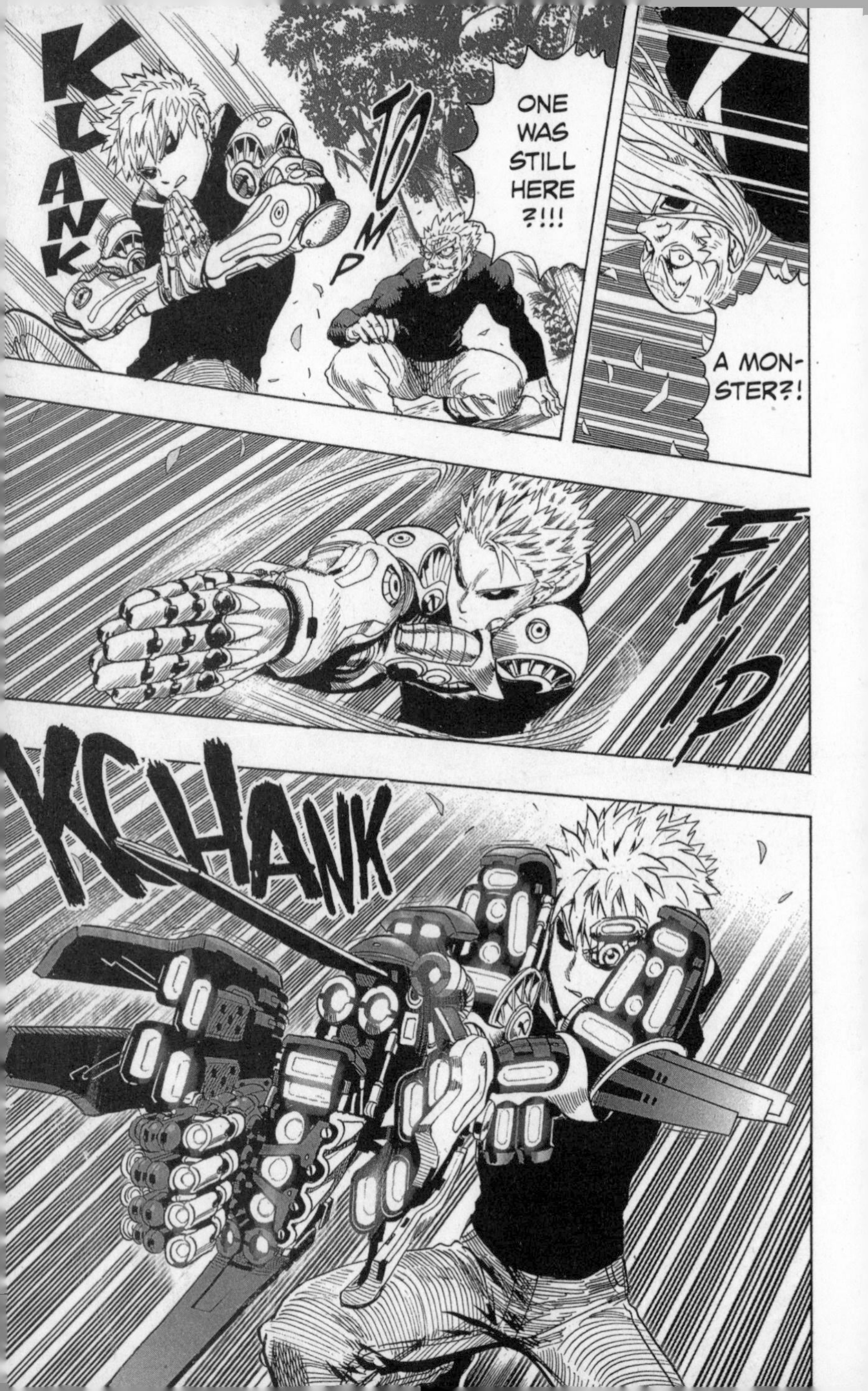
A MON-
STER?!
ONE WAS STILL HERE?!!!
TOMP
KLANK
FWIP
KCHANK

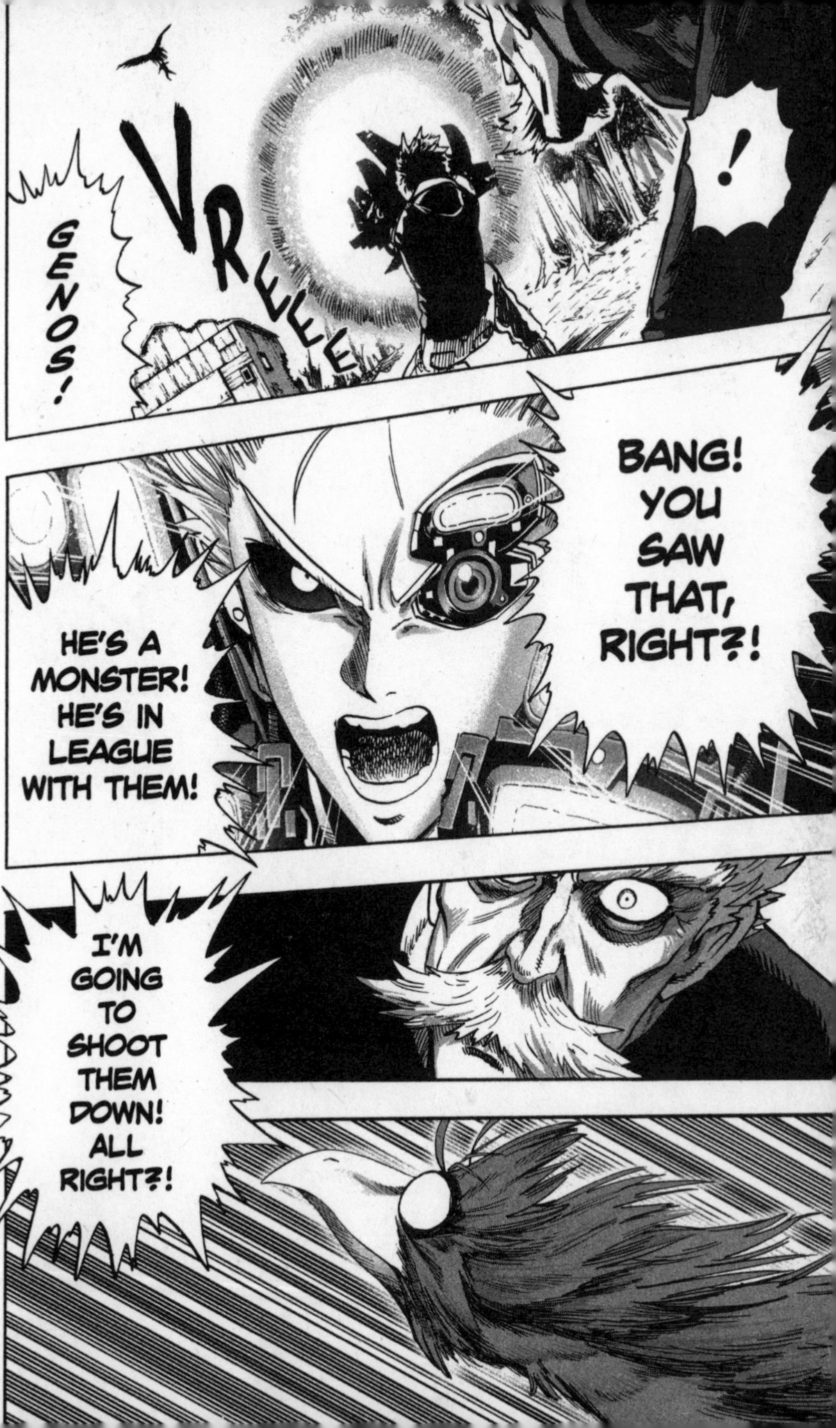
!
VRREEE
GENOS!
BANG! YOU SAW THAT, RIGHT?!
HE'S A MONSTER! HE'S IN LEAGUE WITH THEM!
I'M GOING TO SHOOT THEM DOWN! ALL RIGHT?!

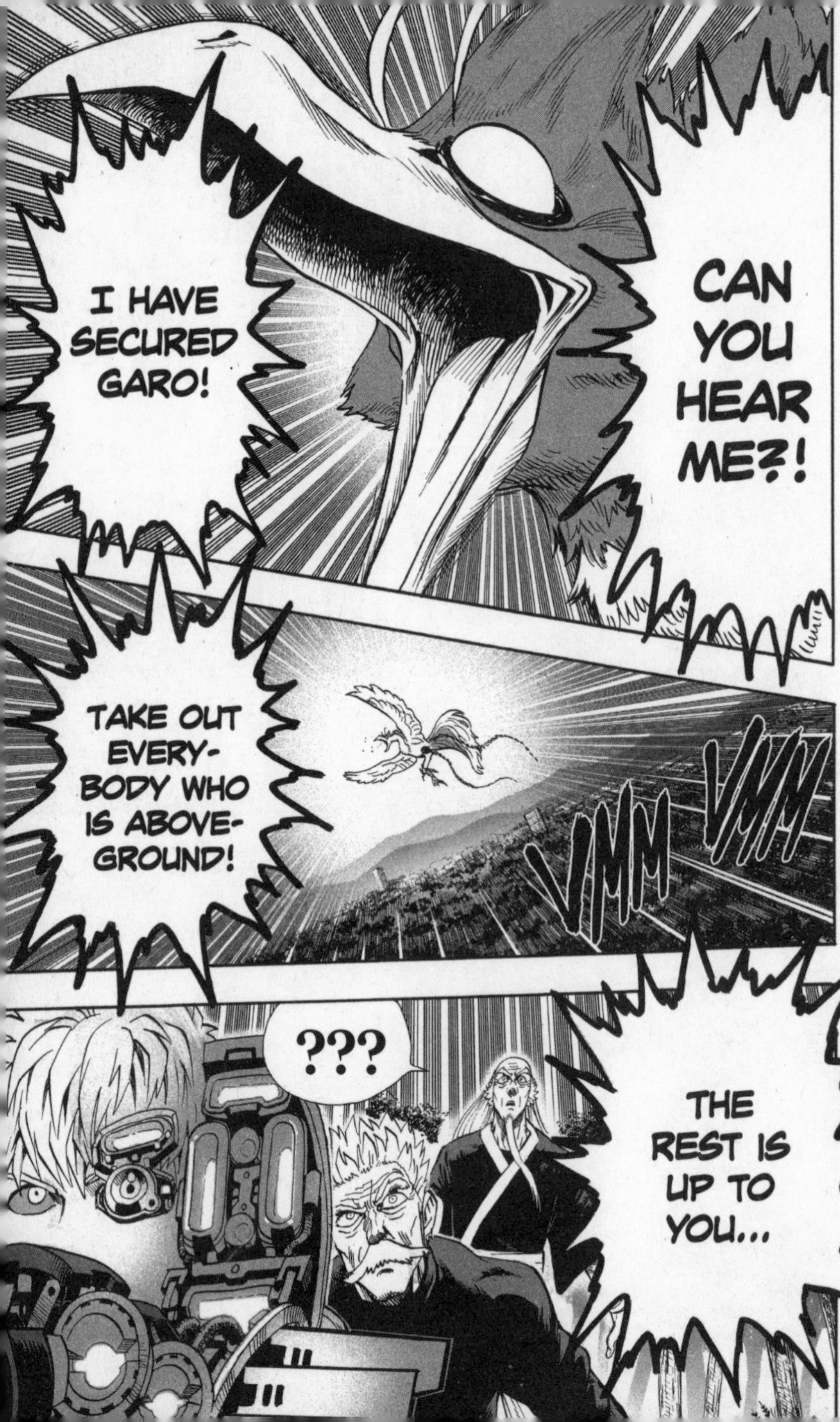
CAN YOU HEAR ME?!
I HAVE SECURED GARO!
VMM VMM
TAKE OUT EVERY-BODY WHO IS ABOVE-GROUND!
THE REST IS UP TO YOU...
???

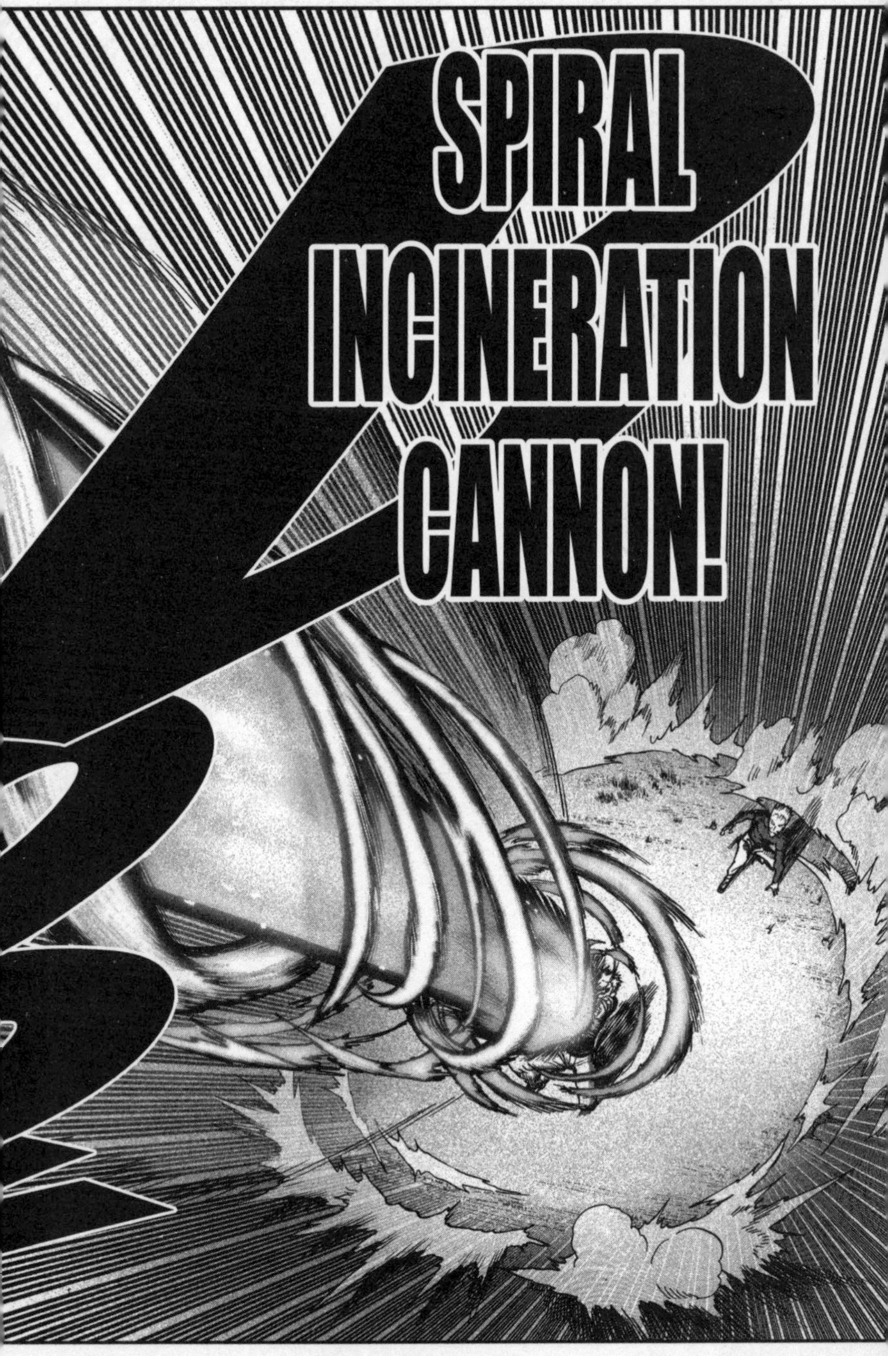
SPIRAL INCINERATION CANNON!

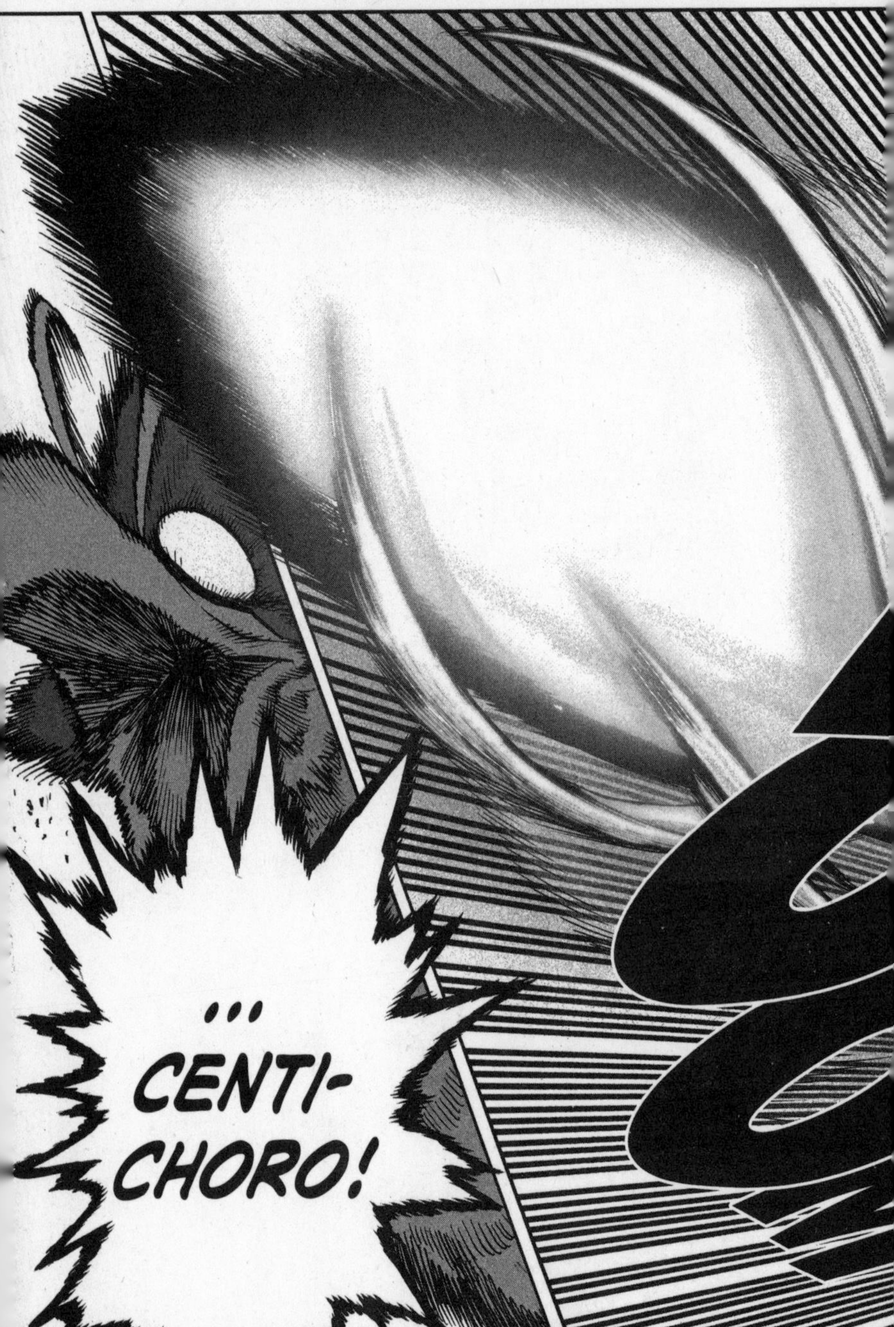
...CENTI-CHORO!

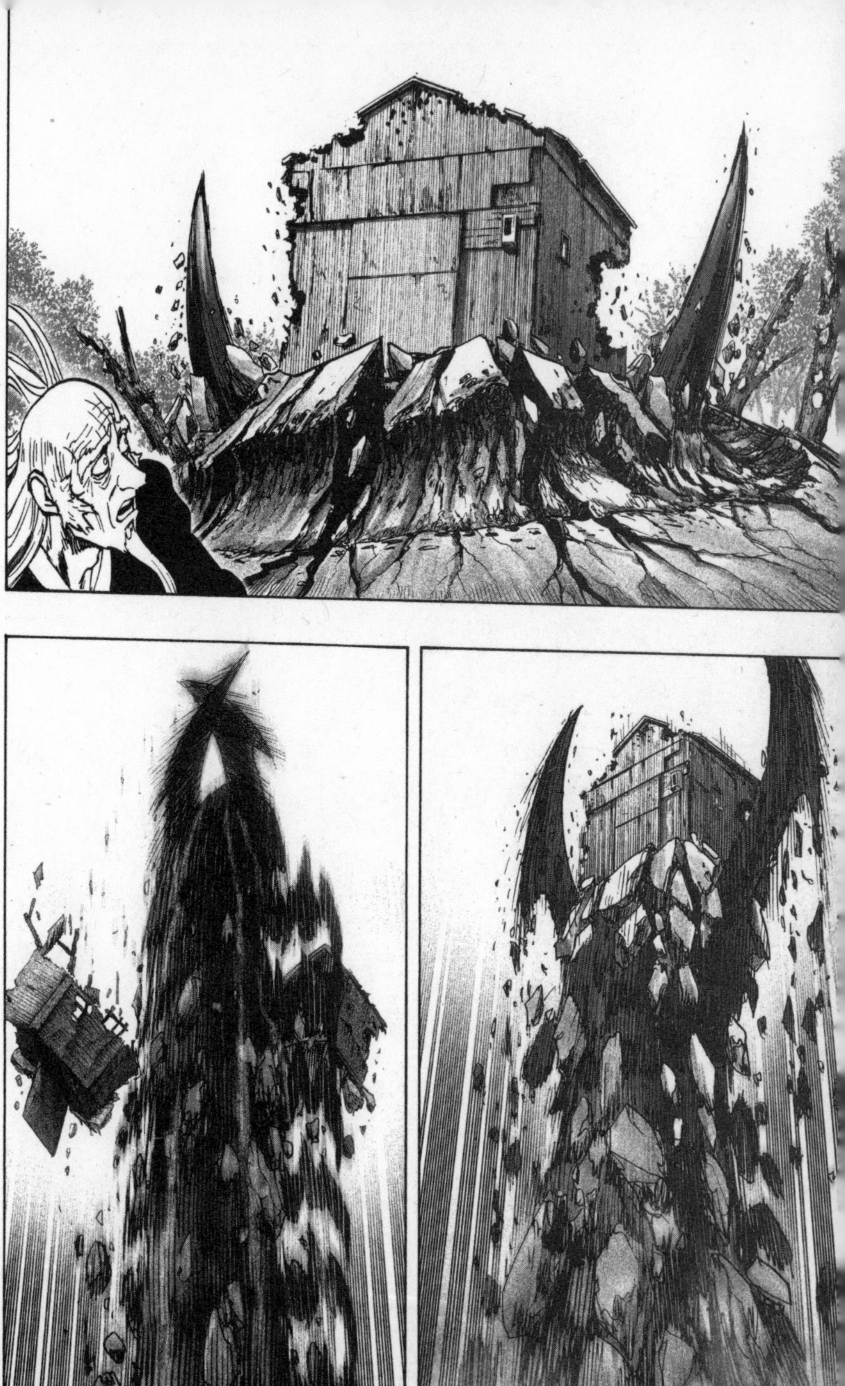

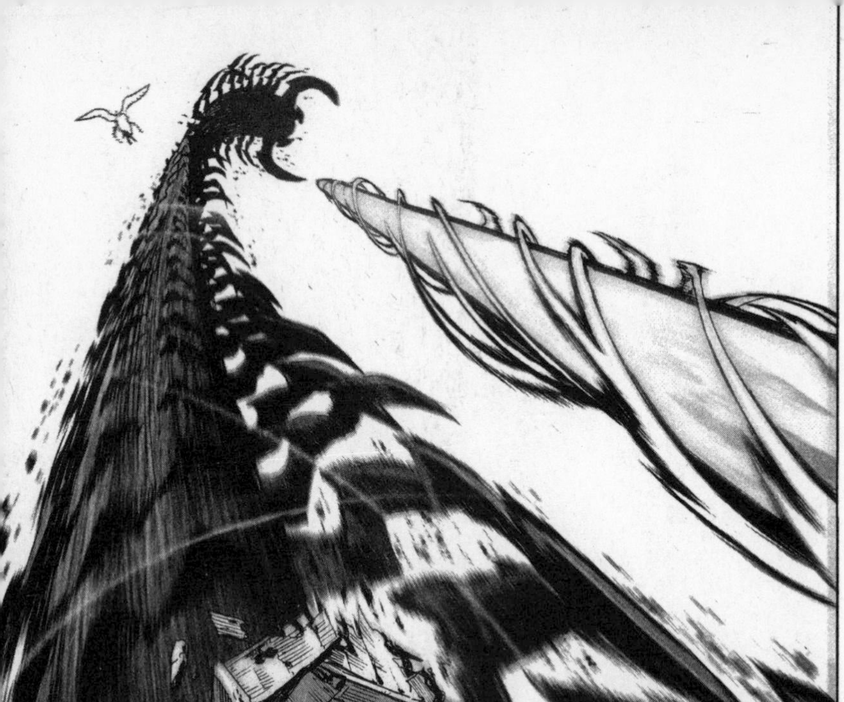

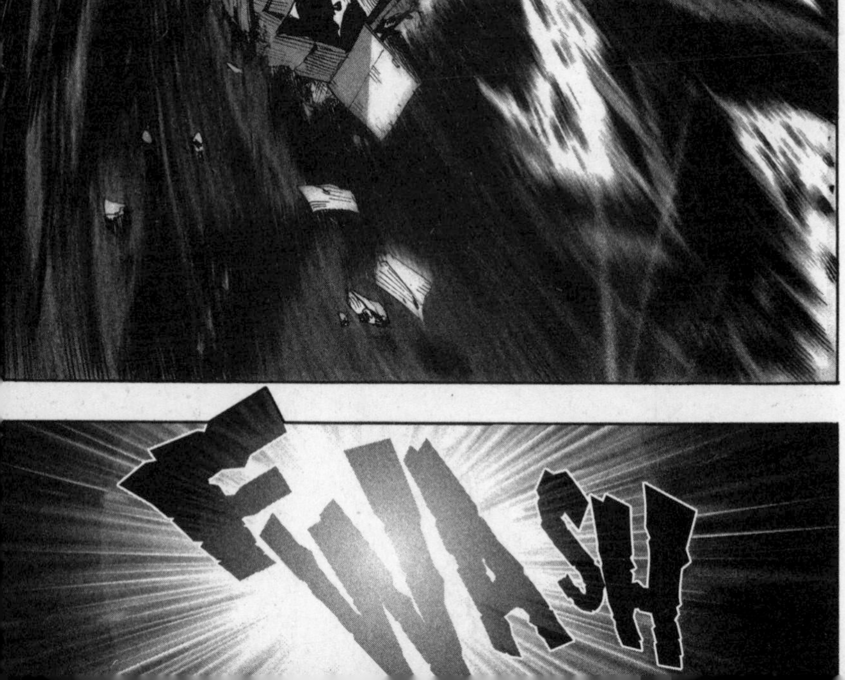
FWASH

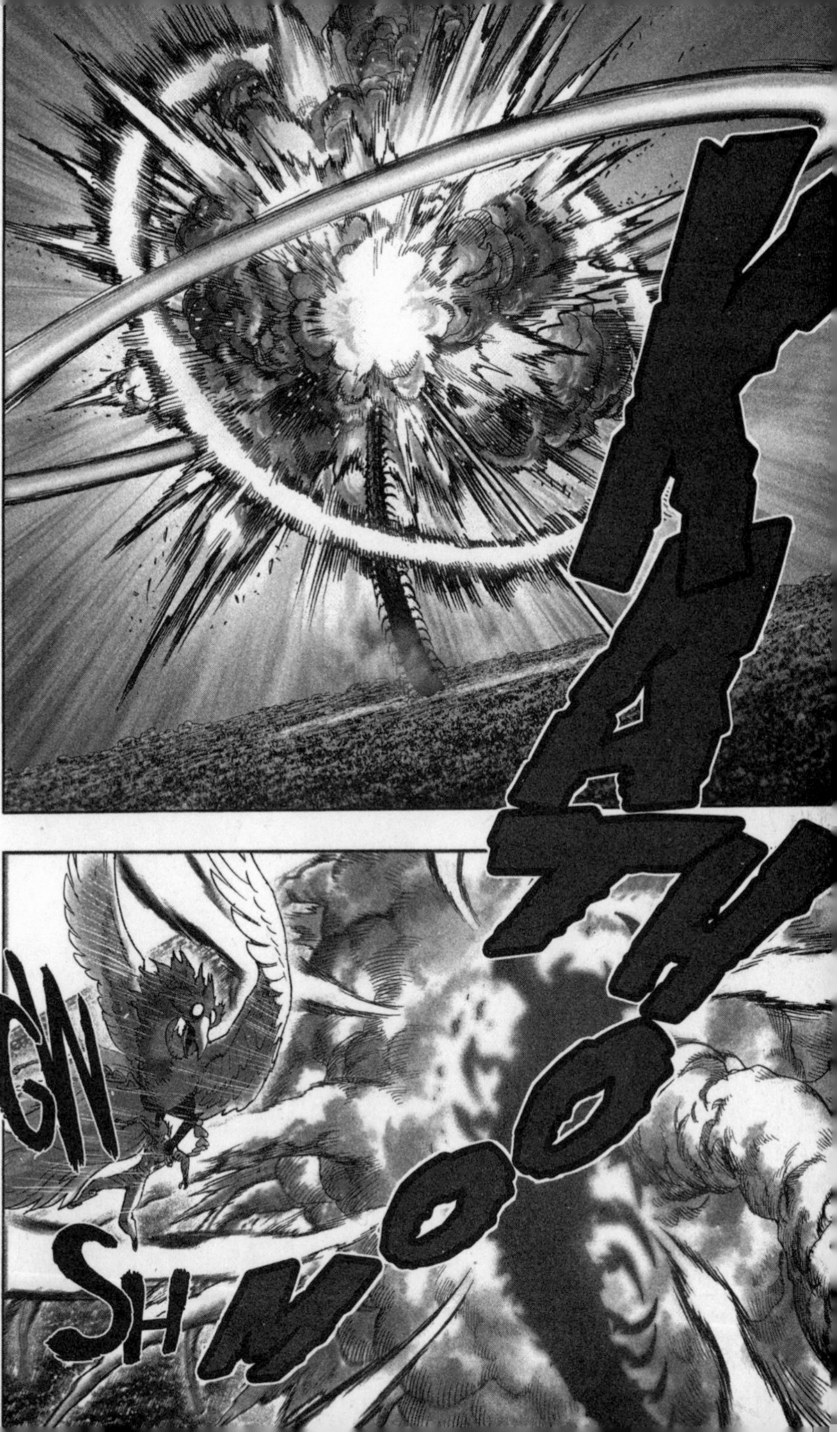
KATHOOOM
GW
SH

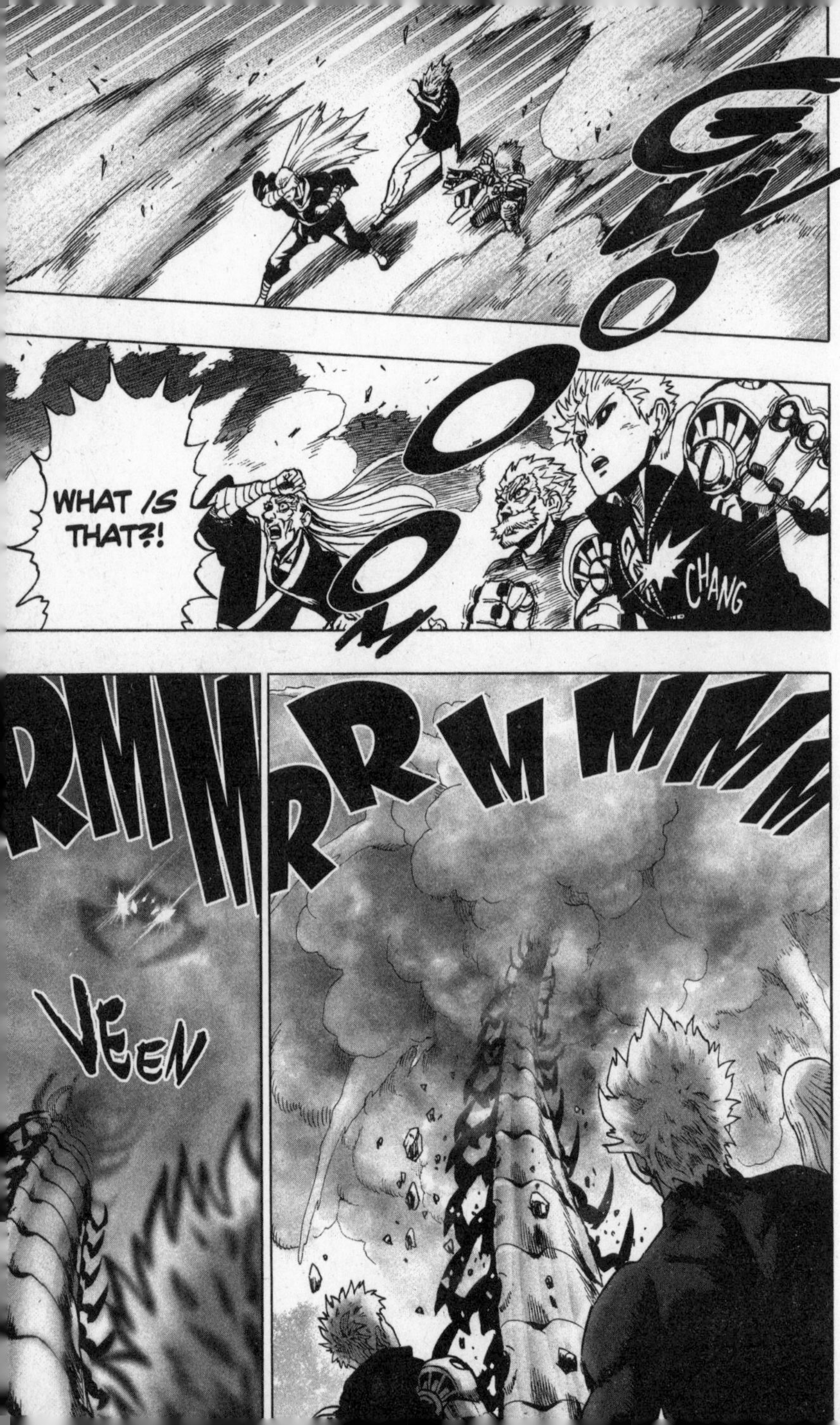

GOOOOOM
WHAT IS THAT?!
CHANG
RRMMMM
RMM
VEEN

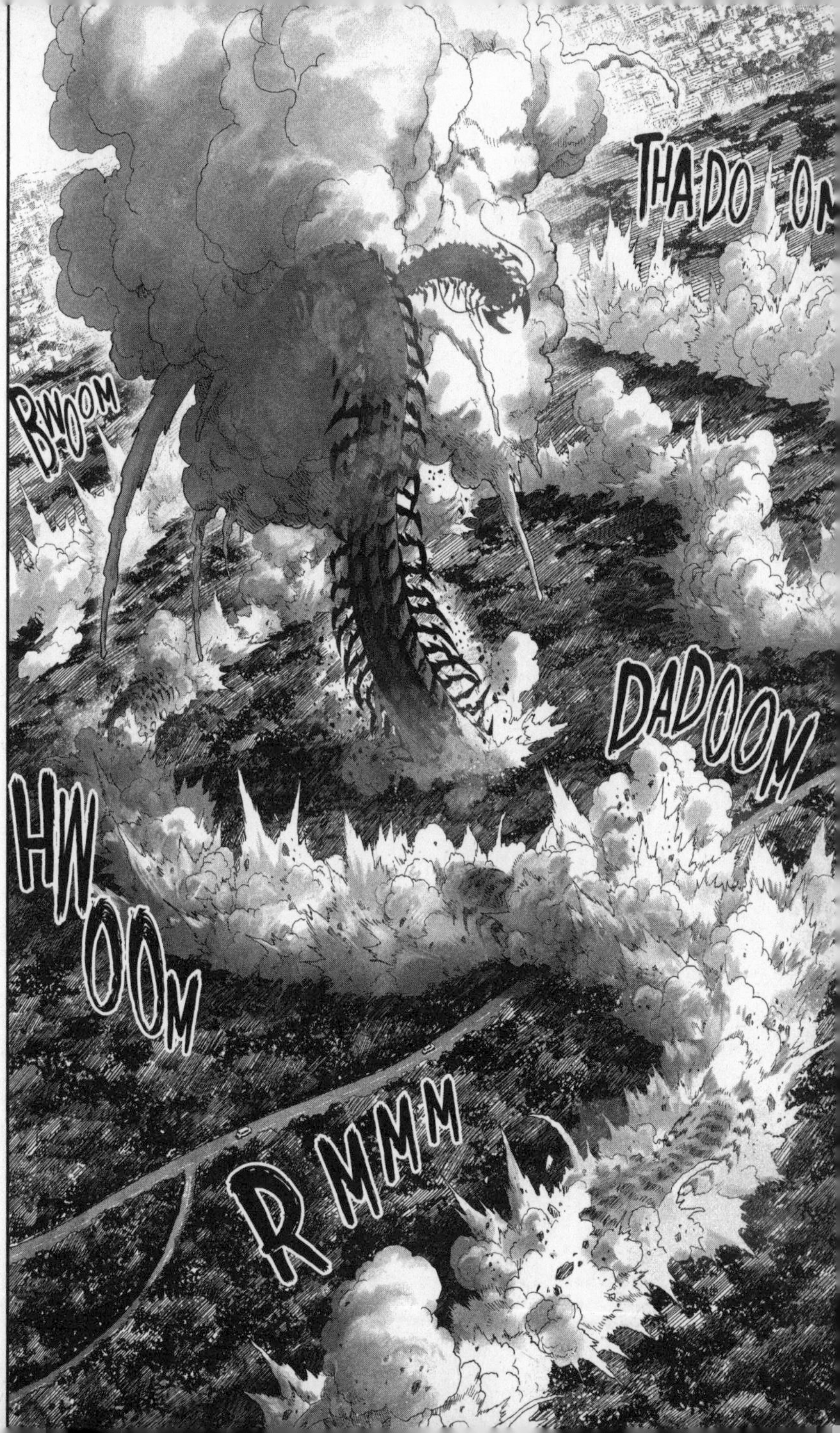
THADO O
RWOOM
DADOOM
HWOOM
RMMM

THWOOM

KN

UNK

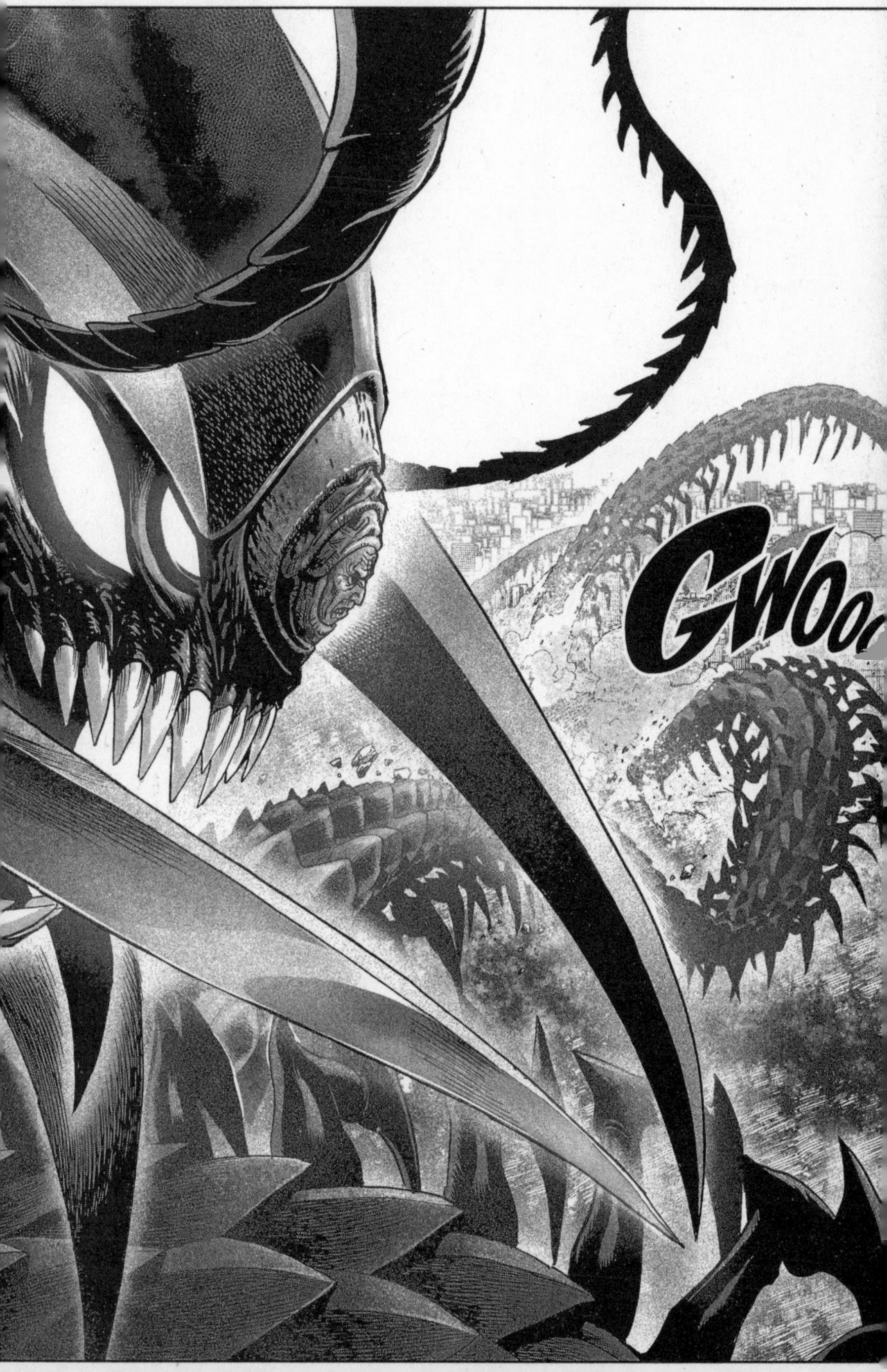
GWOO

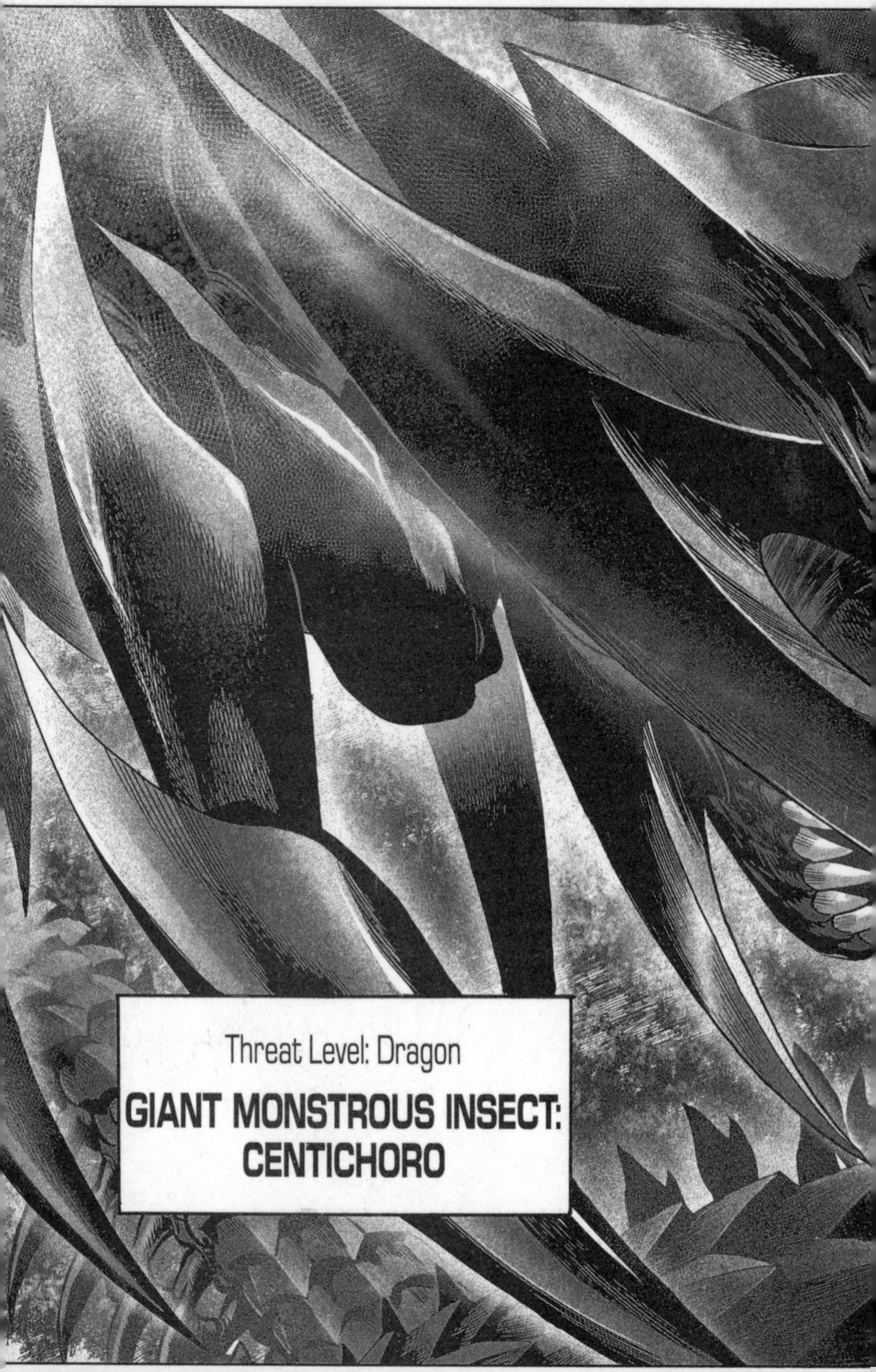
Threat Level: Dragon
GIANT MONSTROUS INSECT: CENTICHORO

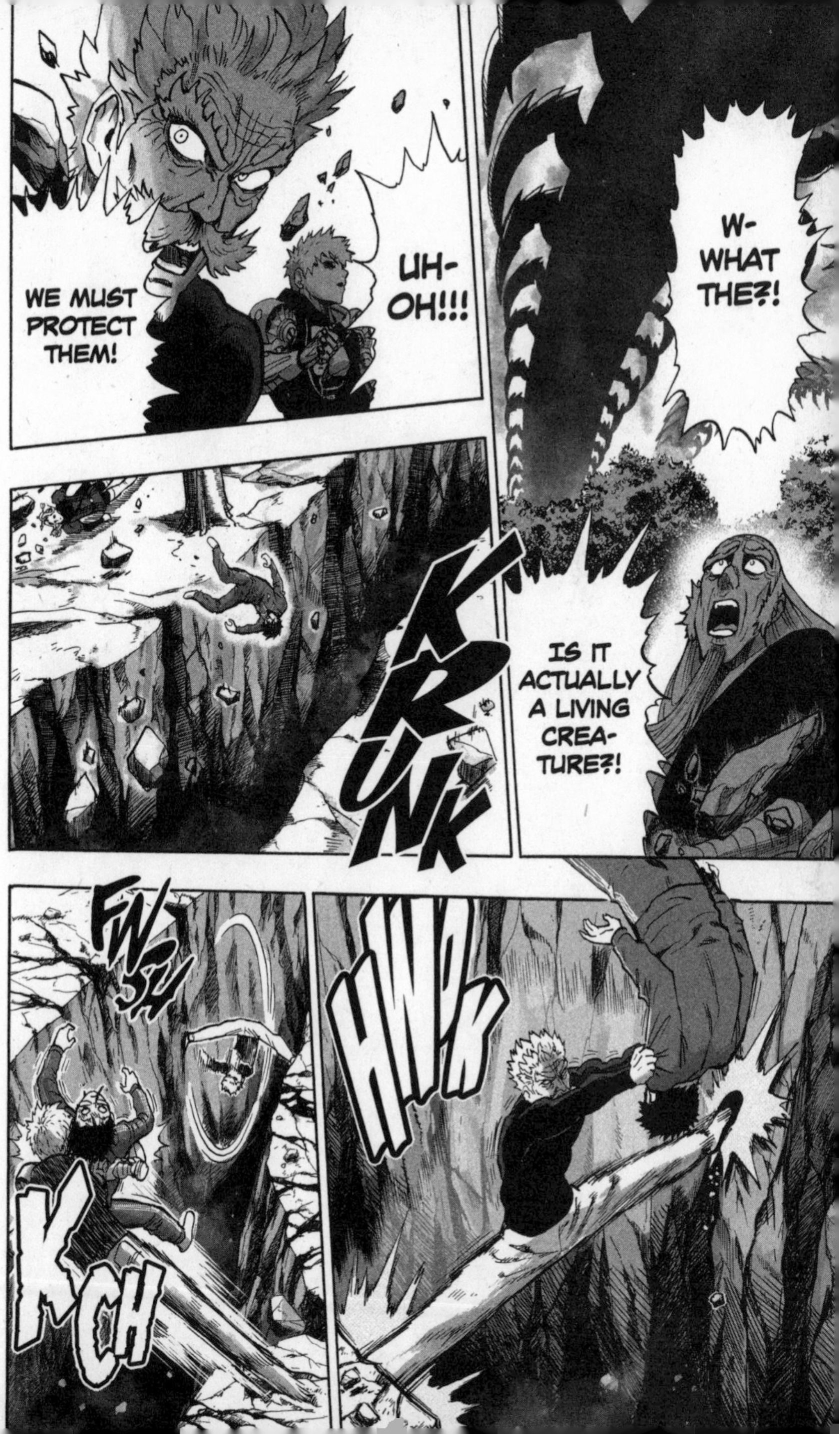
W-WHAT THE?!
IS IT ACTUALLY A LIVING CREATURE?!
UH-OH!!!
WE MUST PROTECT THEM!
KRUNK
HWAK
FWSH
KCH

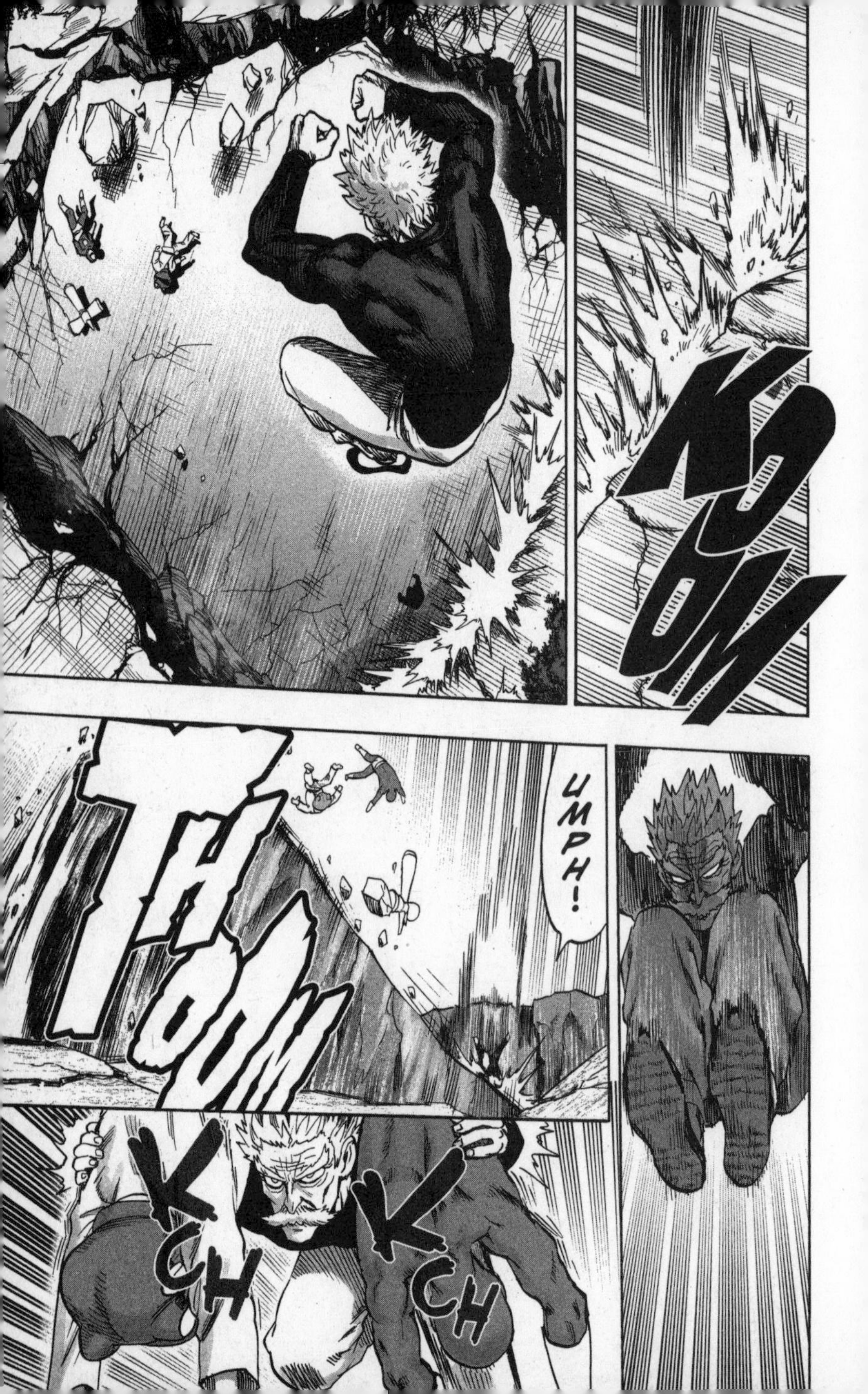

UMPH!
KCH
KCH

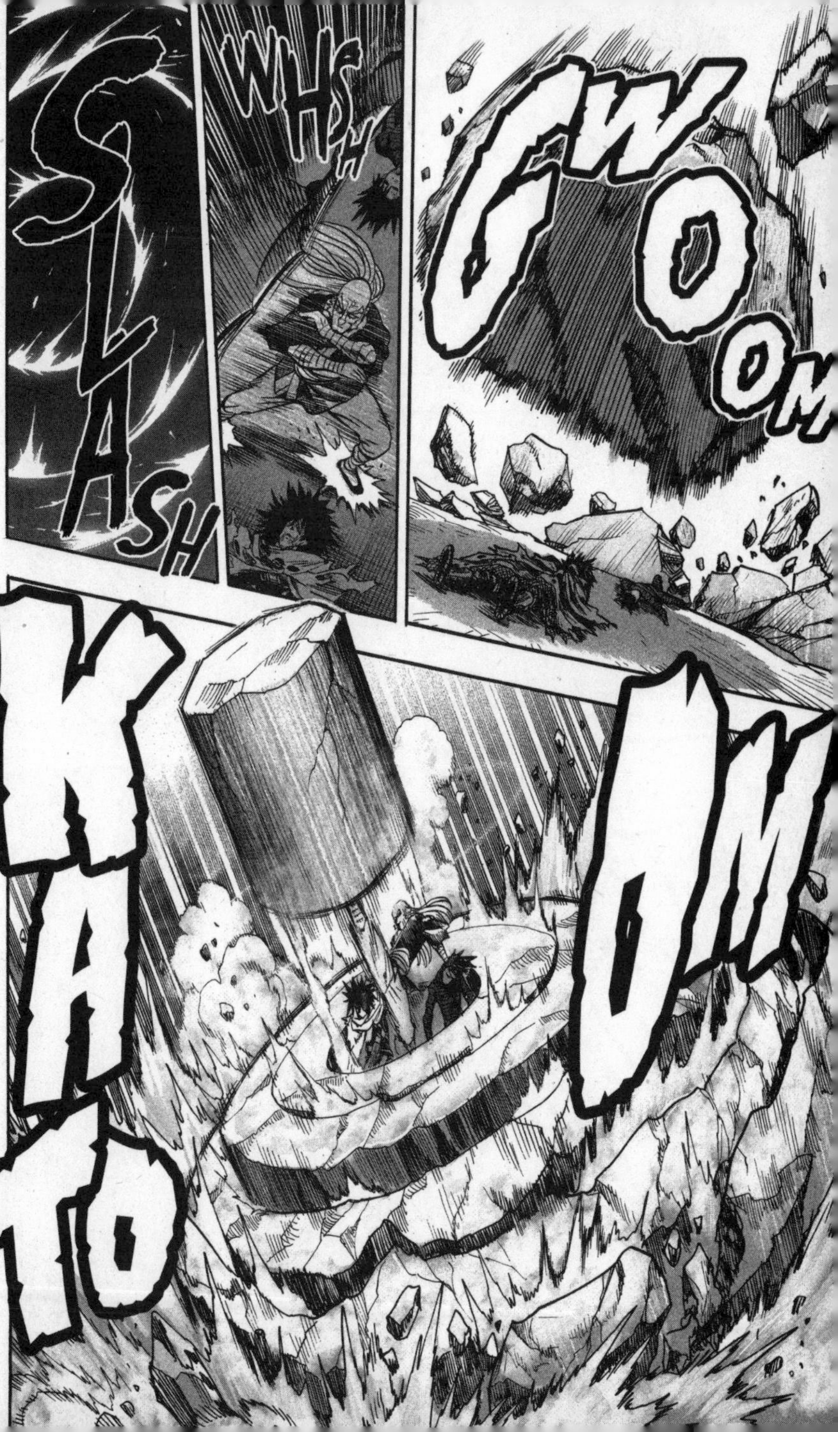
GWOOM
WHSH
SLASH
KATOOM

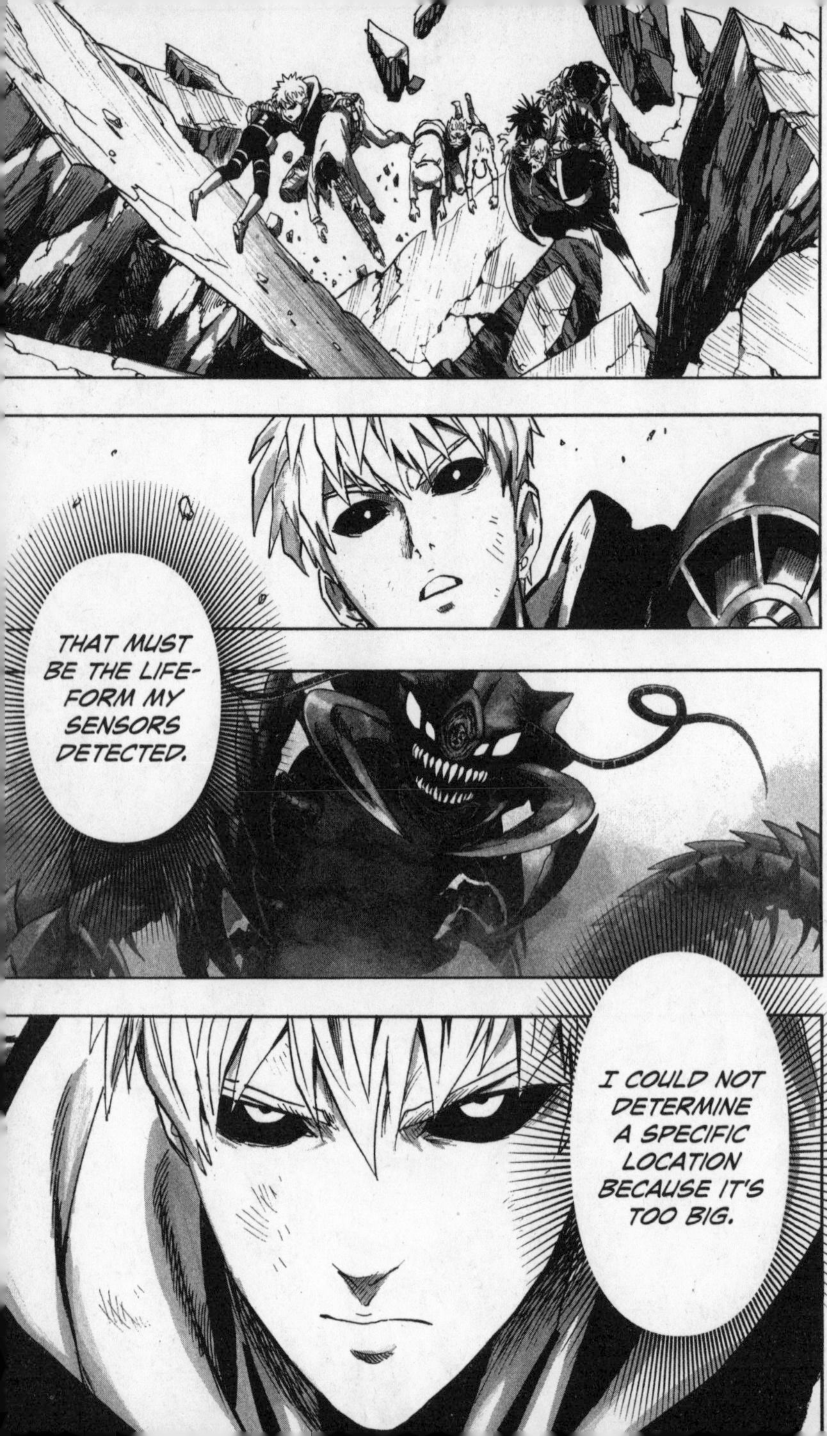
THAT MUST BE THE LIFE-FORM MY SENSORS DETECTED.
I COULD NOT DETERMINE A SPECIFIC LOCATION BECAUSE IT'S TOO BIG.

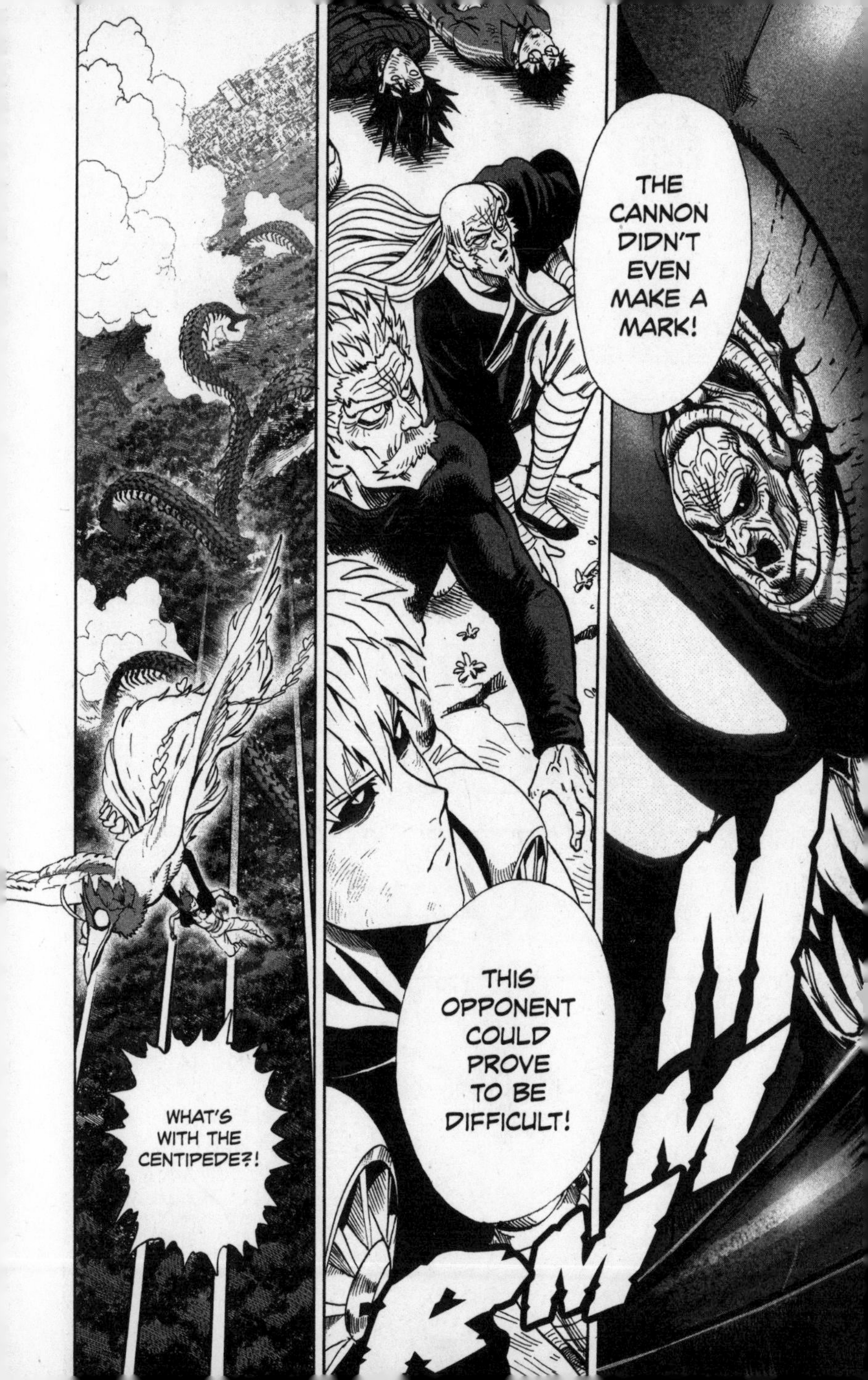
THE CANNON DIDN'T EVEN MAKE A MARK!
THIS OPPONENT COULD PROVE TO BE DIFFICULT!
WHAT'S WITH THE CENTIPEDE?!

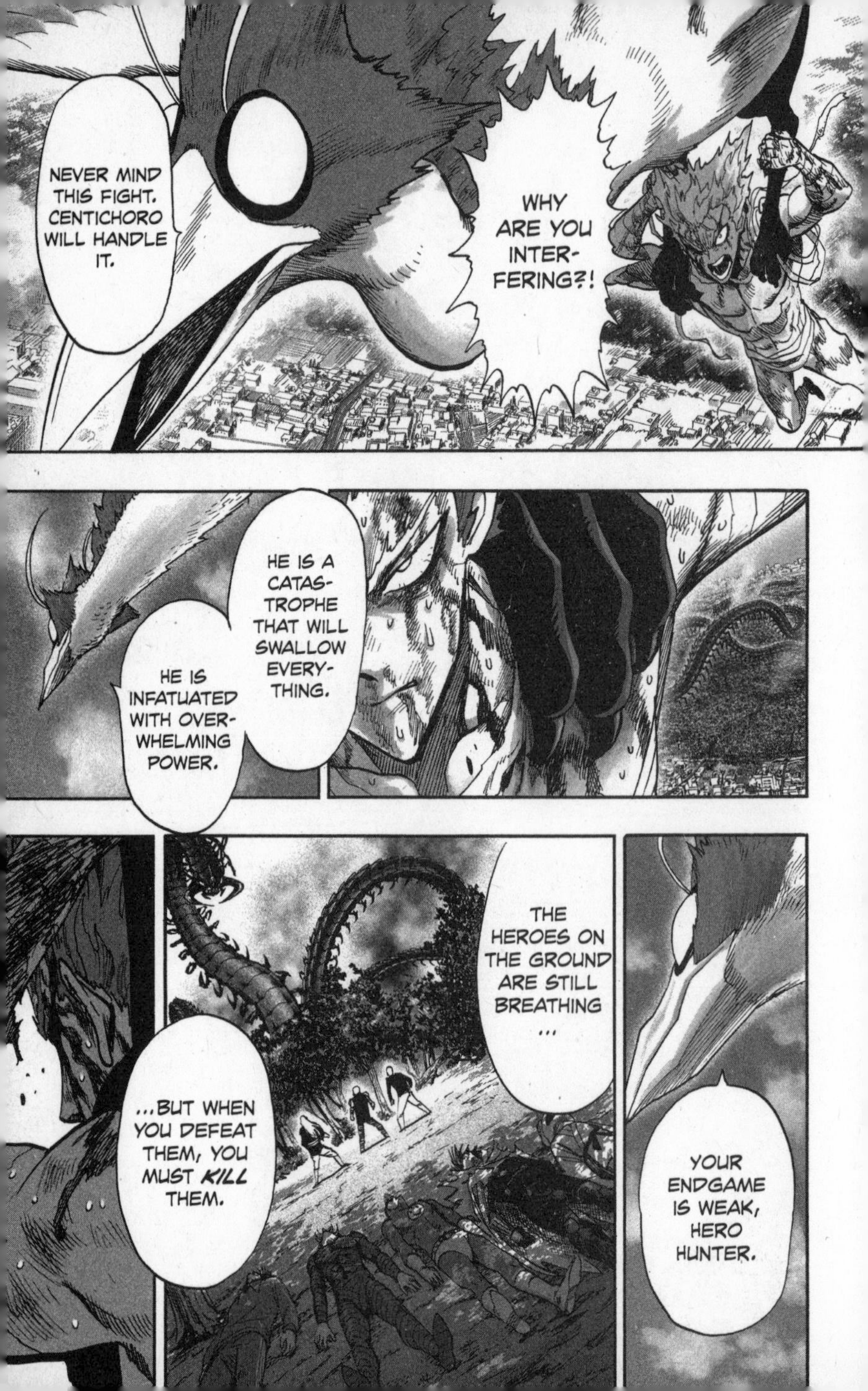
WHY ARE YOU INTERFERING?!
NEVER MIND THIS FIGHT. CENTICHORO WILL HANDLE IT.
HE IS A CATASTROPHE THAT WILL SWALLOW EVERYTHING.
HE IS INFATUATED WITH OVERWHELMING POWER.
YOUR ENDGAME IS WEAK, HERO HUNTER.
THE HEROES ON THE GROUND ARE STILL BREATHING ...
...BUT WHEN YOU DEFEAT THEM, YOU MUST *KILL* THEM.

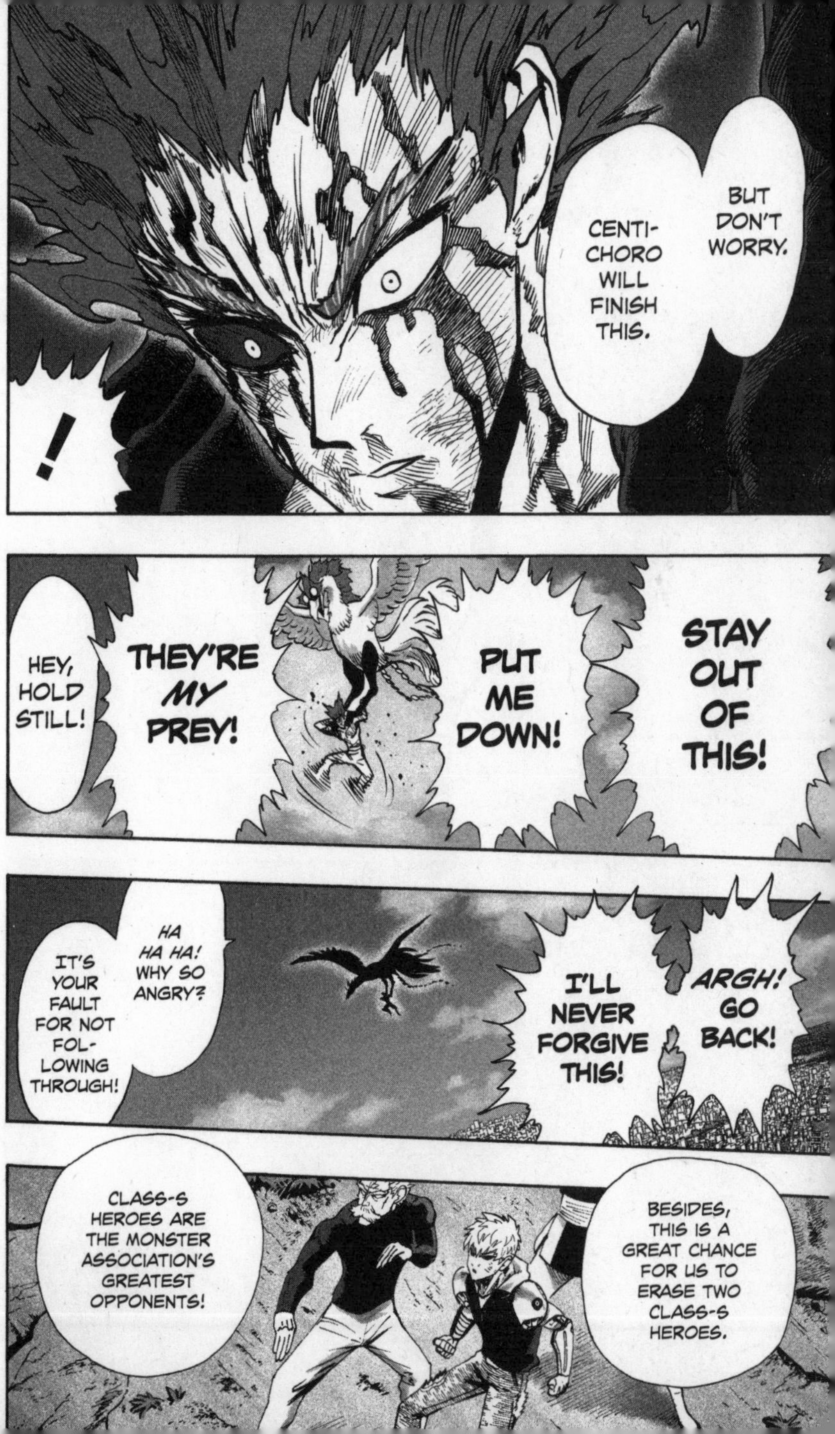
BUT DON'T WORRY.
CENTI-CHORO WILL FINISH THIS.
!
STAY OUT OF THIS!
PUT ME DOWN!
THEY'RE *MY* PREY!
HEY, HOLD STILL!
ARGH! GO BACK!
I'LL NEVER FORGIVE THIS!
HA HA HA! WHY SO ANGRY?
IT'S YOUR FAULT FOR NOT FOL-LOWING THROUGH!
BESIDES, THIS IS A GREAT CHANCE FOR US TO ERASE TWO CLASS-S HEROES.
CLASS-S HEROES ARE THE MONSTER ASSOCIATION'S GREATEST OPPONENTS!

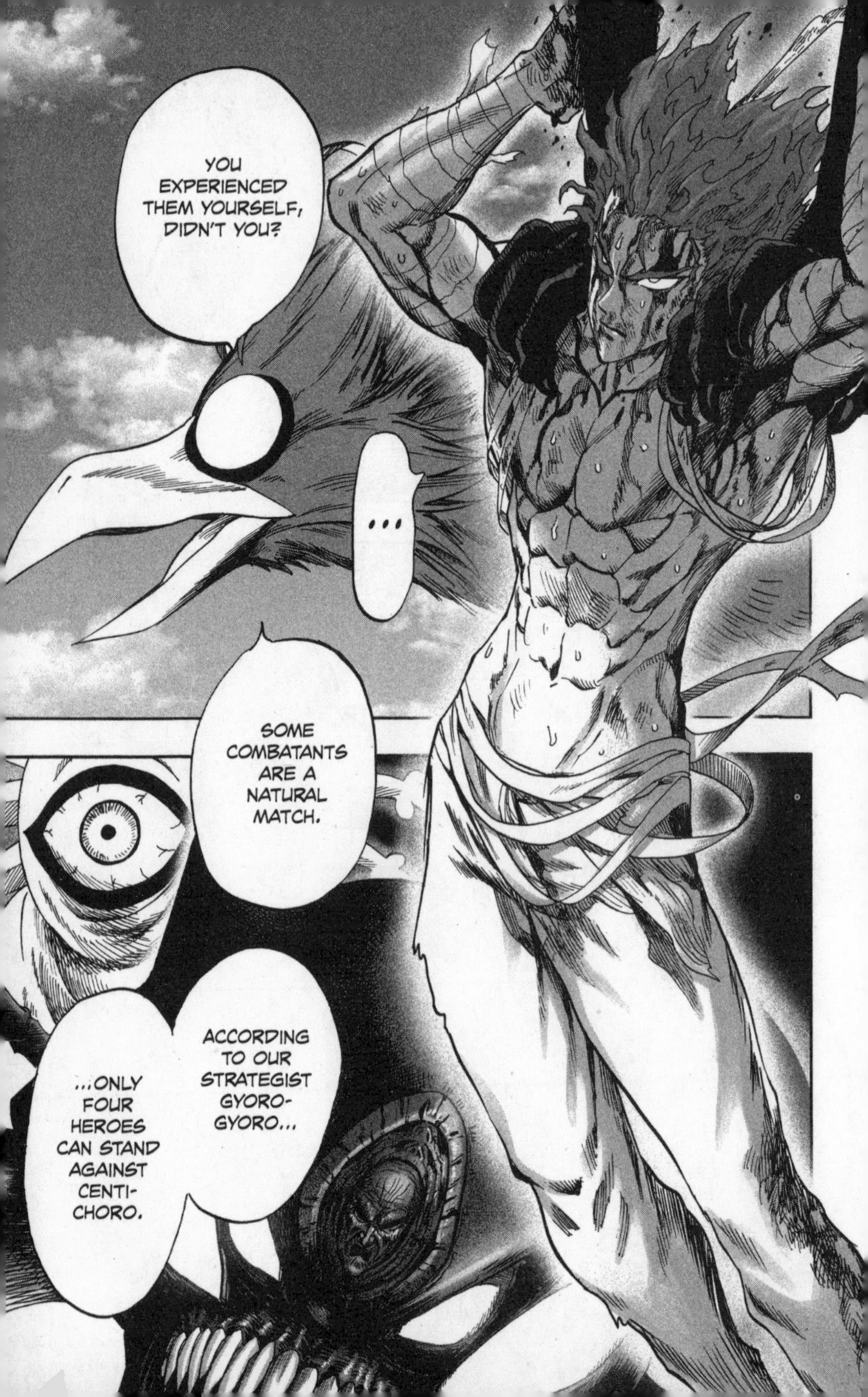
YOU EXPERIENCED THEM YOURSELF, DIDN'T YOU?
...
SOME COMBATANTS ARE A NATURAL MATCH.
ACCORDING TO OUR STRATEGIST GYORO-GYORO...
...ONLY FOUR HEROES CAN STAND AGAINST CENTI-CHORO.

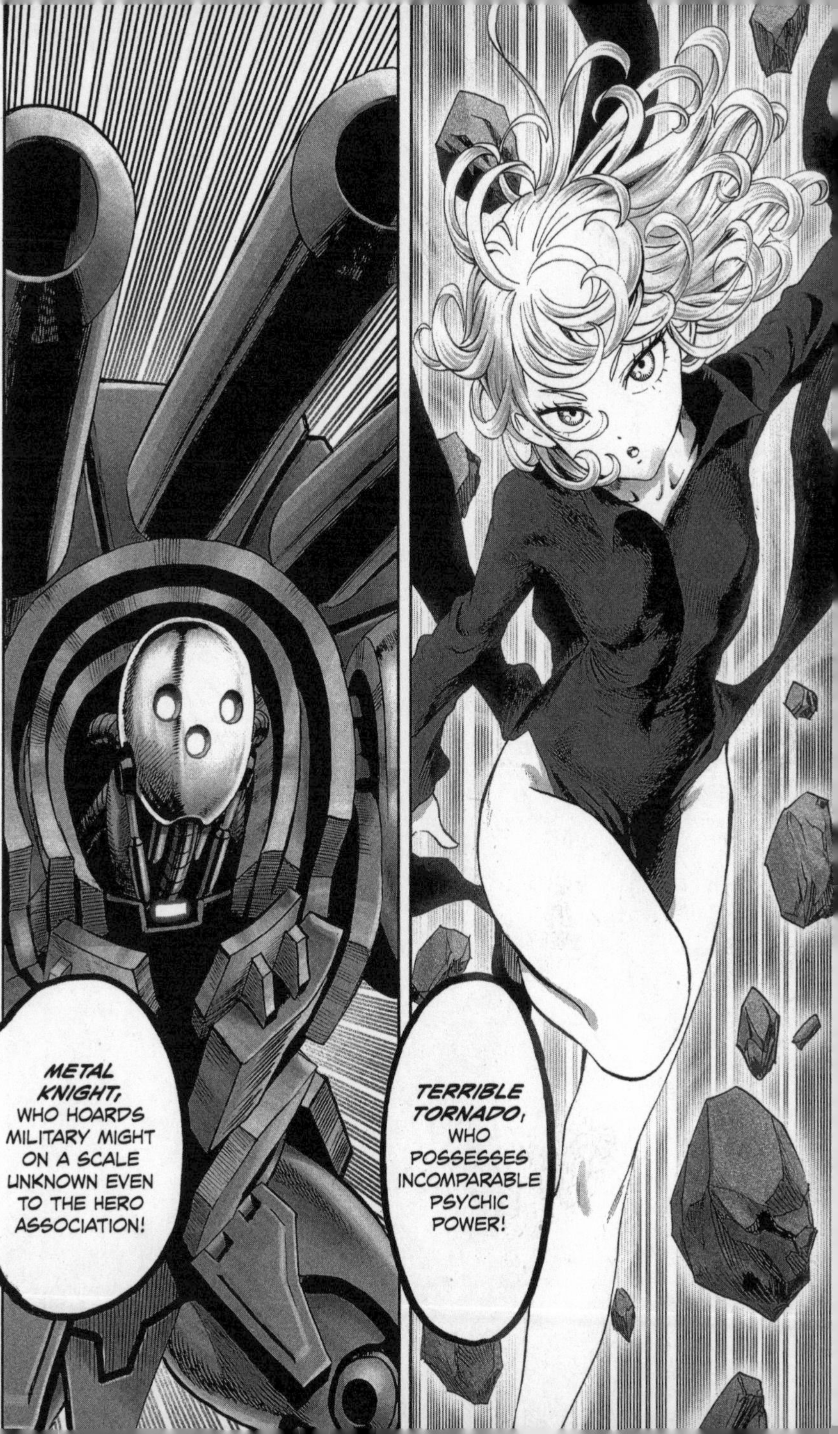
TERRIBLE TORNADO, WHO POSSESSES INCOMPARABLE PSYCHIC POWER!
METAL KNIGHT, WHO HOARDS MILITARY MIGHT ON A SCALE UNKNOWN EVEN TO THE HERO ASSOCIATION!

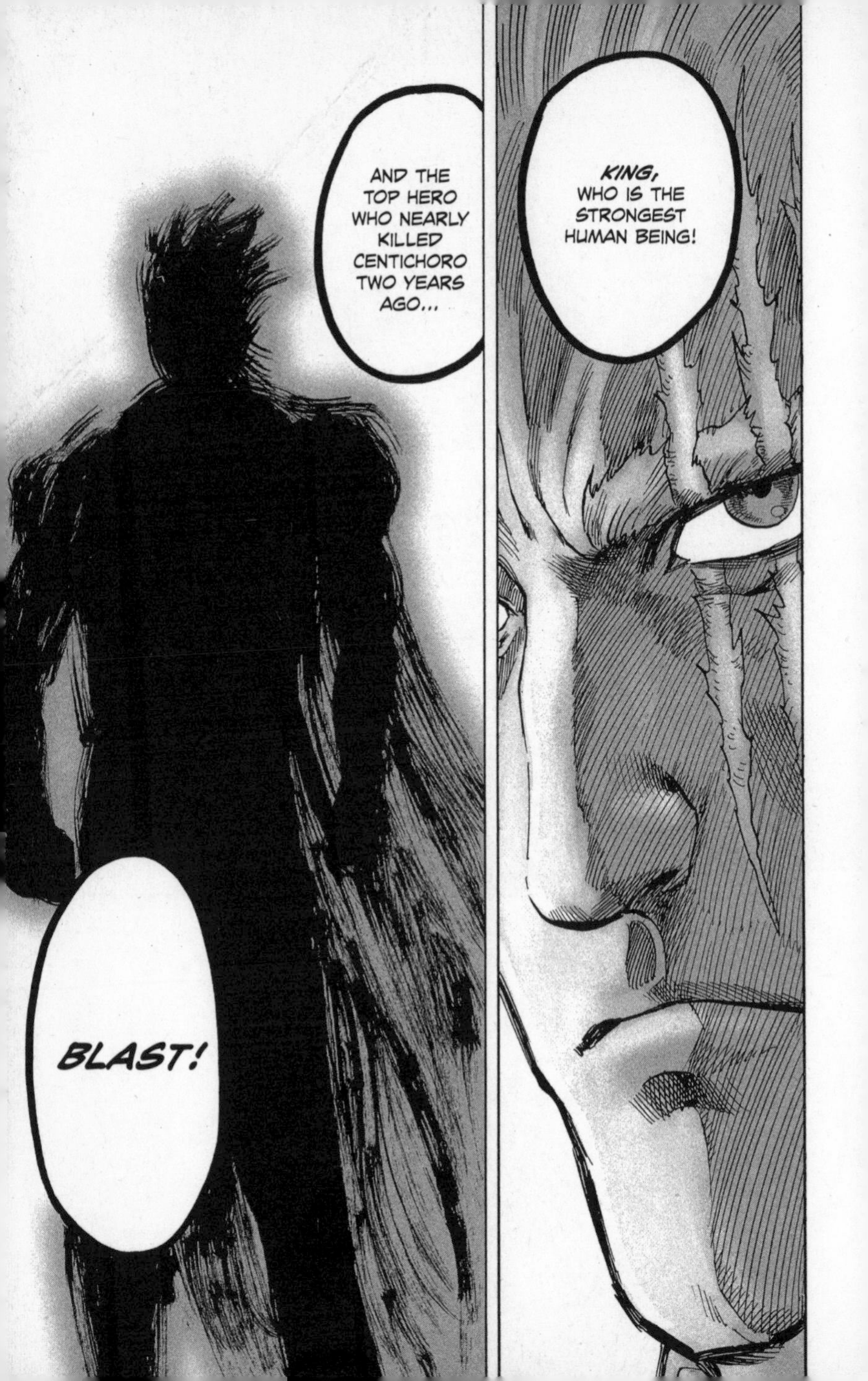
KING, WHO IS THE STRONGEST HUMAN BEING!
AND THE TOP HERO WHO NEARLY KILLED CENTICHORO TWO YEARS AGO...
BLAST!

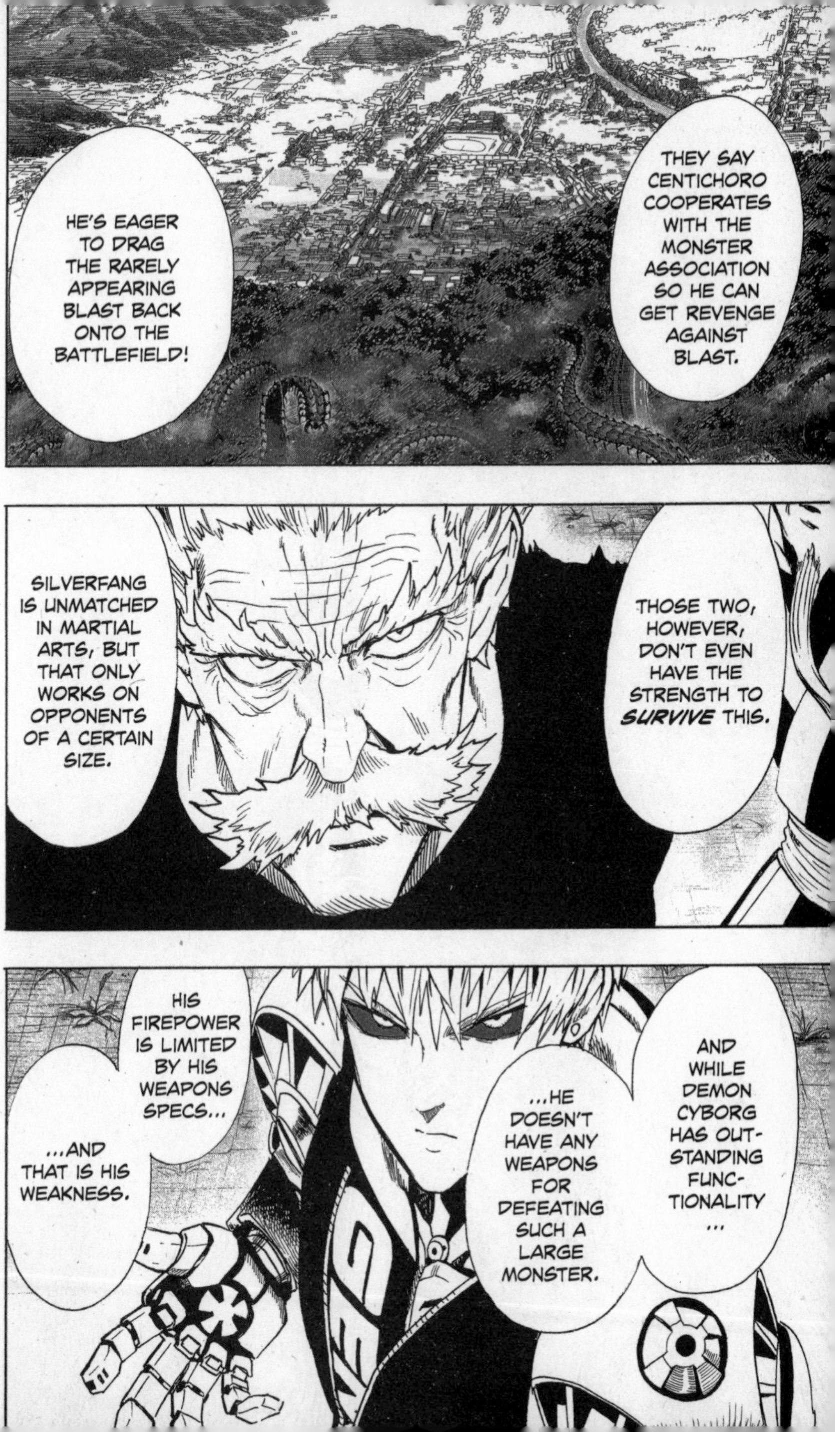
THEY SAY CENTICHORO COOPERATES WITH THE MONSTER ASSOCIATION SO HE CAN GET REVENGE AGAINST BLAST.
HE'S EAGER TO DRAG THE RARELY APPEARING BLAST BACK ONTO THE BATTLEFIELD!
THOSE TWO, HOWEVER, DON'T EVEN HAVE THE STRENGTH TO *SURVIVE* THIS.
SILVERFANG IS UNMATCHED IN MARTIAL ARTS, BUT THAT ONLY WORKS ON OPPONENTS OF A CERTAIN SIZE.
AND WHILE DEMON CYBORG HAS OUT-STANDING FUNC-TIONALITY...
...HE DOESN'T HAVE ANY WEAPONS FOR DEFEATING SUCH A LARGE MONSTER.
HIS FIREPOWER IS LIMITED BY HIS WEAPONS SPECS...
...AND THAT IS HIS WEAKNESS.

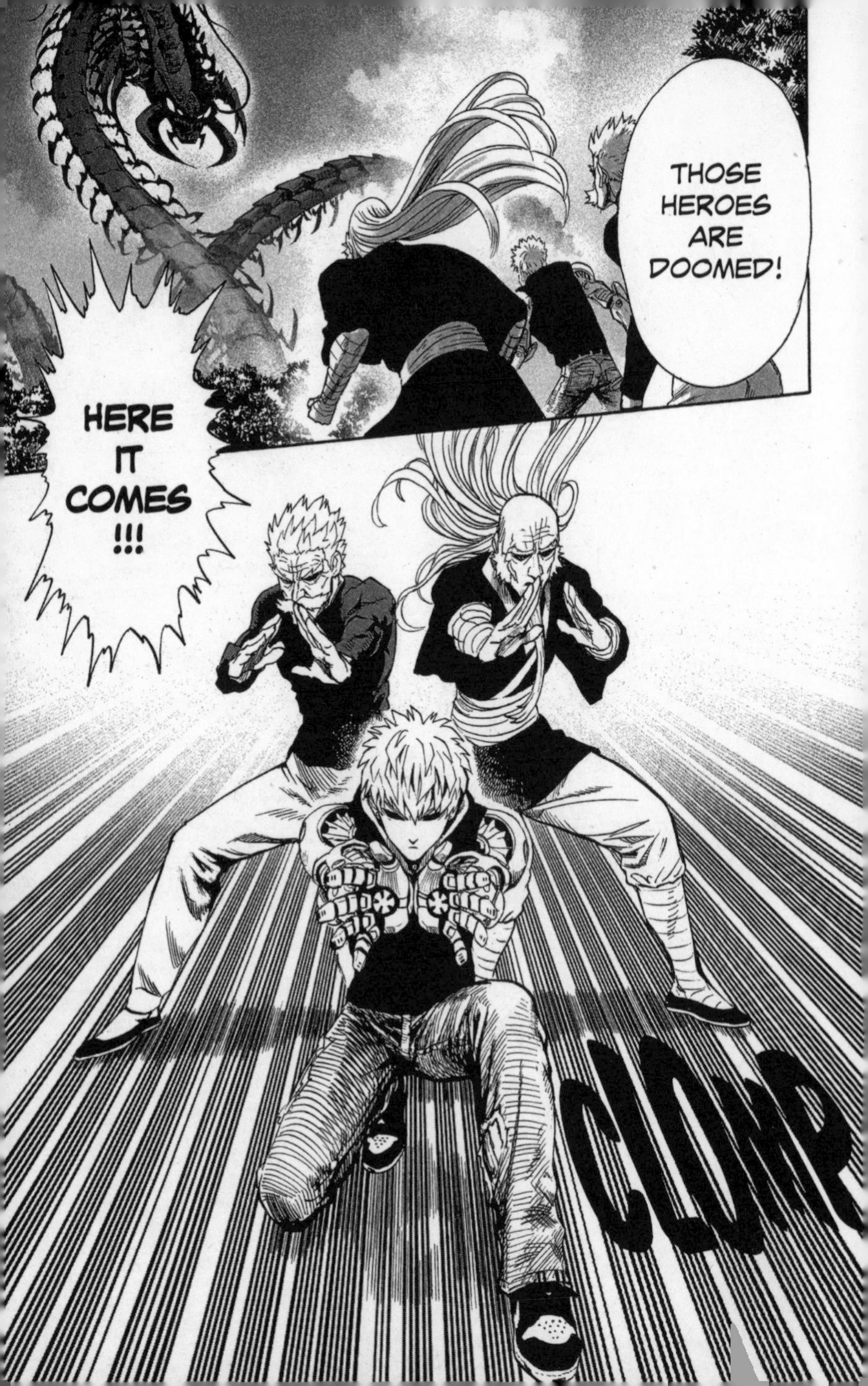
THOSE HEROES ARE DOOMED!
HERE IT COMES!!!
CLOMP

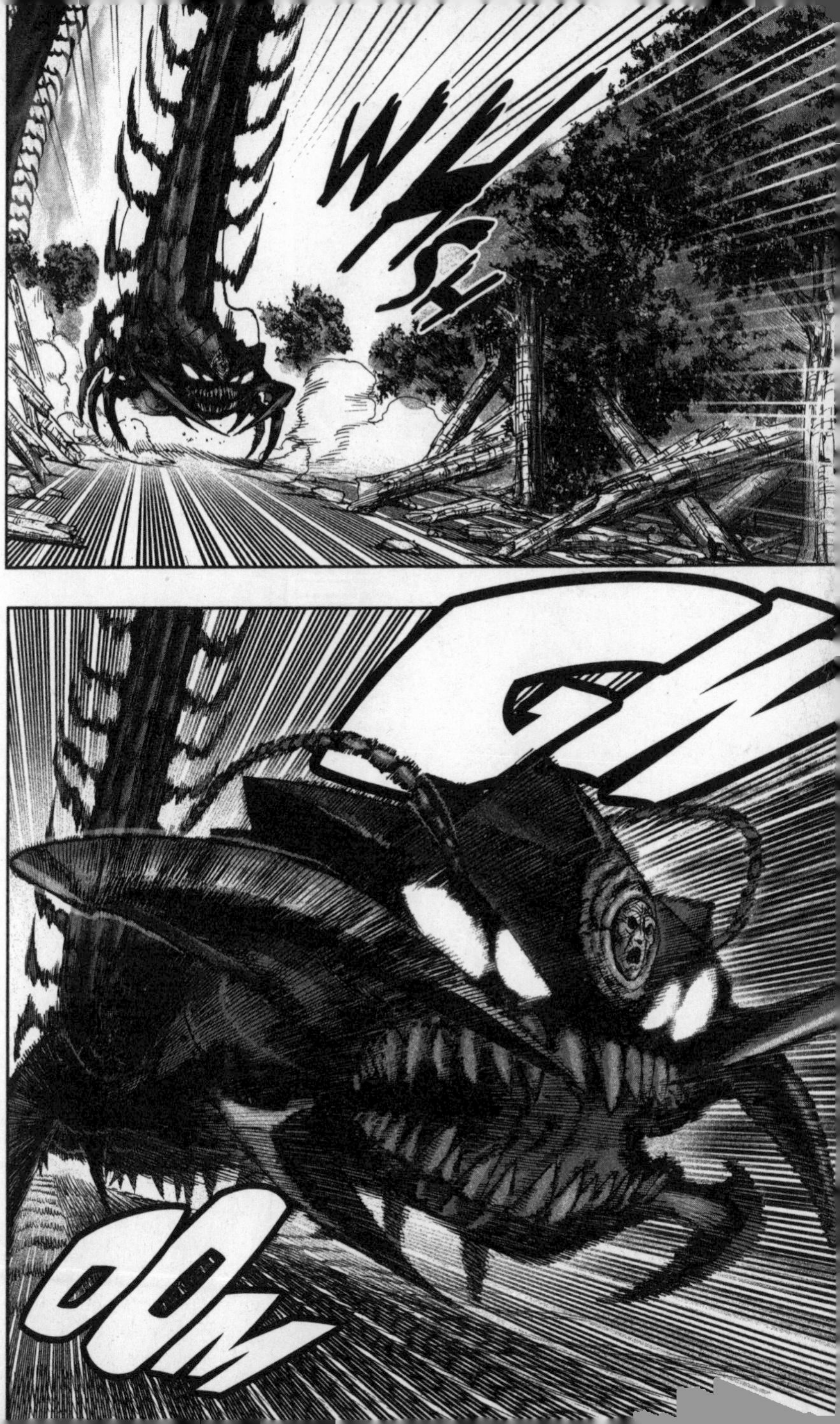
WHSH

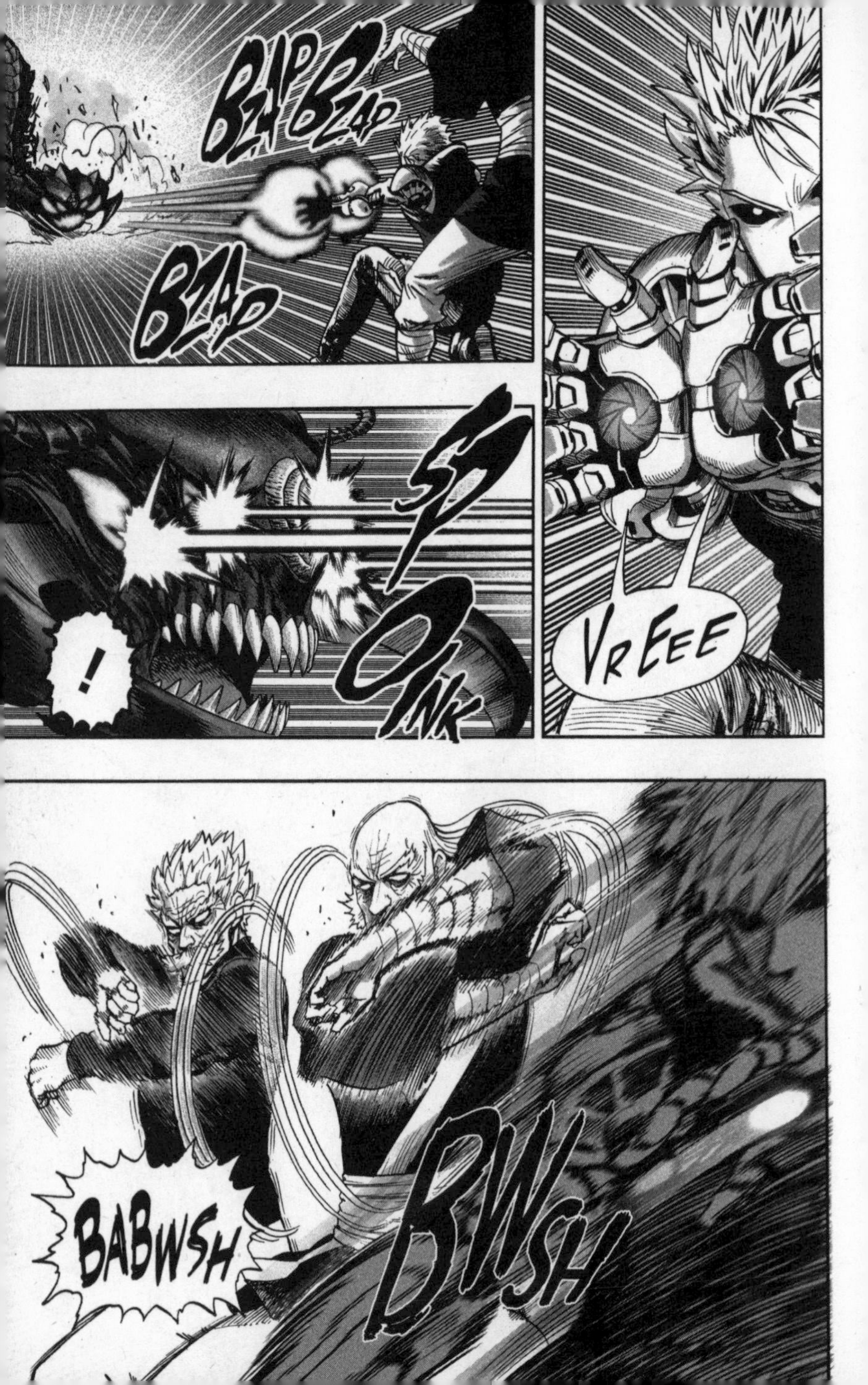
VrEEE
BZAP BZAP
BZAP
SPOINK
!
BWSH
BABWSH

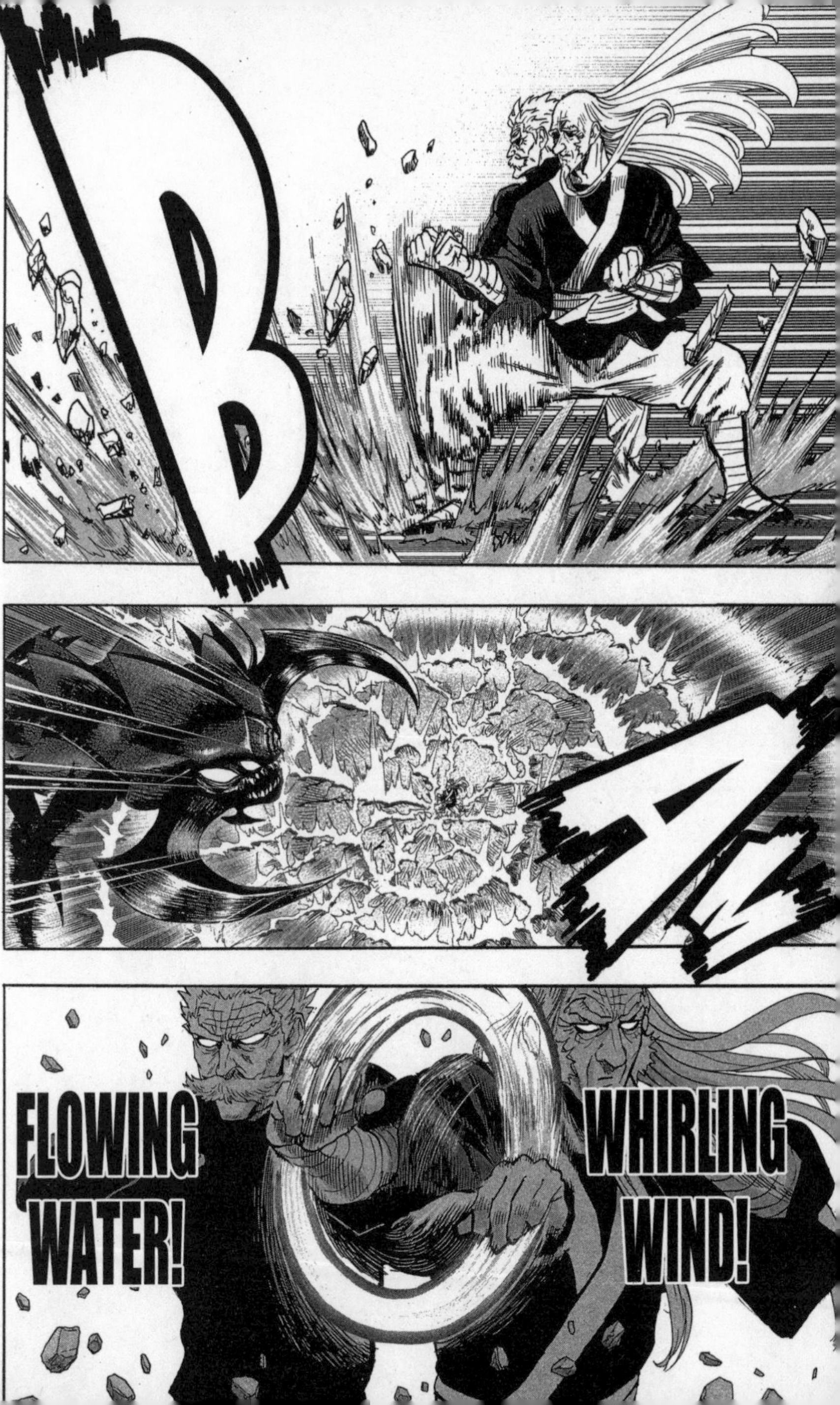
B
A
WHIRLING WIND!
FLOWING WATER!

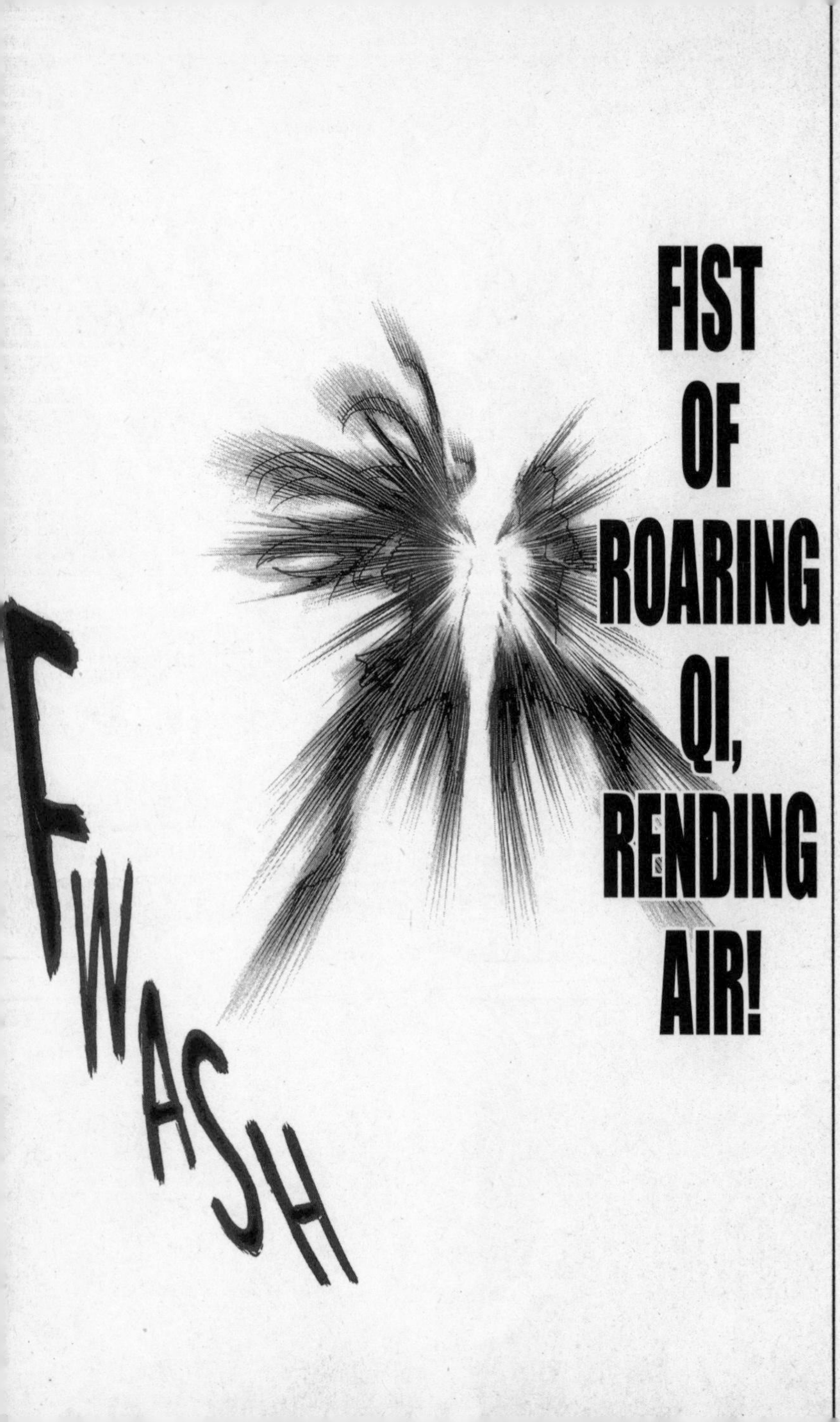
FIST OF ROARING QI, RENDING AIR!
FWASH

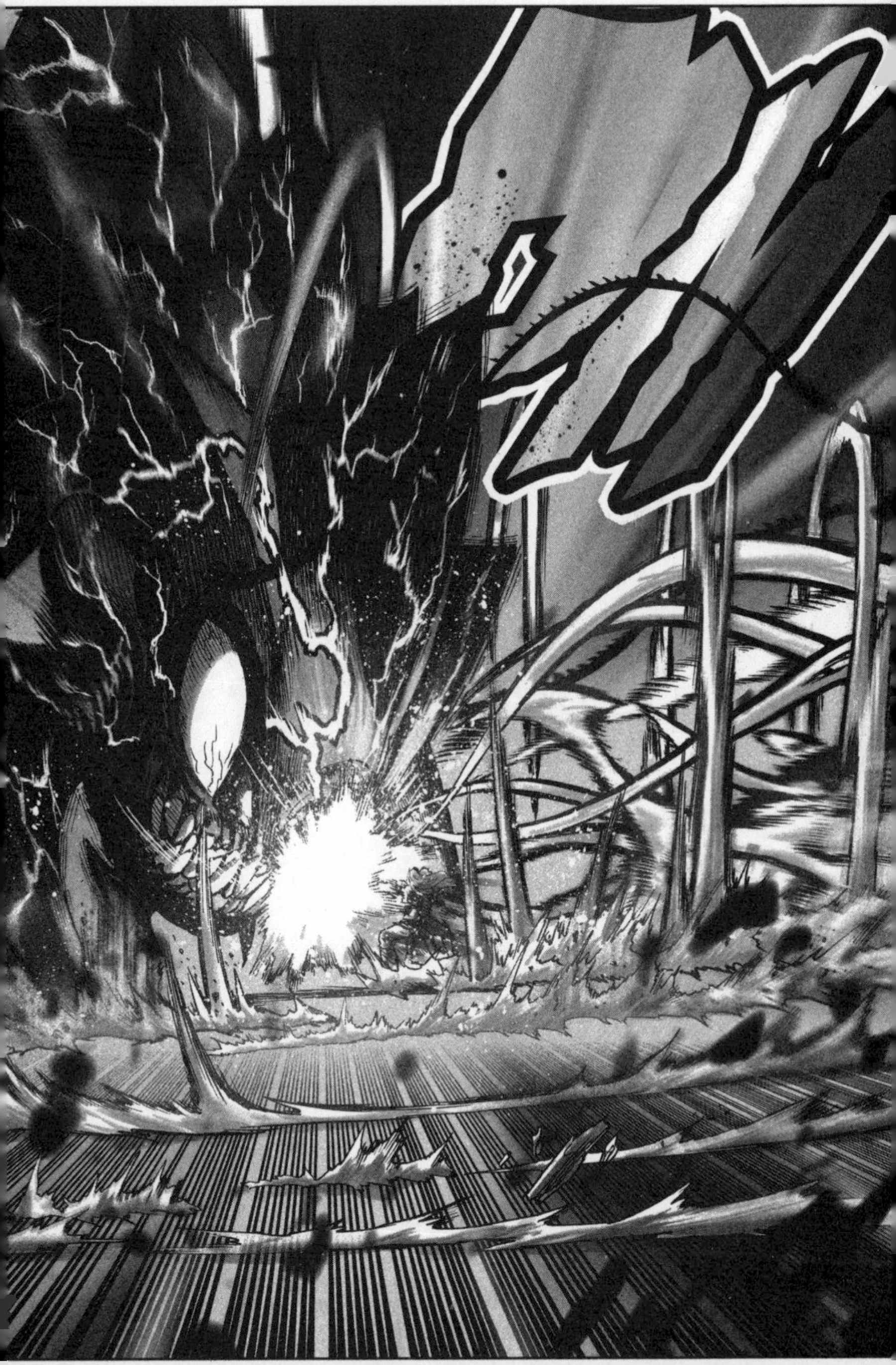

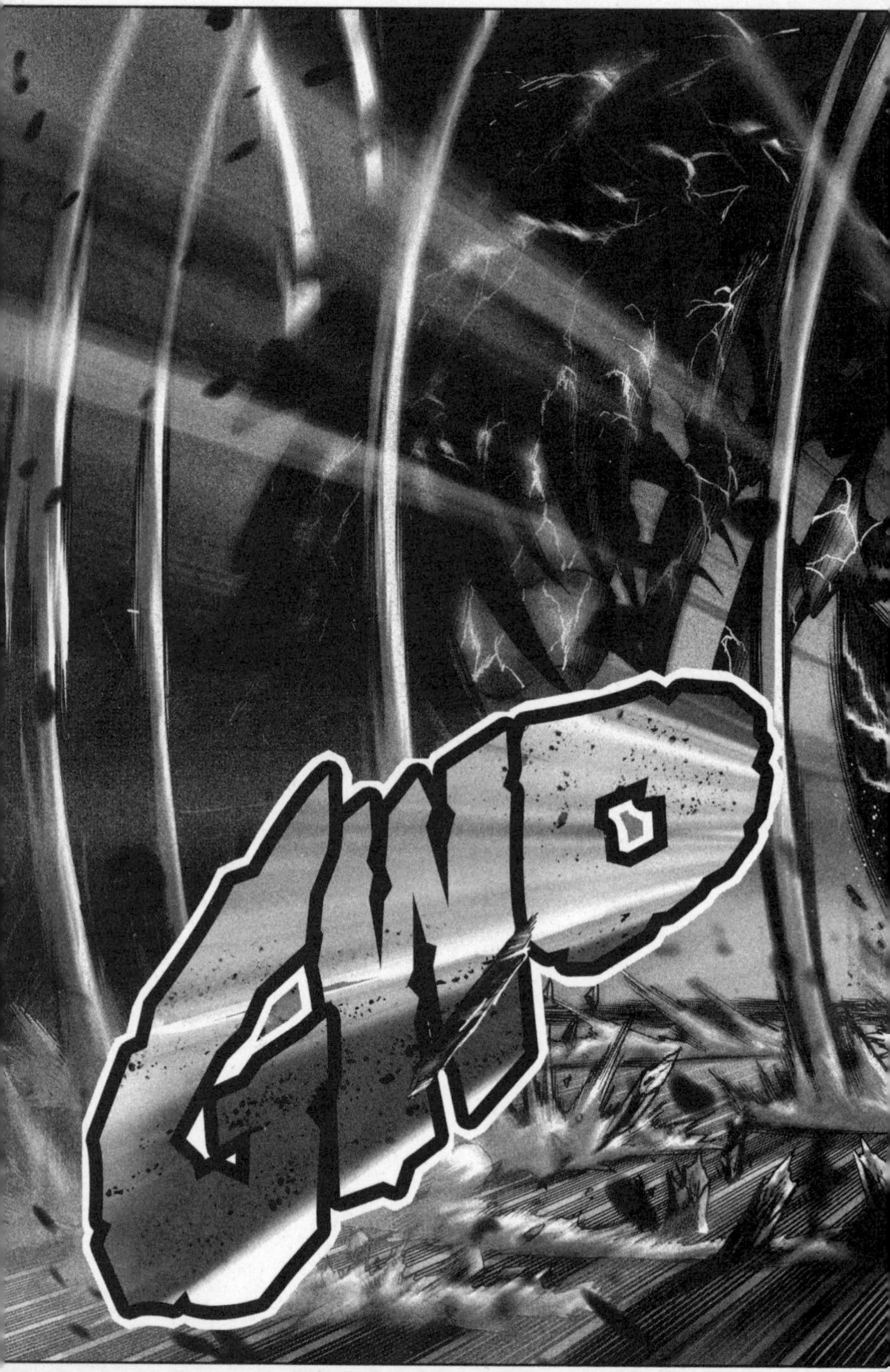

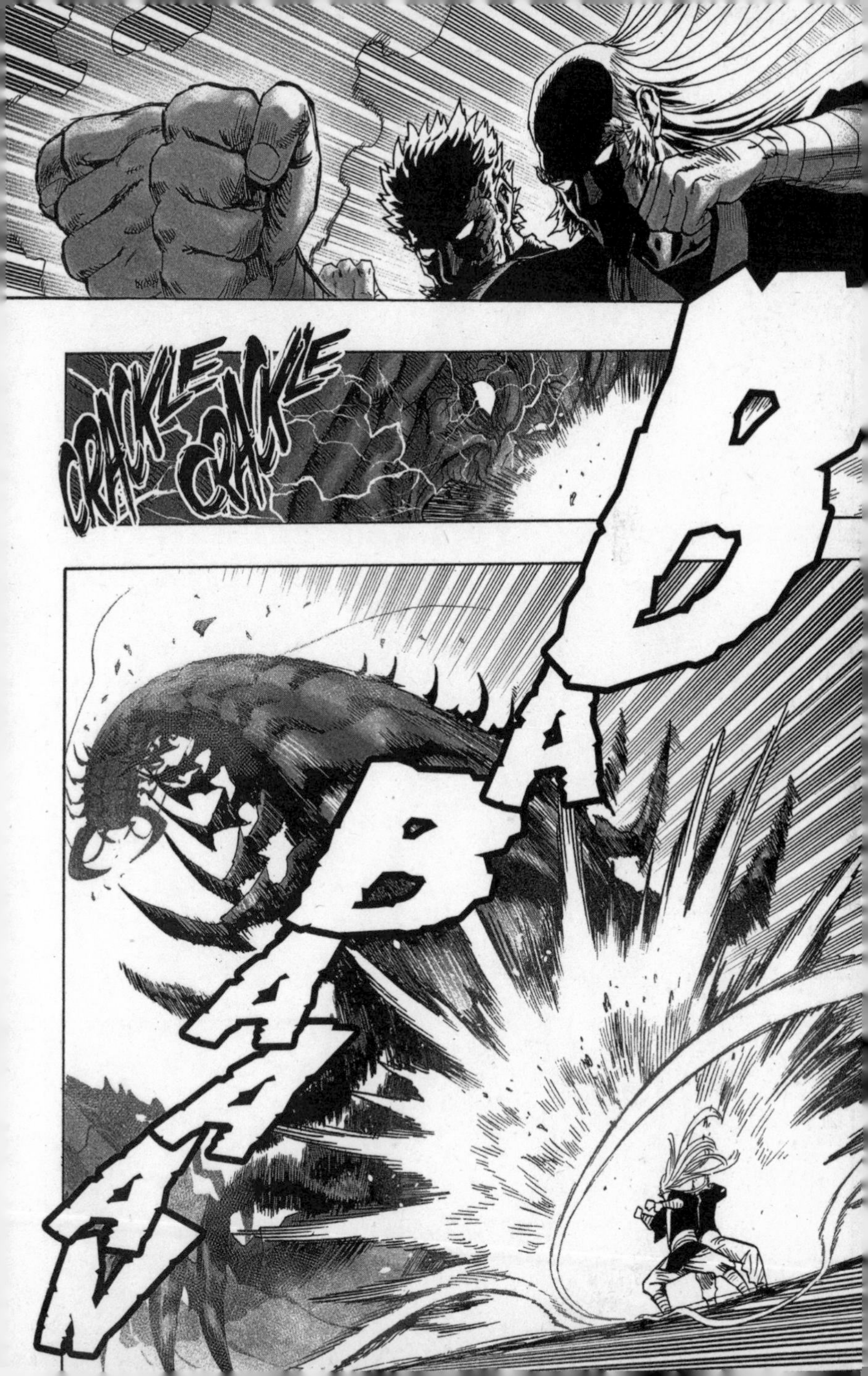
CRACKLE CRACKLE

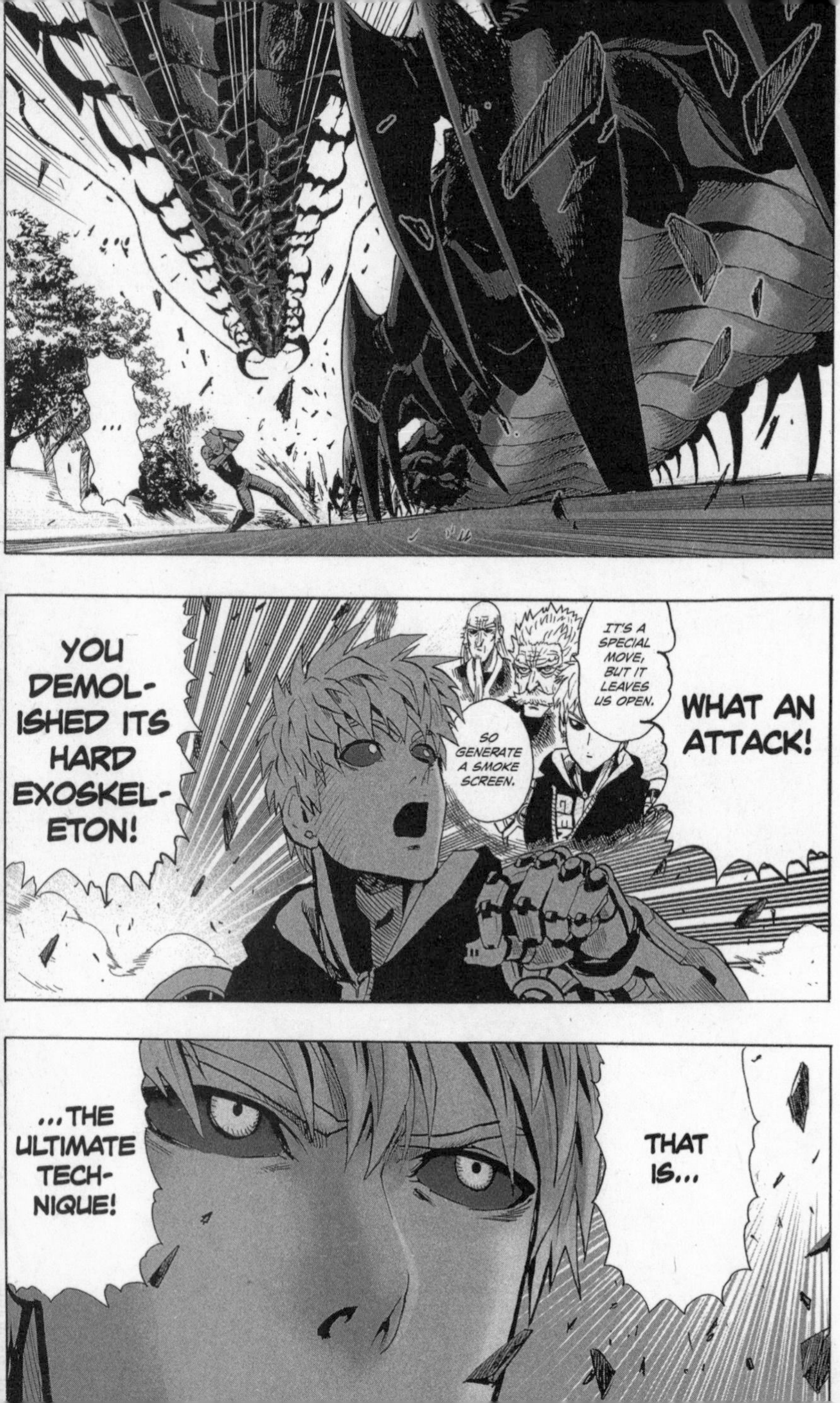
...
WHAT AN ATTACK!
IT'S A SPECIAL MOVE, BUT IT LEAVES US OPEN.
SO GENERATE A SMOKE SCREEN.
YOU DEMOLISHED ITS HARD EXOSKELETON!
THAT IS...
...THE ULTIMATE TECHNIQUE!

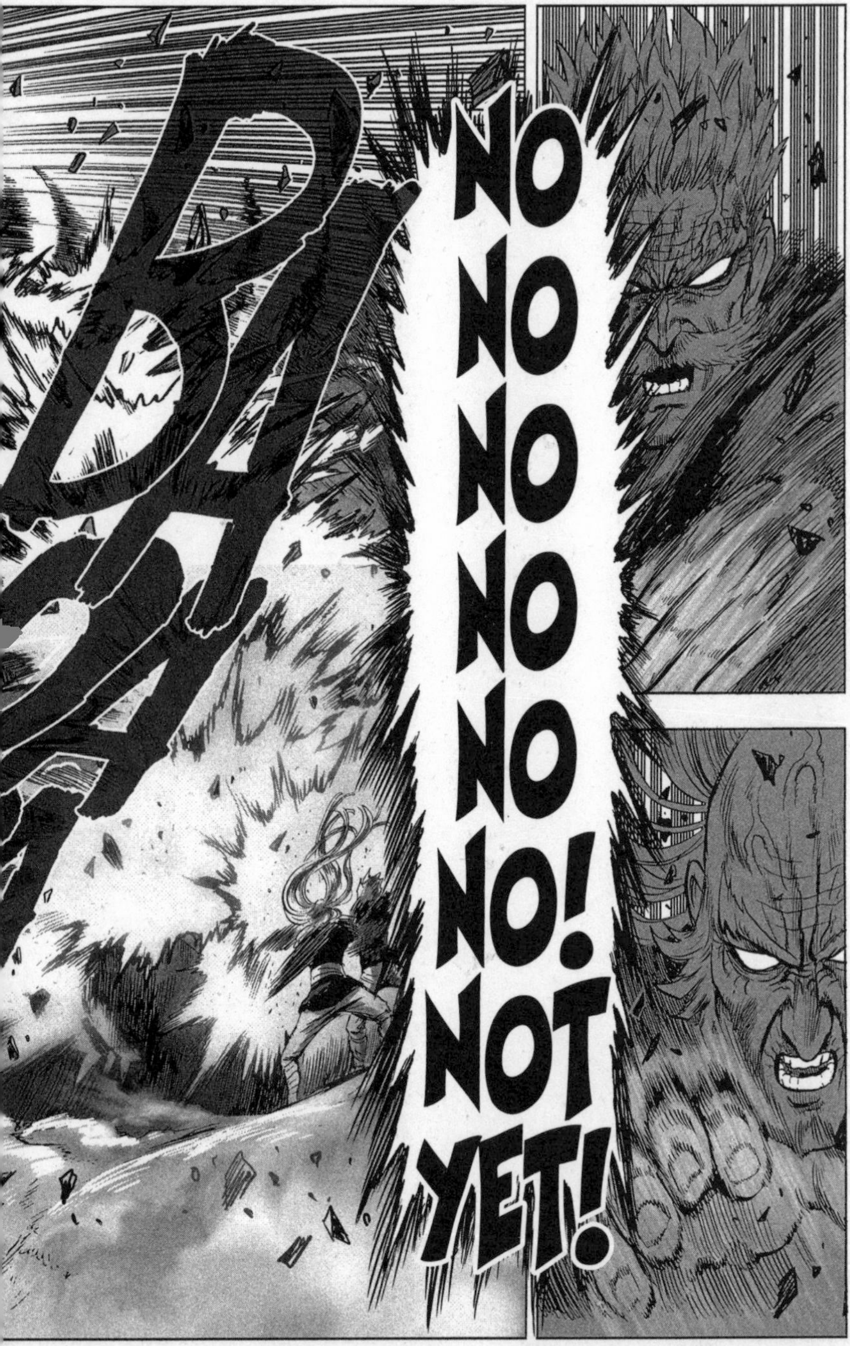
NO NO NO NO NO NO NO! NOT YET!

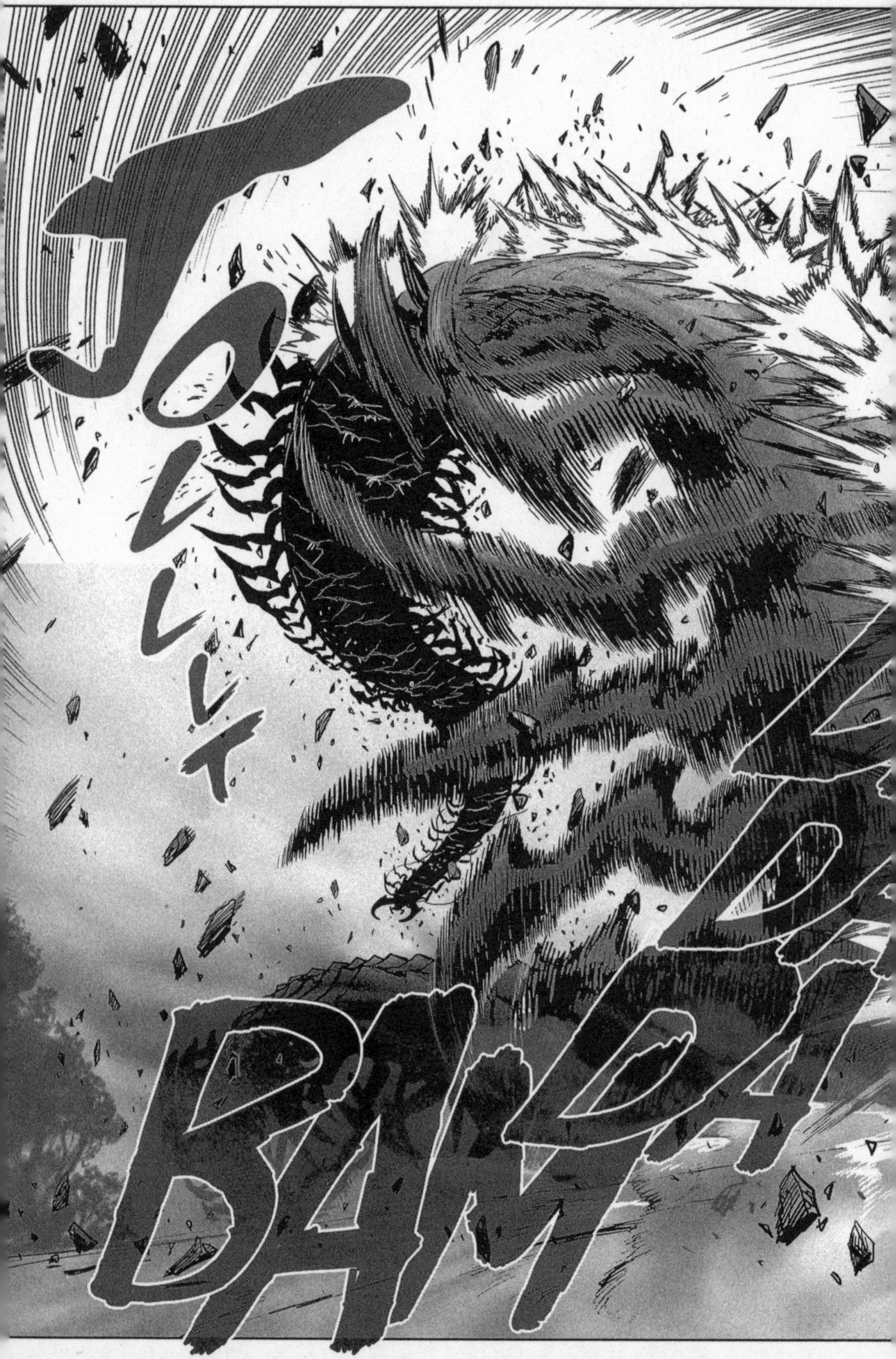
BAM

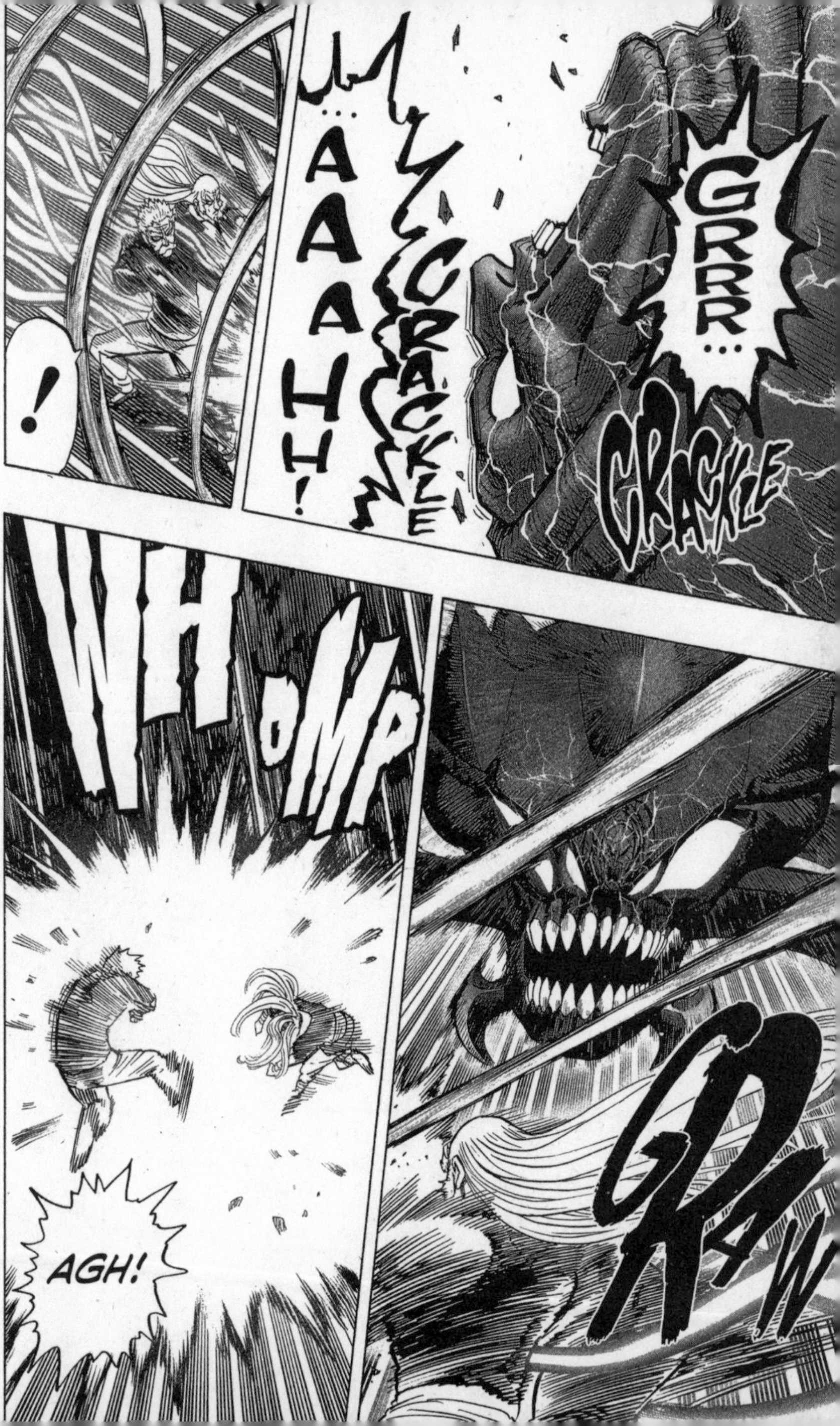
GRRR...
CRACKLE
CRACKLE
...AAAH!
!
GRAW
WHOMP
AGH!

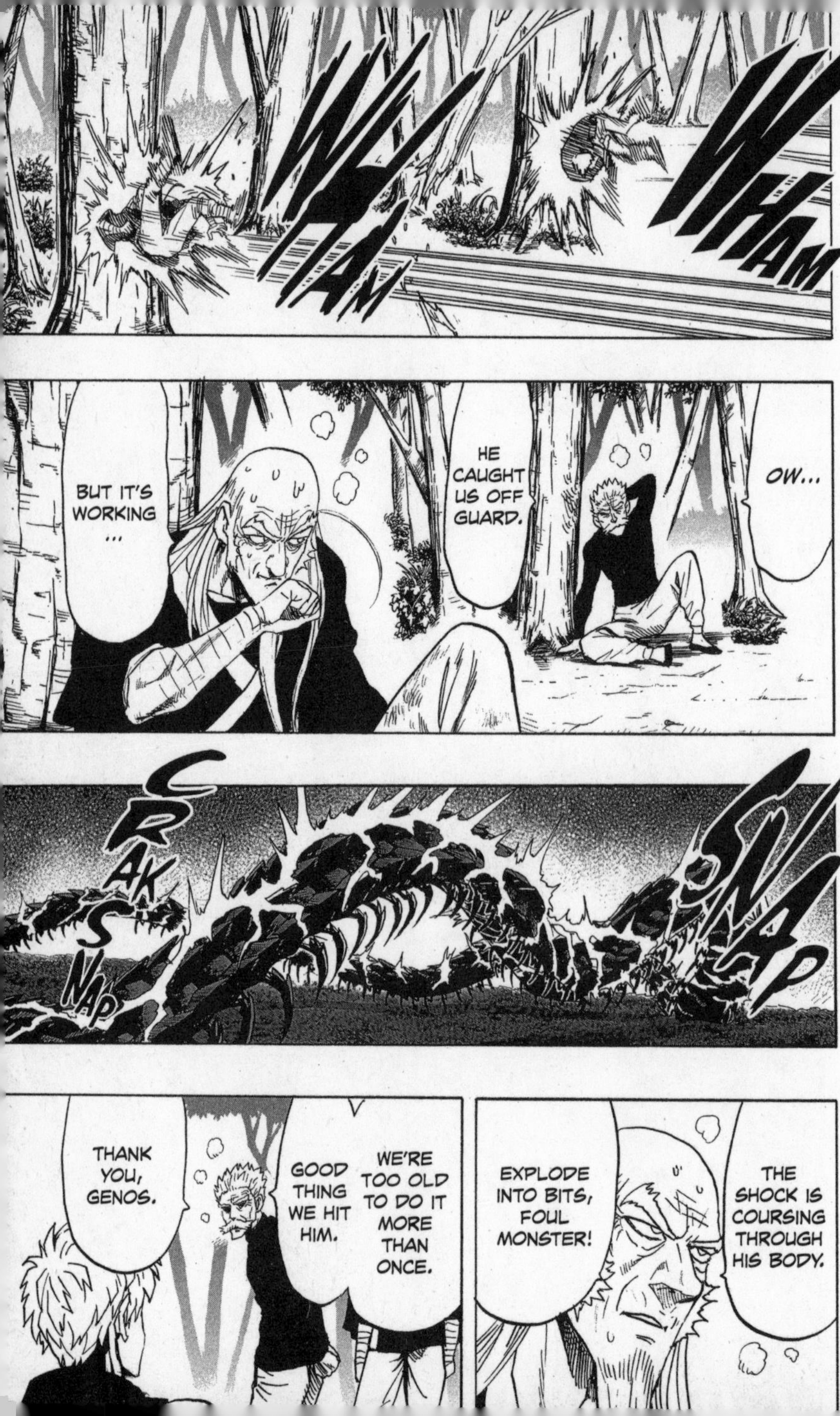
WHAM
WHAM
OW...
HE CAUGHT US OFF GUARD.
BUT IT'S WORKING ...
SNAP
CRAK
SNAP
THE SHOCK IS COURSING THROUGH HIS BODY.
EXPLODE INTO BITS, FOUL MONSTER!
WE'RE TOO OLD TO DO IT MORE THAN ONCE.
GOOD THING WE HIT HIM.
THANK YOU, GENOS.

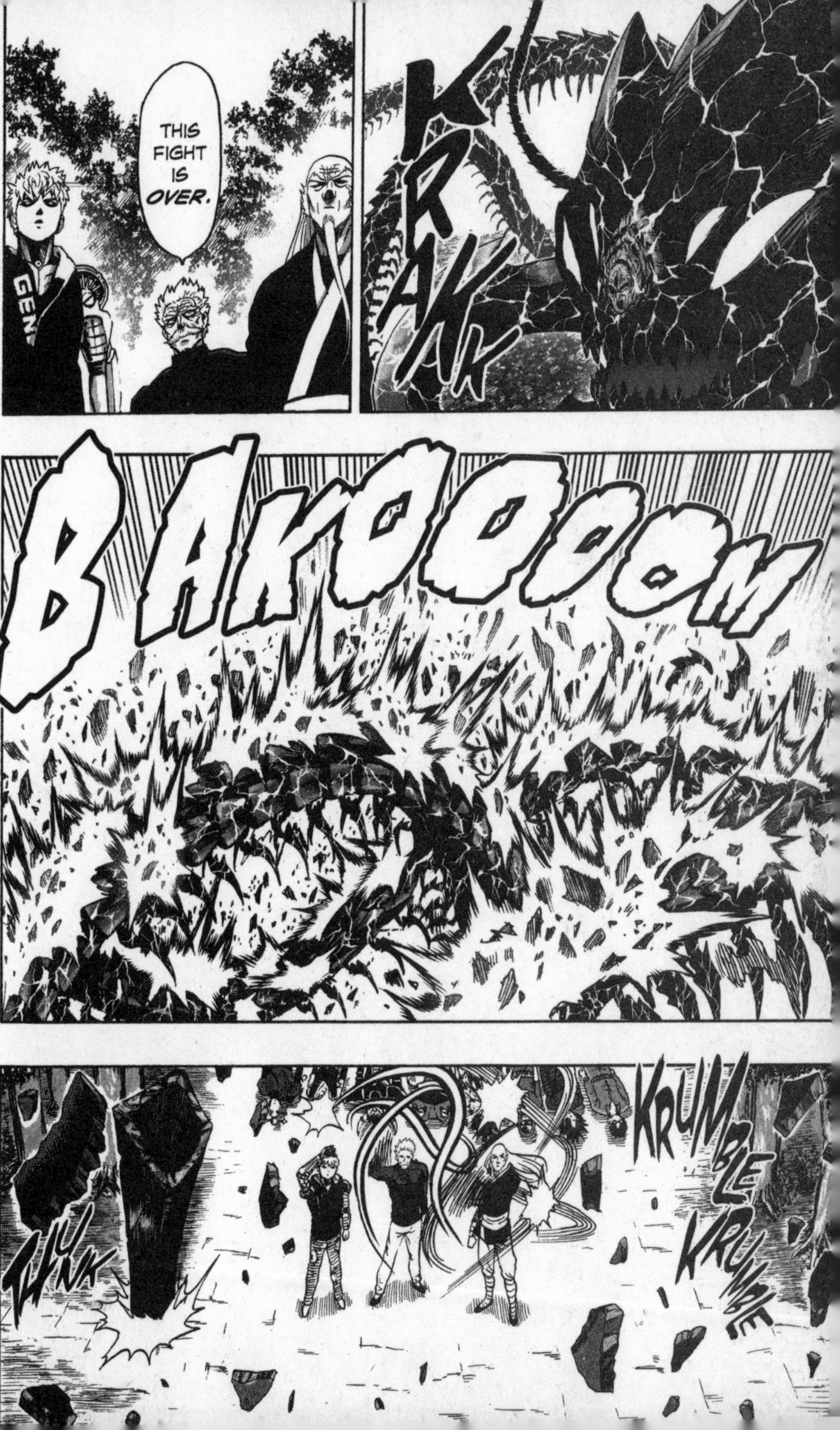
KRAKK
THIS FIGHT IS OVER.
BAKOOOOM
KRUMBLE KRUMBLE
THUNK

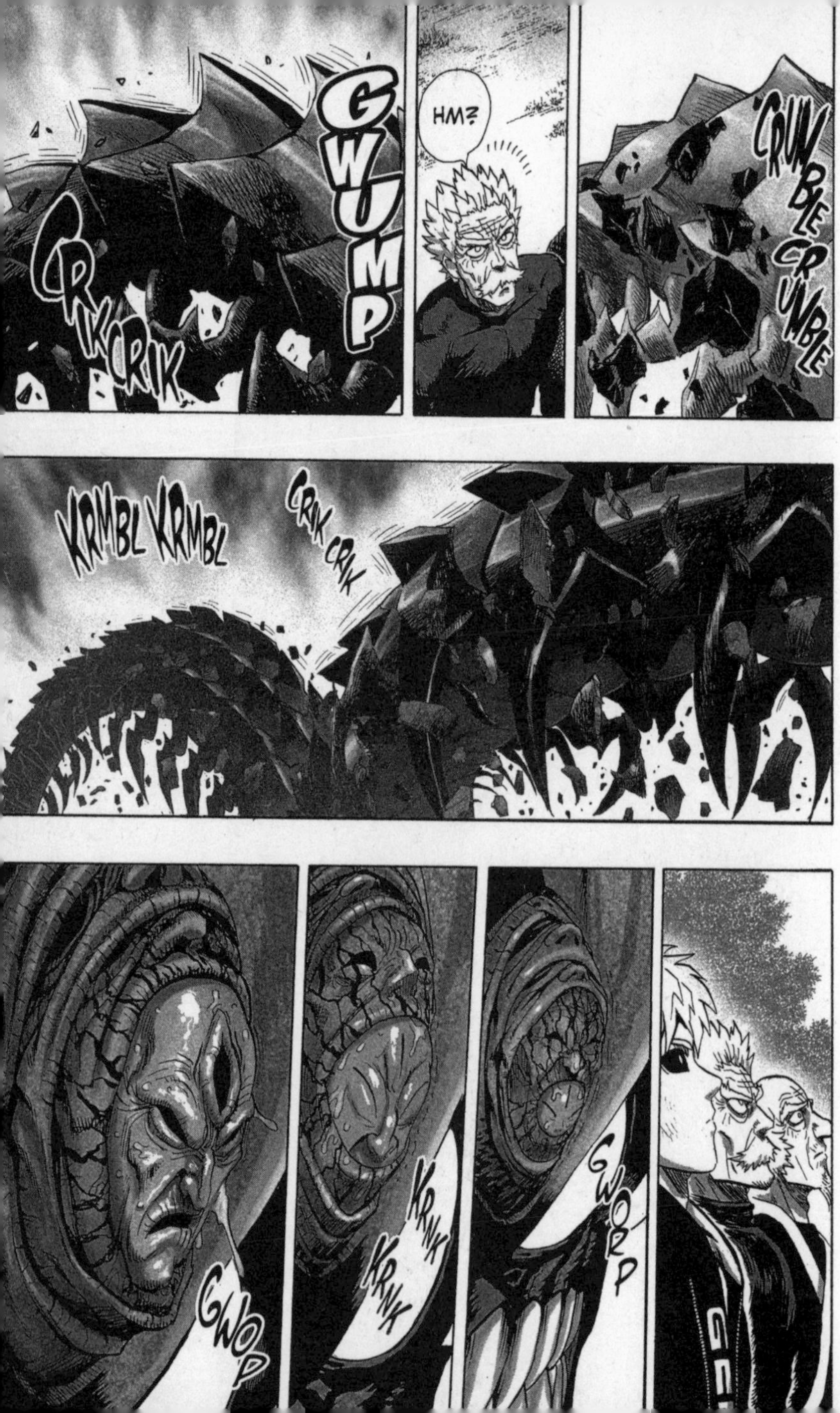
CRUMBLE CRUMBLE
HM?
GWUMP
CRIK CRIK
CRIK CRIK
KRMBL KRMBL
GWORP
KRNK KRNK
GWOP

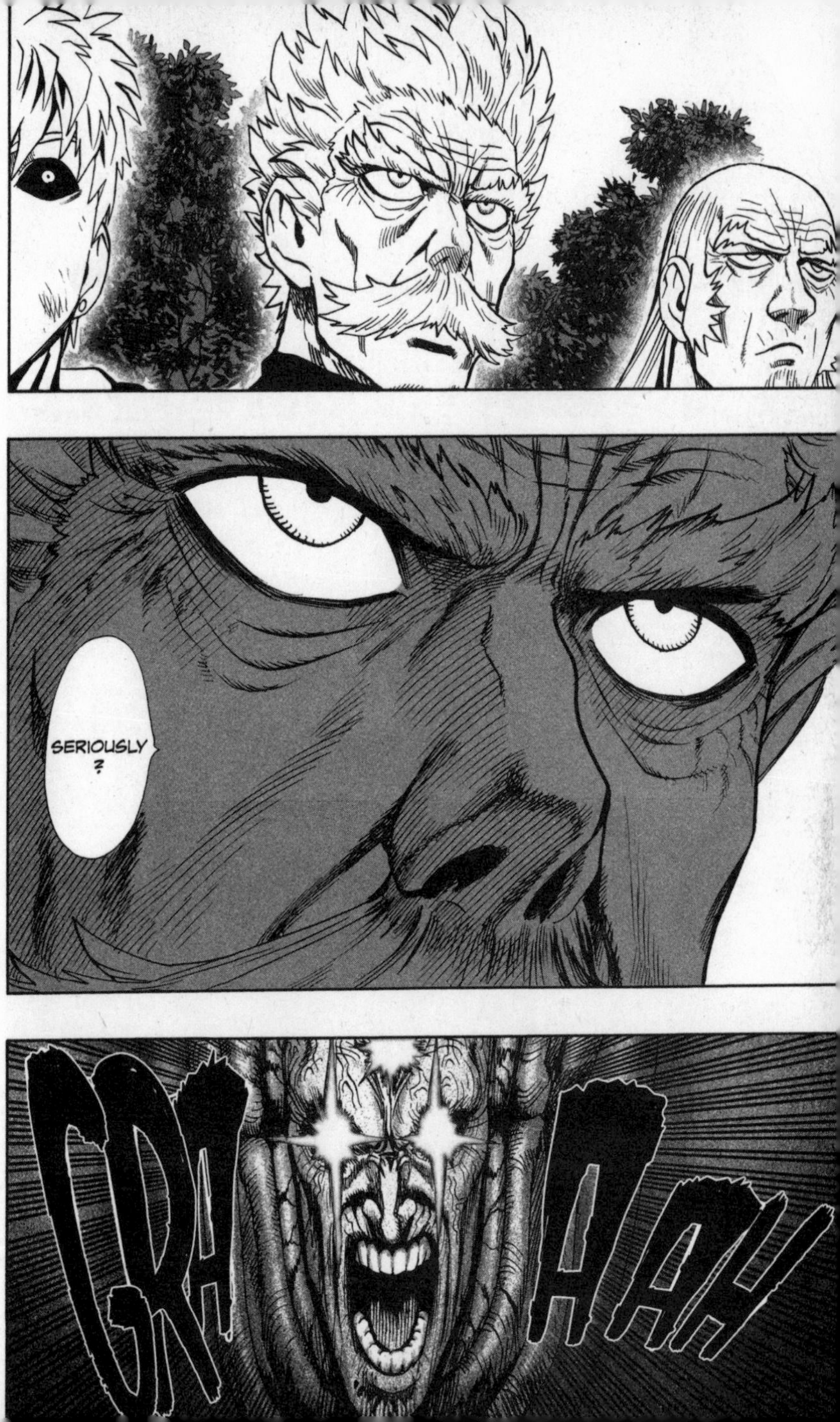
SERIOUSLY?
GRAAAH

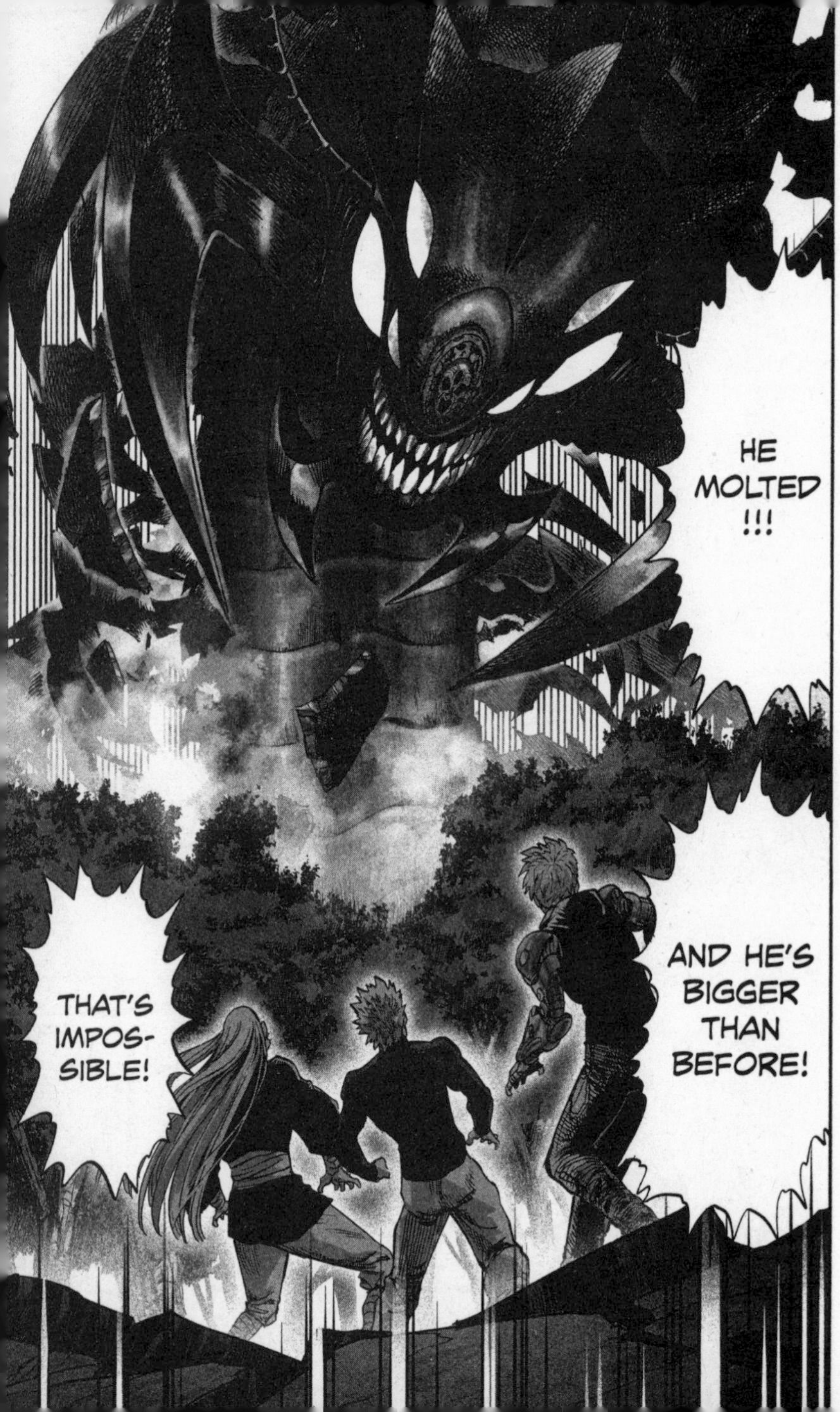
HE MOLTED !!!
AND HE'S BIGGER THAN BEFORE!
THAT'S IMPOS-SIBLE!

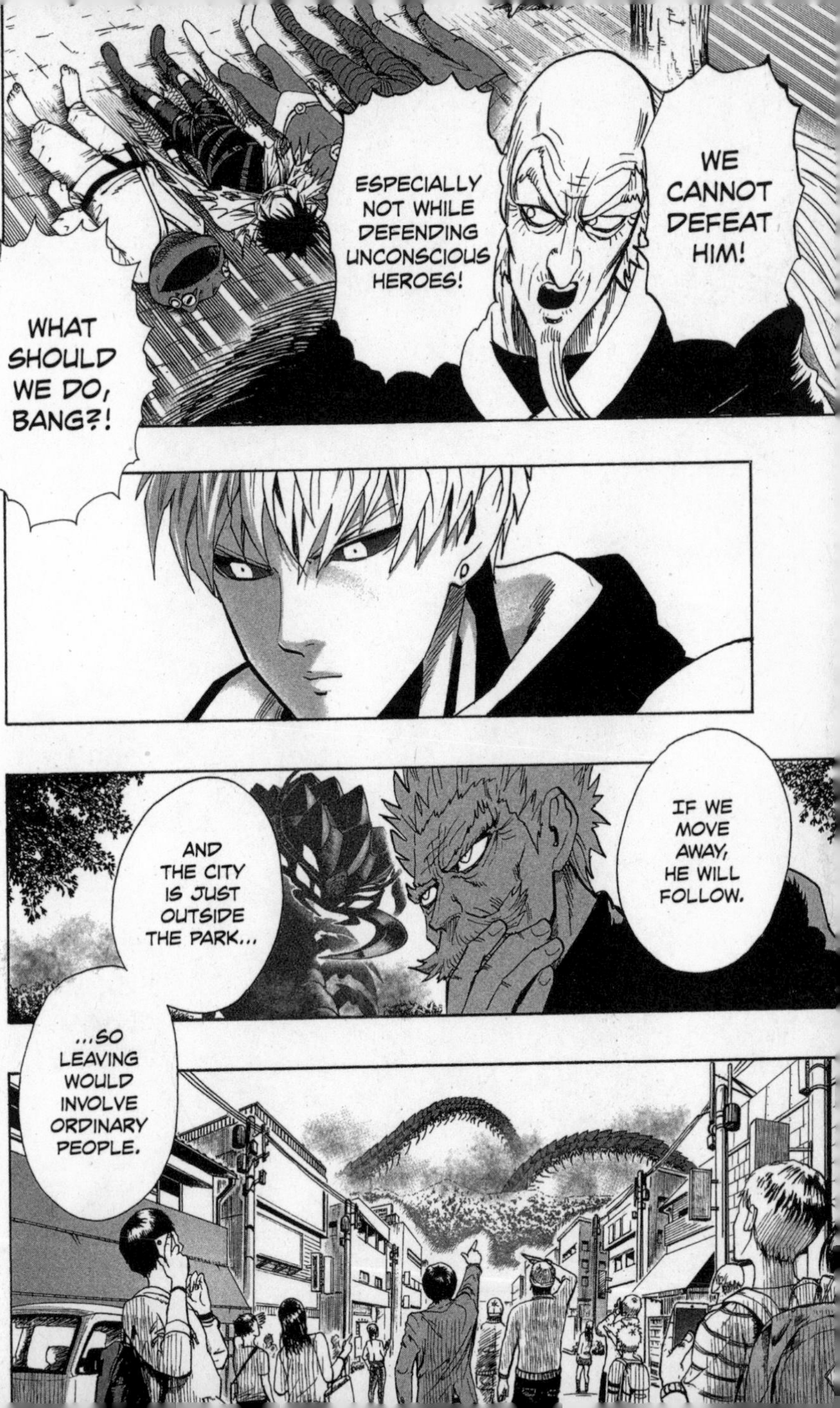
WE CANNOT DEFEAT HIM!
ESPECIALLY NOT WHILE DEFENDING UNCONSCIOUS HEROES!
WHAT SHOULD WE DO, BANG?!
IF WE MOVE AWAY, HE WILL FOLLOW.
AND THE CITY IS JUST OUTSIDE THE PARK...
...SO LEAVING WOULD INVOLVE ORDINARY PEOPLE.

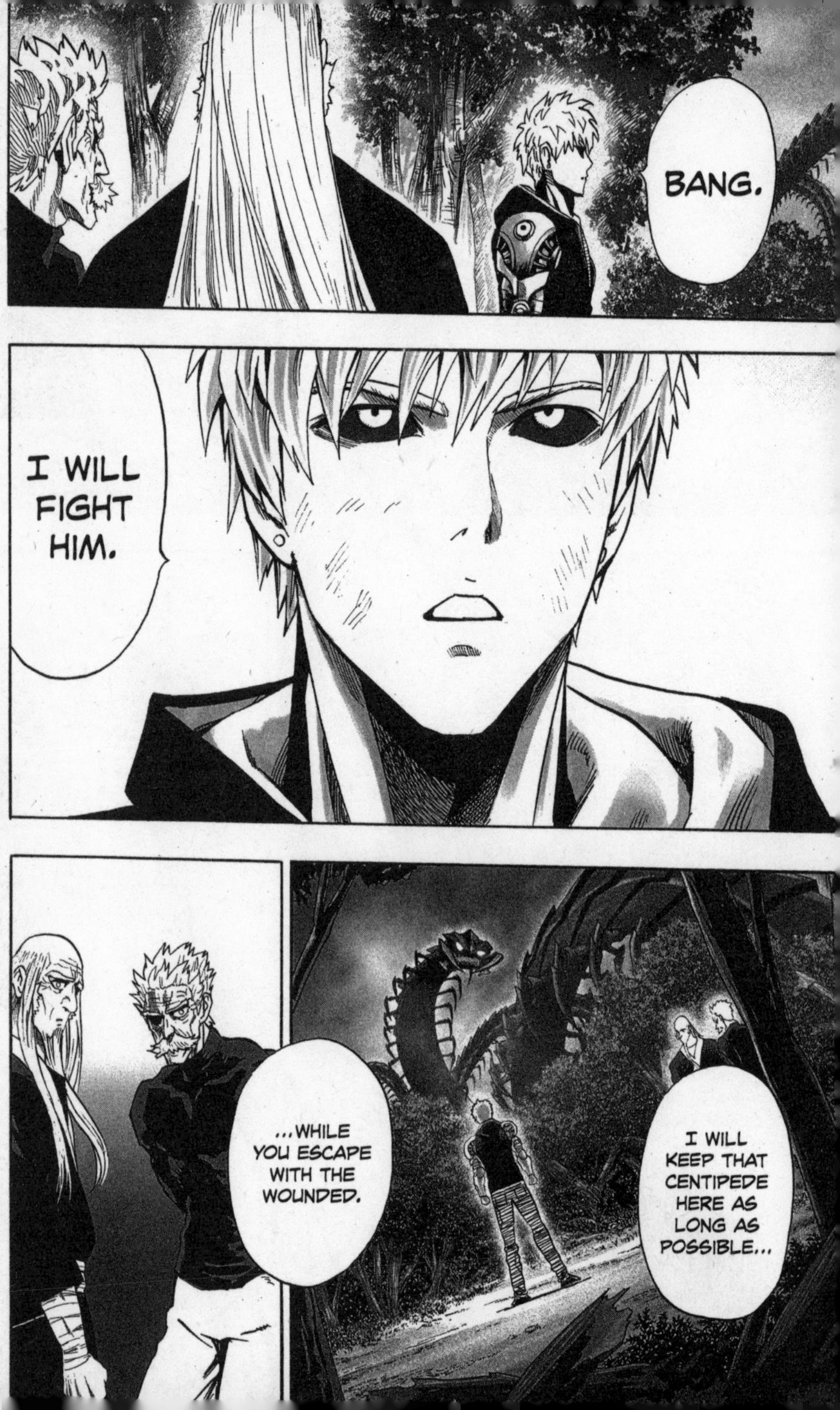
BANG.
I WILL FIGHT HIM.
I WILL KEEP THAT CENTIPEDE HERE AS LONG AS POSSIBLE...
...WHILE YOU ESCAPE WITH THE WOUNDED.

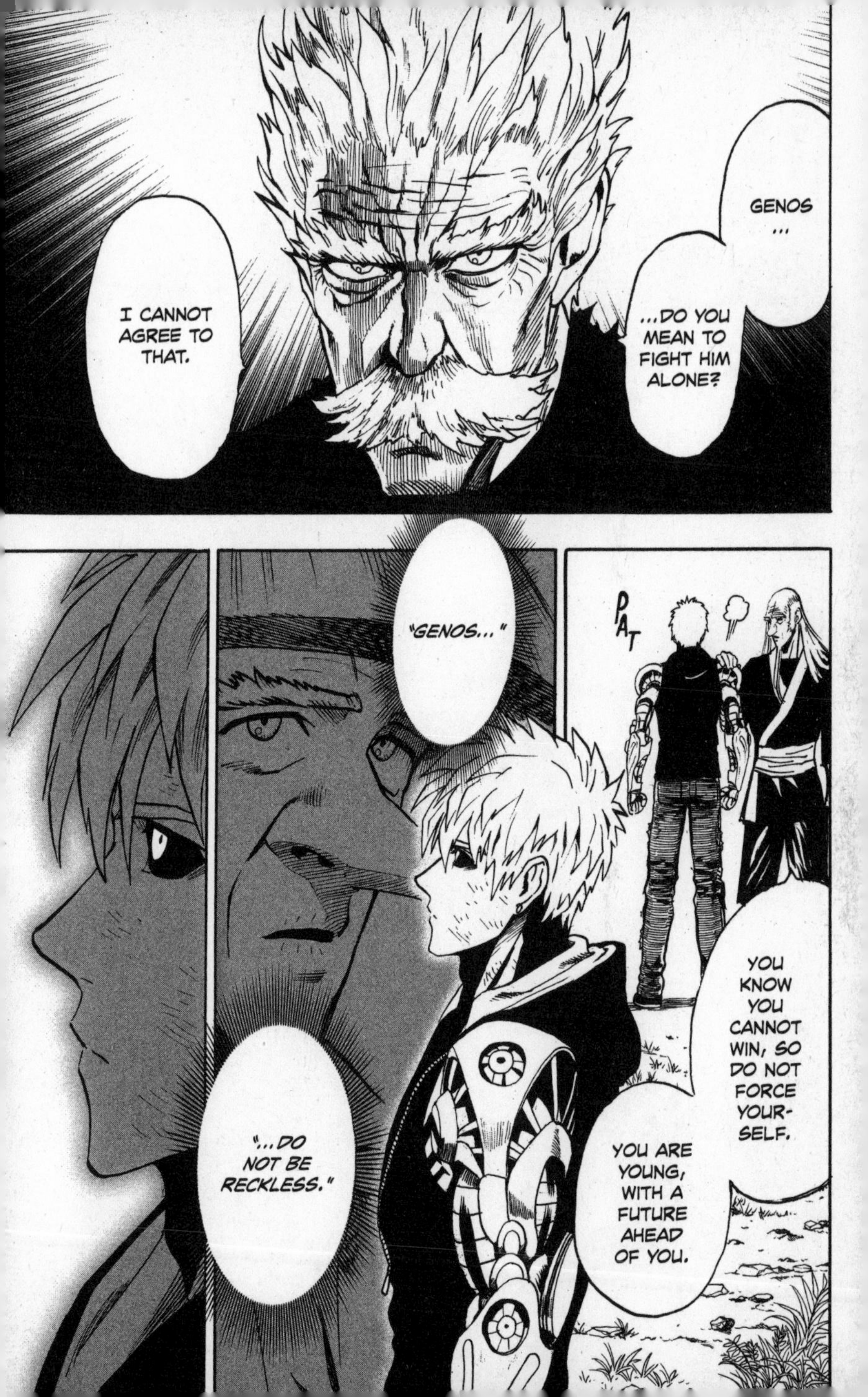
GENOS ...
...DO YOU MEAN TO FIGHT HIM ALONE?
I CANNOT AGREE TO THAT.
PAT
YOU KNOW YOU CANNOT WIN, SO DO NOT FORCE YOUR-SELF.
YOU ARE YOUNG, WITH A FUTURE AHEAD OF YOU.
"GENOS..."
"...DO NOT BE RECKLESS."

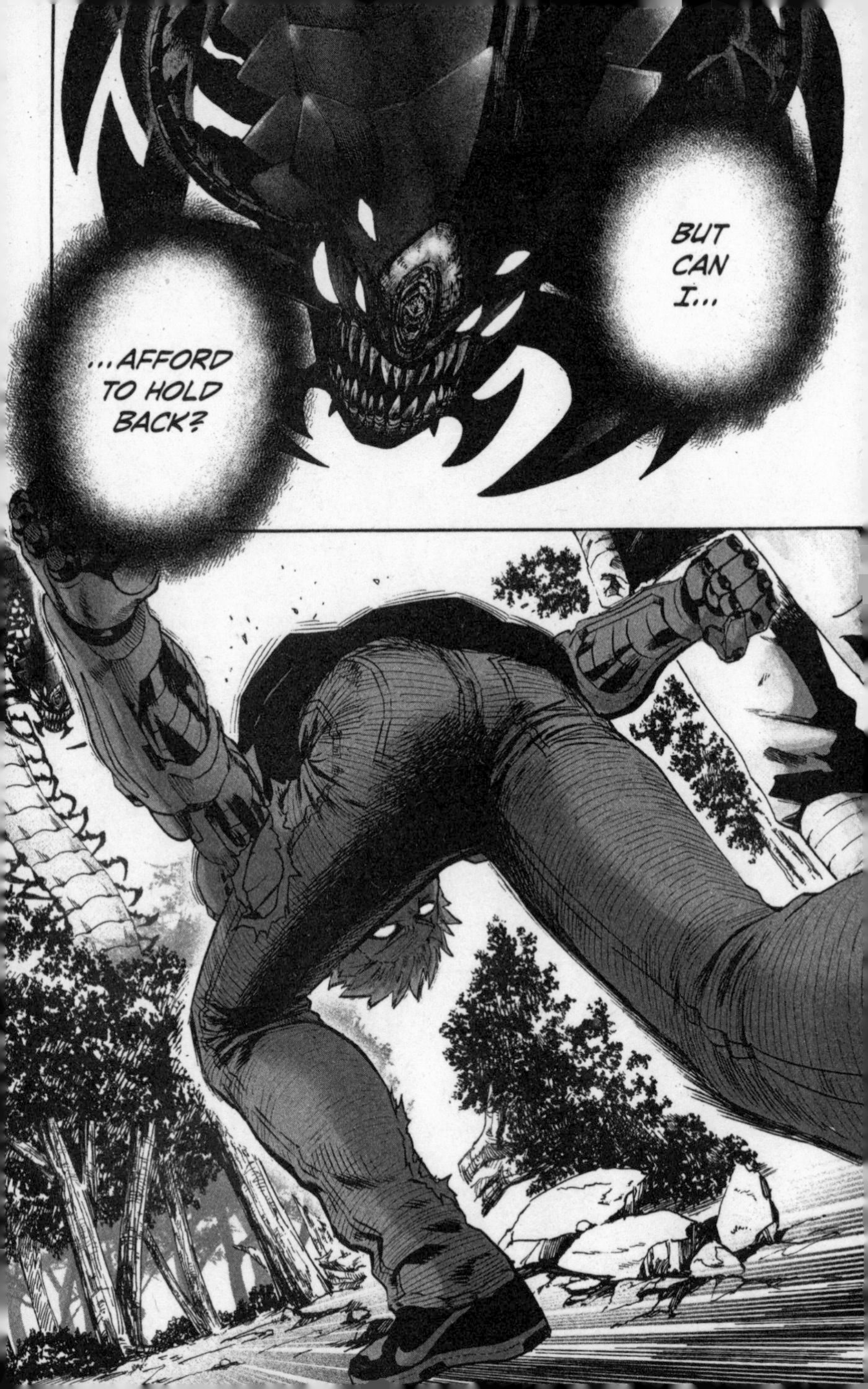
BUT CAN I...
...AFFORD TO HOLD BACK?

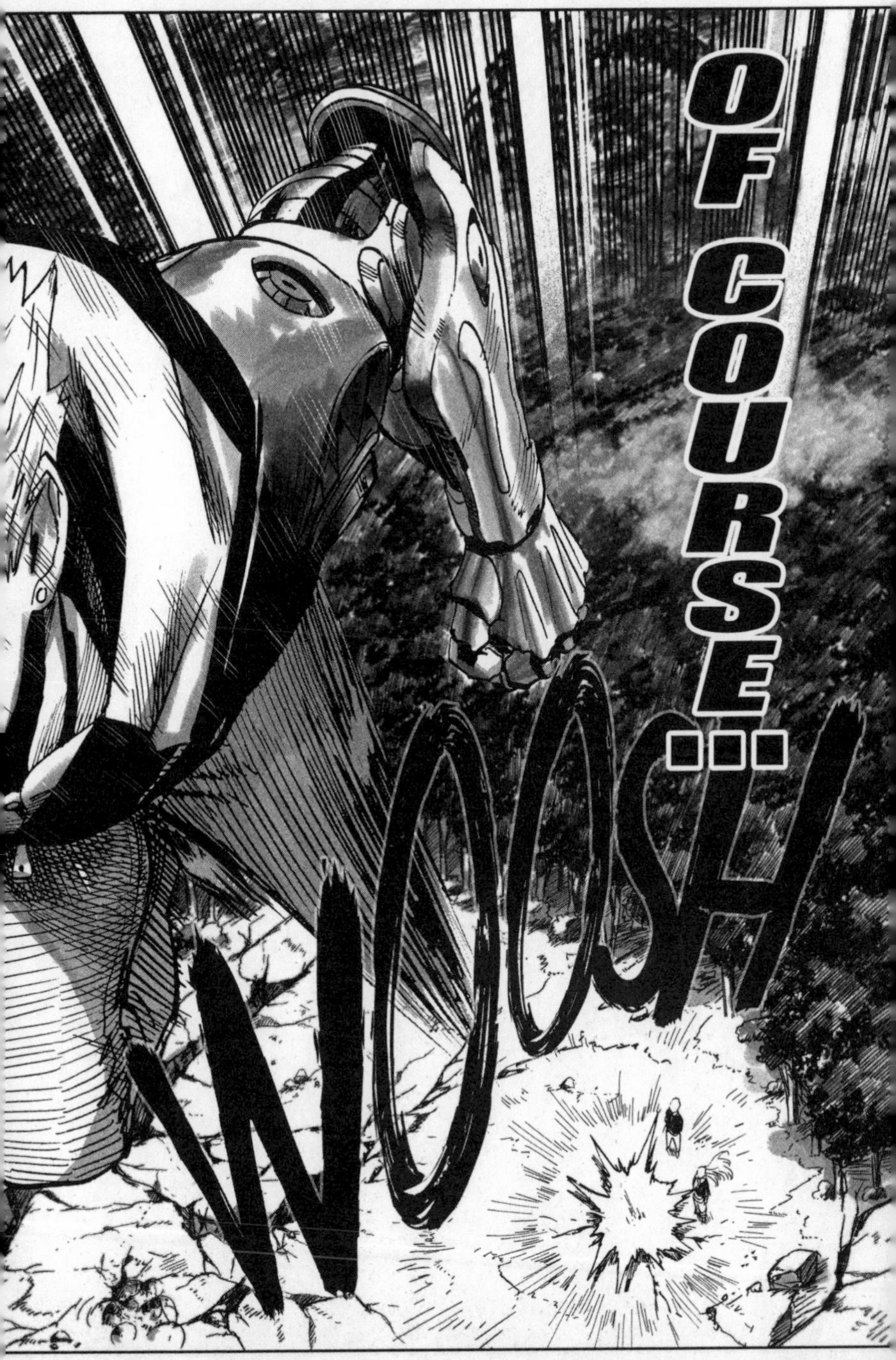
OF COURSE...
WOOSH

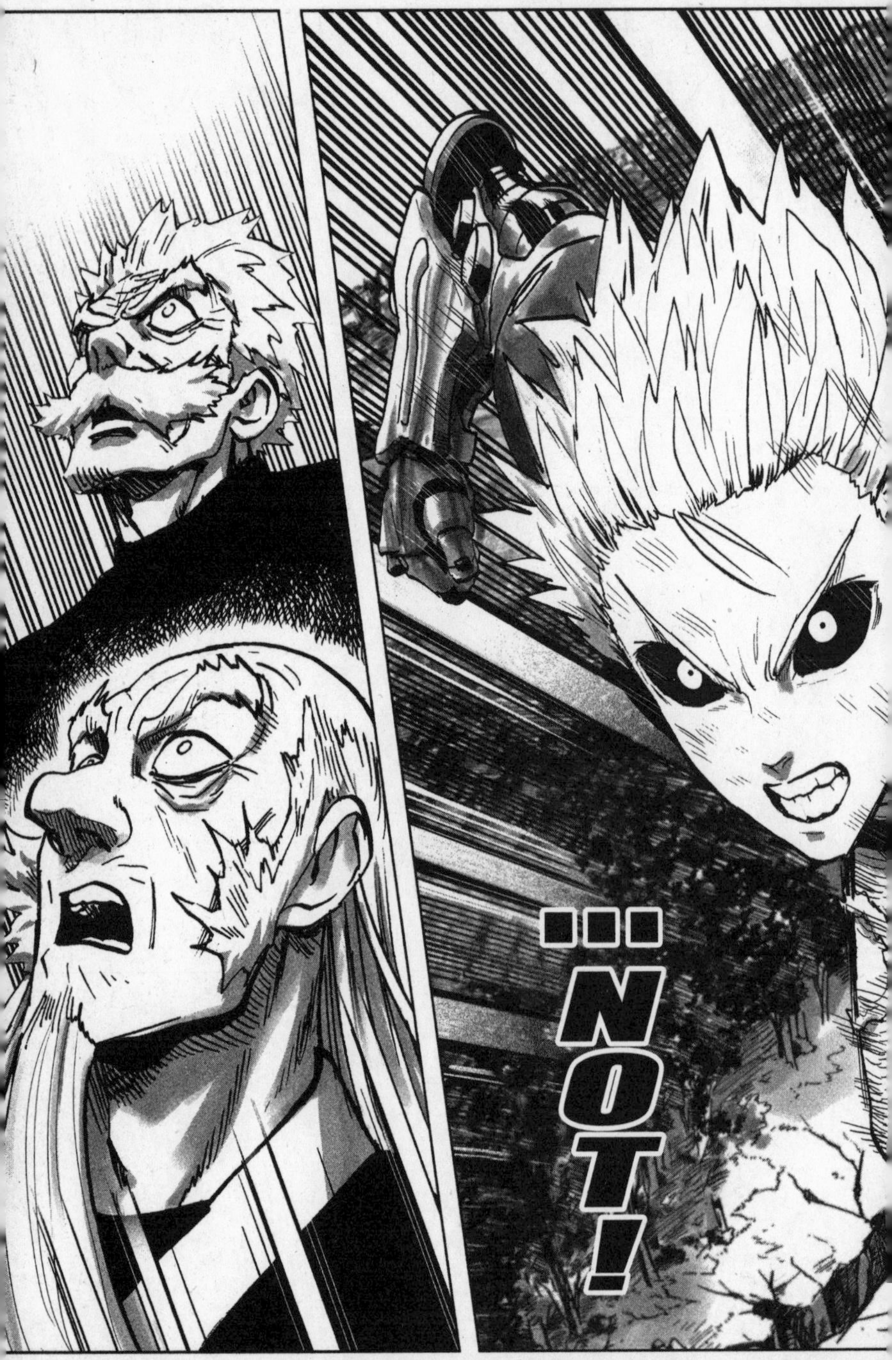
...NOT!

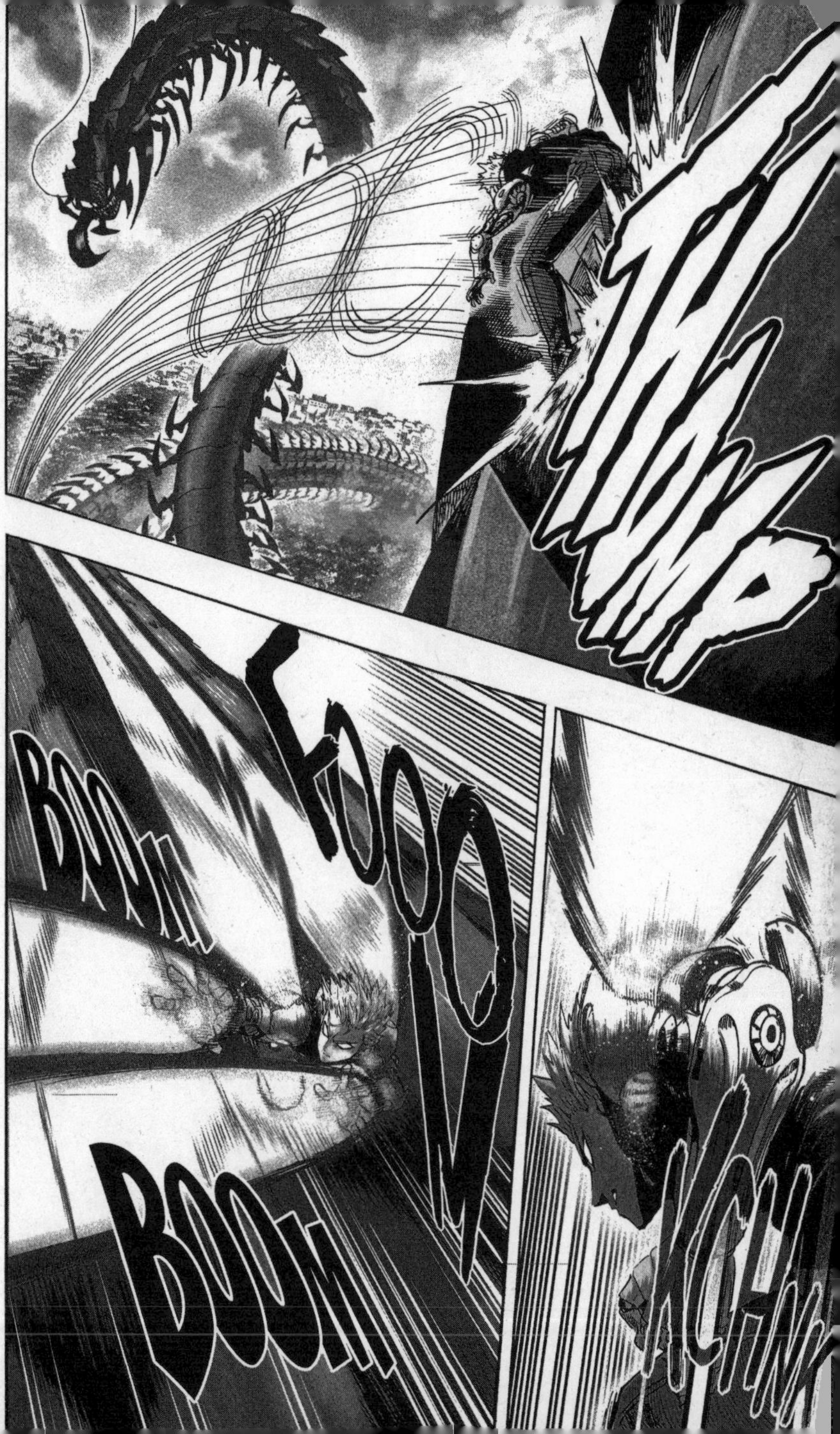
THUMP
BOOOM...
FOOOOM
BOOOM...
KCHN

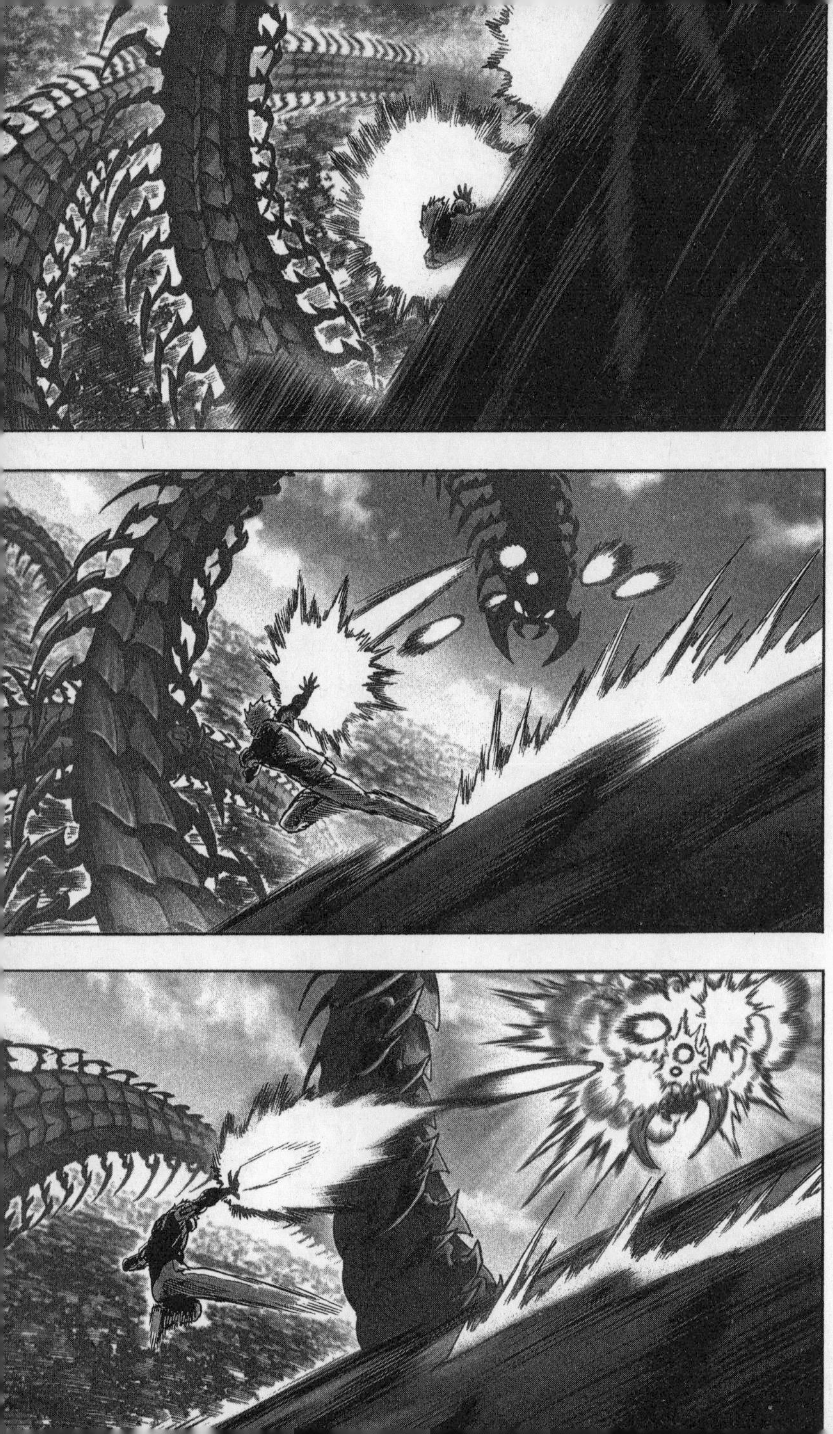

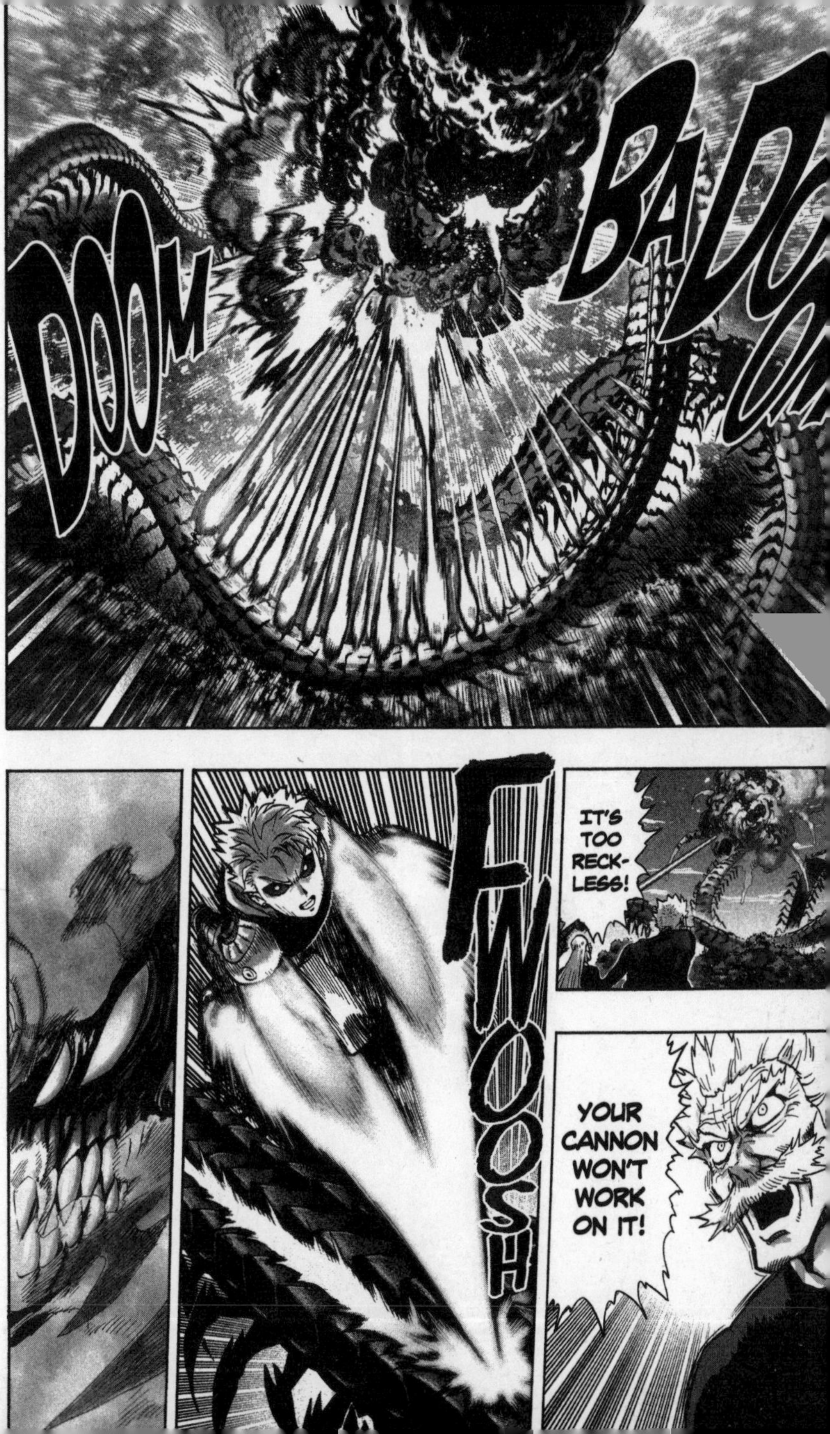
DOOM
IT'S TOO RECK-LESS!
YOUR CANNON WON'T WORK ON IT!
FWOOSH

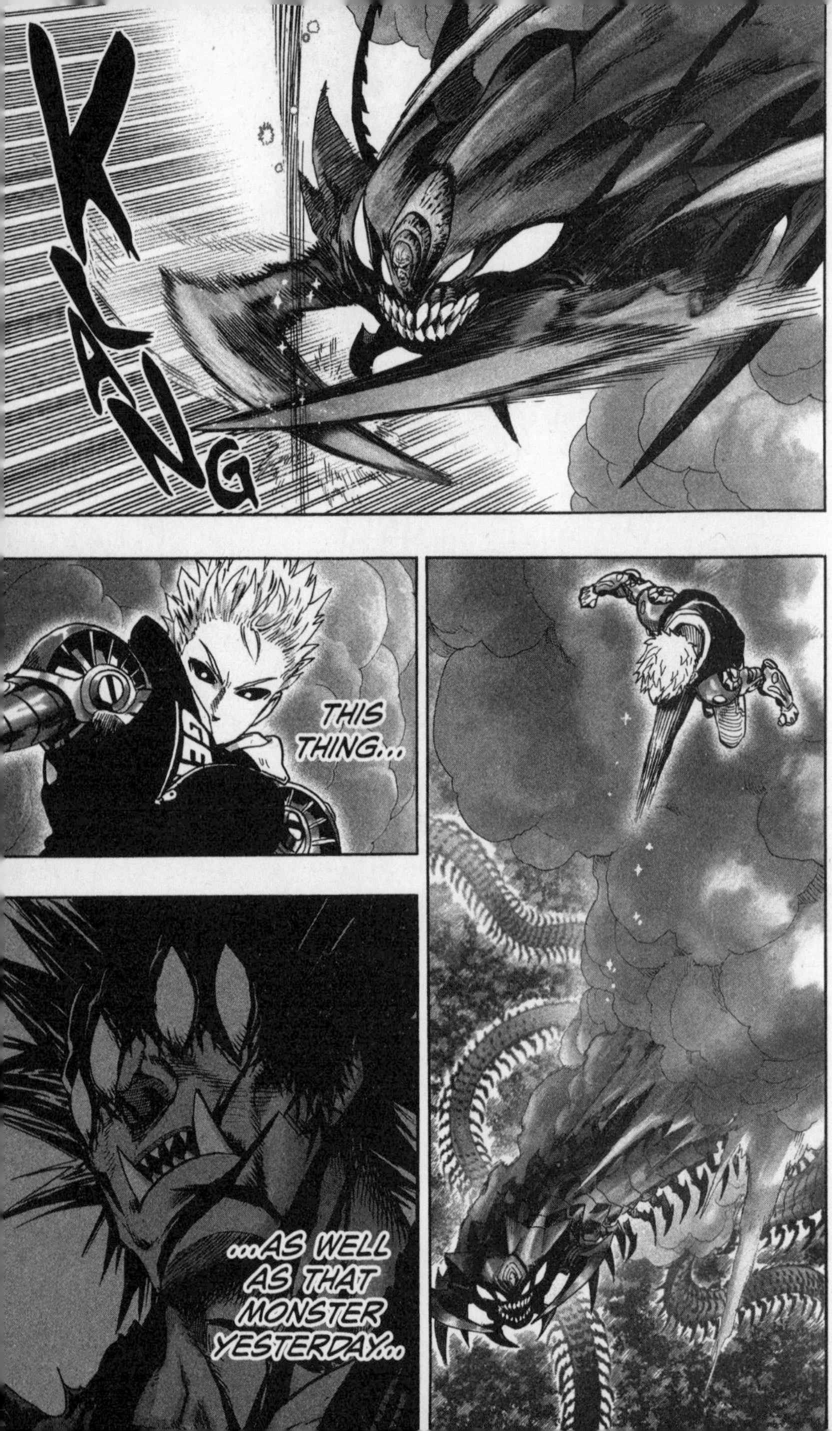
KLANG
THIS THING...
...AS WELL AS THAT MONSTER YESTERDAY...

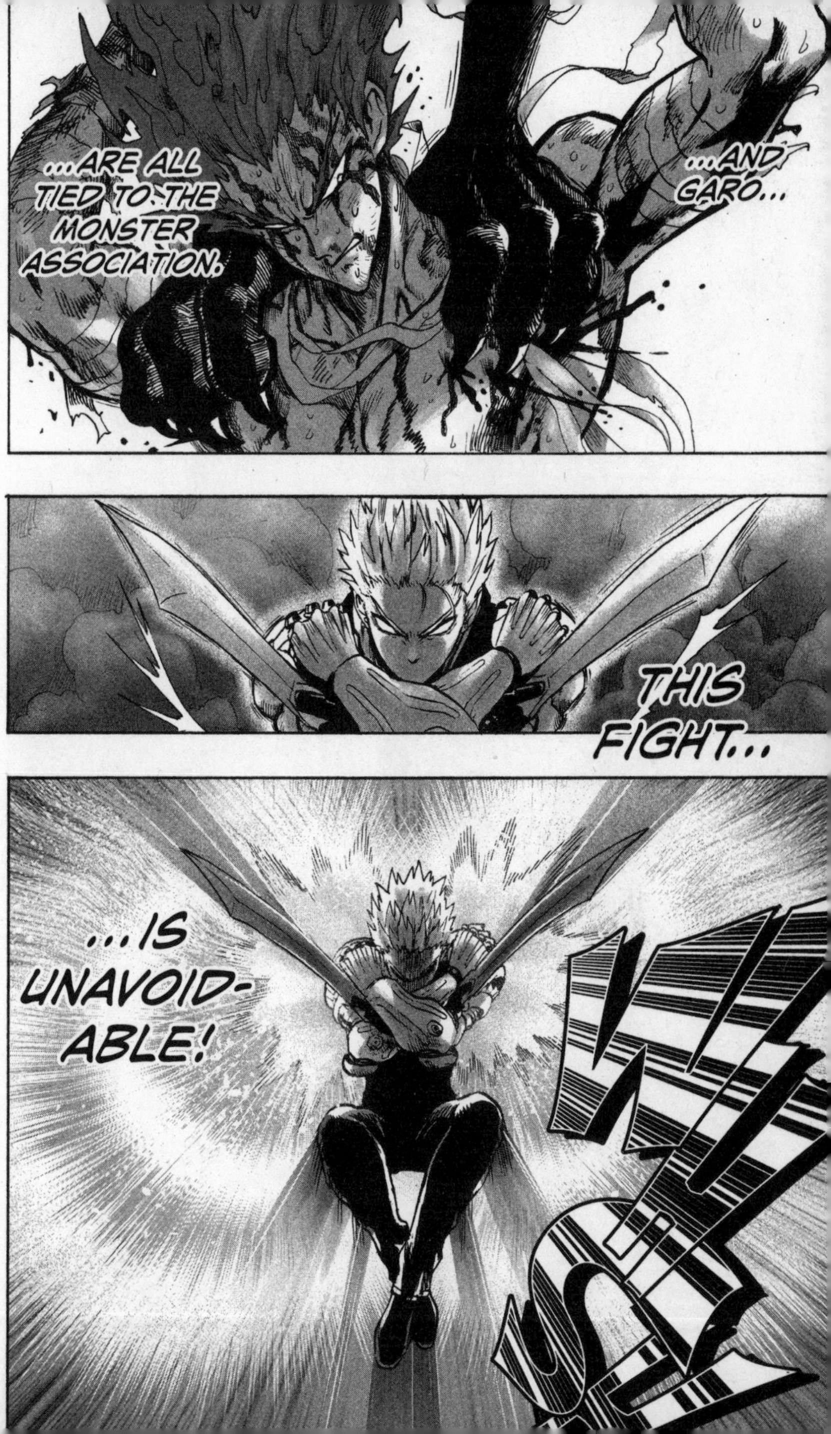
...AND GARO...
...ARE ALL TIED TO THE MONSTER ASSOCIATION.
THIS FIGHT...
...IS UNAVOID-ABLE!

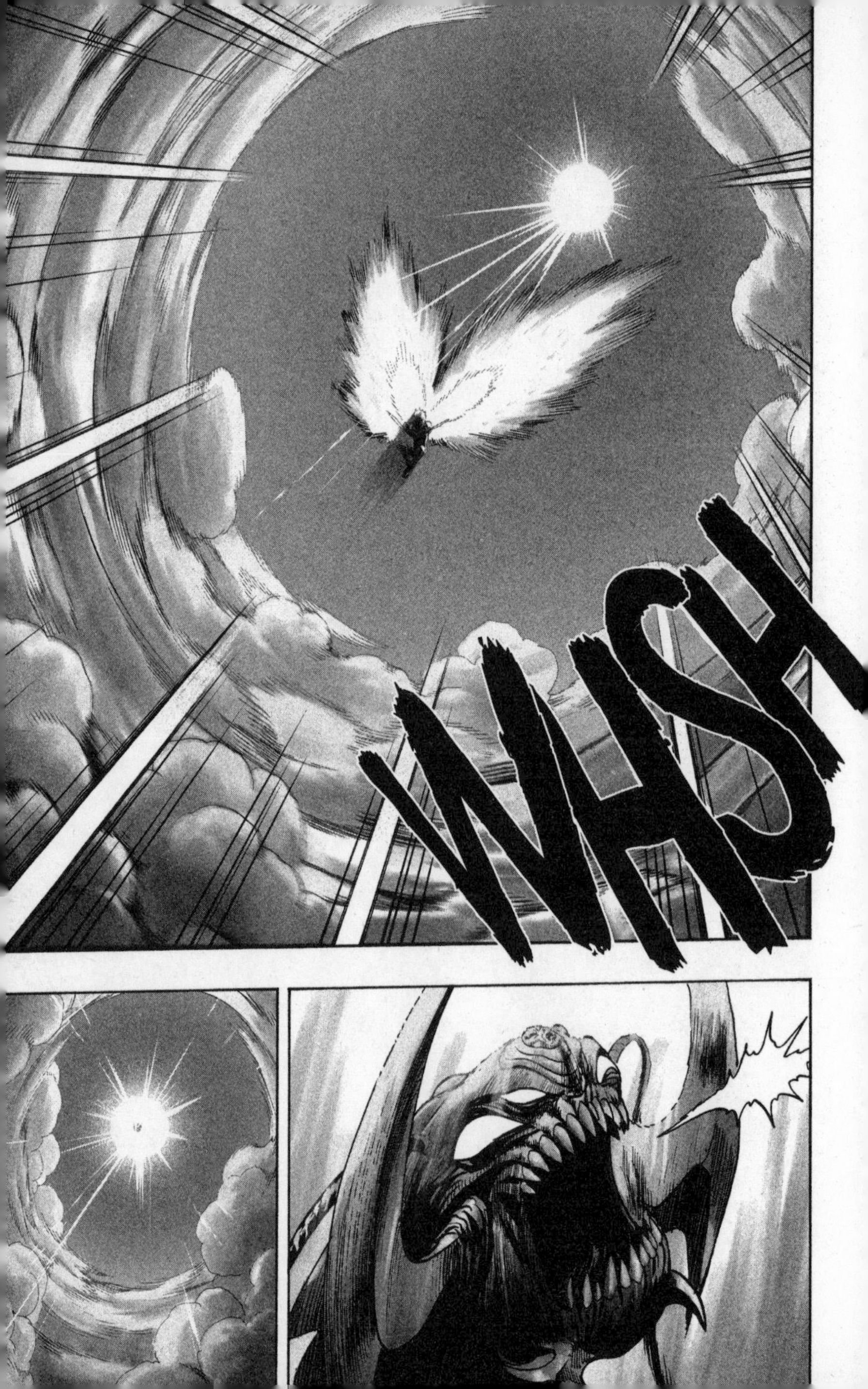
WHSH

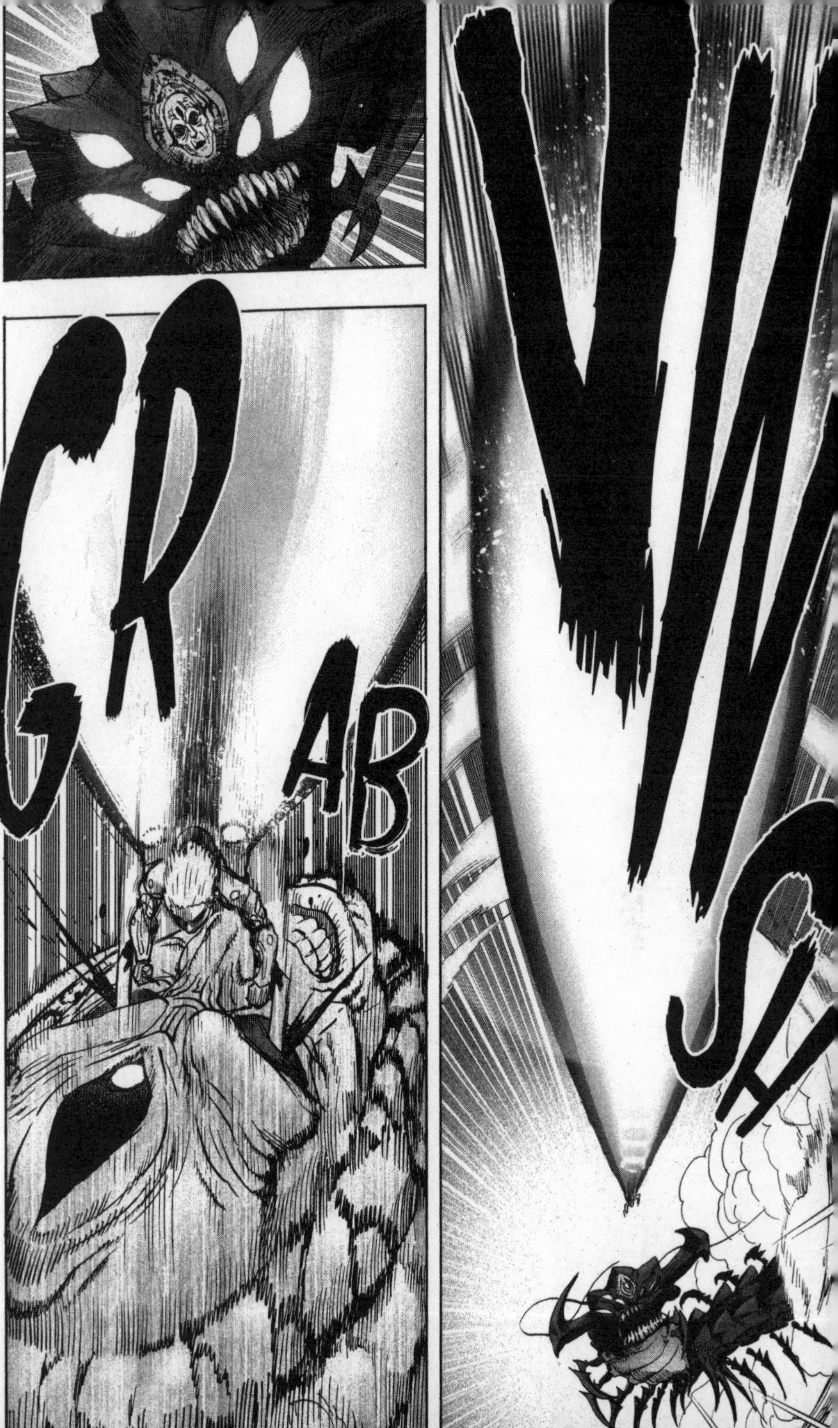
VWSH
GRAB

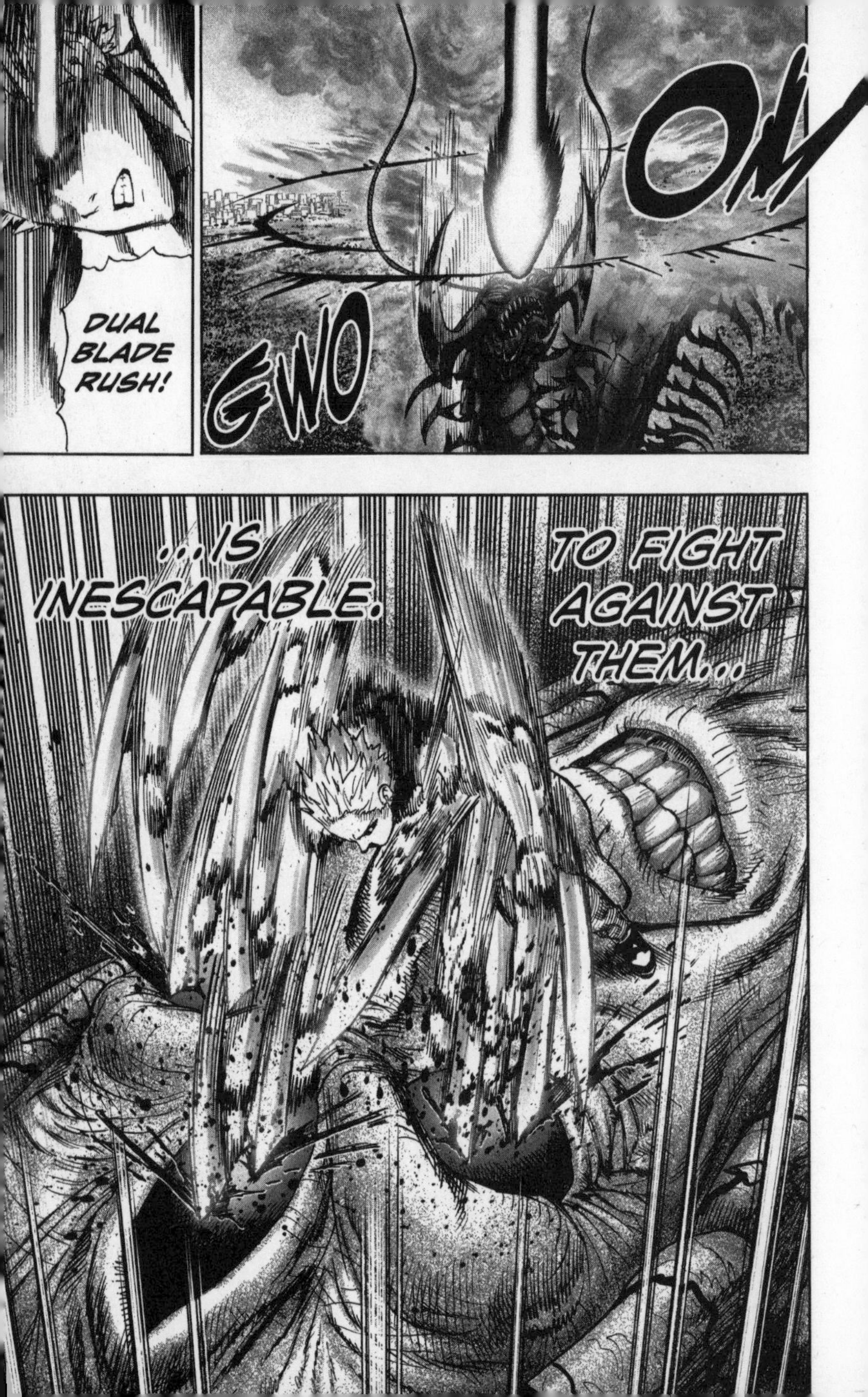
GWO
OM
DUAL BLADE RUSH!
TO FIGHT AGAINST THEM...
...IS INESCAPABLE.

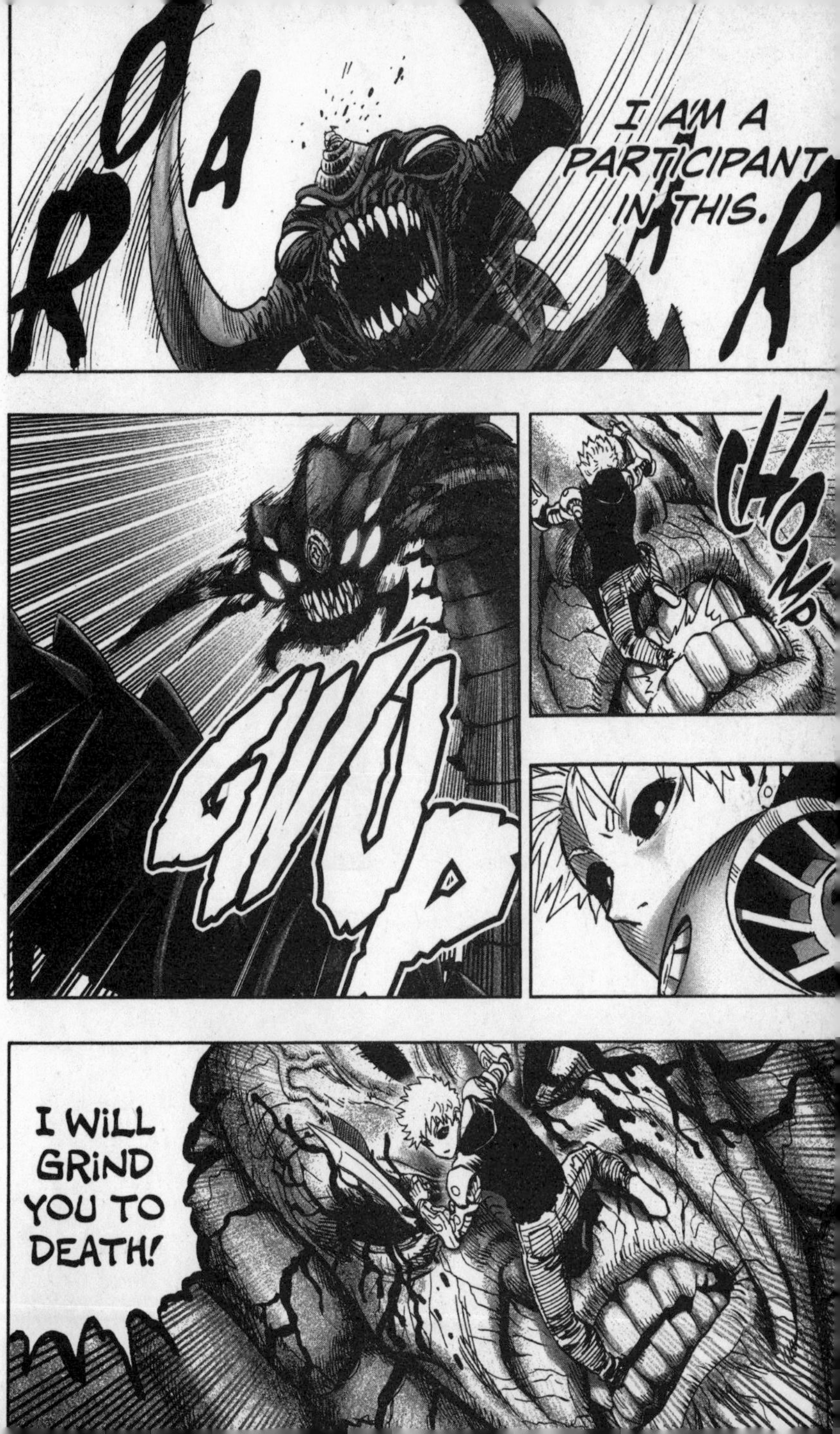
I AM A PARTICIPANT IN THIS.
CHOMP
I WILL GRIND YOU TO DEATH!

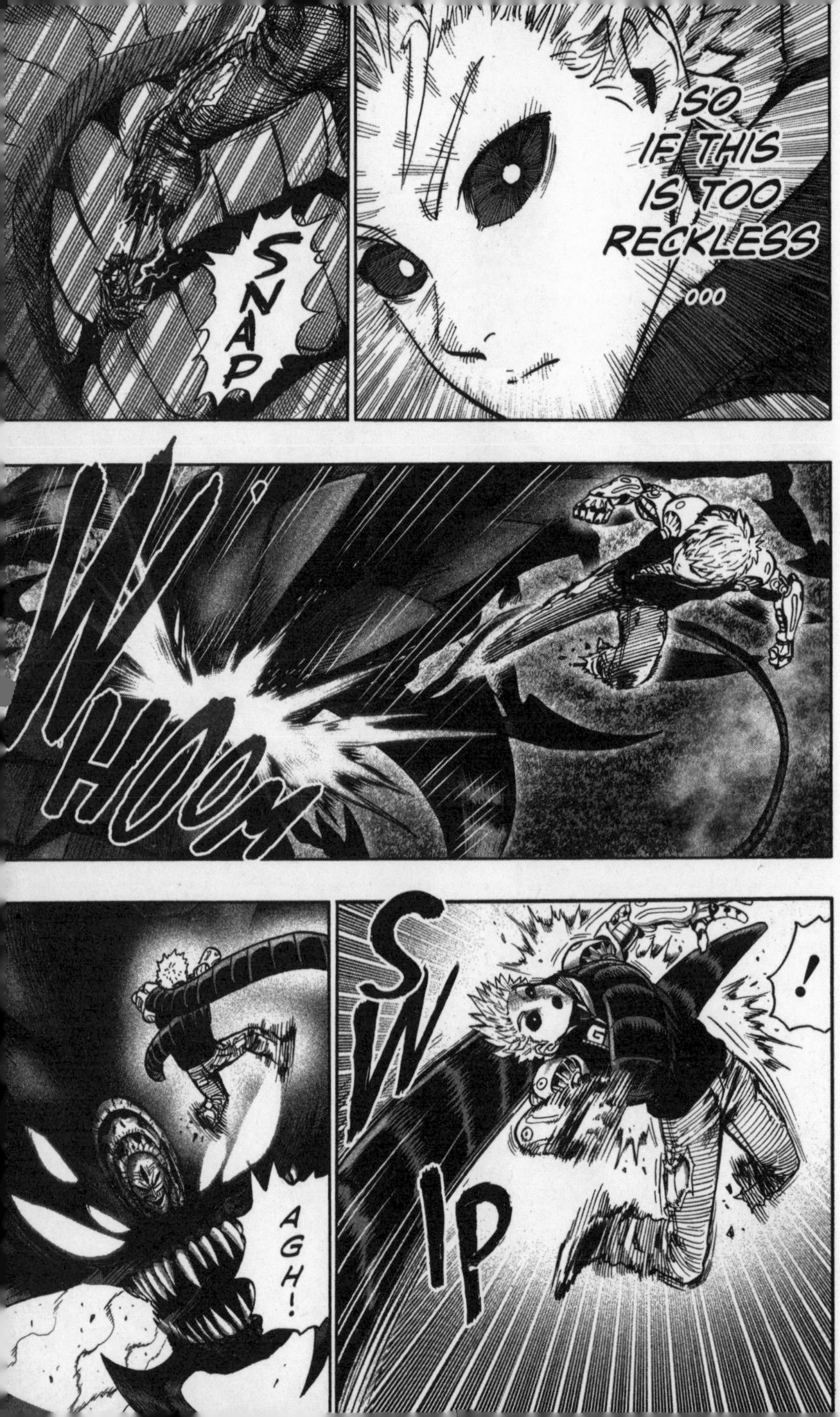
SO IF THIS IS TOO RECKLESS
...
SNAP
WHOOM
!
SWIP
AGH!

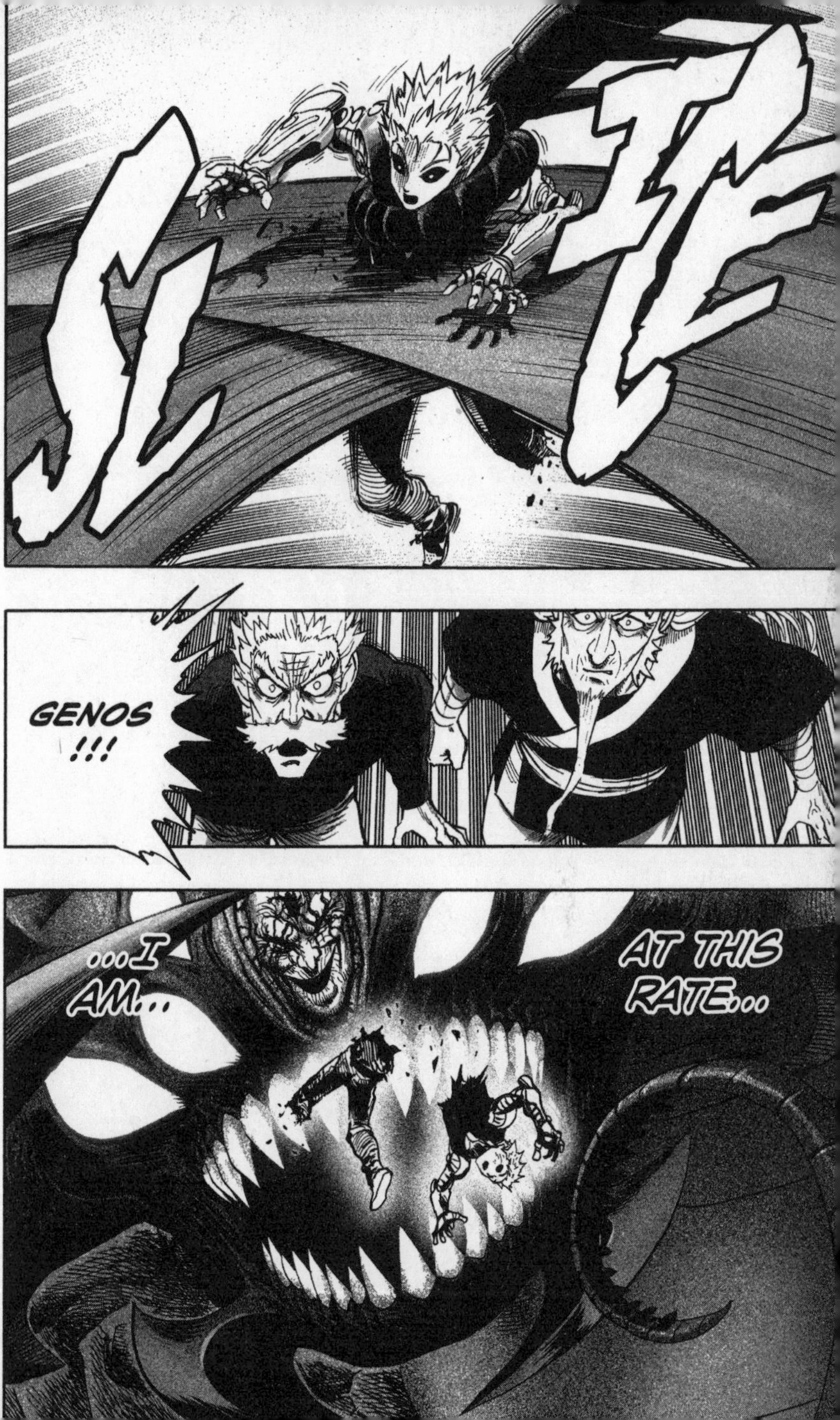
GENOS !!!
AT THIS RATE...
...I AM...

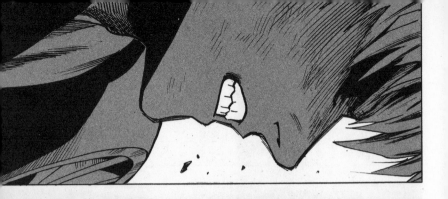

...UNWORTHY.

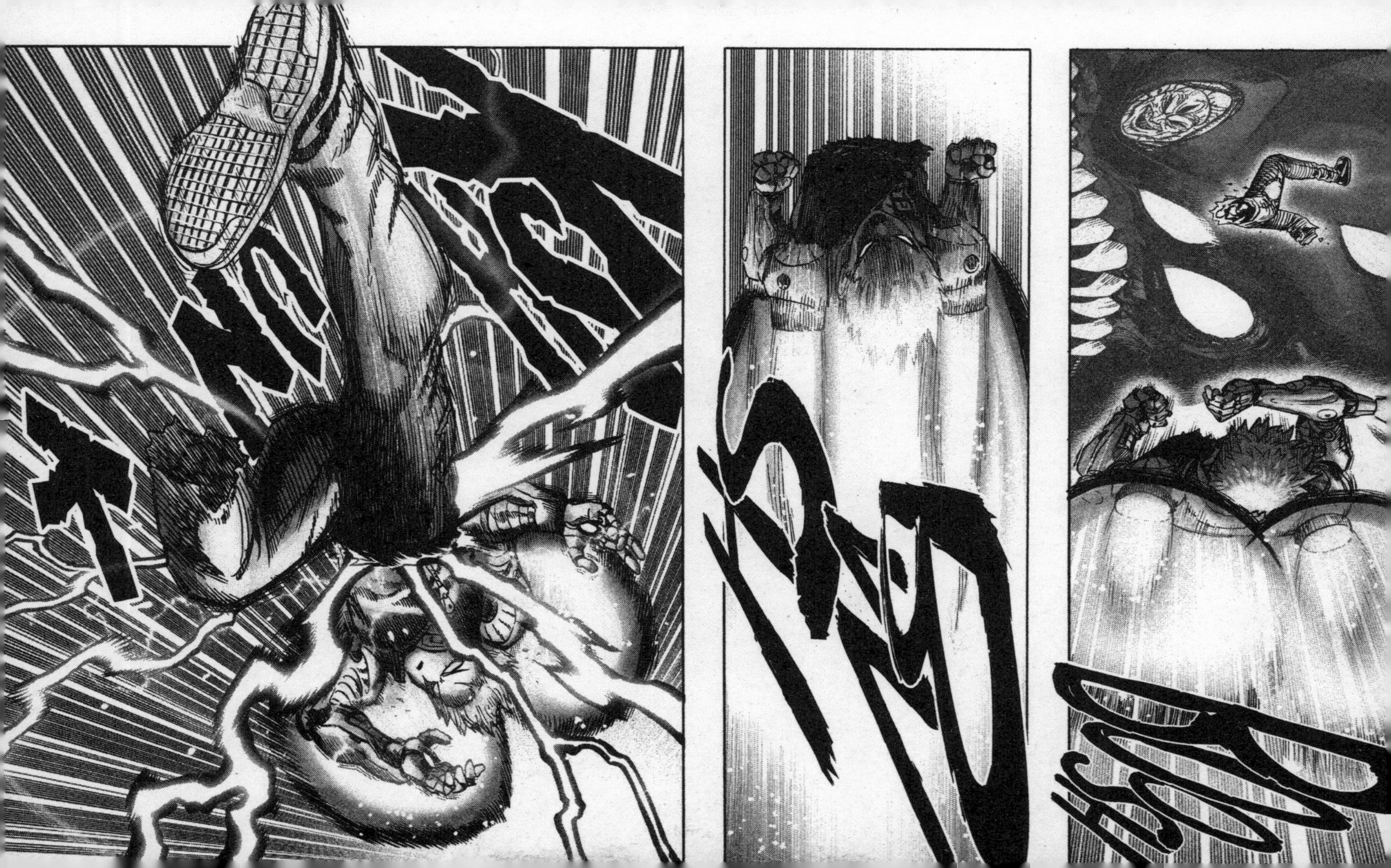
BOSH
DASH

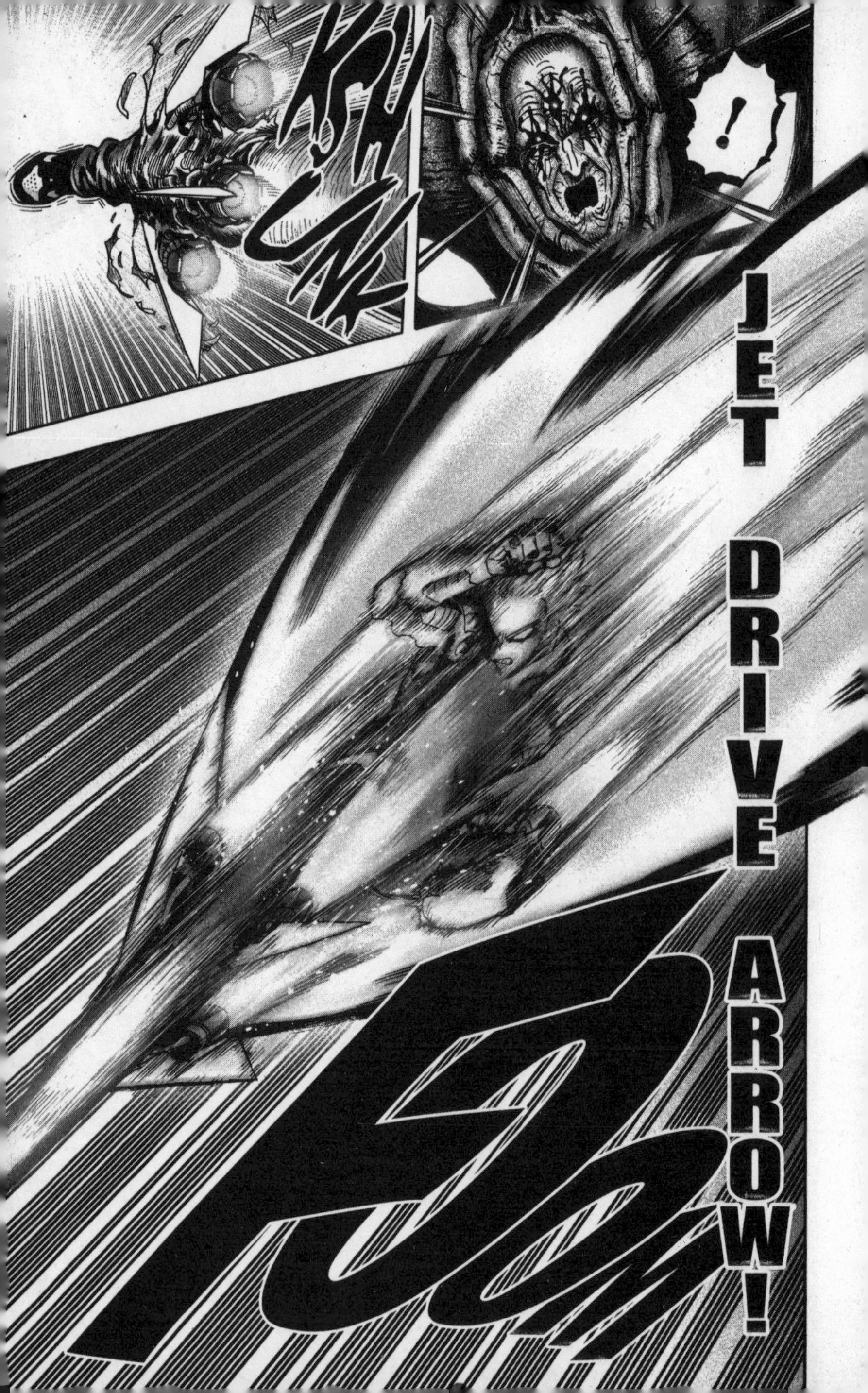
!
KSH UNK
JET DRIVE ARROW!

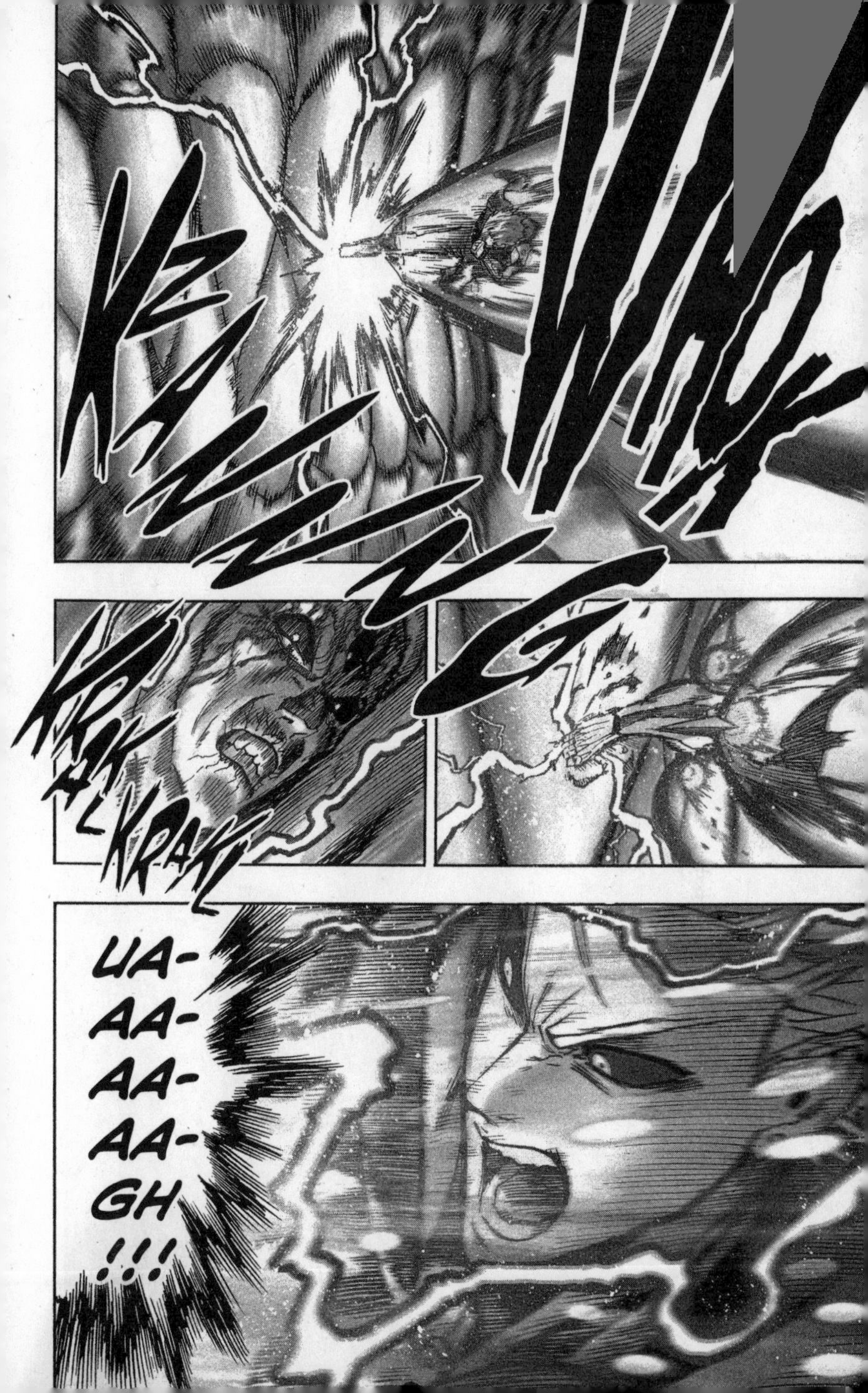
WHAK
KZANNNNG
KRAK KRAK KRAK!
UA-AA-AA-AA-GH!!!

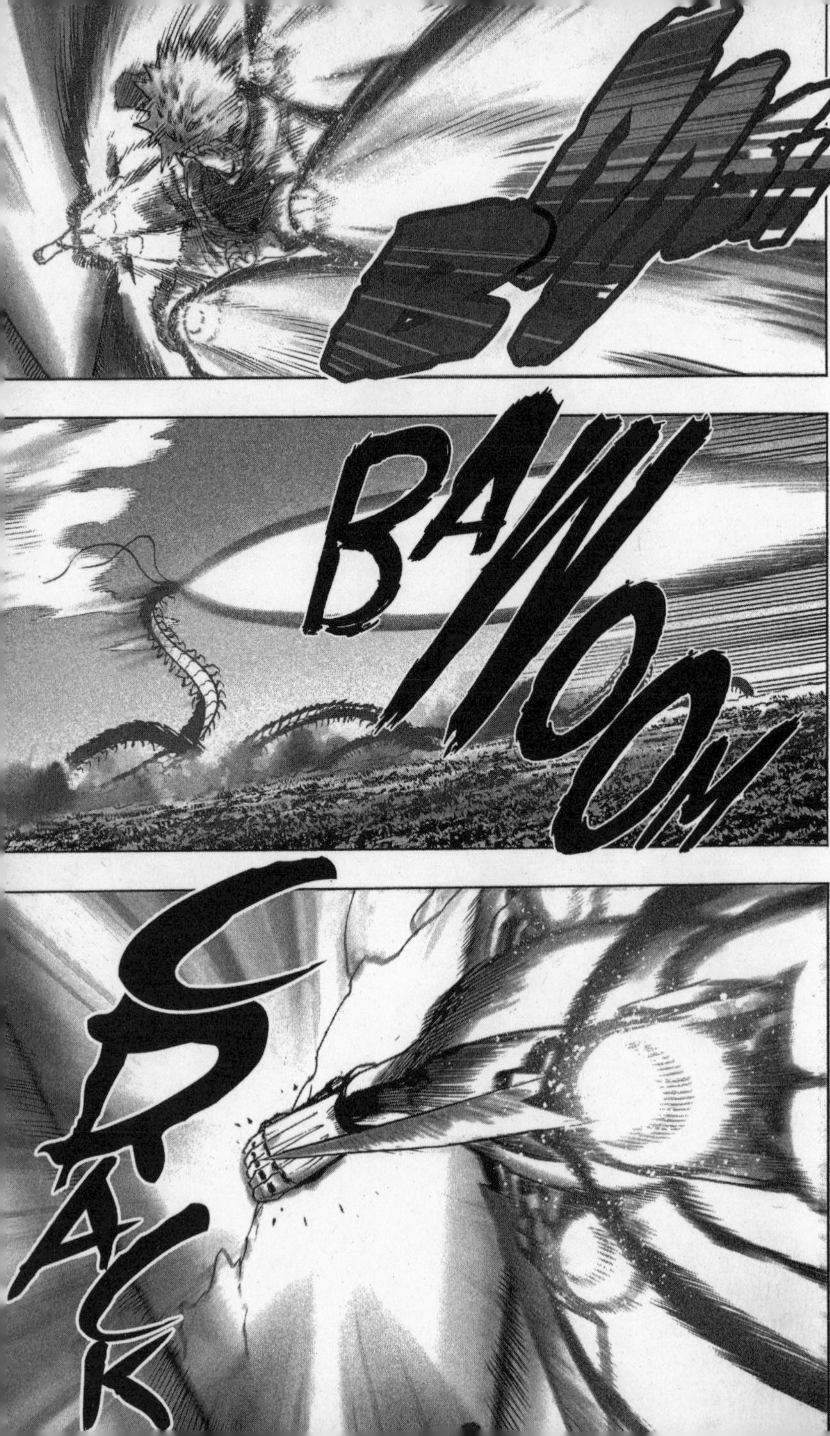
BAWOOM
SDACK

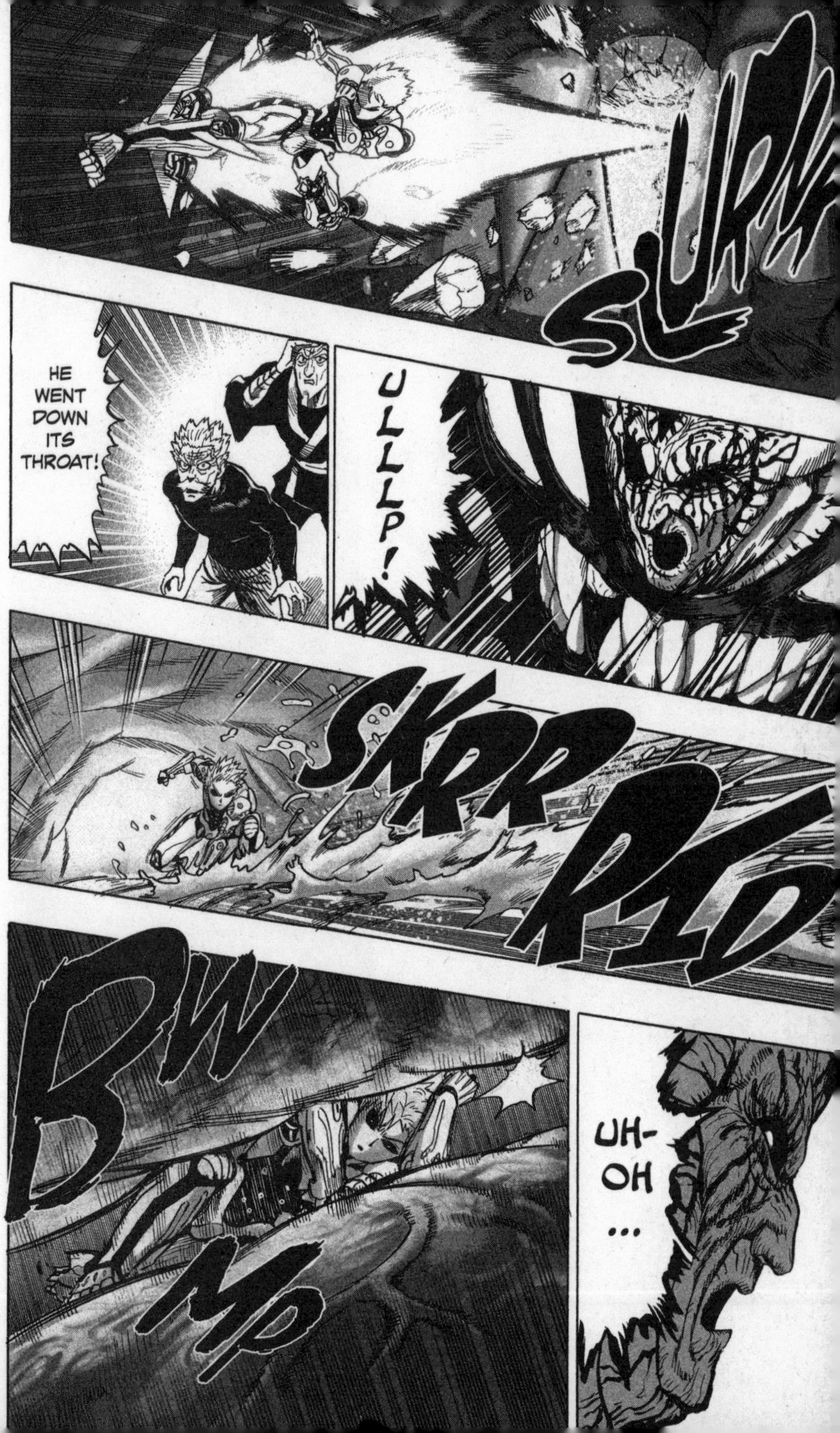
SLURP
ULLLP!
HE WENT DOWN ITS THROAT!
SKRR
RIID
UH-OH ...
BUMP
DW

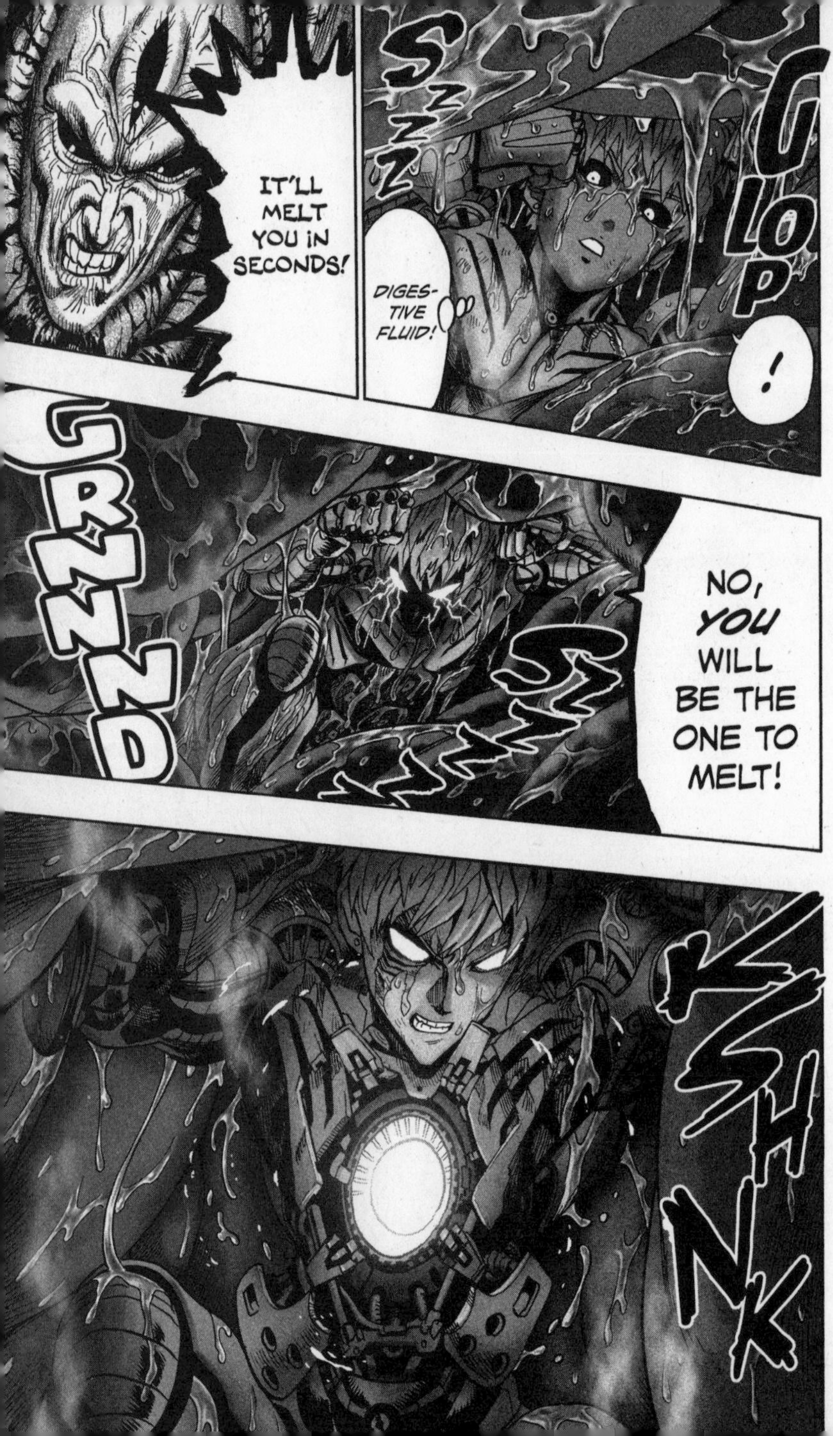
SZZZ
GLOP
!
DIGES-TIVE FLUID!
IT'LL MELT YOU IN SECONDS!
NO, *YOU* WILL BE THE ONE TO MELT!
SZZZZ
GRNND
KSHNK

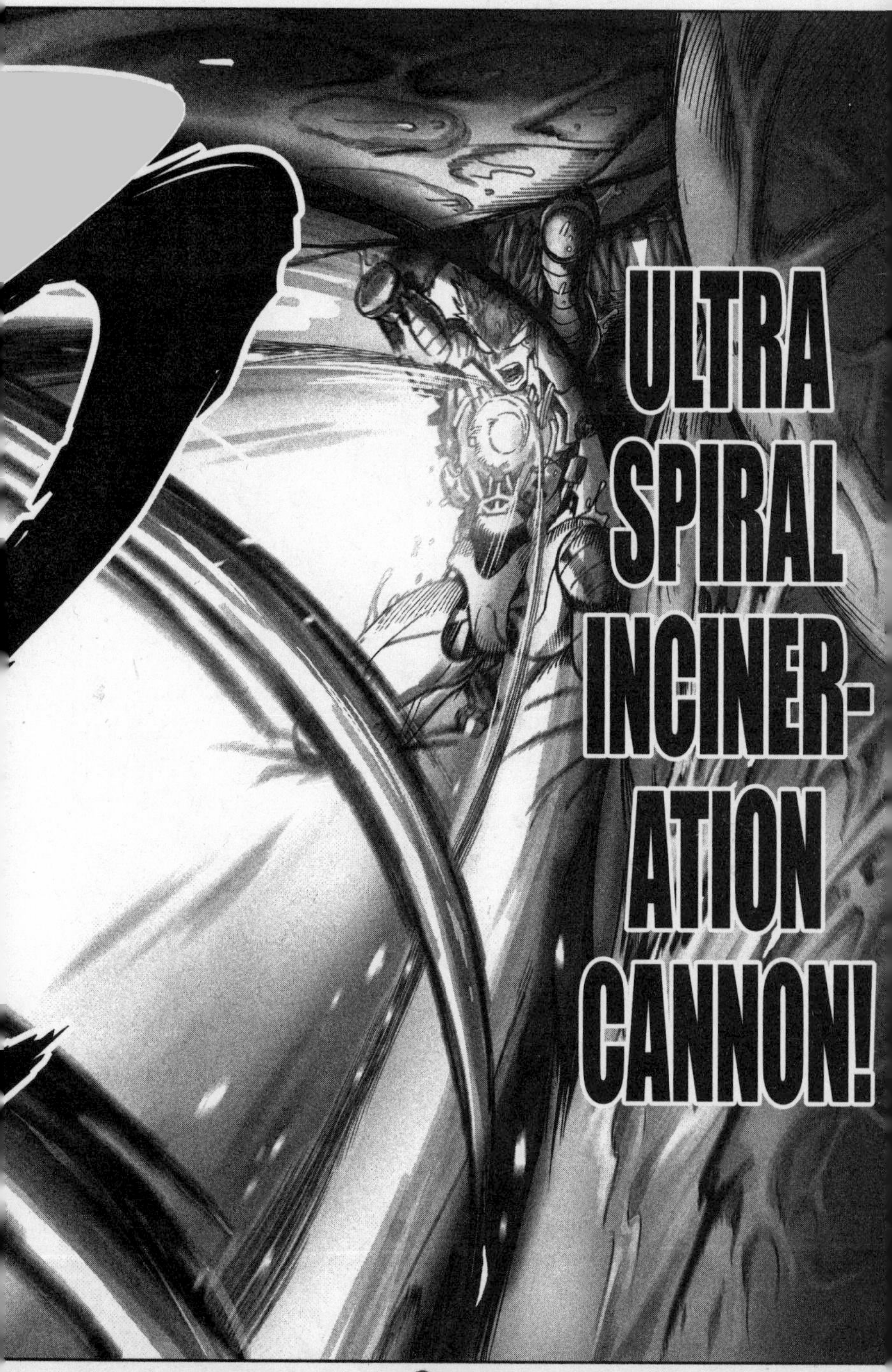
ULTRA SPIRAL INCINER-ATION CANNON!

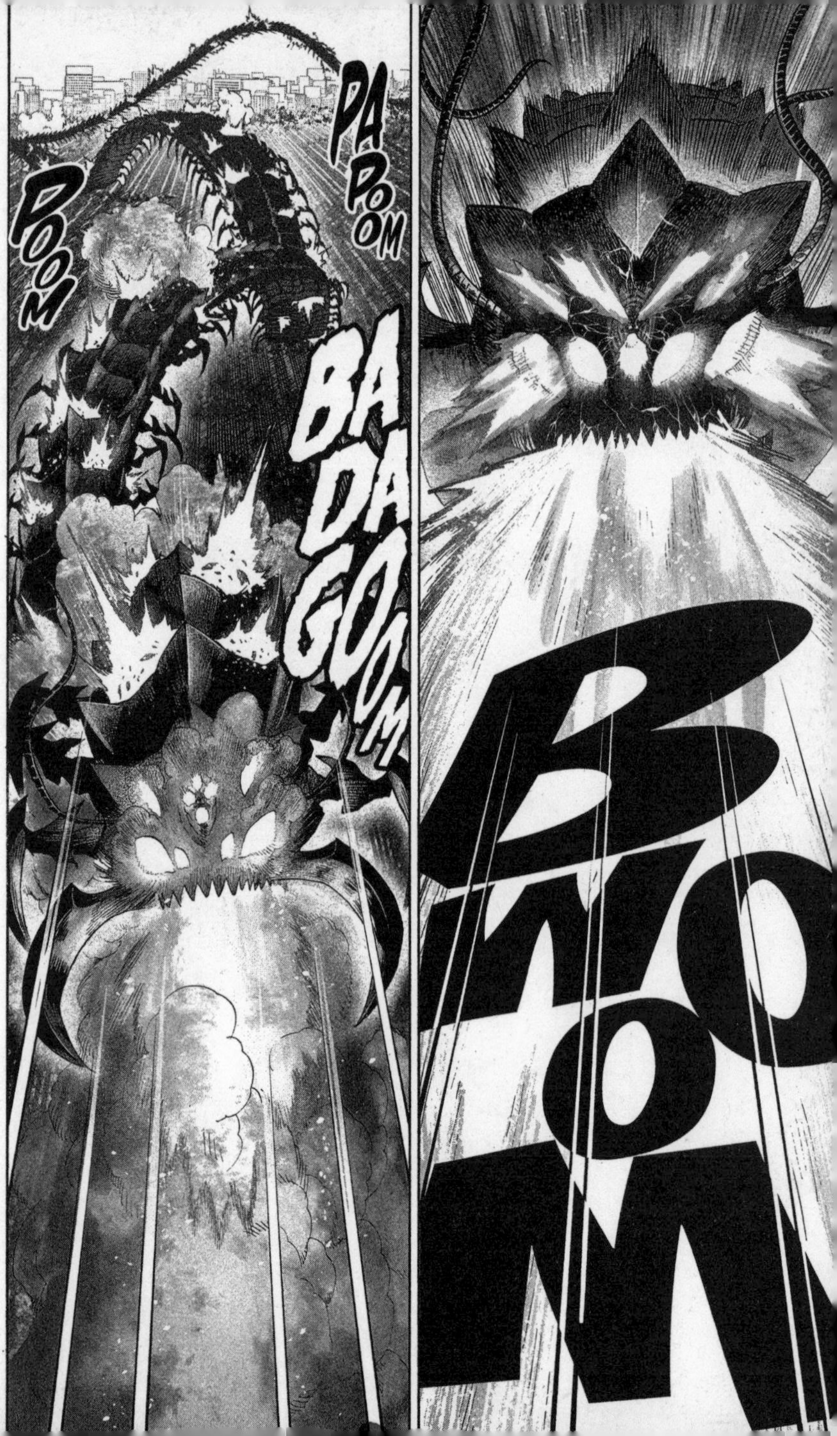
BWOOM
PAPOOM
POOM
BADAGOOM

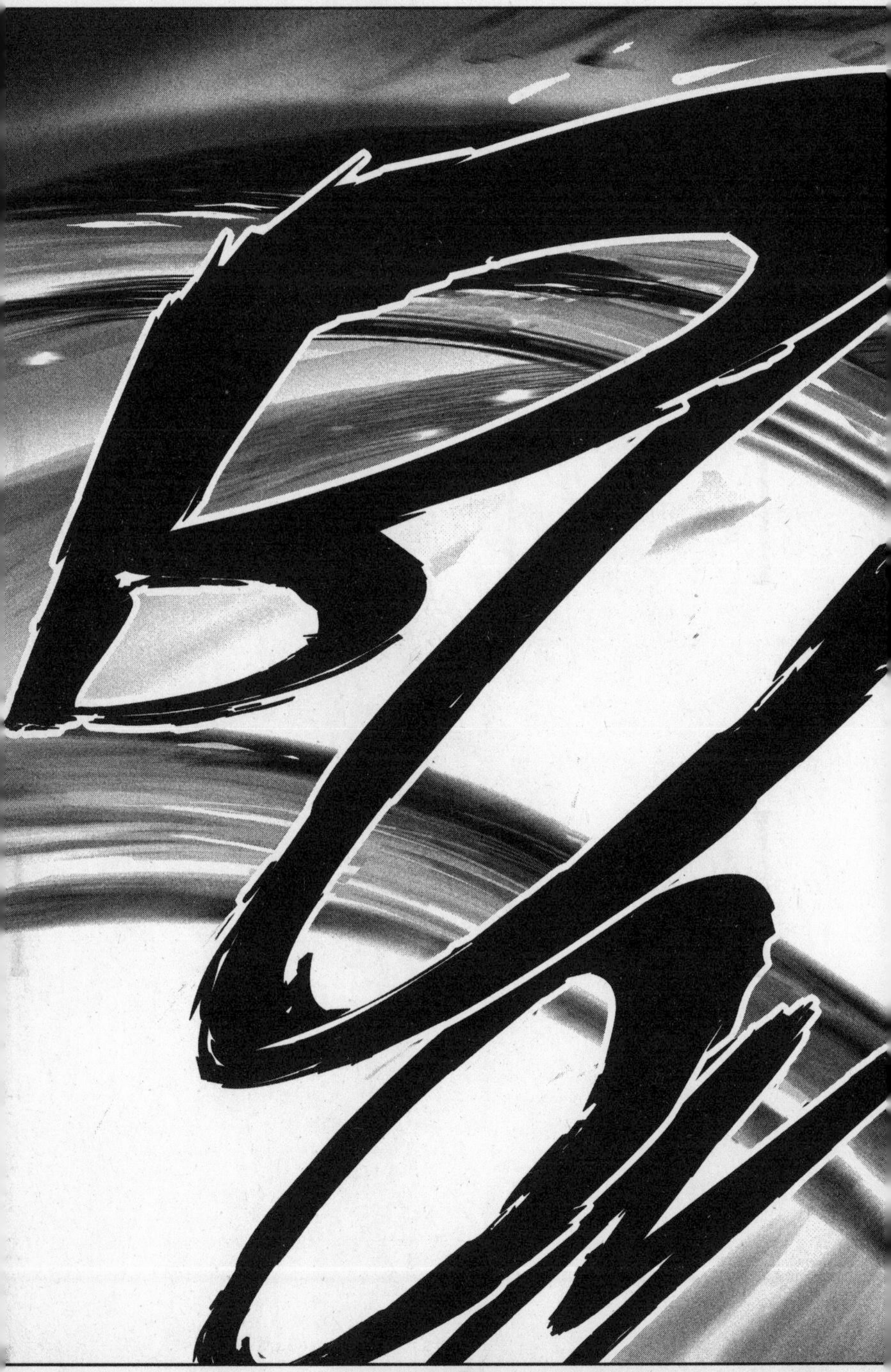

IT'S ALMOST BEEN 24 HOURS, SO WHY HAVEN'T YOU ATTACKED ?!

WHY DO YOU THINK I GIVE YOU SO MUCH MONEY?!

MR. NARINKI...

PLEASE, CALM DOWN.

THOSE MONSTERS TOOK MY SON!

WE *WILL* RESCUE HIM.

YOU HAVE MY PROMISE.

BAL-
DER-
DASH!

HOW-
EVER...

...HE WILL AID US WHEN HUMANITY FACES A TRUE CRISIS!

THIS RIGHT HERE...

...IS ONE SUCH CRISIS!!!

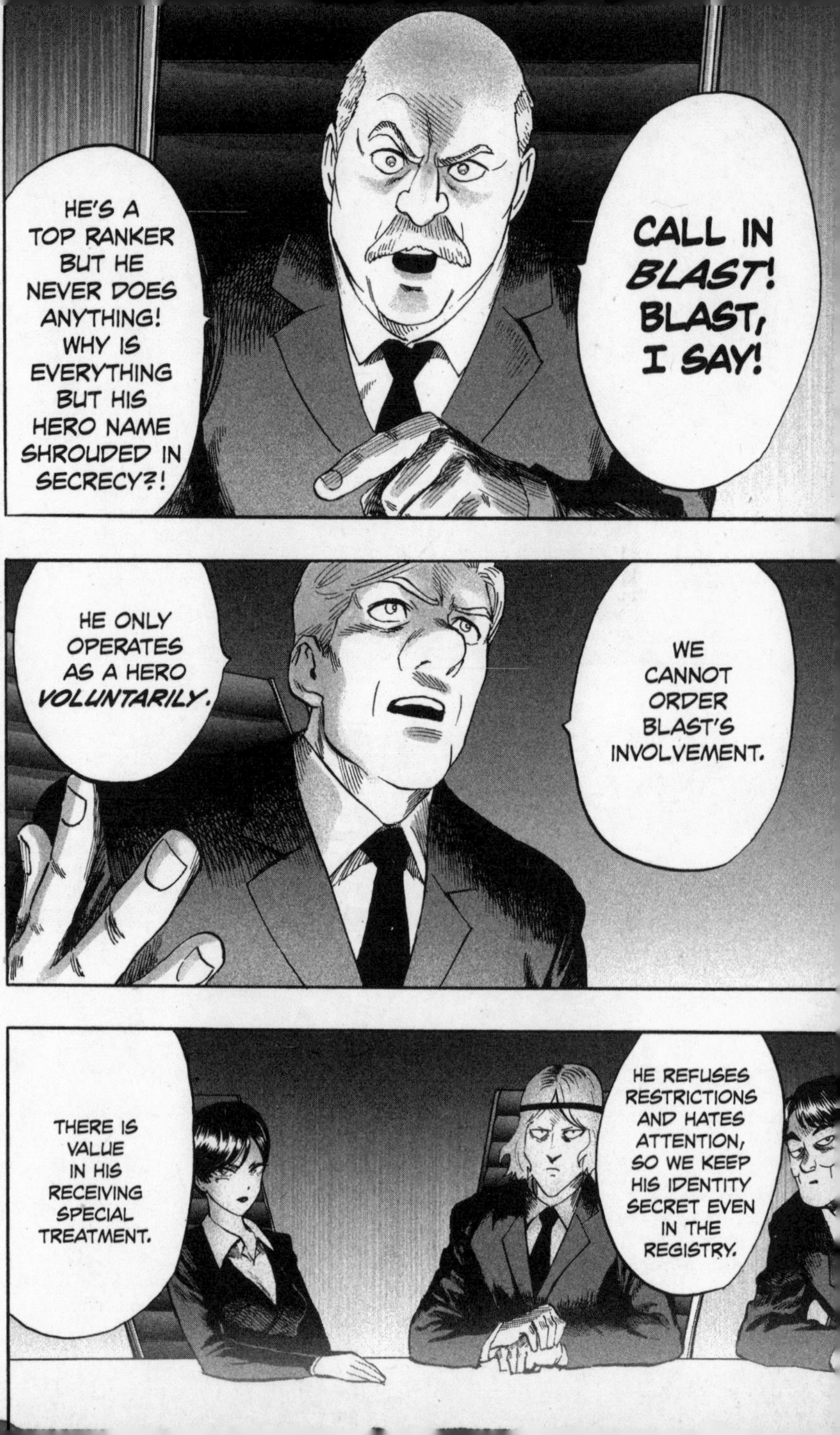
CALL IN BLAST! BLAST, I SAY!
HE'S A TOP RANKER BUT HE NEVER DOES ANYTHING! WHY IS EVERYTHING BUT HIS HERO NAME SHROUDED IN SECRECY?!
WE CANNOT ORDER BLAST'S INVOLVEMENT.
HE ONLY OPERATES AS A HERO VOLUNTARILY.
HE REFUSES RESTRICTIONS AND HATES ATTENTION, SO WE KEEP HIS IDENTITY SECRET EVEN IN THE REGISTRY.
THERE IS VALUE IN HIS RECEIVING SPECIAL TREATMENT.

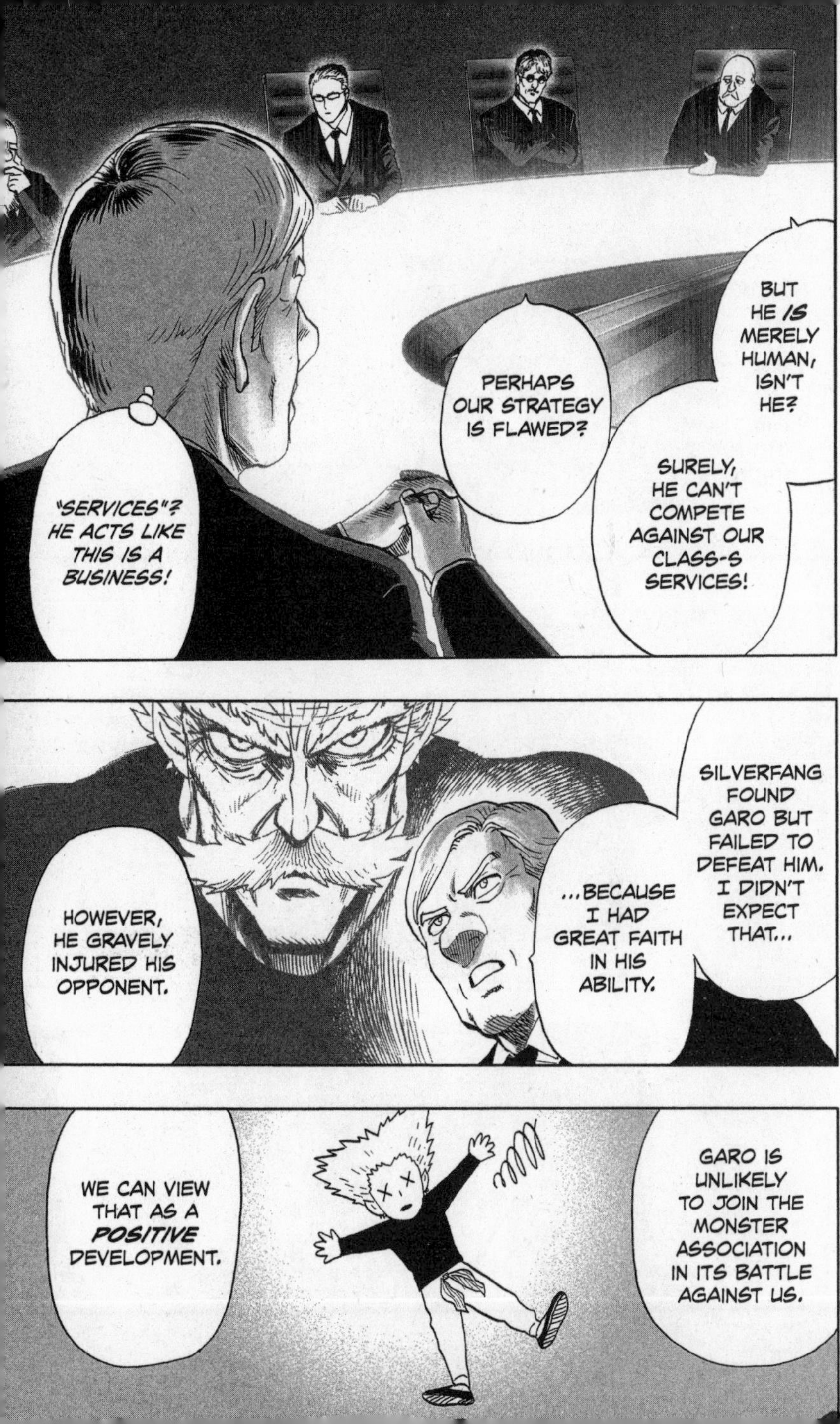
BUT HE *IS* MERELY HUMAN, ISN'T HE?
SURELY, HE CAN'T COMPETE AGAINST OUR CLASS-S SERVICES!
PERHAPS OUR STRATEGY IS FLAWED?
"SERVICES"? HE ACTS LIKE THIS IS A BUSINESS!
SILVERFANG FOUND GARO BUT FAILED TO DEFEAT HIM. I DIDN'T EXPECT THAT...
...BECAUSE I HAD GREAT FAITH IN HIS ABILITY.
HOWEVER, HE GRAVELY INJURED HIS OPPONENT.
GARO IS UNLIKELY TO JOIN THE MONSTER ASSOCIATION IN ITS BATTLE AGAINST US.
WE CAN VIEW THAT AS A *POSITIVE* DEVELOPMENT.

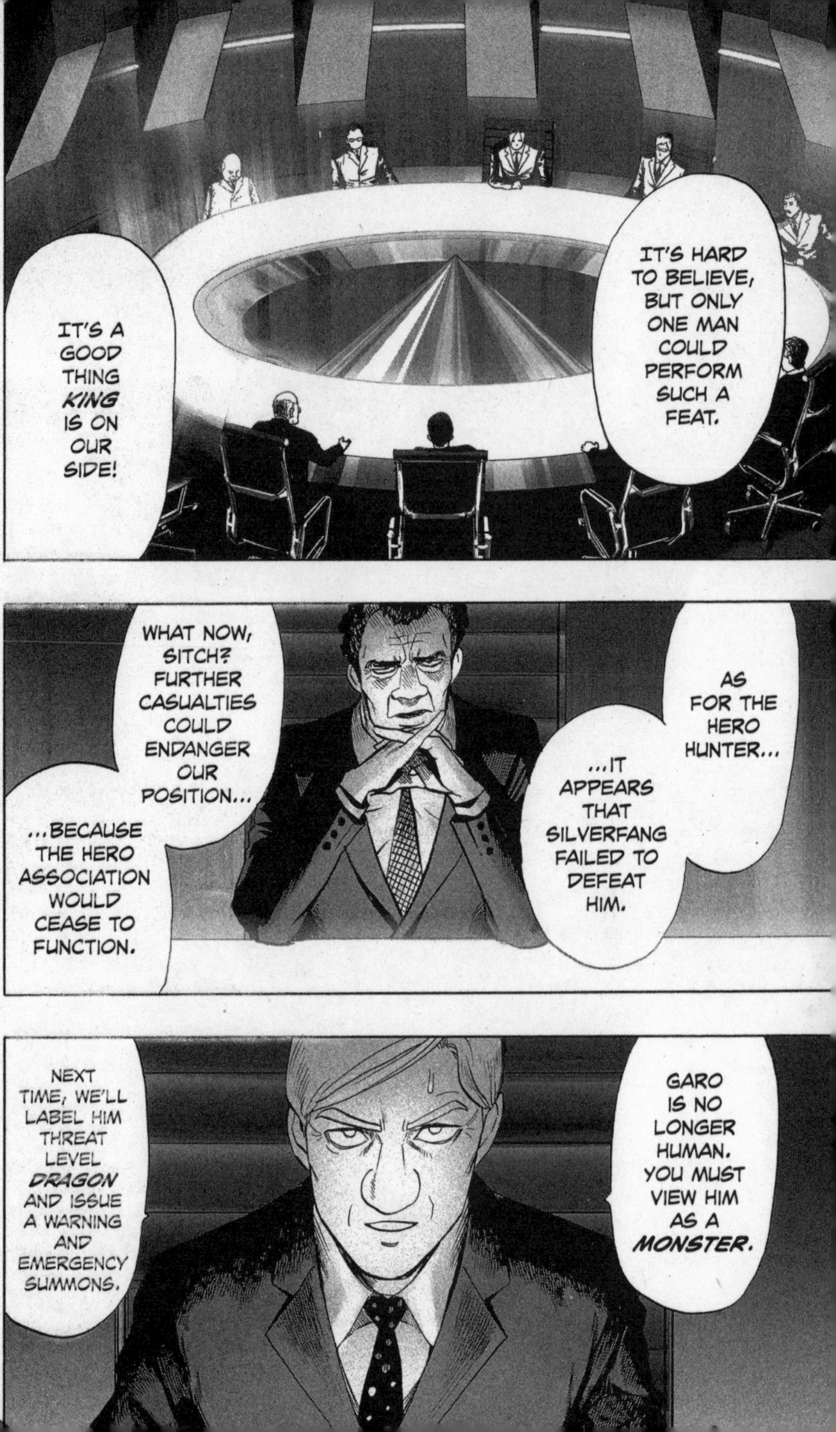
IT'S HARD TO BELIEVE, BUT ONLY ONE MAN COULD PERFORM SUCH A FEAT.
IT'S A GOOD THING *KING* IS ON OUR SIDE!
AS FOR THE HERO HUNTER...
...IT APPEARS THAT SILVERFANG FAILED TO DEFEAT HIM.
WHAT NOW, SITCH? FURTHER CASUALTIES COULD ENDANGER OUR POSITION...
...BECAUSE THE HERO ASSOCIATION WOULD CEASE TO FUNCTION.
GARO IS NO LONGER HUMAN. YOU MUST VIEW HIM AS A *MONSTER*.
NEXT TIME, WE'LL LABEL HIM THREAT LEVEL *DRAGON* AND ISSUE A WARNING AND EMERGENCY SUMMONS.

SNIFF
SNIFF

...

YOU SMELL THAT?

YES.

I CAN WALK.

ARE YOU MOBILE, GENOS?

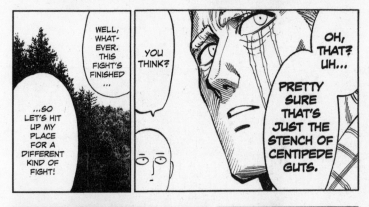

WELL, WHATEVER. THIS FIGHT'S FINISHED...

...SO LET'S HIT UP MY PLACE FOR A DIFFERENT KIND OF FIGHT!

YOU THINK?

OH, THAT? UH...

PRETTY SURE THAT'S JUST THE STENCH OF CENTIPEDE GUTS.

I KINDA NEED TO GET SOME NEW PANTS.

MIND IF I STOP BY A DEPARTMENT STORE FIRST?

WHY?

GARO, DID YOU FINALLY PASS OUT?

REST WELL...

FWIP FWIP

...FOR WE WILL SOON REACH OROCHI.

NOOOOO-
OOOOOO-
OOOOOO-
OOOOOO!

GENOS, YOU SHOULDN'T USE SAITAMA AS A GOOD EXAMPLE!

...!!!

THANK YOU VERY MUCH!

MASTER'S FIGHT HAS SHOWN ME THE WAY!

...TOWARD WHICH I TOO MUST TRAVEL!

HE HAS SHOWN ME TRUE STRENGTH...

...AND THE DESTINATION...

WELL, I JUST WANTED TO SHOW YOU THAT CONTINUING TO FIGHT THE SAME WAY IS NO GOOD.

HE WAS STILL IRRI- TATED?

I WAS STRESSED FROM LOSING AGAINST YOU AT VIDEO GAMES.

WHAT IS IT?

CLINK

TUNK

MASTER SAITAMA, MAY I ASK A QUESTION?

HUH?

WHAT IS IT I LACK?

MAYBE IT'S POWER?

SPWORSH

YOU WERE RIGHT.

HE *WAS* HERE!

YEAH, AND IT LOOKS LIKE HE BARELY SURVIVED.

PSHOOK

GOOD THING WE CAME.

BABABOOM

WELL, THAT FELT PRETTY GOOD.

PHEW!

WHAT HAPPENED?

HM? SAITAMA, YOU SEEM RELIEVED.

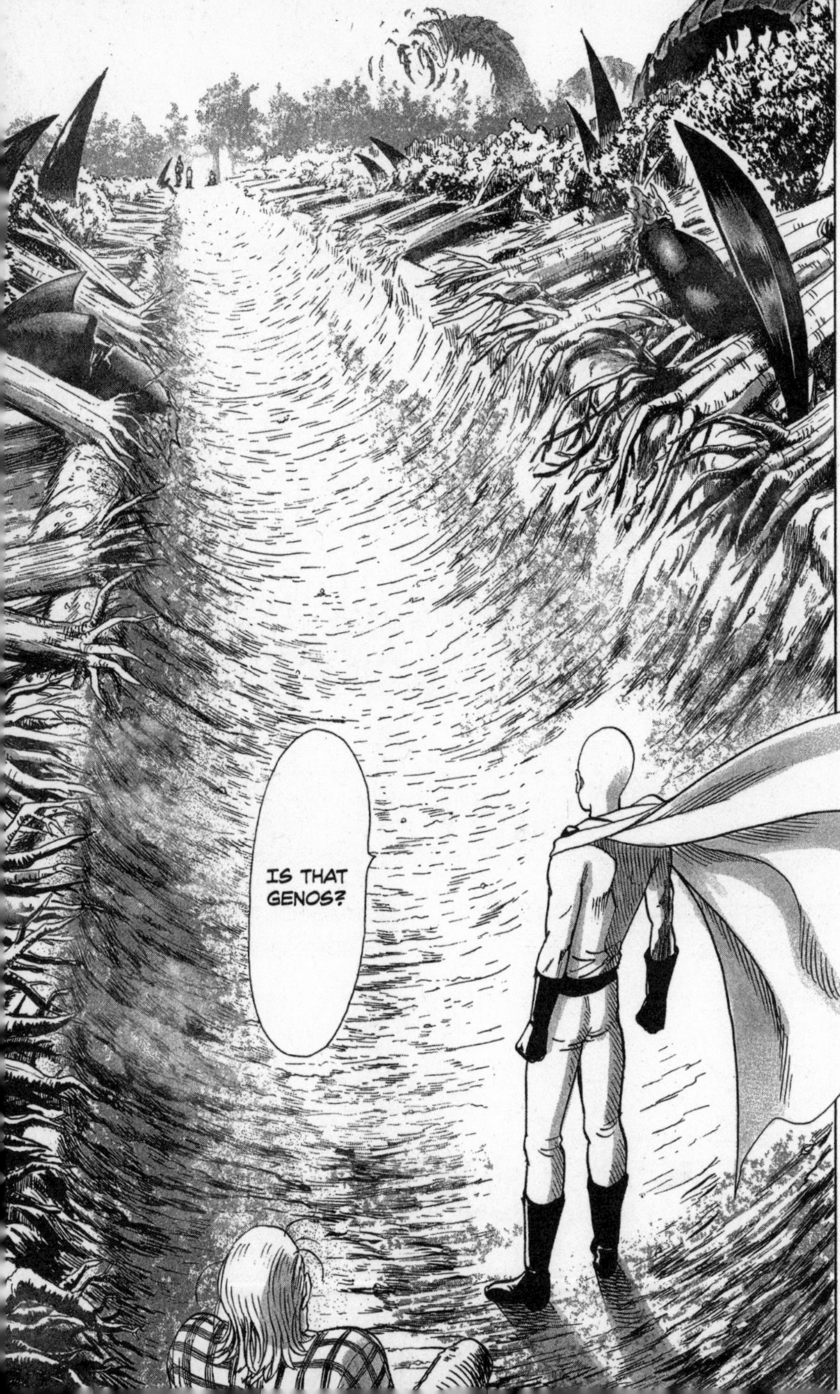
IS THAT GENOS?

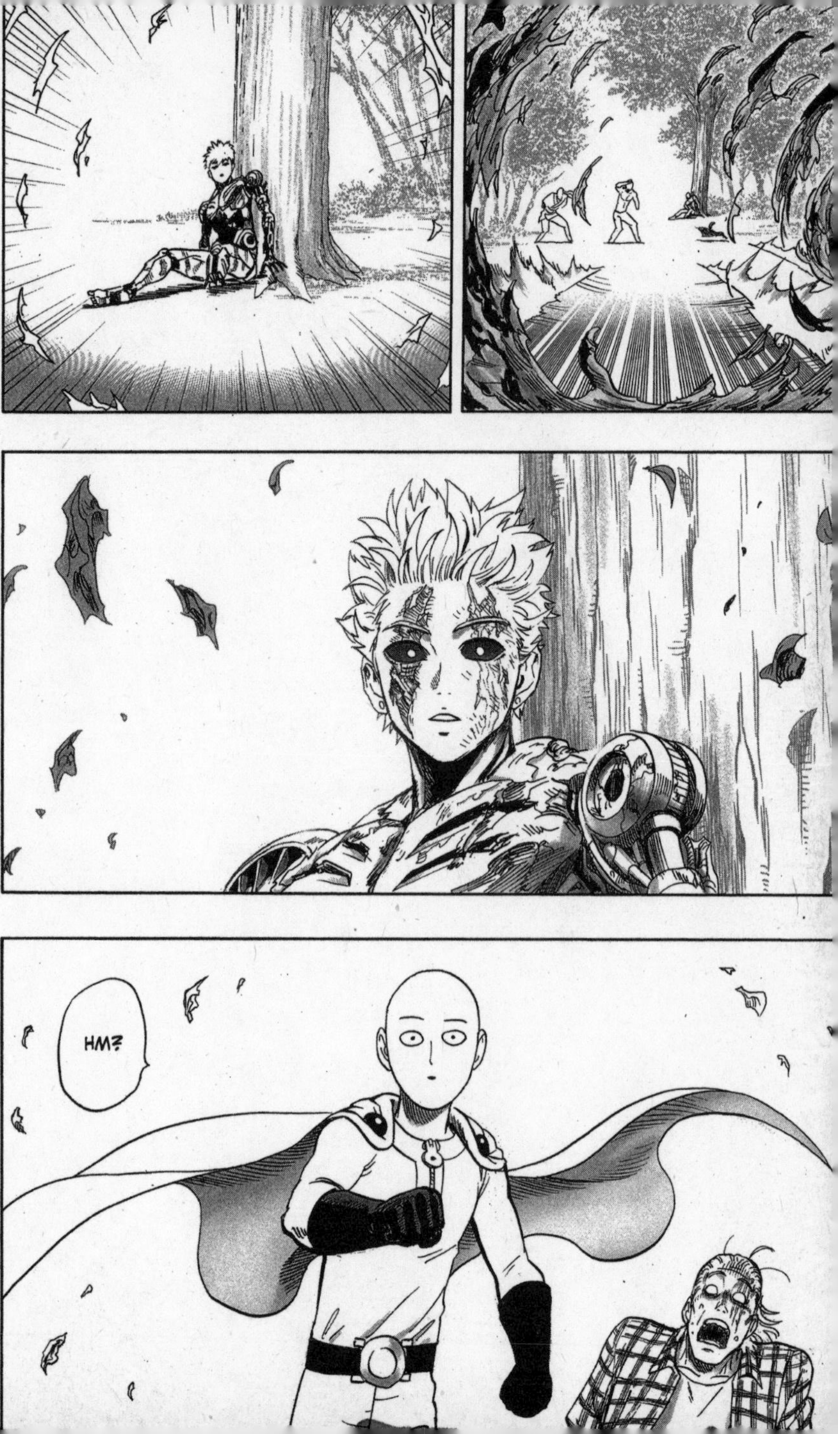
HM?

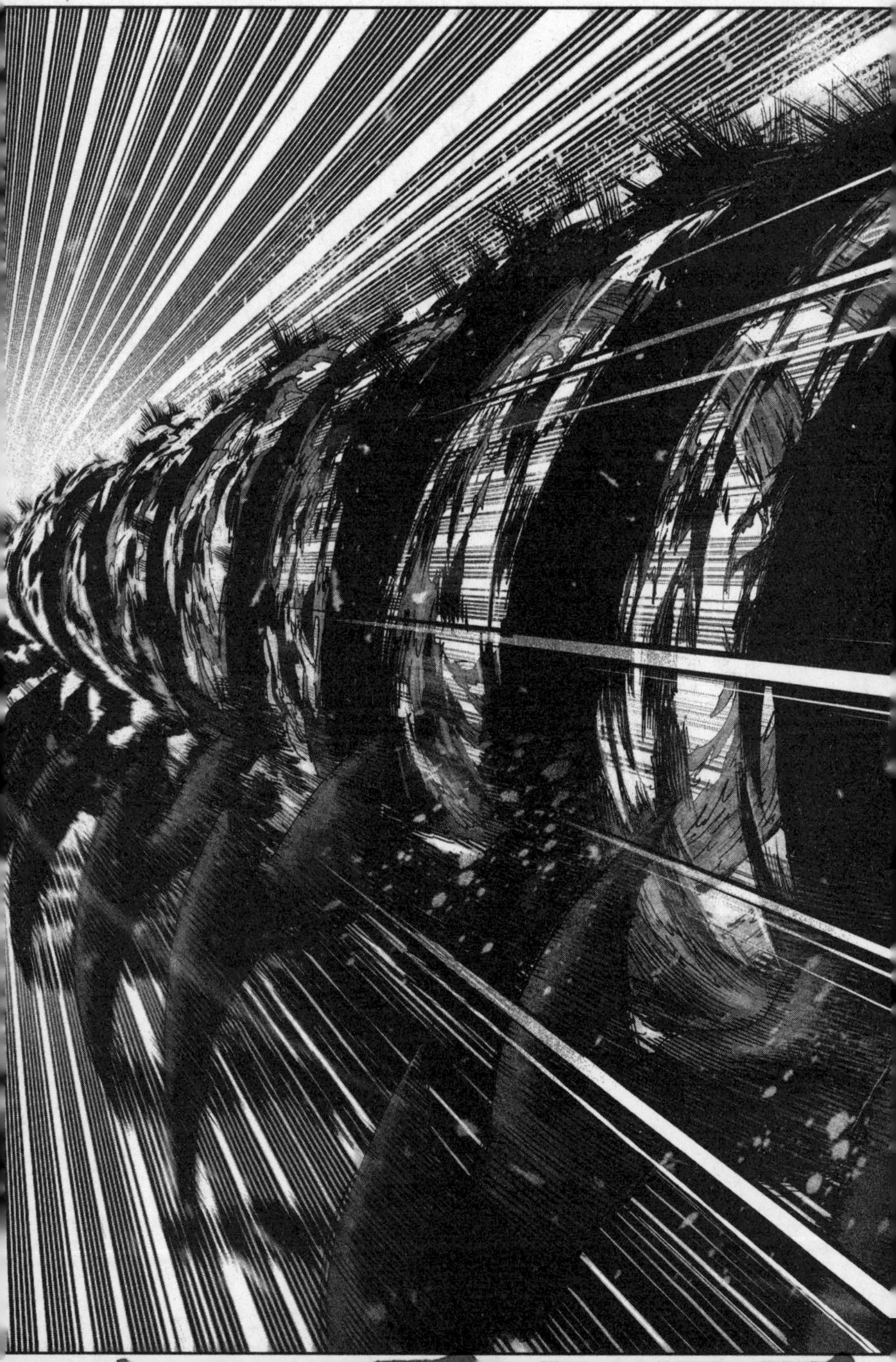

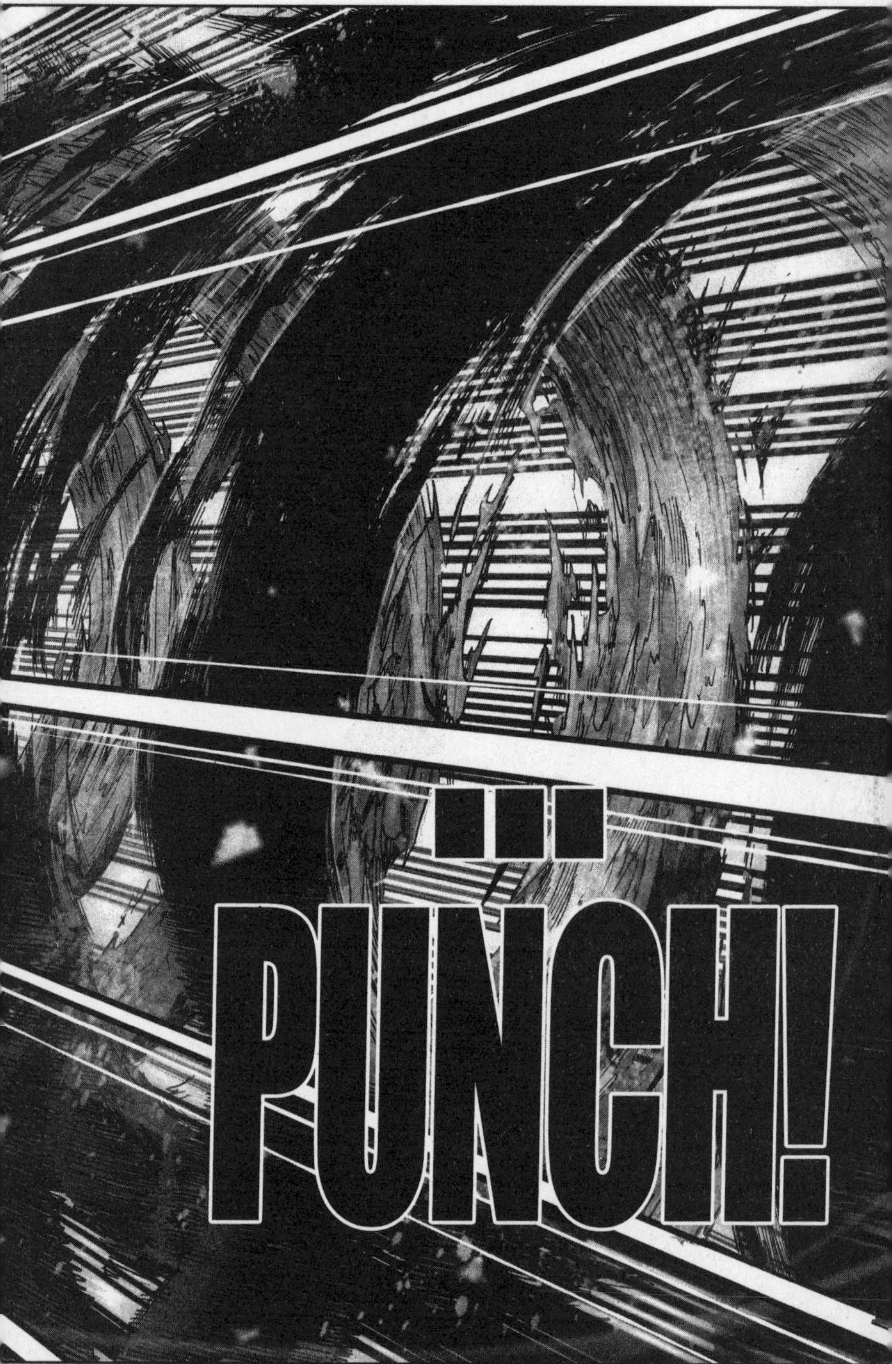
...
PUNCH!

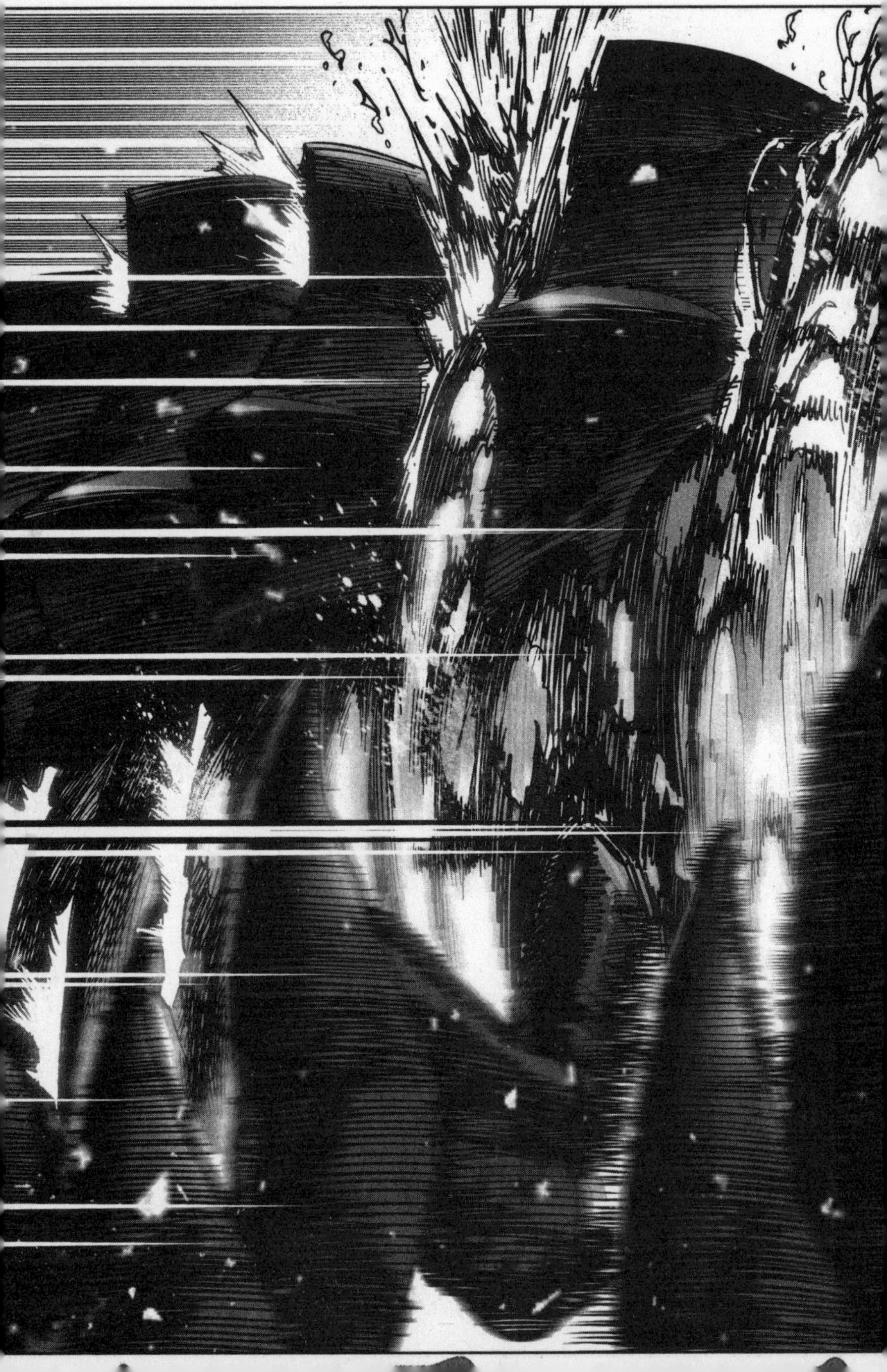

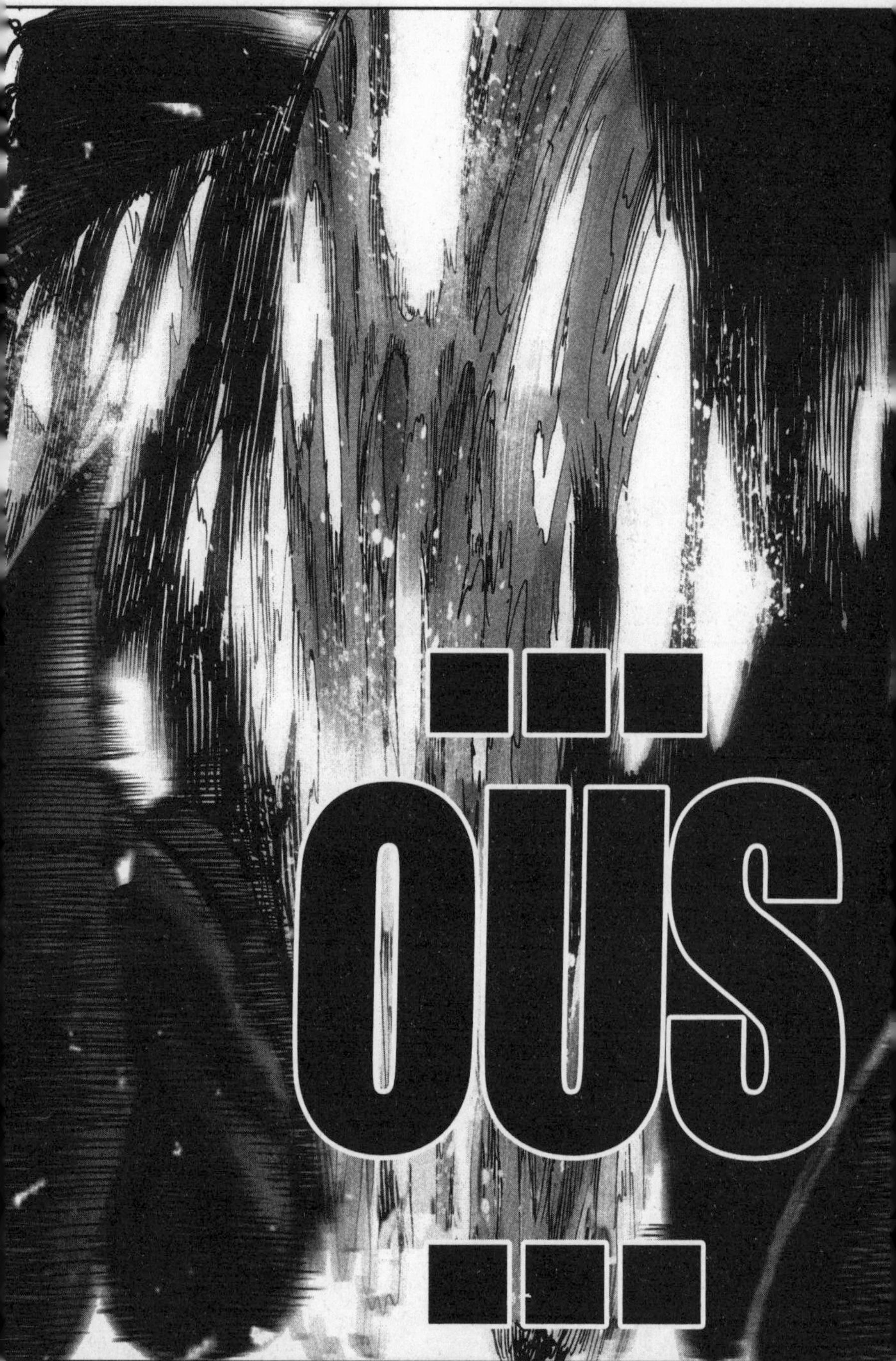
...
OUS
...

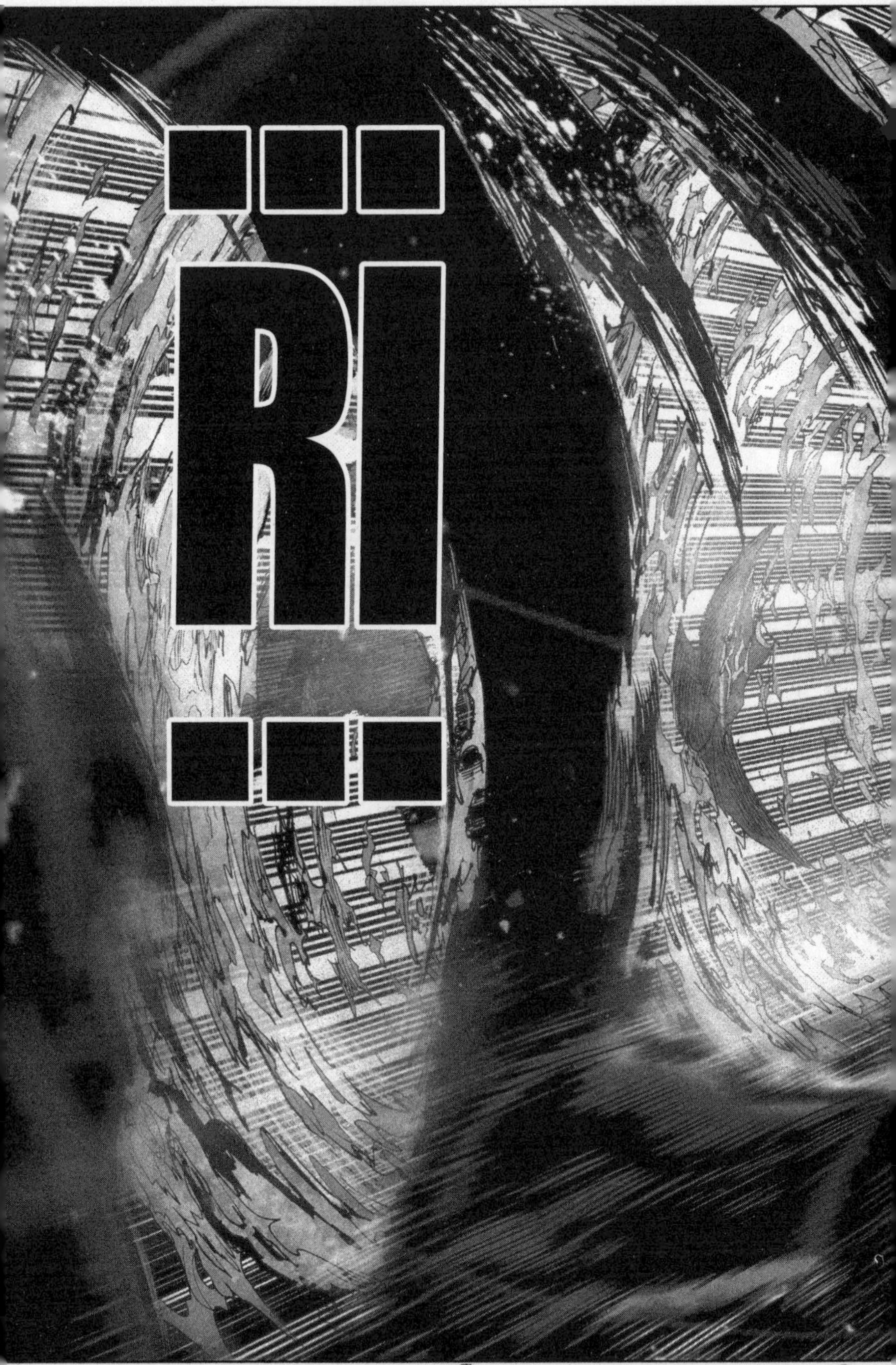
RI

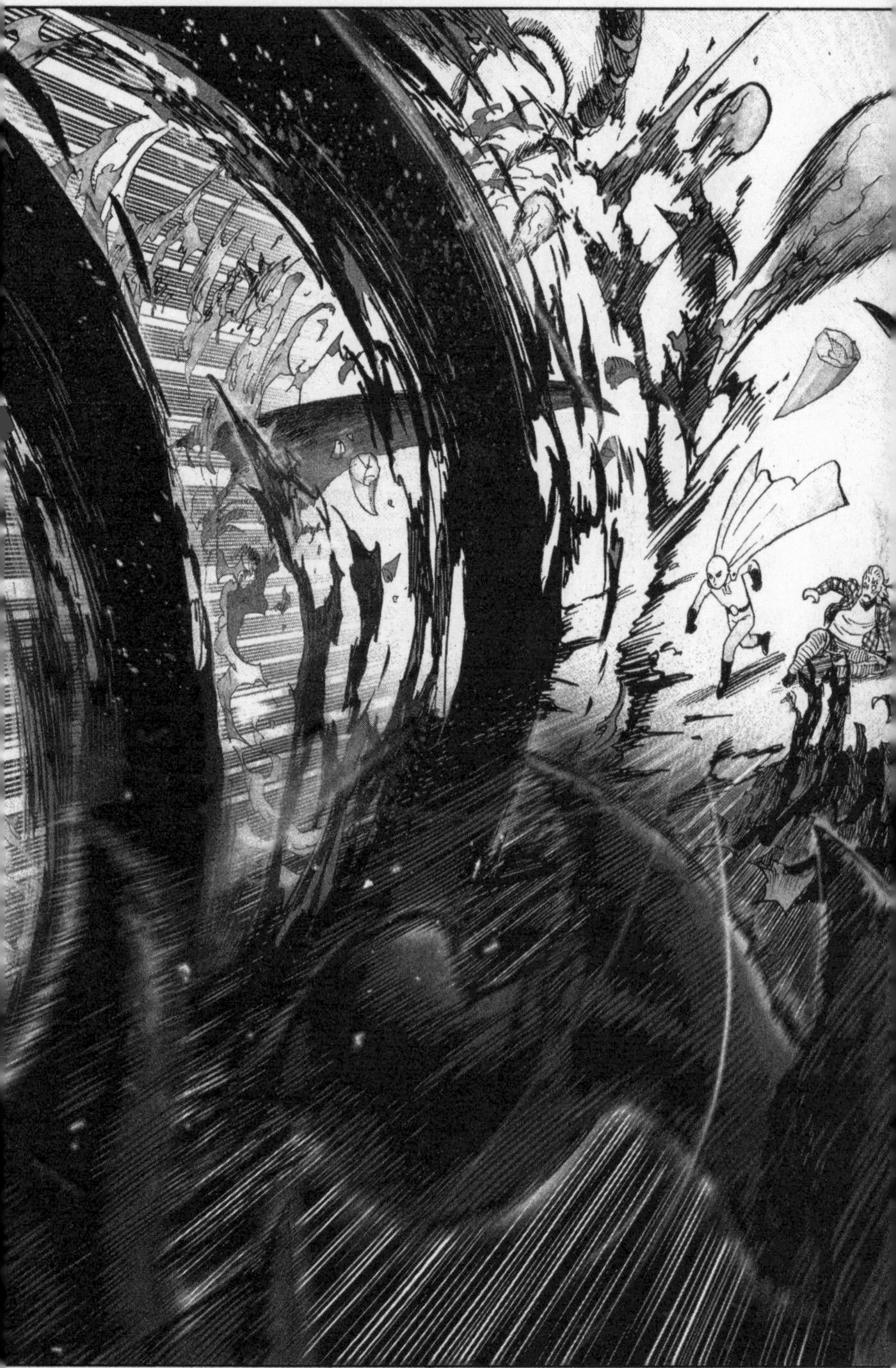

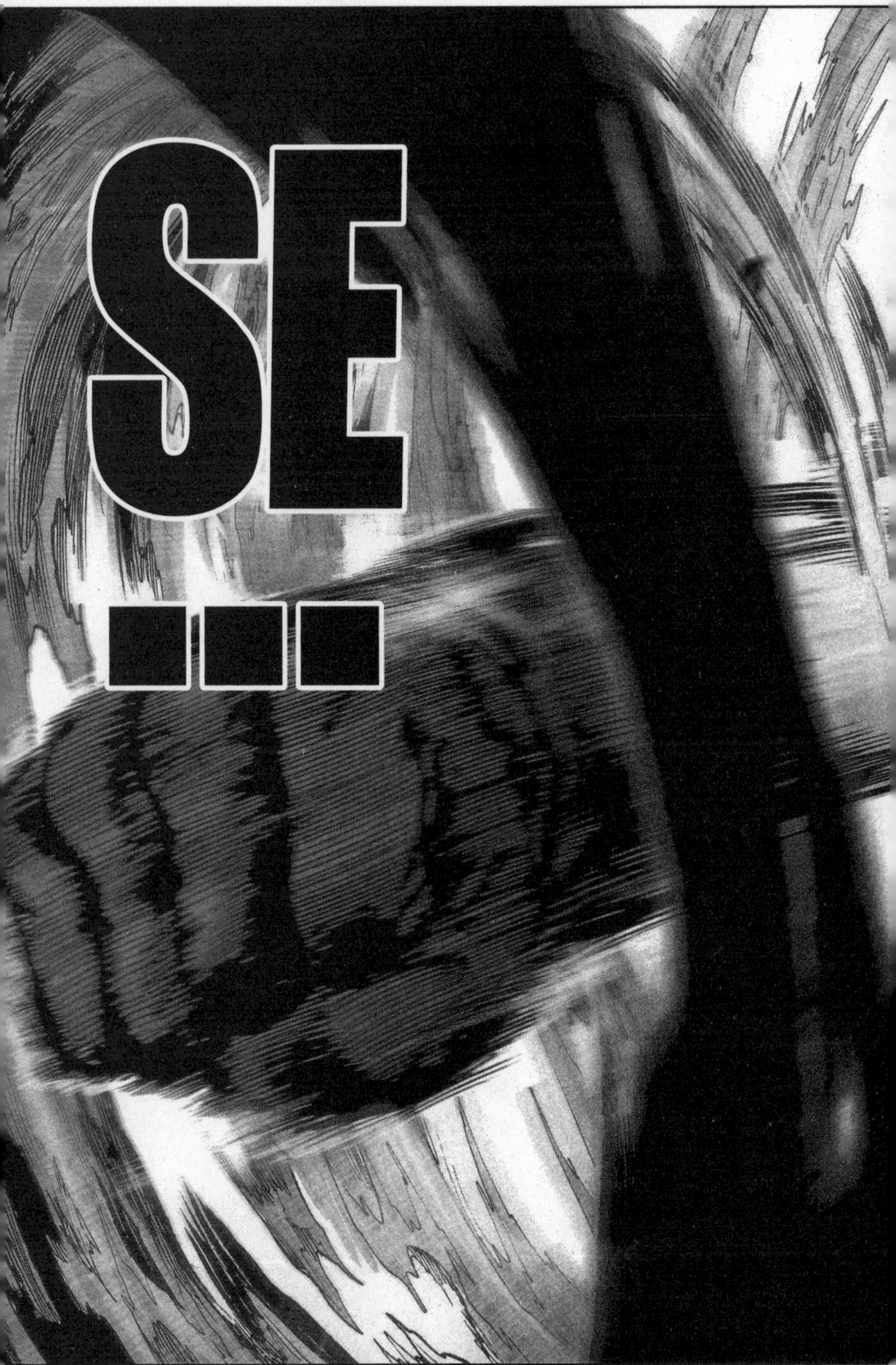
SE...

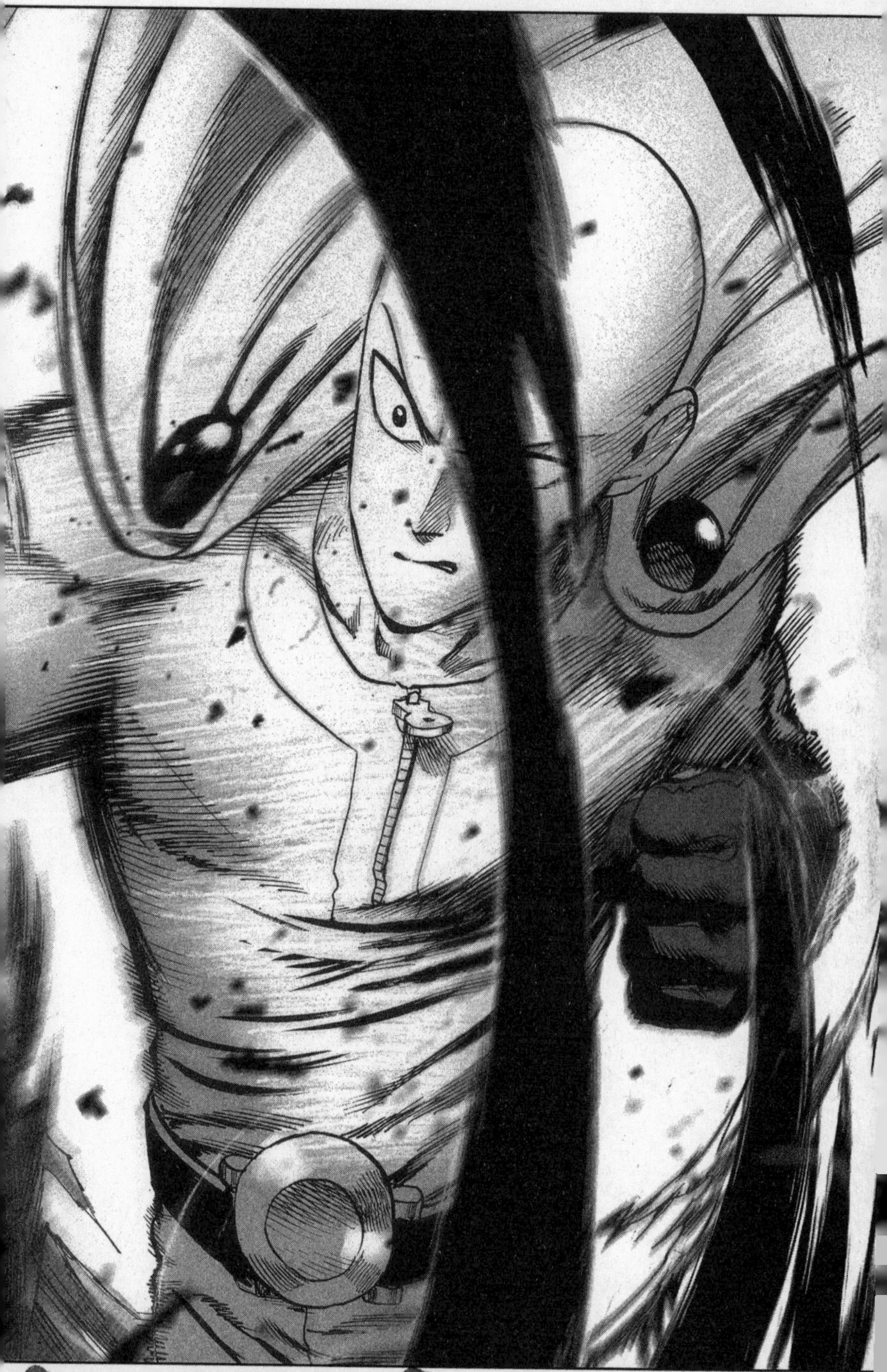

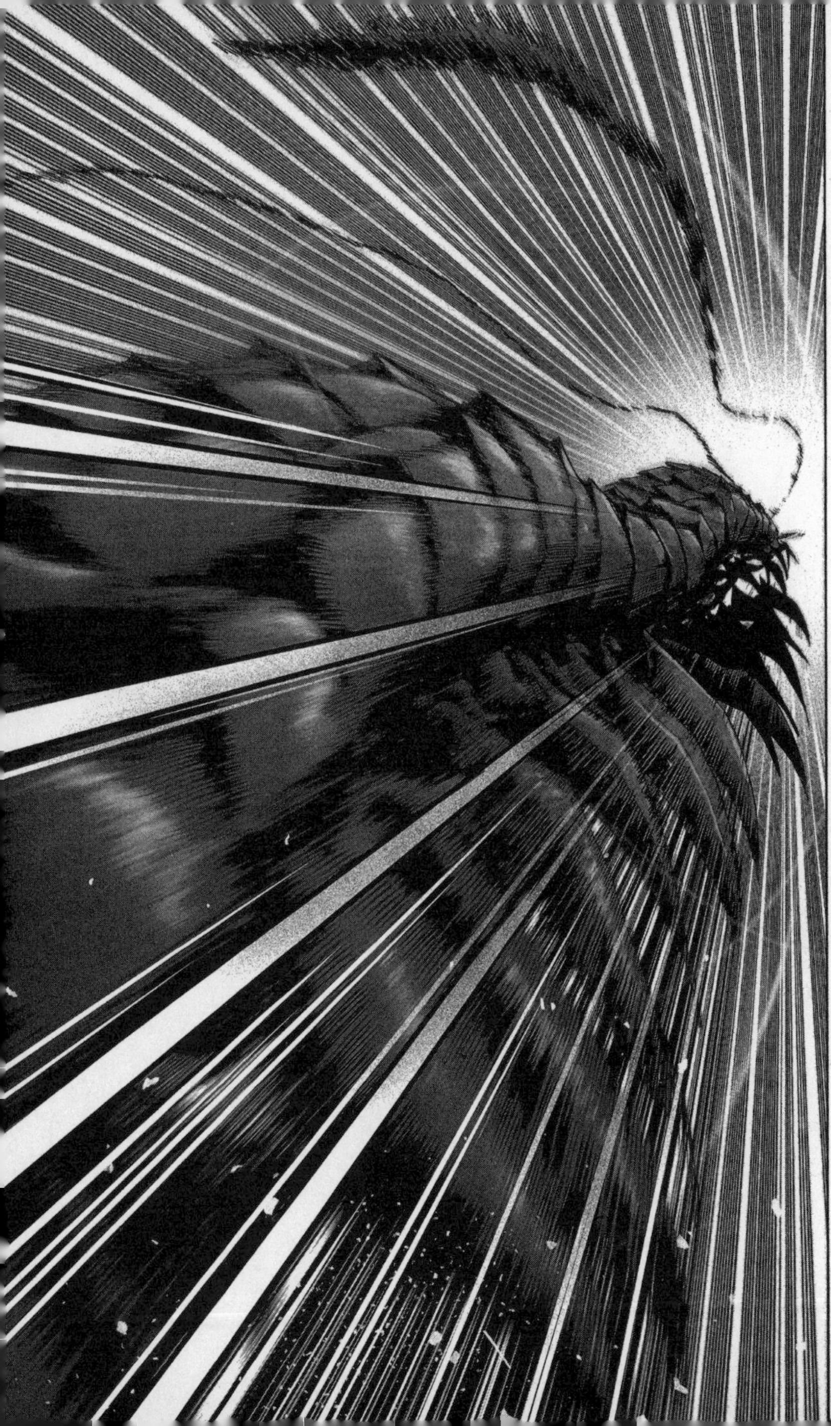

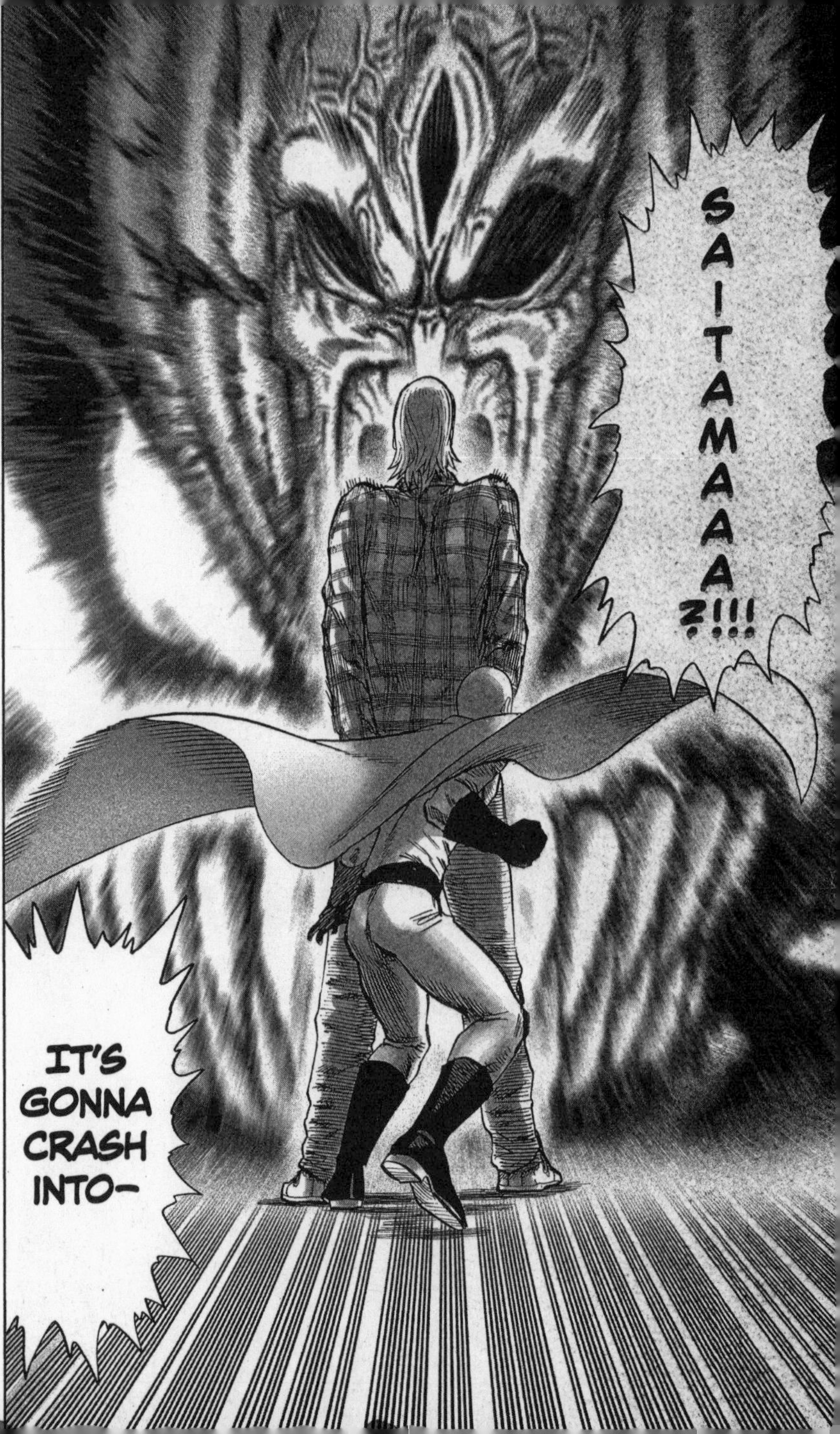
SAITAMAAAA?!!!
IT'S GONNA CRASH INTO-

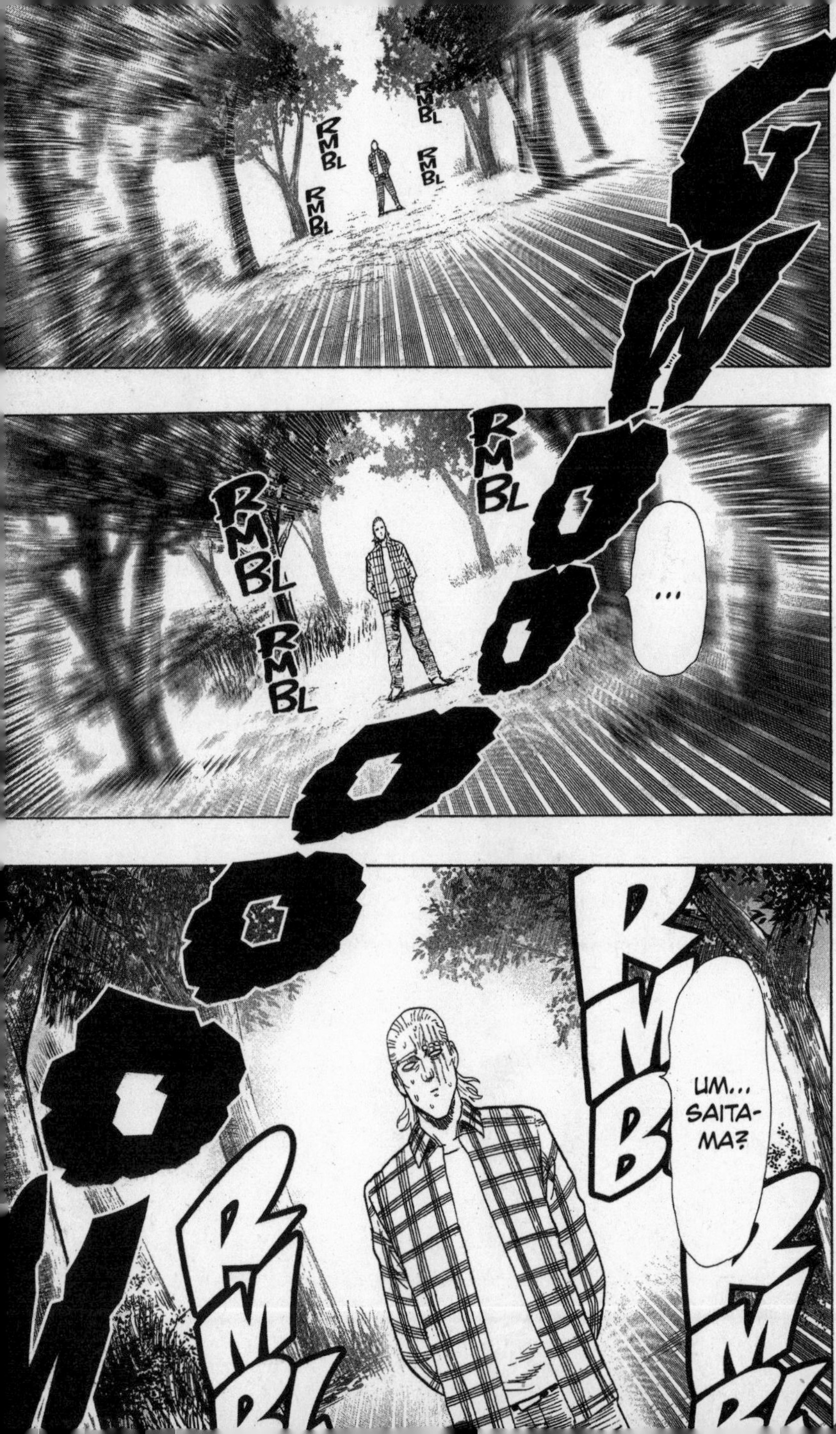
GGWOOOOOOM
RMBL
RMBL
RMBL
RMBL
RMBL
...
RMBL
RMBL
UM... SAITAMA?
RMBL
RMBL
RMBL

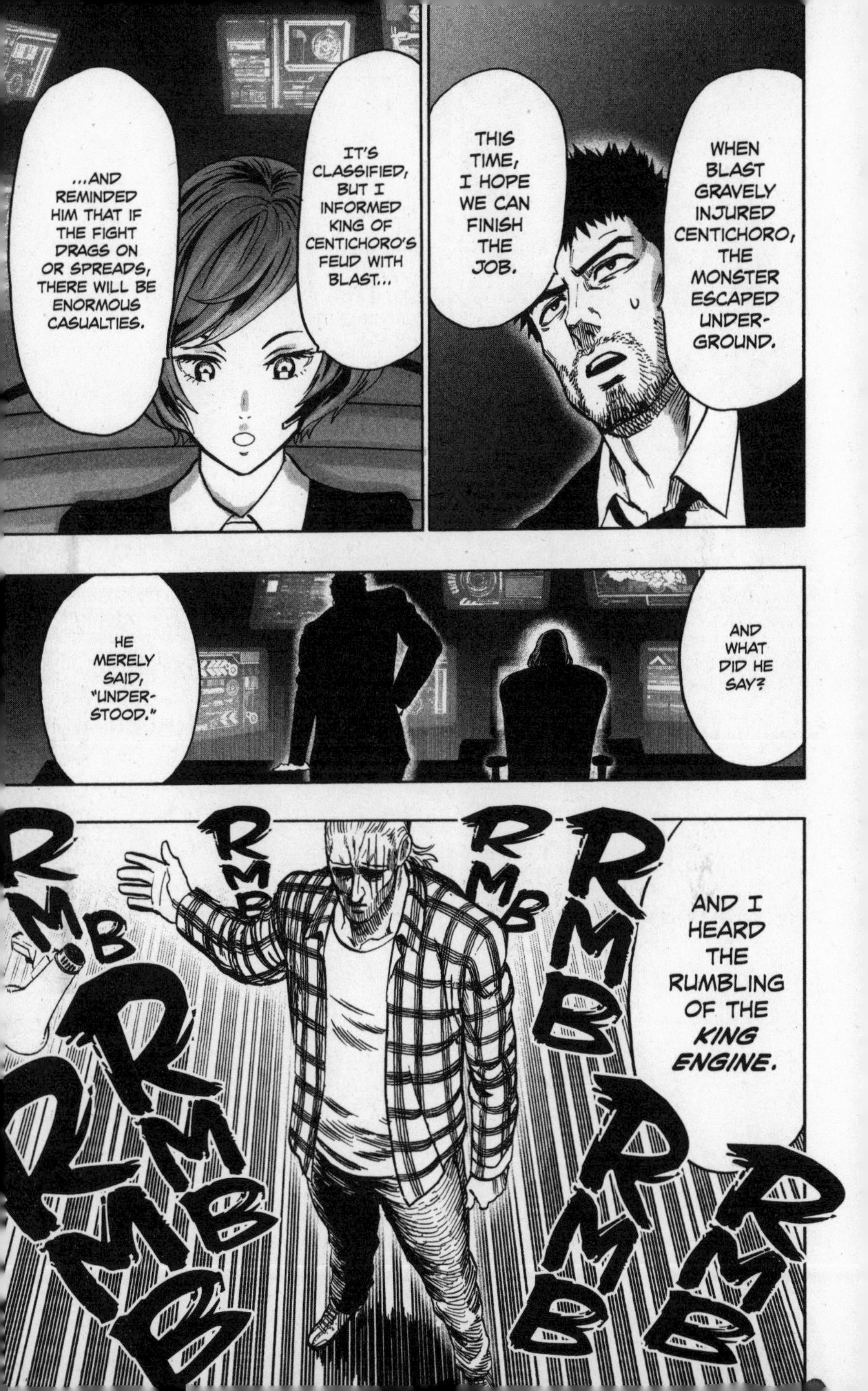
WHEN BLAST GRAVELY INJURED CENTICHORO, THE MONSTER ESCAPED UNDER-GROUND.
THIS TIME, I HOPE WE CAN FINISH THE JOB.
IT'S CLASSIFIED, BUT I INFORMED KING OF CENTICHORO'S FEUD WITH BLAST...
...AND REMINDED HIM THAT IF THE FIGHT DRAGS ON OR SPREADS, THERE WILL BE ENORMOUS CASUALTIES.
AND WHAT DID HE SAY?
HE MERELY SAID, "UNDER-STOOD."
RMB
RMB
AND I HEARD THE RUMBLING OF THE *KING ENGINE*.
RMB
RMB
RMB
RMB
RMB
RMB
RMB

EXCELLENT! KING IS SURE TO HANDLE THIS!

KING HAS REACHED THE SCENE OF THE FIGHT IN CITY S!!!

...HE ASKED FOR INFORMATION ON HOW TO PROVOKE CENTICHORO.

...STILL THREATENS THE LIVES OF SEVERAL HEROES...

WHEN I TOLD HIM THAT THE FIGHT...

I BELIEVE HE MEANS TO FIGHT IT *ALONE.*

IF YOU WANT TO FIGHT HIM, COME THIS WAY!

YES, THAT'S RIGHT! THE HERO WHO BEAT YOU SO BAD THAT YOU PEED YOURSELF AND SLITHERED AWAY!

BLAST?

A WIMPY BUG LIKE YOU SHOULD GO BACK UNDER-GROUND AND SUCK YOUR MOMMY'S BOOBY!!!

WHAT'S WRONG? TOO SCARED TO MOVE?! WHAT A COWARD!!! BUT IF YOU'RE GONNA *POOP* YOURSELF, DO IT AT HOME!

RMB RMB RMB RMB RMB RMB RMB

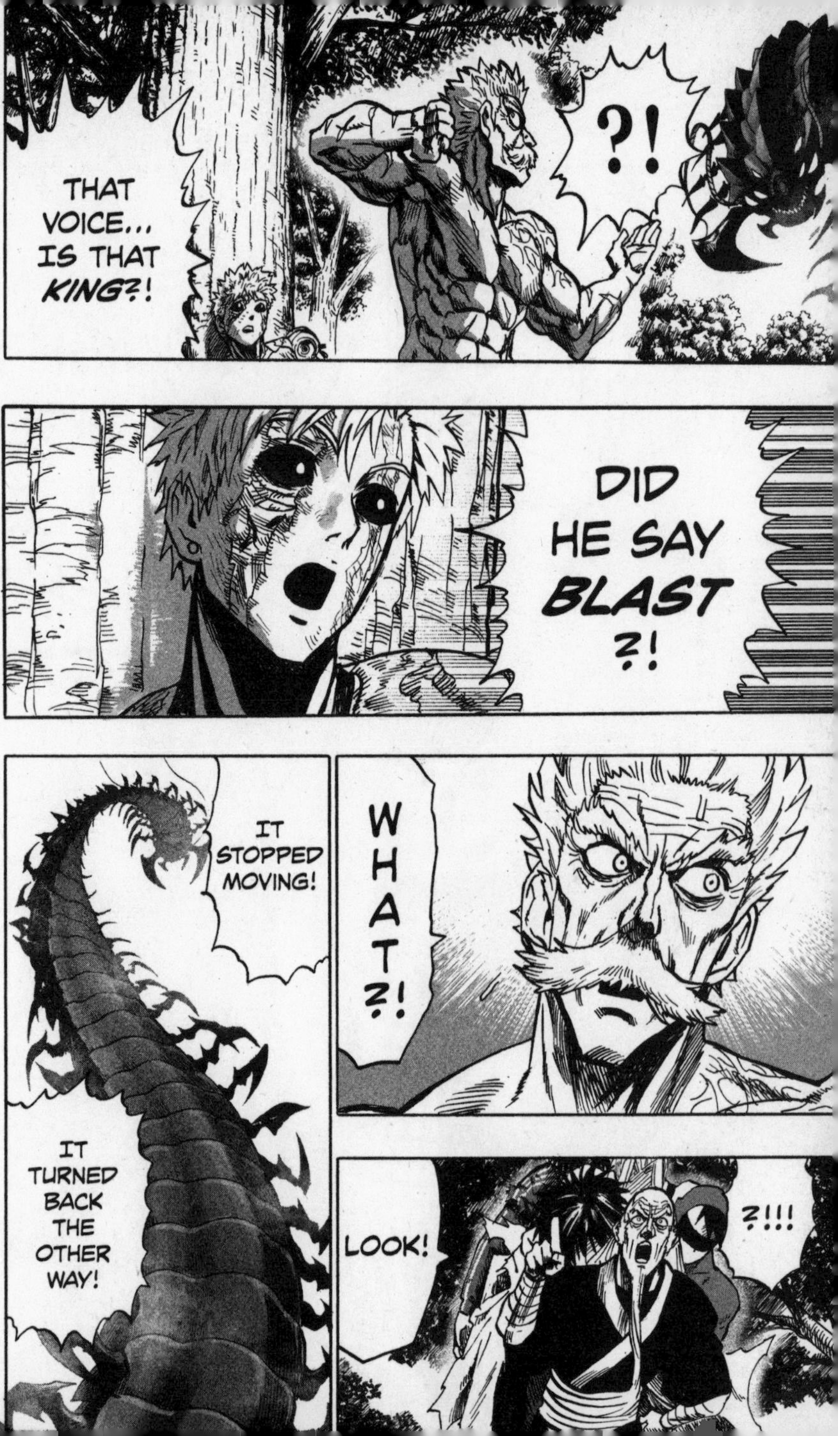
?!
THAT VOICE... IS THAT KING?!
DID HE SAY BLAST?!
WHAT?!
?!!!
LOOK!
IT STOPPED MOVING!
IT TURNED BACK THE OTHER WAY!

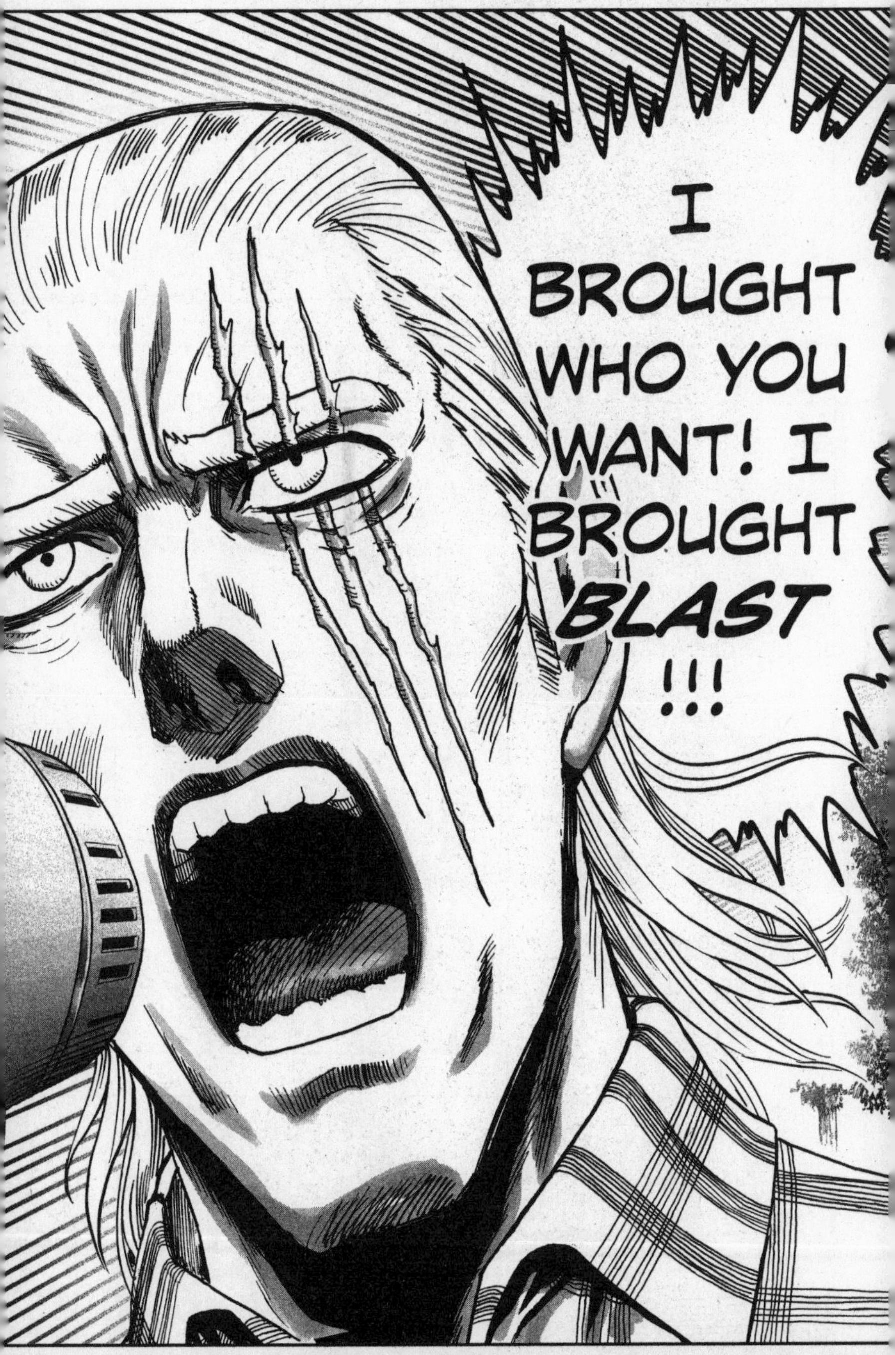
I BROUGHT WHO YOU WANT! I BROUGHT BLAST !!!

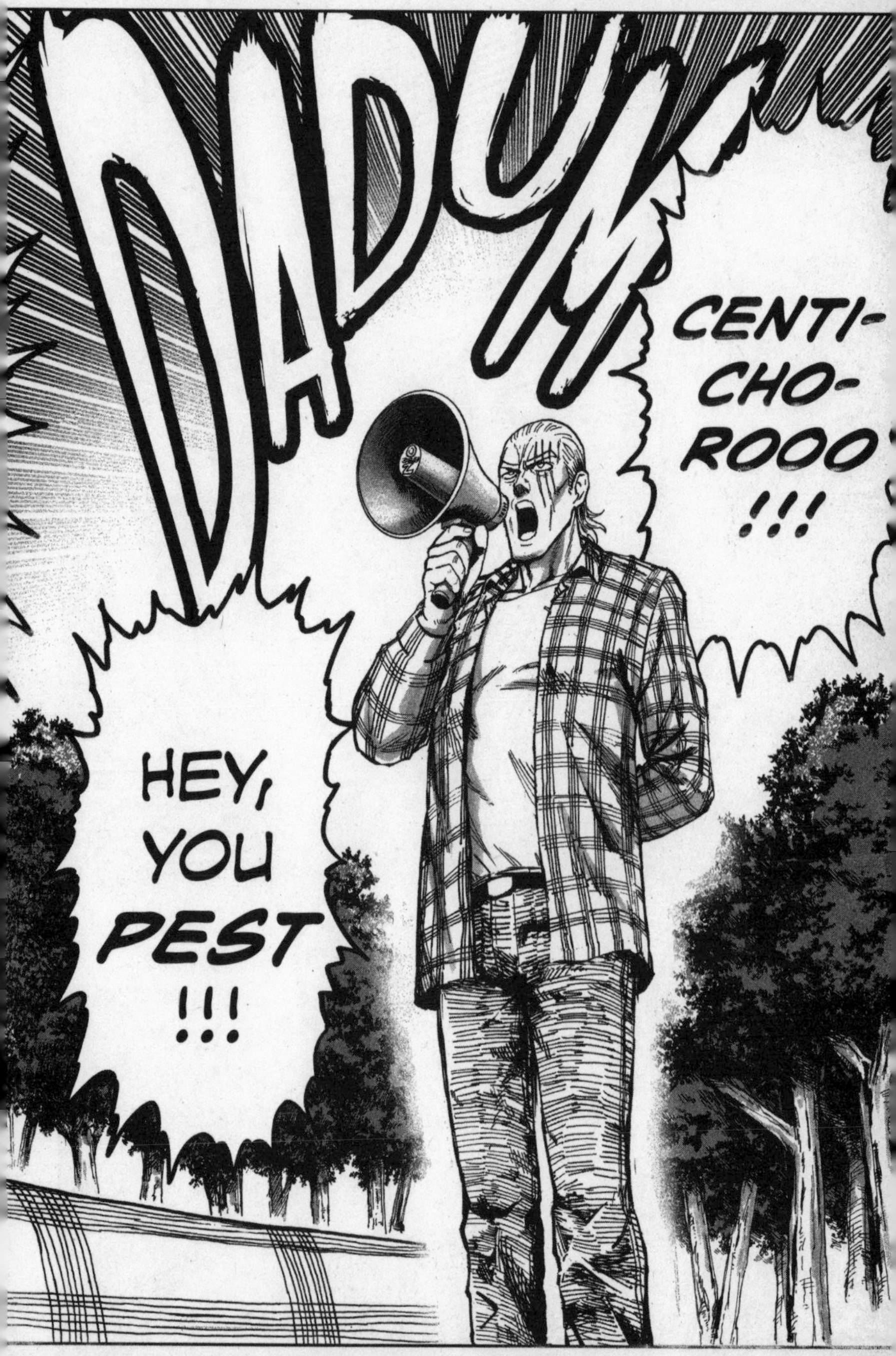
DADUN
CENTI-CHO-ROOO !!!
HEY, YOU PEST !!!

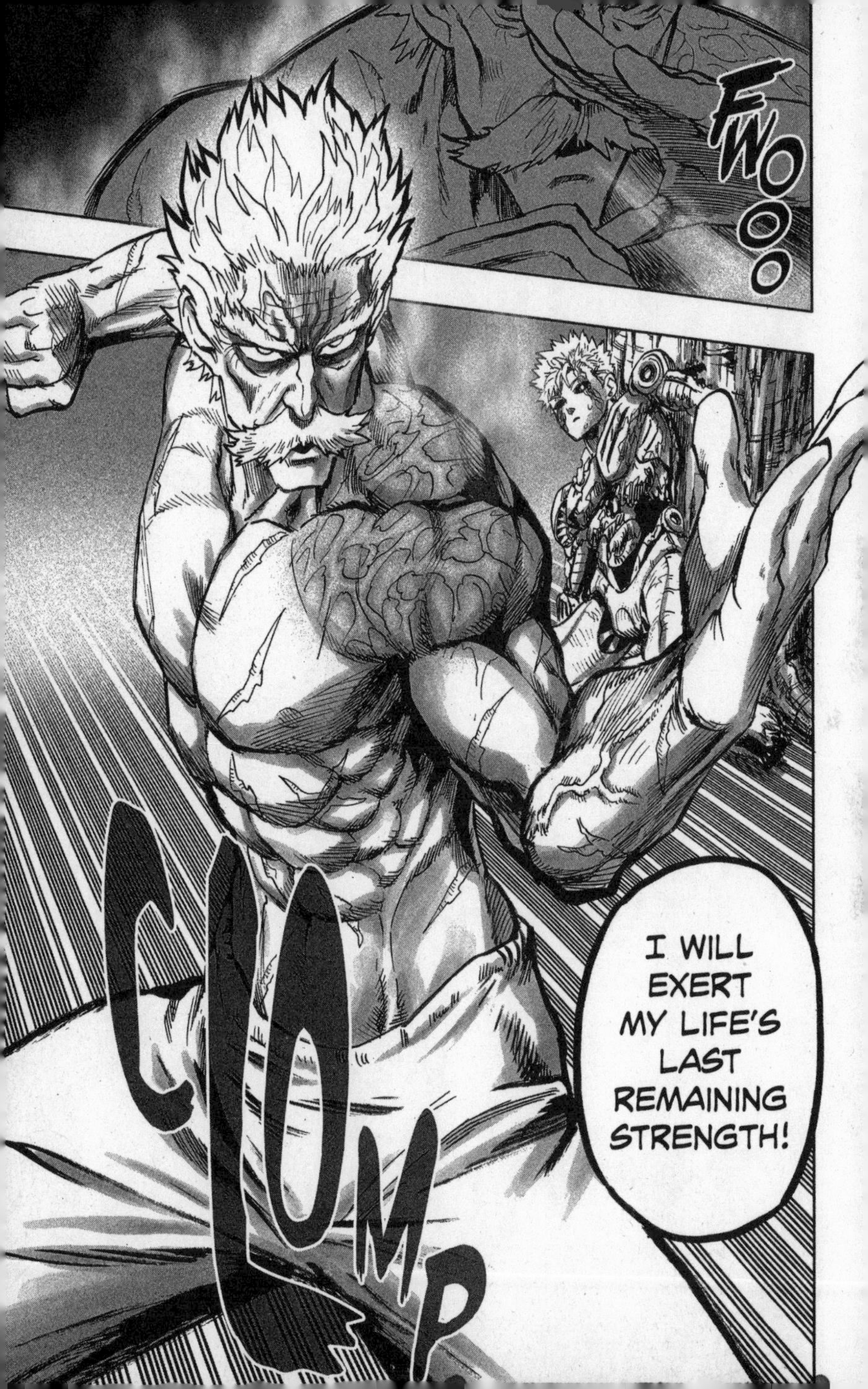
FWOOO
I WILL EXERT MY LIFE'S LAST REMAINING STRENGTH!
CLOMP

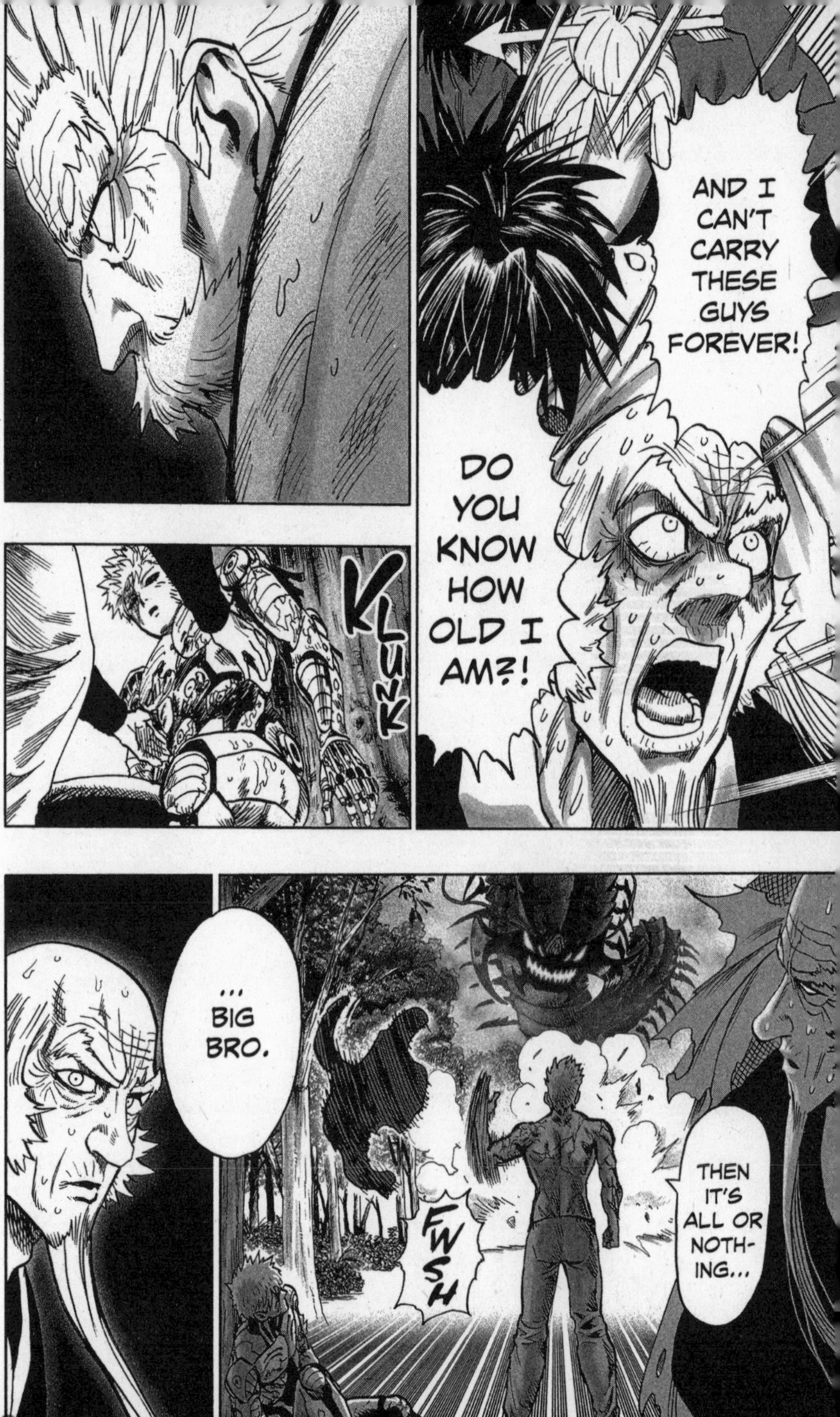
AND I CAN'T CARRY THESE GUYS FOREVER!
DO YOU KNOW HOW OLD I AM?!
KLUNK
THEN IT'S ALL OR NOTH-ING...
FWSH
... BIG BRO.

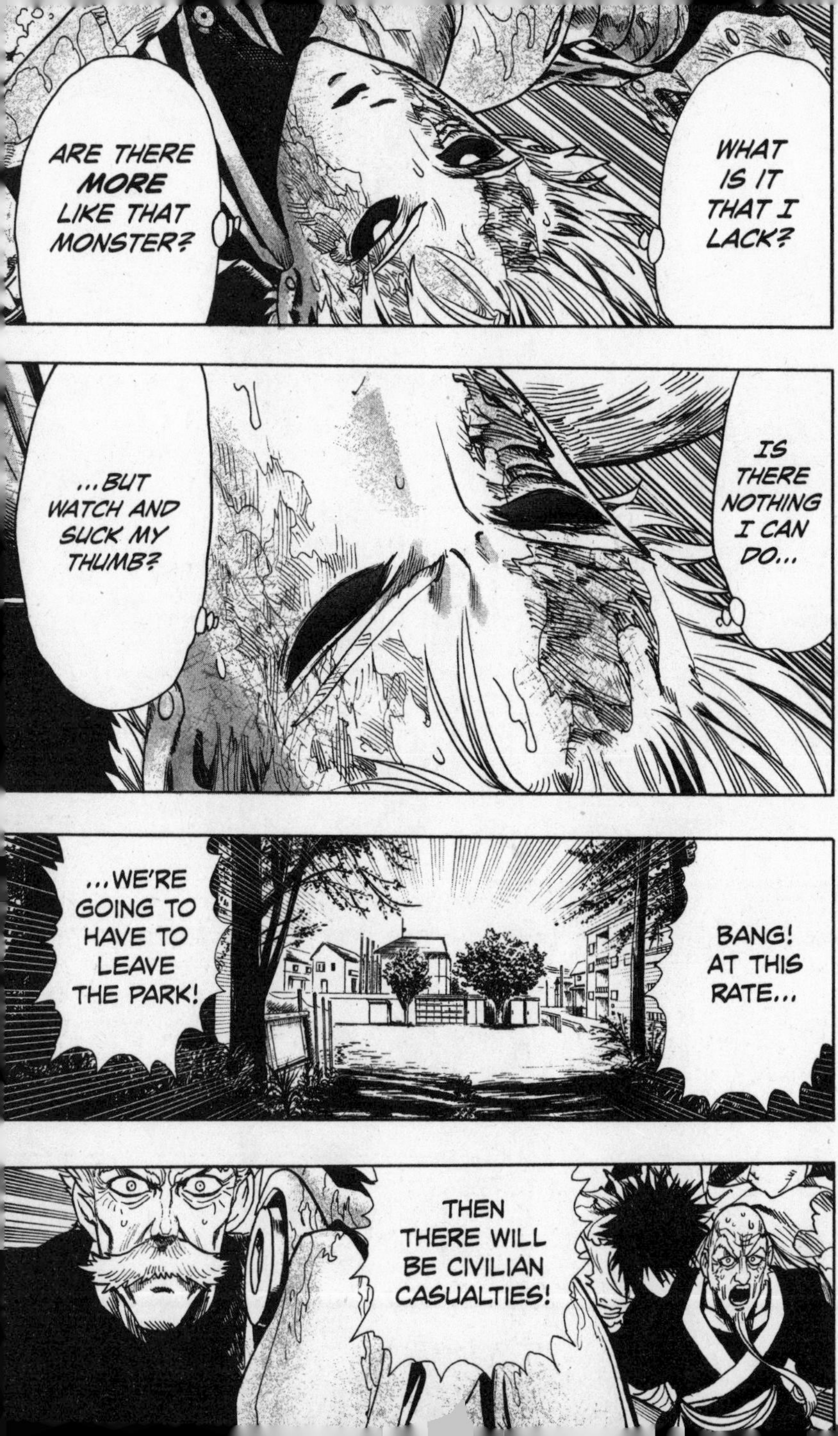
WHAT IS IT THAT I LACK?
ARE THERE MORE LIKE THAT MONSTER?
IS THERE NOTHING I CAN DO...
...BUT WATCH AND SUCK MY THUMB?
BANG! AT THIS RATE...
...WE'RE GOING TO HAVE TO LEAVE THE PARK!
THEN THERE WILL BE CIVILIAN CASUALTIES!

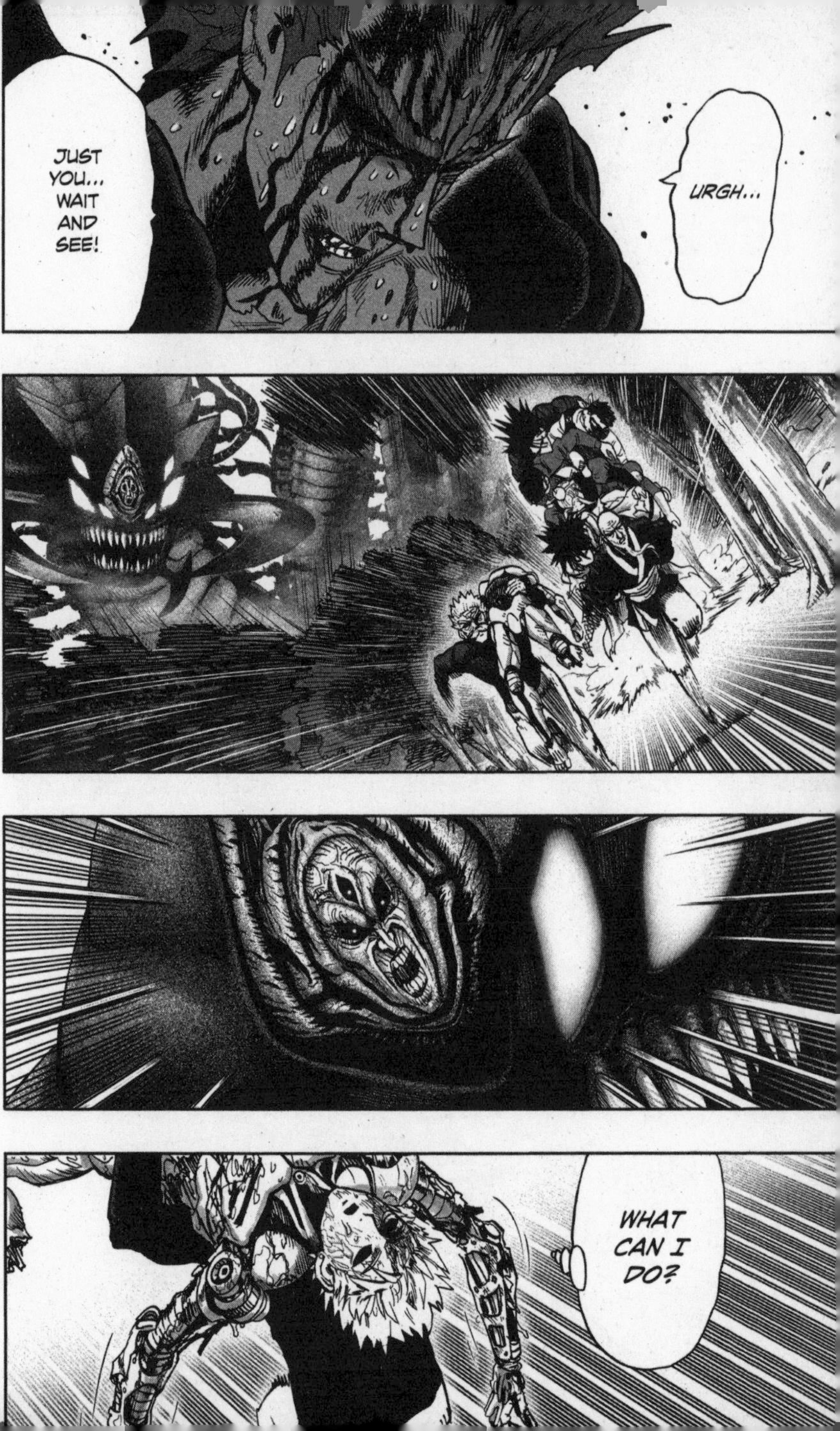
URGH...
JUST YOU... WAIT AND SEE!
WHAT CAN I DO?

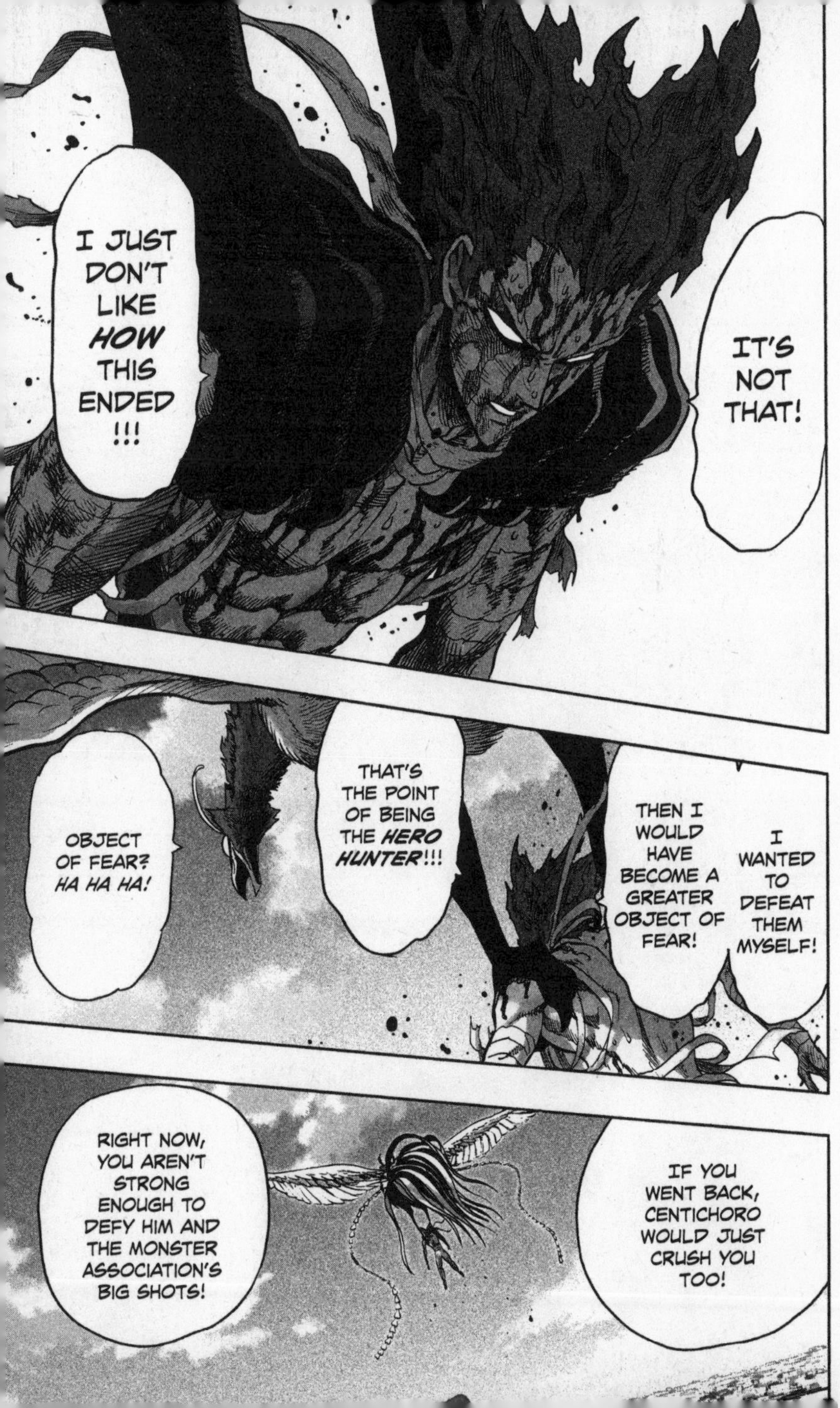
IT'S NOT THAT!
I JUST DON'T LIKE *HOW* THIS ENDED!!!
I WANTED TO DEFEAT THEM MYSELF!
THEN I WOULD HAVE BECOME A GREATER OBJECT OF FEAR!
THAT'S THE POINT OF BEING THE *HERO HUNTER*!!!
OBJECT OF FEAR? *HA HA HA!*
IF YOU WENT BACK, CENTICHORO WOULD JUST CRUSH YOU TOO!
RIGHT NOW, YOU AREN'T STRONG ENOUGH TO DEFY HIM AND THE MONSTER ASSOCIATION'S BIG SHOTS!

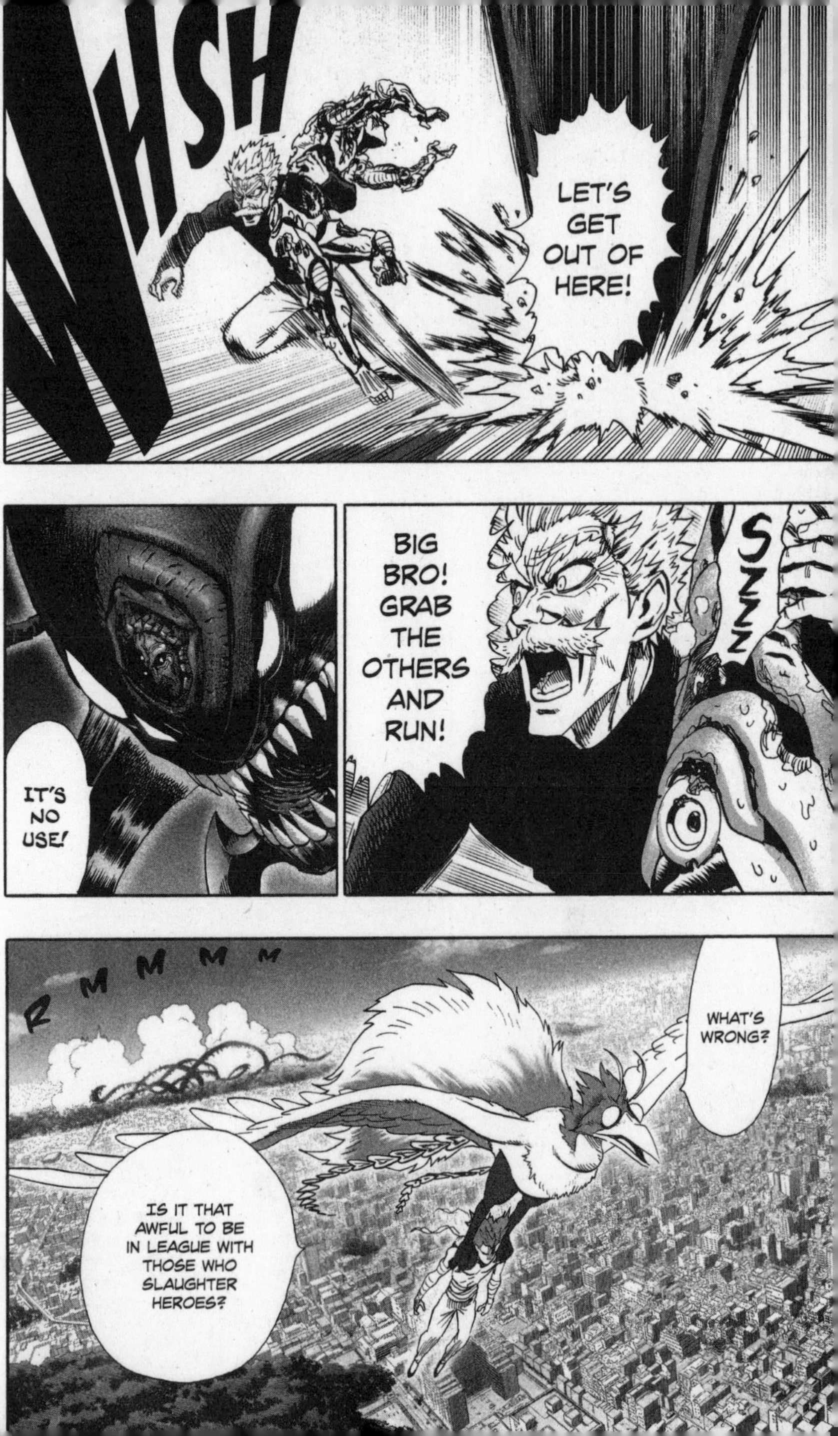
WHSH
LET'S GET OUT OF HERE!
SZZZ
BIG BRO! GRAB THE OTHERS AND RUN!
IT'S NO USE!
RMMMMM
WHAT'S WRONG?
IS IT THAT AWFUL TO BE IN LEAGUE WITH THOSE WHO SLAUGHTER HEROES?

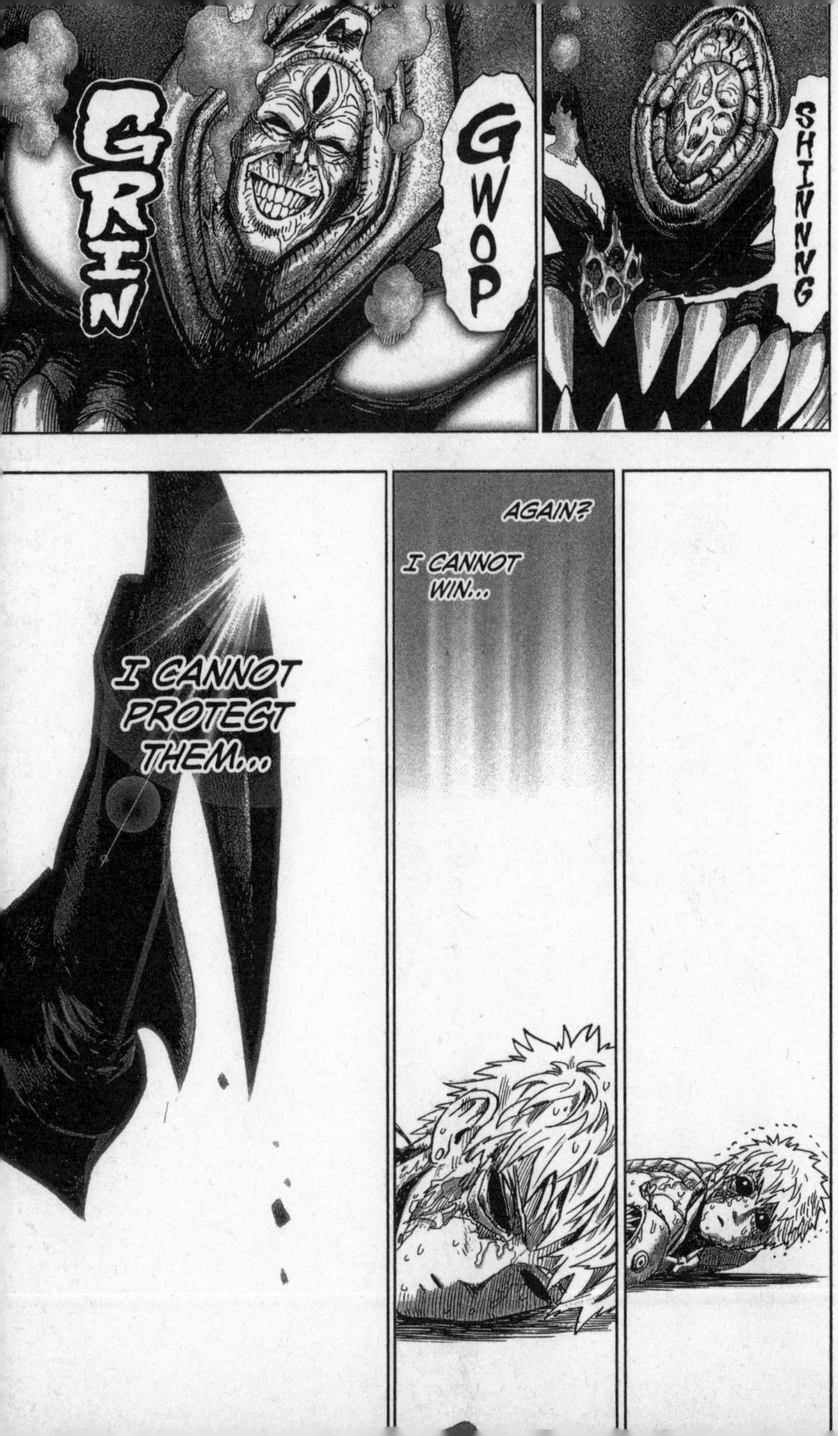
SHINNNG
GWOP
GRIN
AGAIN?
I CANNOT WIN...
I CANNOT PROTECT THEM...

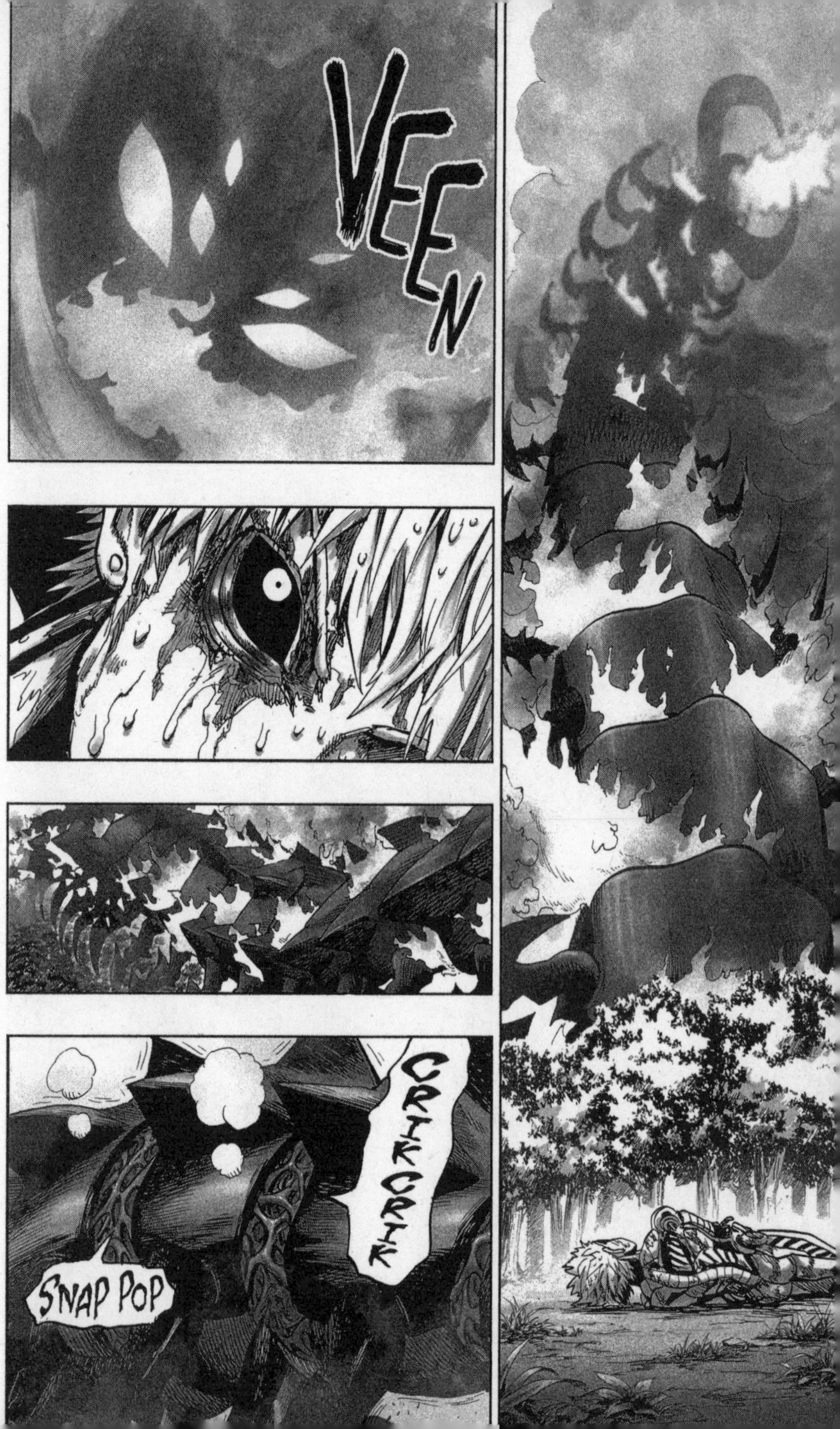
VEEN
CRIK CRIK
SNAP POP

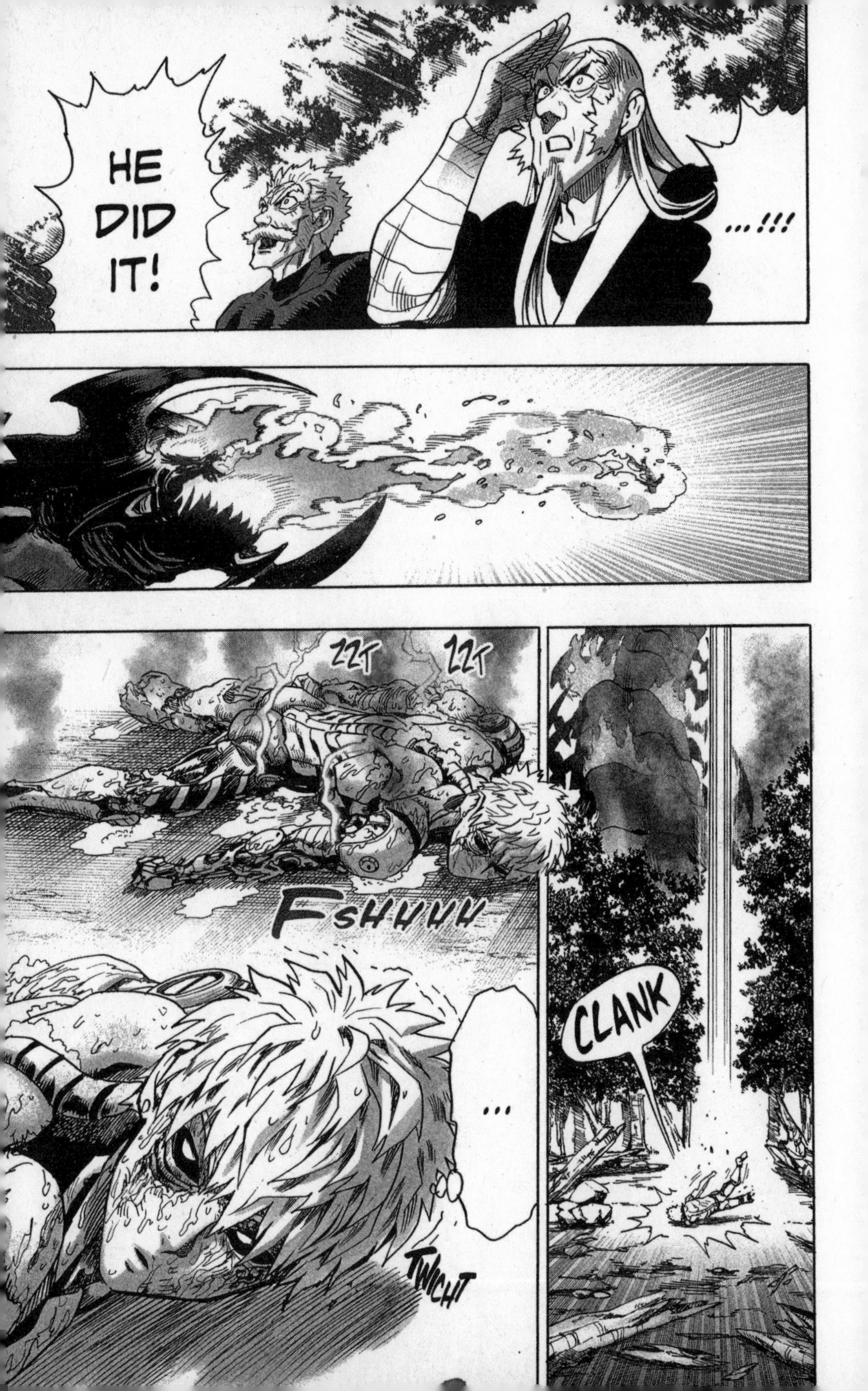

...!!!
HE DID IT!
CLANK
ZZT
ZZT
FSHHHH
...
TWICHT

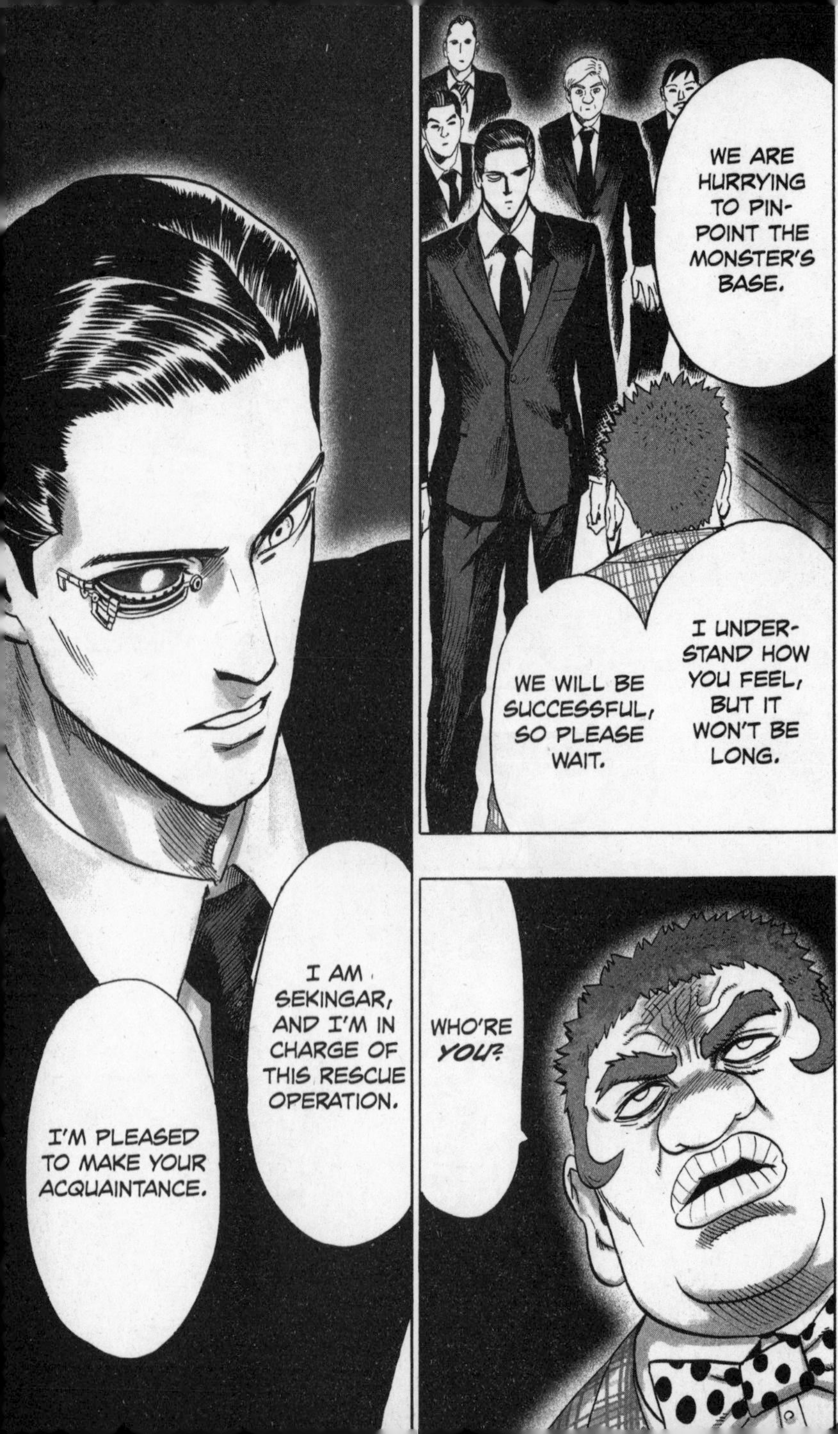
WE ARE HURRYING TO PIN-POINT THE MONSTER'S BASE.
I UNDER-STAND HOW YOU FEEL, BUT IT WON'T BE LONG.
WE WILL BE SUCCESSFUL, SO PLEASE WAIT.
WHO'RE YOU?
I AM SEKINGAR, AND I'M IN CHARGE OF THIS RESCUE OPERATION.
I'M PLEASED TO MAKE YOUR ACQUAINTANCE.

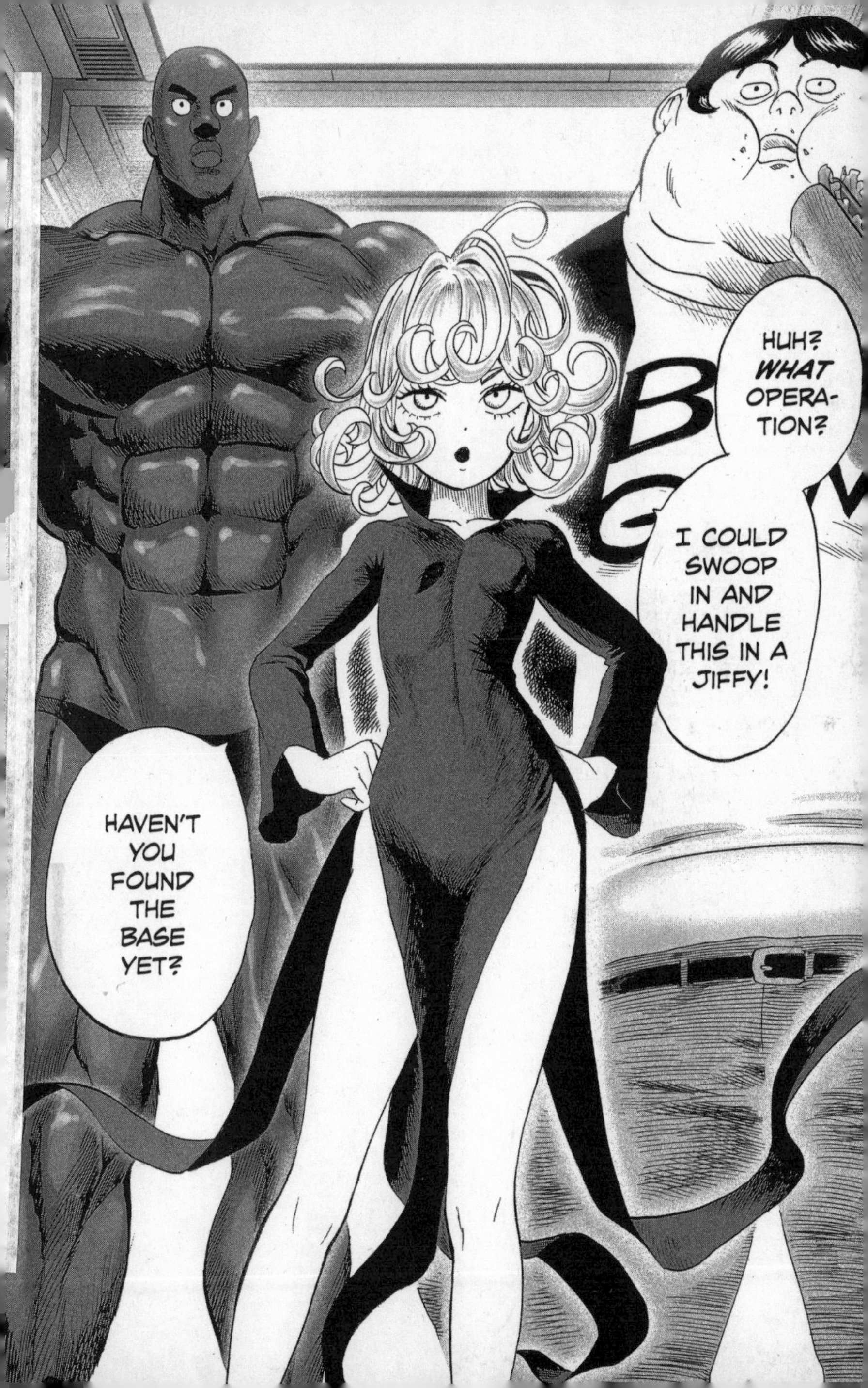
HUH? ***WHAT*** OPERATION?
I COULD SWOOP IN AND HANDLE THIS IN A JIFFY!
HAVEN'T YOU FOUND THE BASE YET?

CHILD EMPEROR IS HURRYING.

BUT WE ONLY HAVE *TWO*.

I ESTIMATE THREE DAYS OR LESS.

I HAVE MULTIPLE TRACKING ROBOTS FOLLOWING CENTICHORO'S UNDERGROUND ROUTE, BUT THE AREA IS SO VAST THAT IT WILL TAKE A LITTLE LONGER.

UGH... THAT MEANS I CAN'T *SLEEP*!

THERE'S A HOSTAGE, SO WE MUST BE CAREFUL.

SHALL I JUST MAKE IT ALL GO BOOM?

IT'S IN CITY Z'S GHOST TOWN, RIGHT?

BOOOM

THEY'RE MAKING IT HARD FOR US, HUH?

OTHERWISE, THERE'D BE NO CONTEST.

THOSE MONSTERS *FEAR* ME!

YEAH, WHAT-EVER.

THEY ARE QUITE STRONG.

DO NOT UNDER-ESTIMATE OUR OPPONENT.

IS THAT WHY YOU CALLED US HERE? TO *WARN* US?

I'M SICK OF HEARING YOU OVERRATE THEM.

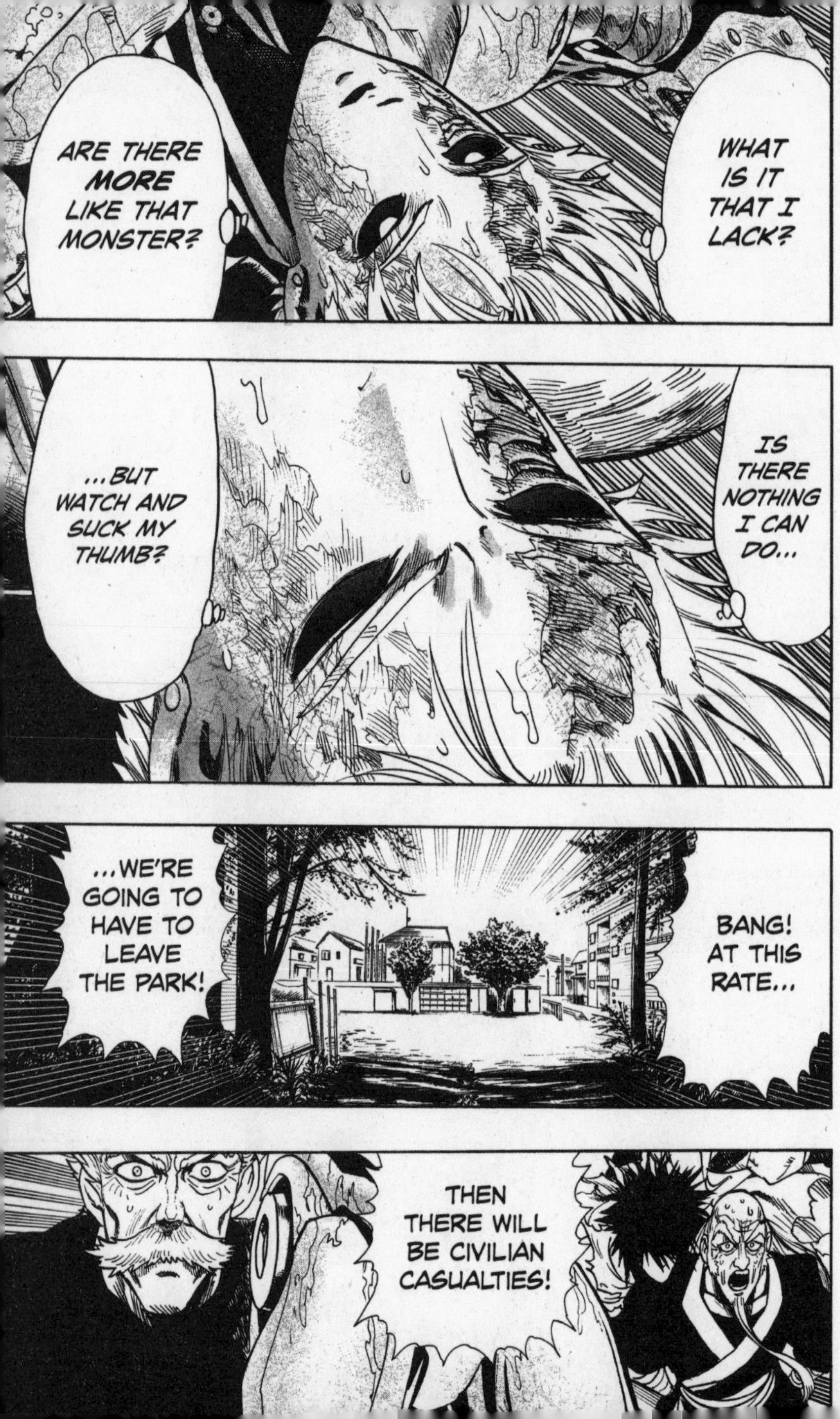
WHAT IS IT THAT I LACK?
ARE THERE MORE LIKE THAT MONSTER?
IS THERE NOTHING I CAN DO...
...BUT WATCH AND SUCK MY THUMB?
BANG! AT THIS RATE...
...WE'RE GOING TO HAVE TO LEAVE THE PARK!
THEN THERE WILL BE CIVILIAN CASUALTIES!

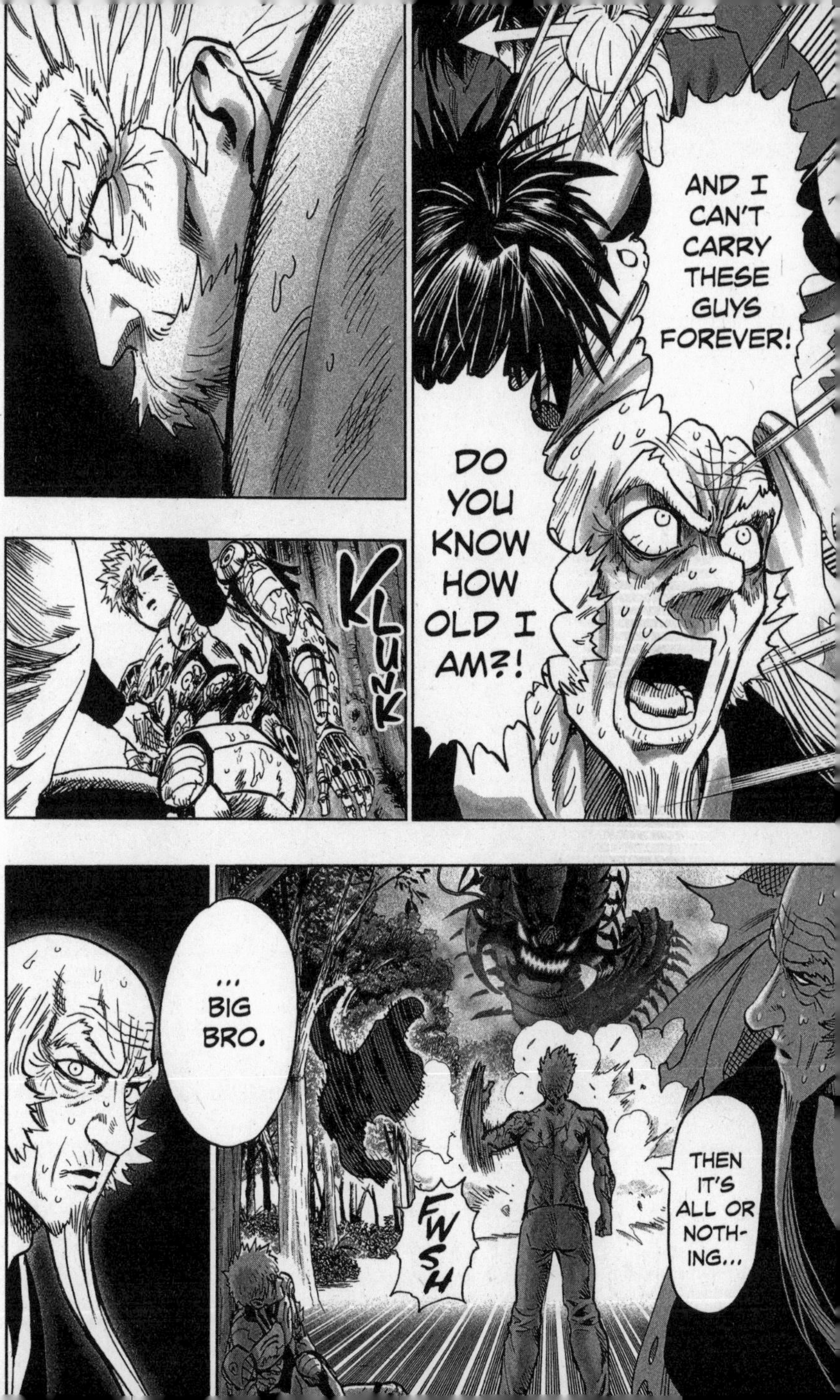
AND I CAN'T CARRY THESE GUYS FOREVER!
DO YOU KNOW HOW OLD I AM?!
KLUNK
THEN IT'S ALL OR NOTH-ING...
FWSH
... BIG BRO.

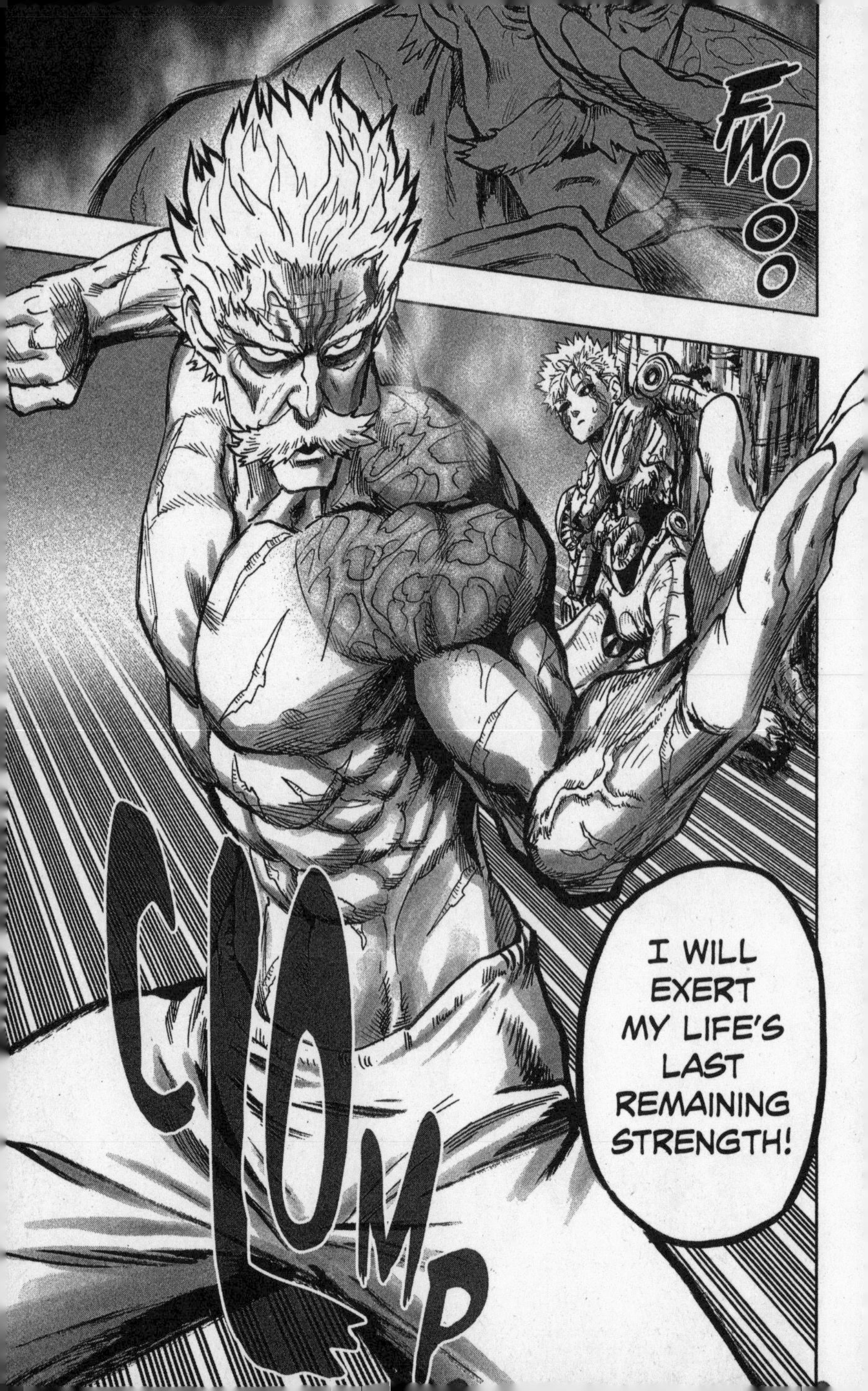
FWOOOO
I WILL EXERT MY LIFE'S LAST REMAINING STRENGTH!
CLOMP

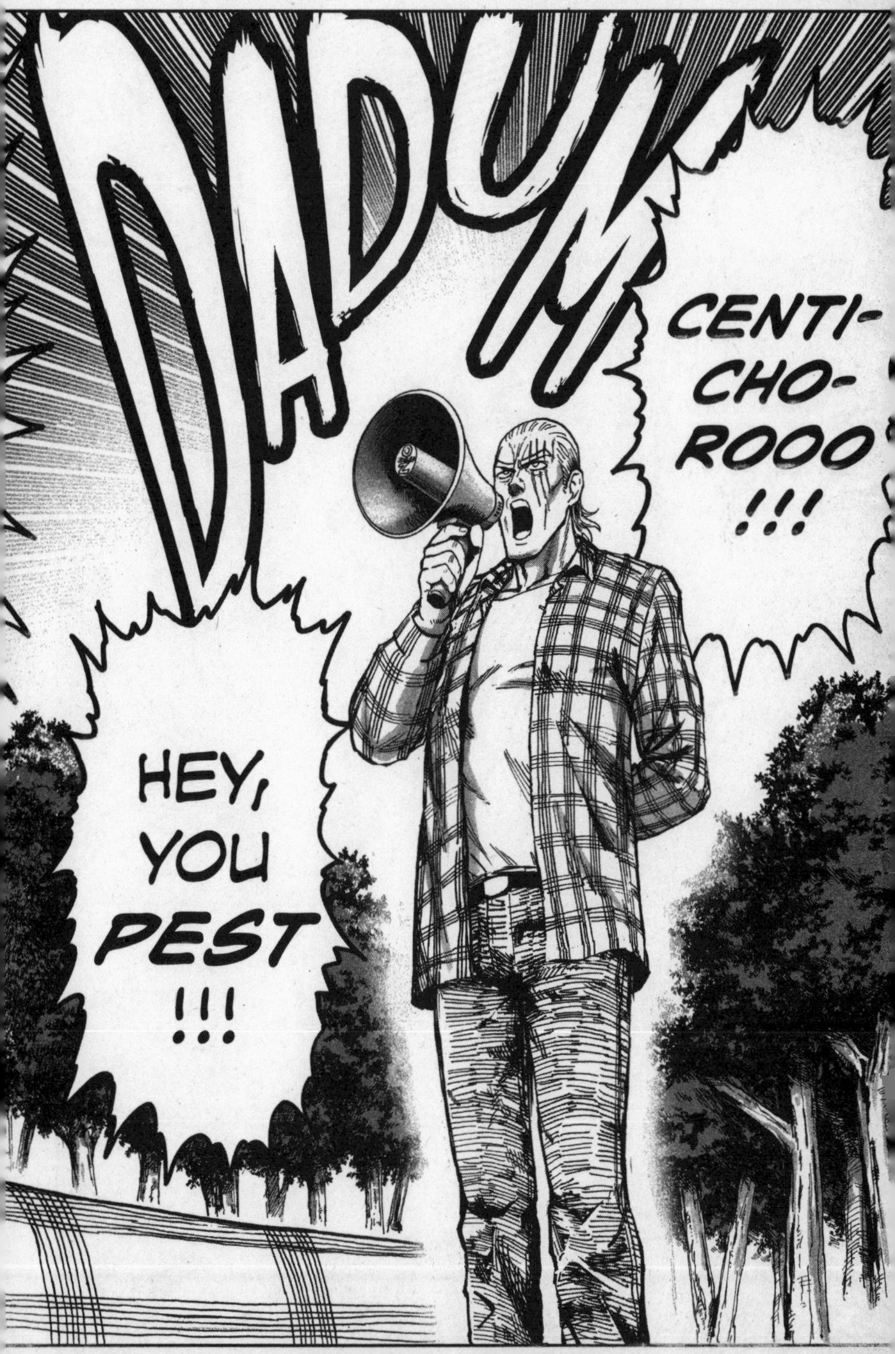
DADUM
CENTI-CHO-ROOO!!!
HEY, YOU PEST!!!

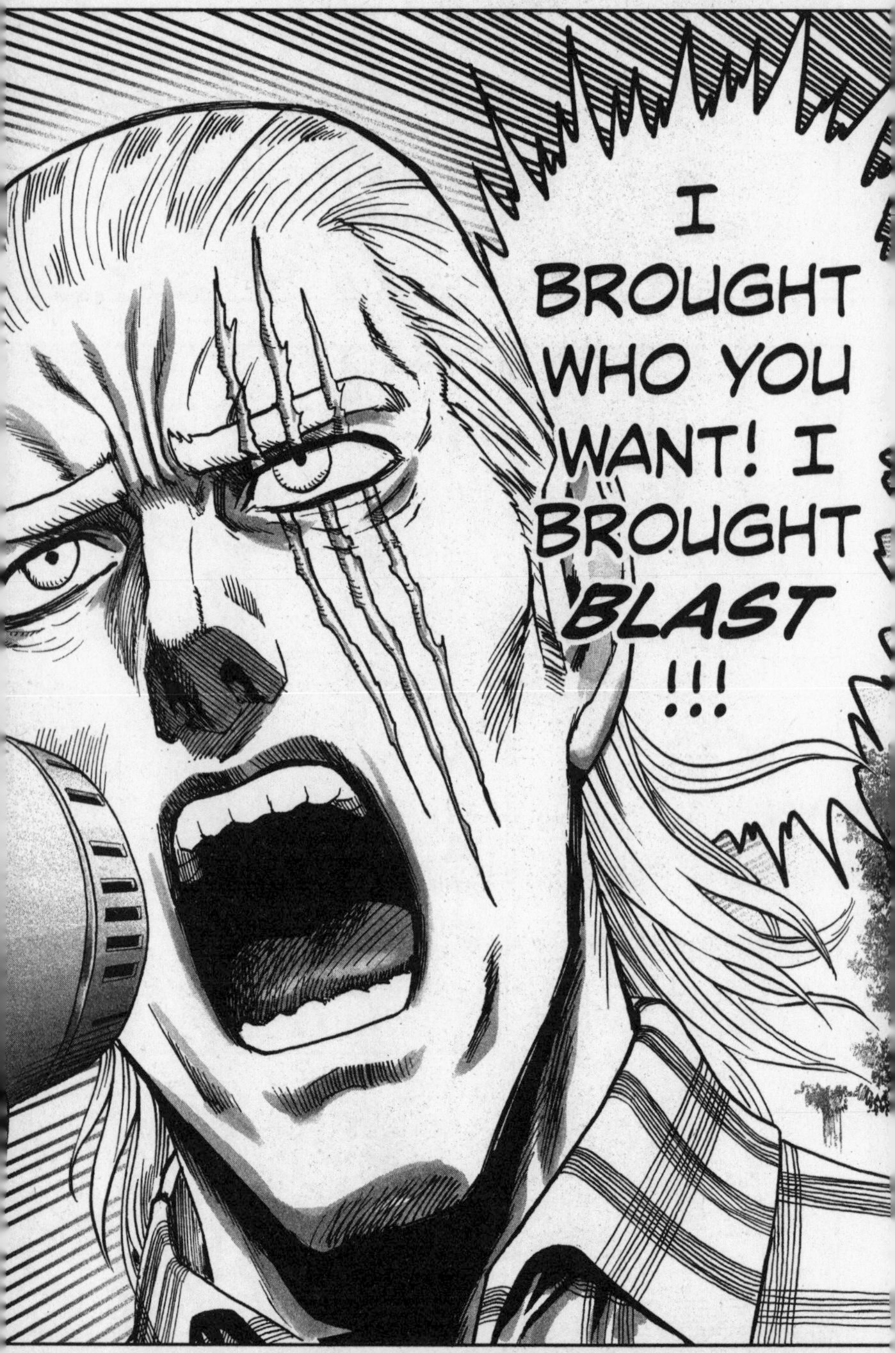
I BROUGHT WHO YOU WANT! I BROUGHT BLAST!!!

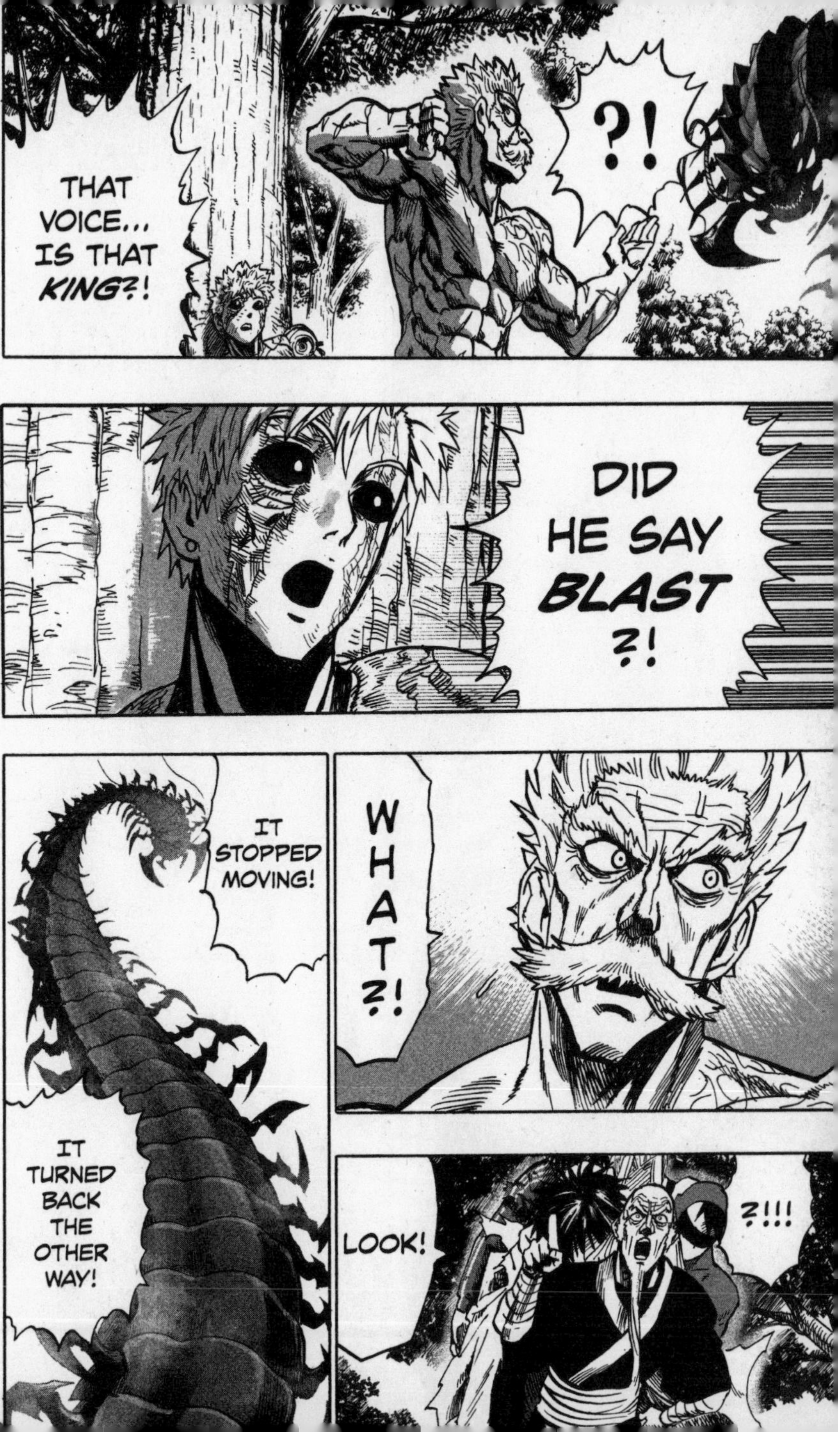
?!
THAT VOICE... IS THAT KING?!
DID HE SAY BLAST?!
WHAT?!
?!!!
LOOK!
IT STOPPED MOVING!
IT TURNED BACK THE OTHER WAY!

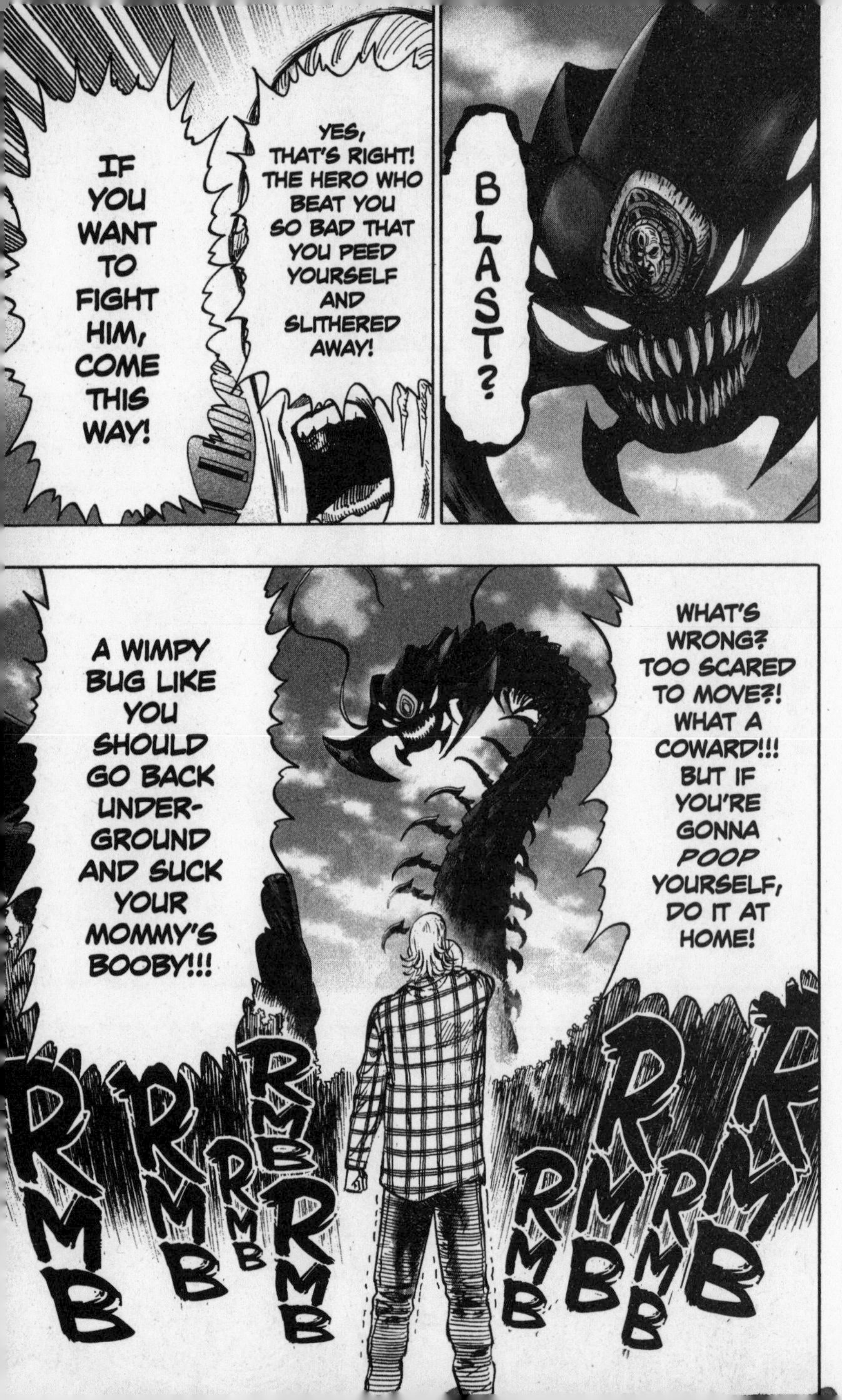
BLAST?
YES, THAT'S RIGHT! THE HERO WHO BEAT YOU SO BAD THAT YOU PEED YOURSELF AND SLITHERED AWAY!
IF YOU WANT TO FIGHT HIM, COME THIS WAY!
WHAT'S WRONG? TOO SCARED TO MOVE?! WHAT A COWARD!!! BUT IF YOU'RE GONNA *POOP* YOURSELF, DO IT AT HOME!
A WIMPY BUG LIKE YOU SHOULD GO BACK UNDERGROUND AND SUCK YOUR MOMMY'S BOOBY!!!
RMMB
RMMB
RMMB
RMMB
RMMB
RMB
RMB
RMMB

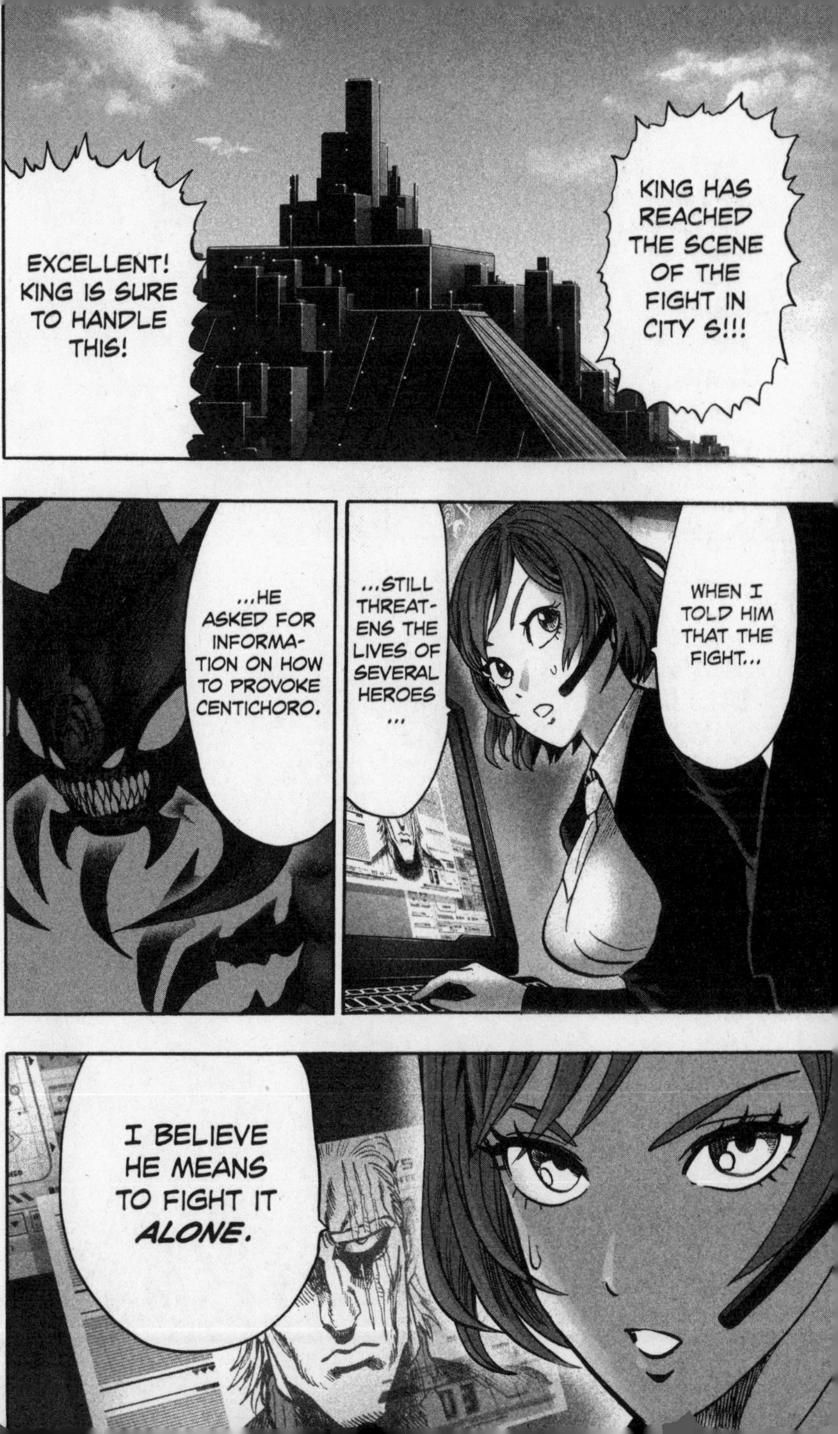
KING HAS REACHED THE SCENE OF THE FIGHT IN CITY S!!!
EXCELLENT! KING IS SURE TO HANDLE THIS!
WHEN I TOLD HIM THAT THE FIGHT...
...STILL THREAT- ENS THE LIVES OF SEVERAL HEROES ...
...HE ASKED FOR INFORMA- TION ON HOW TO PROVOKE CENTICHORO.
I BELIEVE HE MEANS TO FIGHT IT *ALONE*.

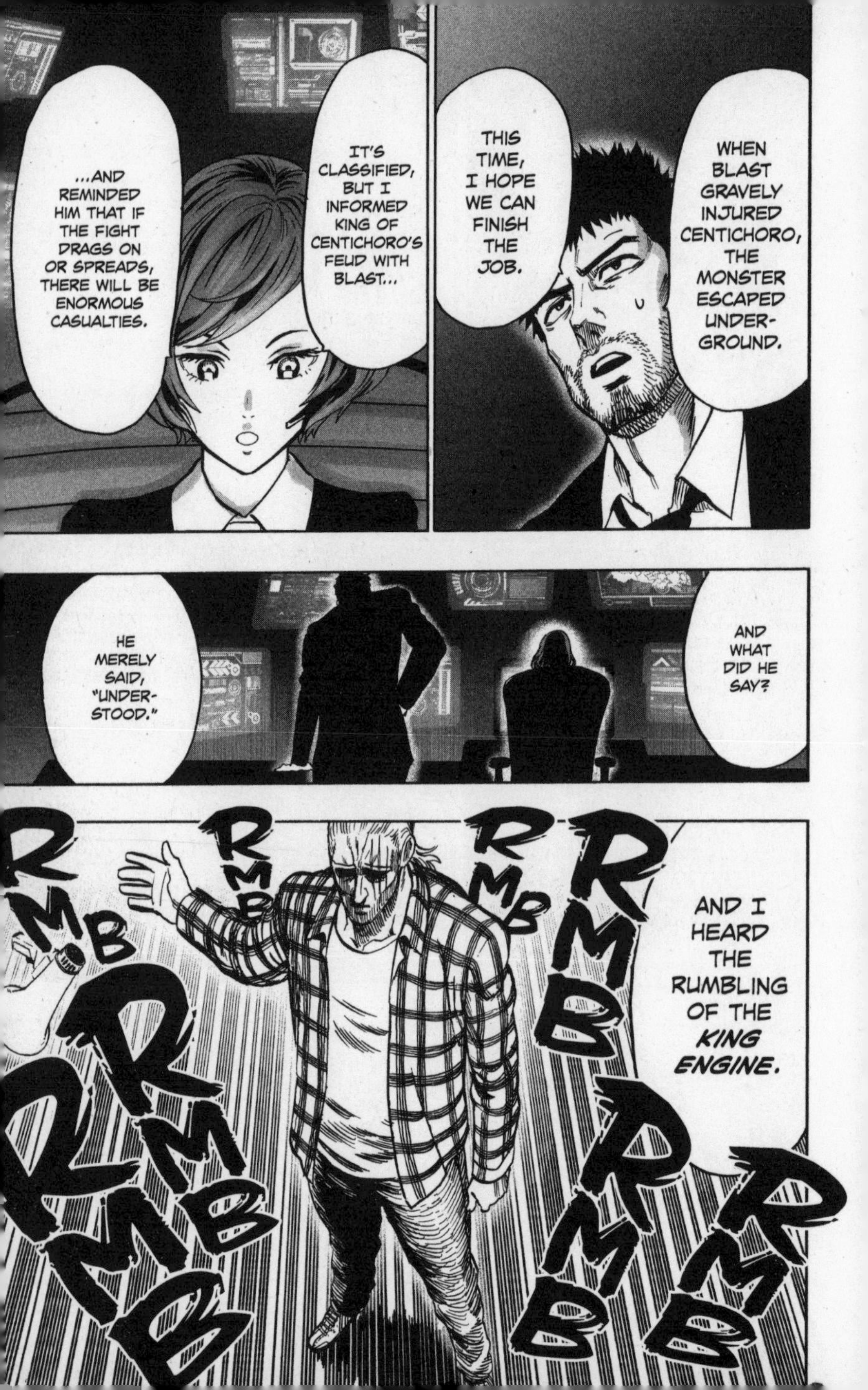
WHEN BLAST GRAVELY INJURED CENTICHORO, THE MONSTER ESCAPED UNDERGROUND.
THIS TIME, I HOPE WE CAN FINISH THE JOB.
IT'S CLASSIFIED, BUT I INFORMED KING OF CENTICHORO'S FEUD WITH BLAST...
...AND REMINDED HIM THAT IF THE FIGHT DRAGS ON OR SPREADS, THERE WILL BE ENORMOUS CASUALTIES.
AND WHAT DID HE SAY?
HE MERELY SAID, "UNDERSTOOD."
AND I HEARD THE RUMBLING OF THE *KING ENGINE*.
RMB
RMB
RMB
RMB
RMB
RMB
RMB
RMB
RMB
RMB

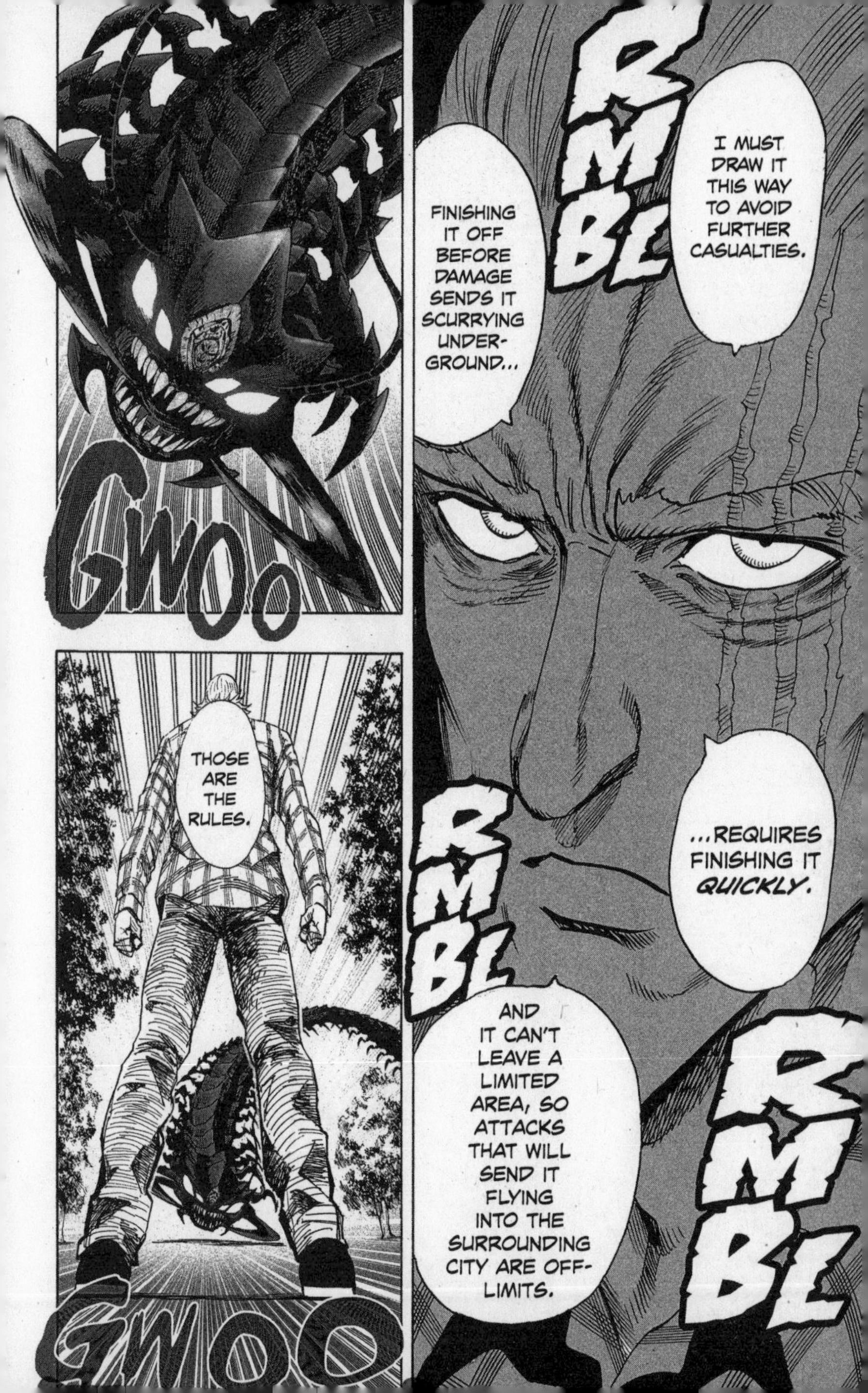
RMBL
I MUST DRAW IT THIS WAY TO AVOID FURTHER CASUALTIES.
FINISHING IT OFF BEFORE DAMAGE SENDS IT SCURRYING UNDER-GROUND...
...REQUIRES FINISHING IT *QUICKLY*.
RMBL
AND IT CAN'T LEAVE A LIMITED AREA, SO ATTACKS THAT WILL SEND IT FLYING INTO THE SURROUNDING CITY ARE OFF-LIMITS.
RMBL
GWOO
THOSE ARE THE RULES.
GWOO

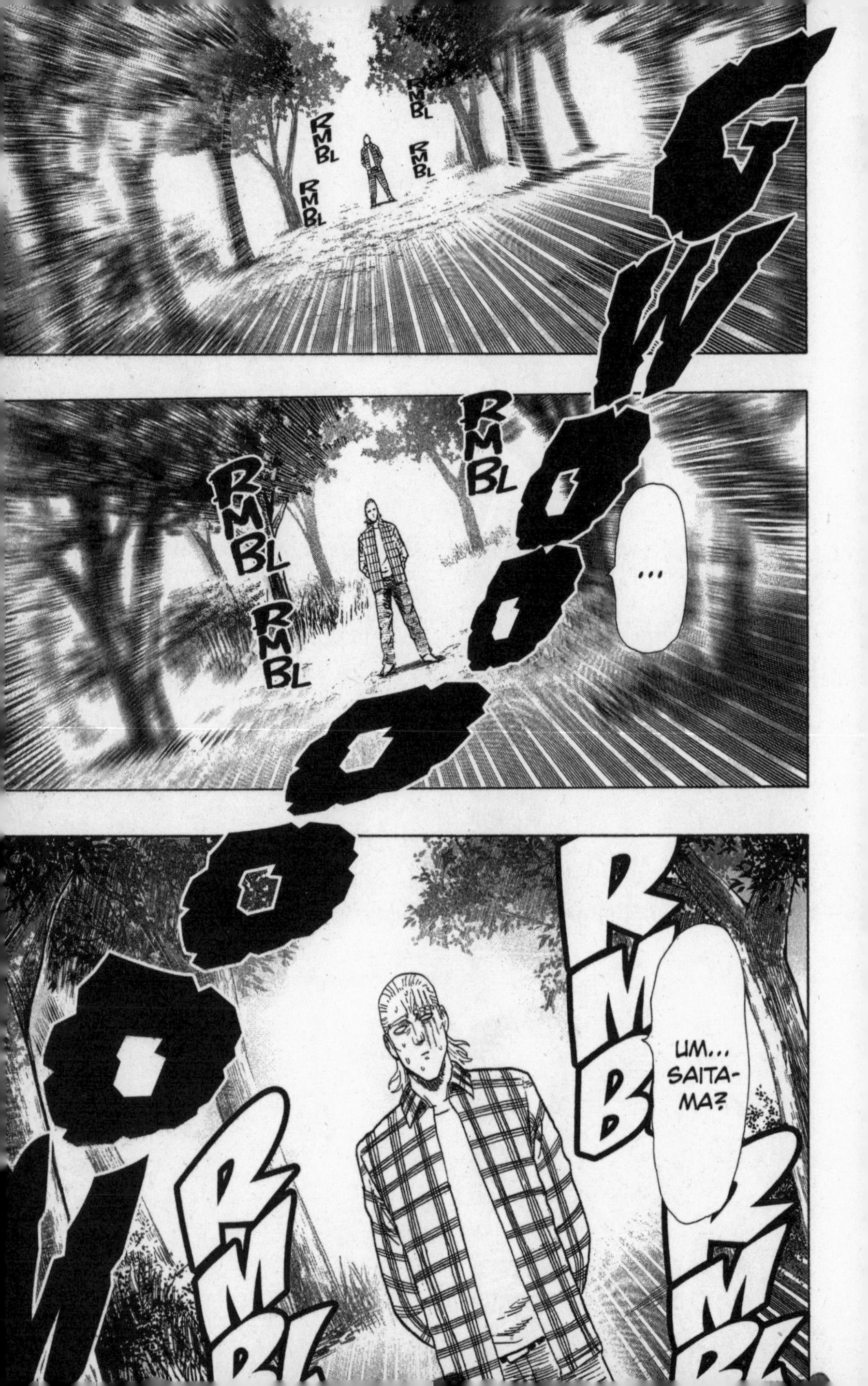
RMBL
RMBL
RMBL
RMBL
GWOOOOOO
RMBL
RMBL
RMBL
...
UM... SAITAMA?

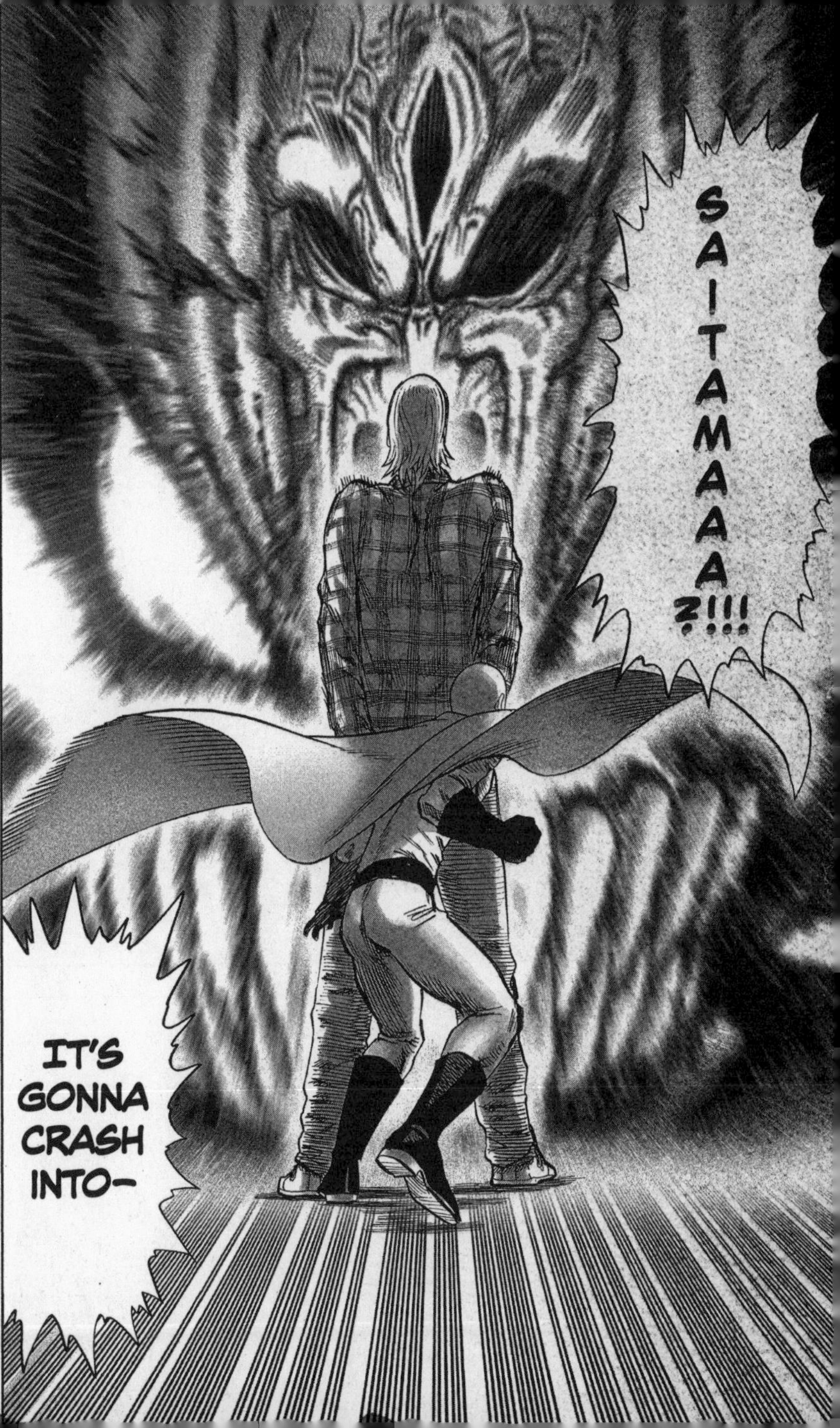
SAITAMAAAA?!!!
IT'S GONNA CRASH INTO-

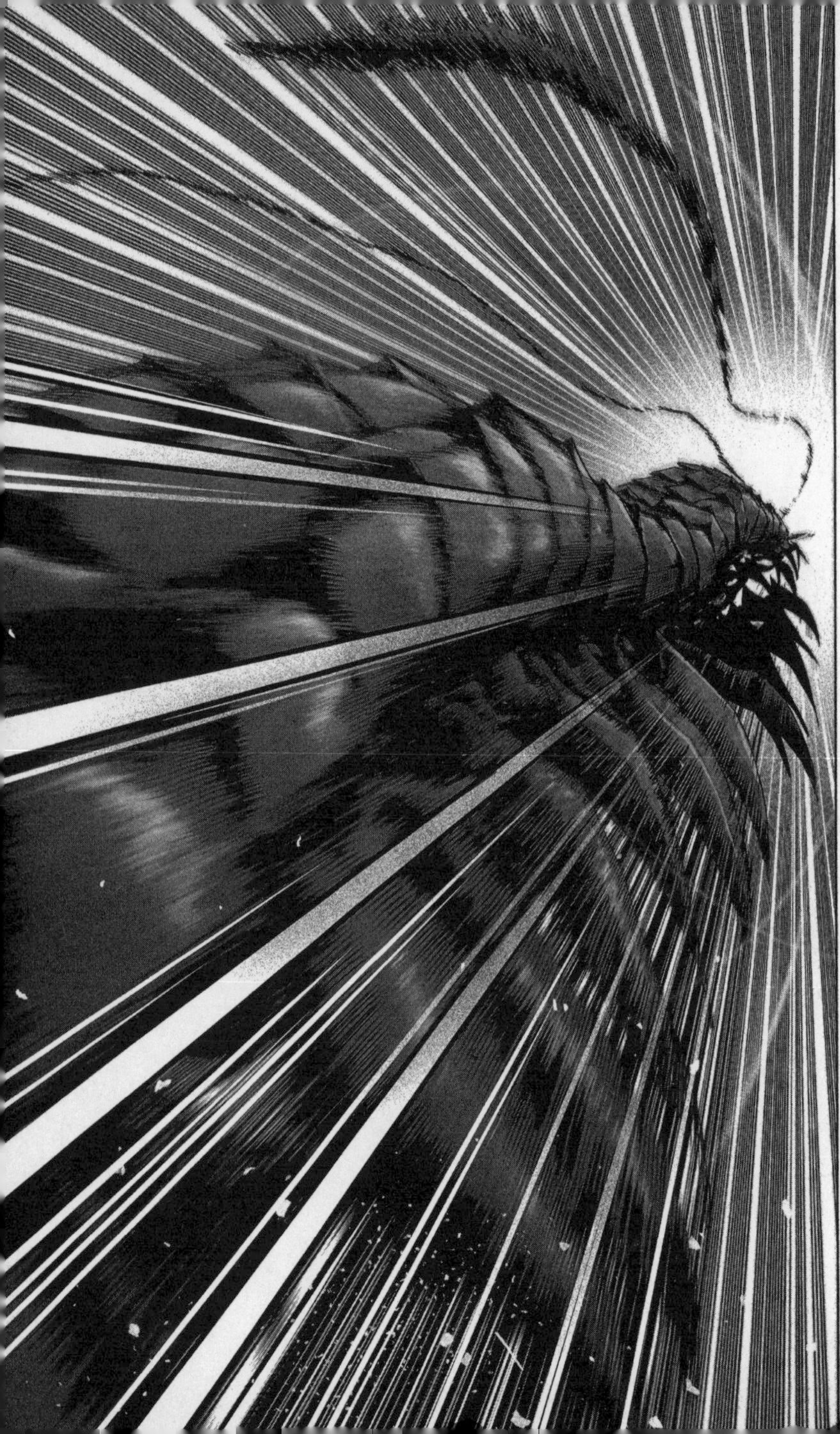

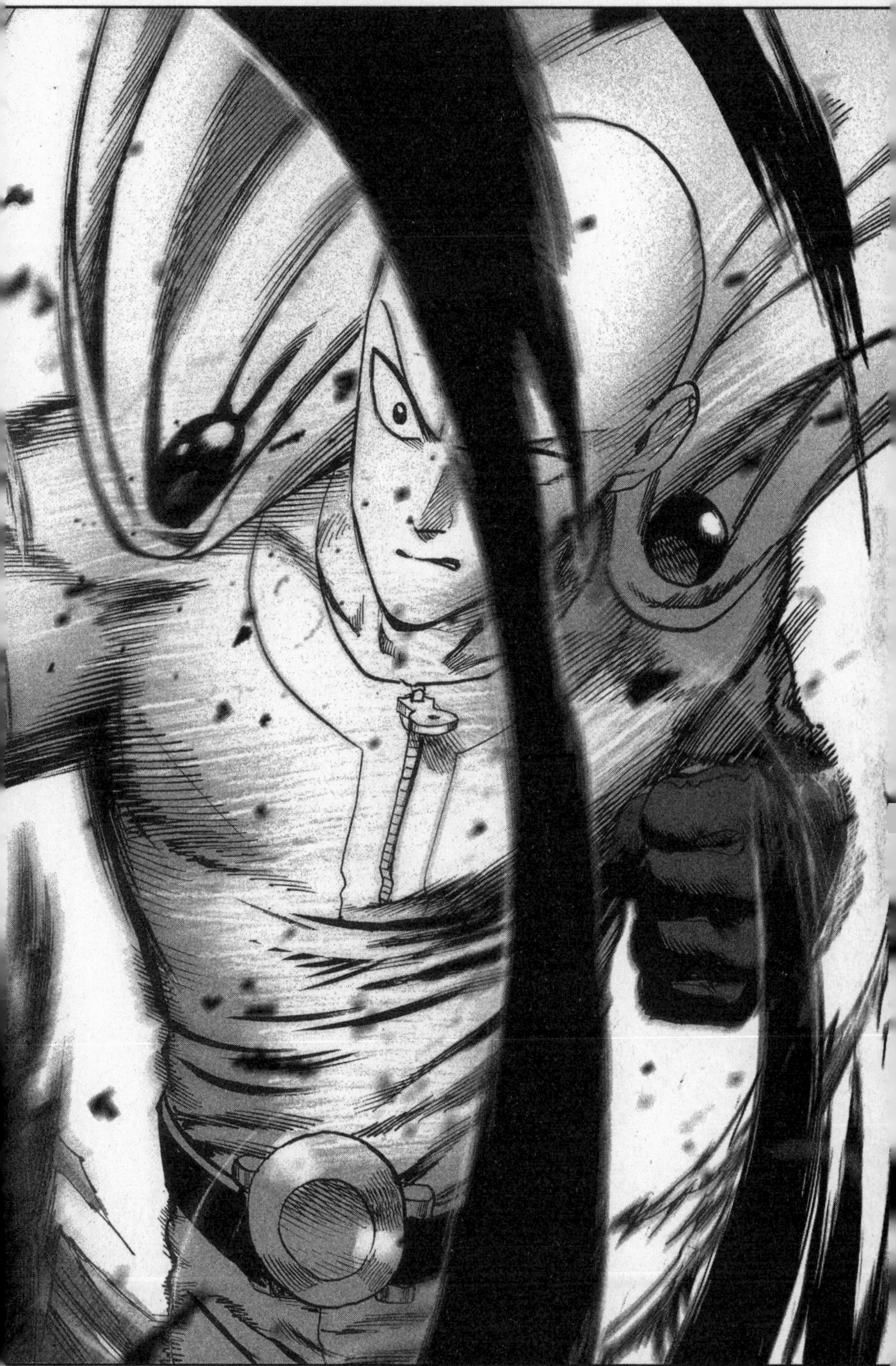

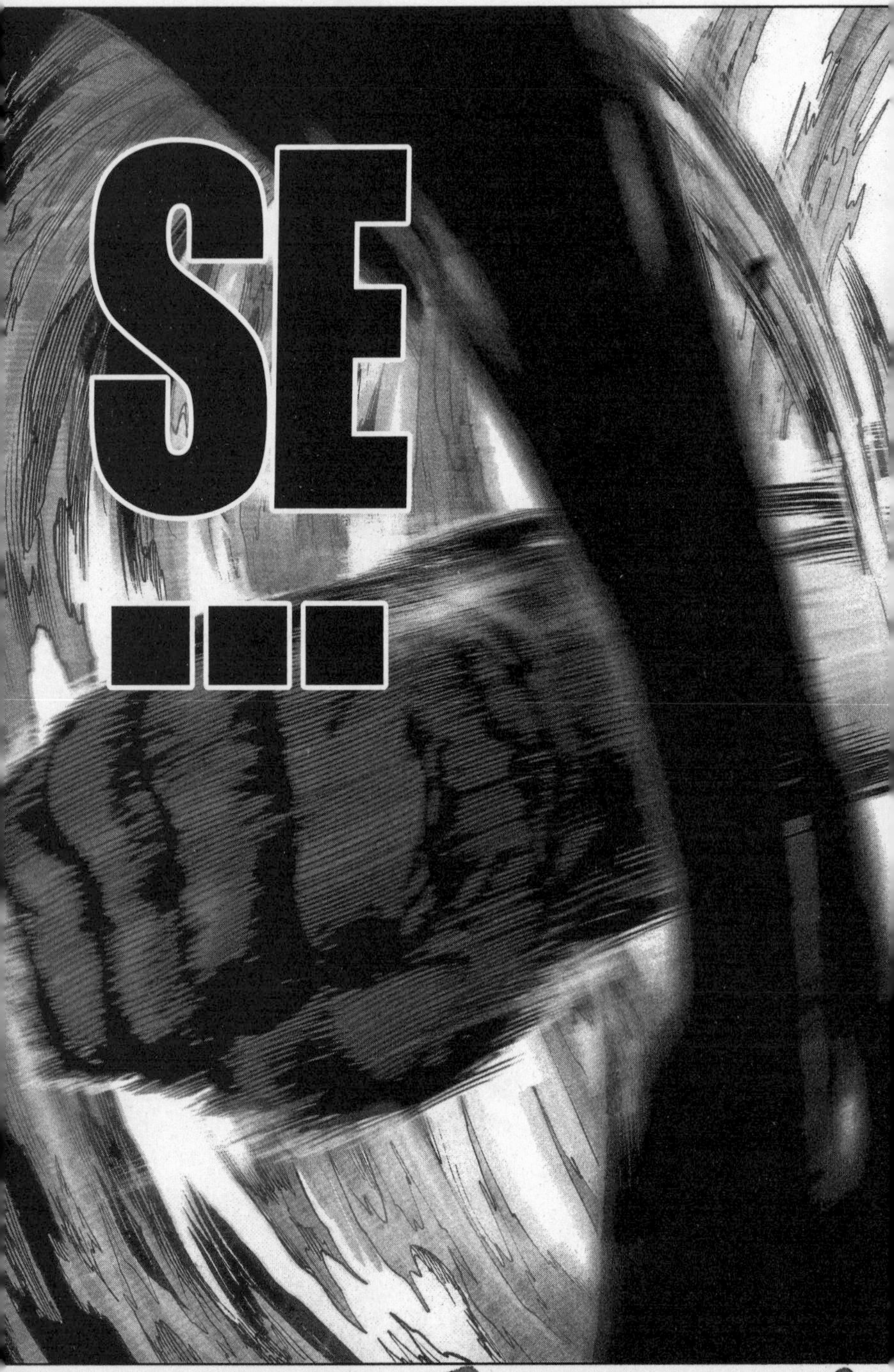
SE...

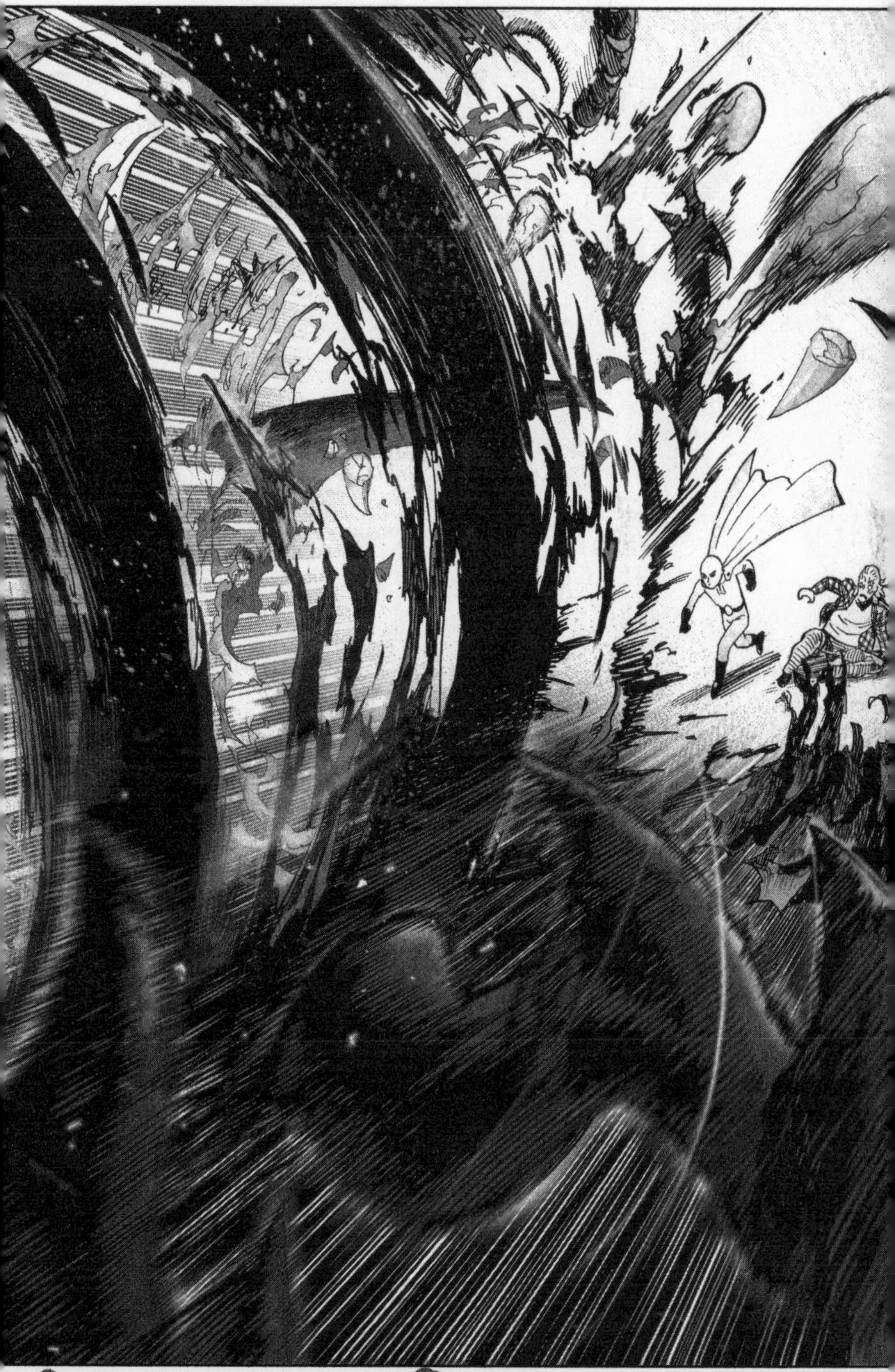

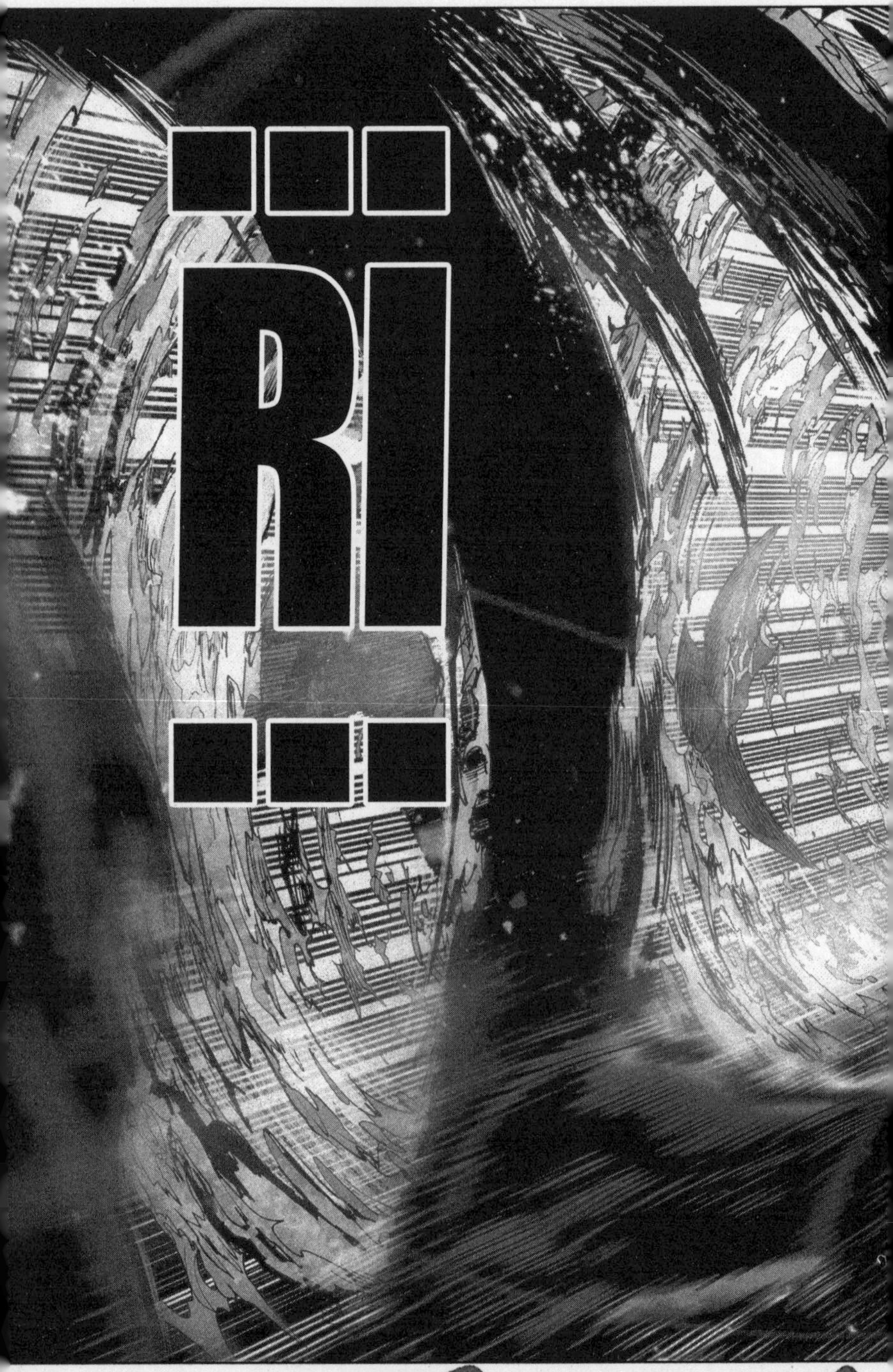
RI

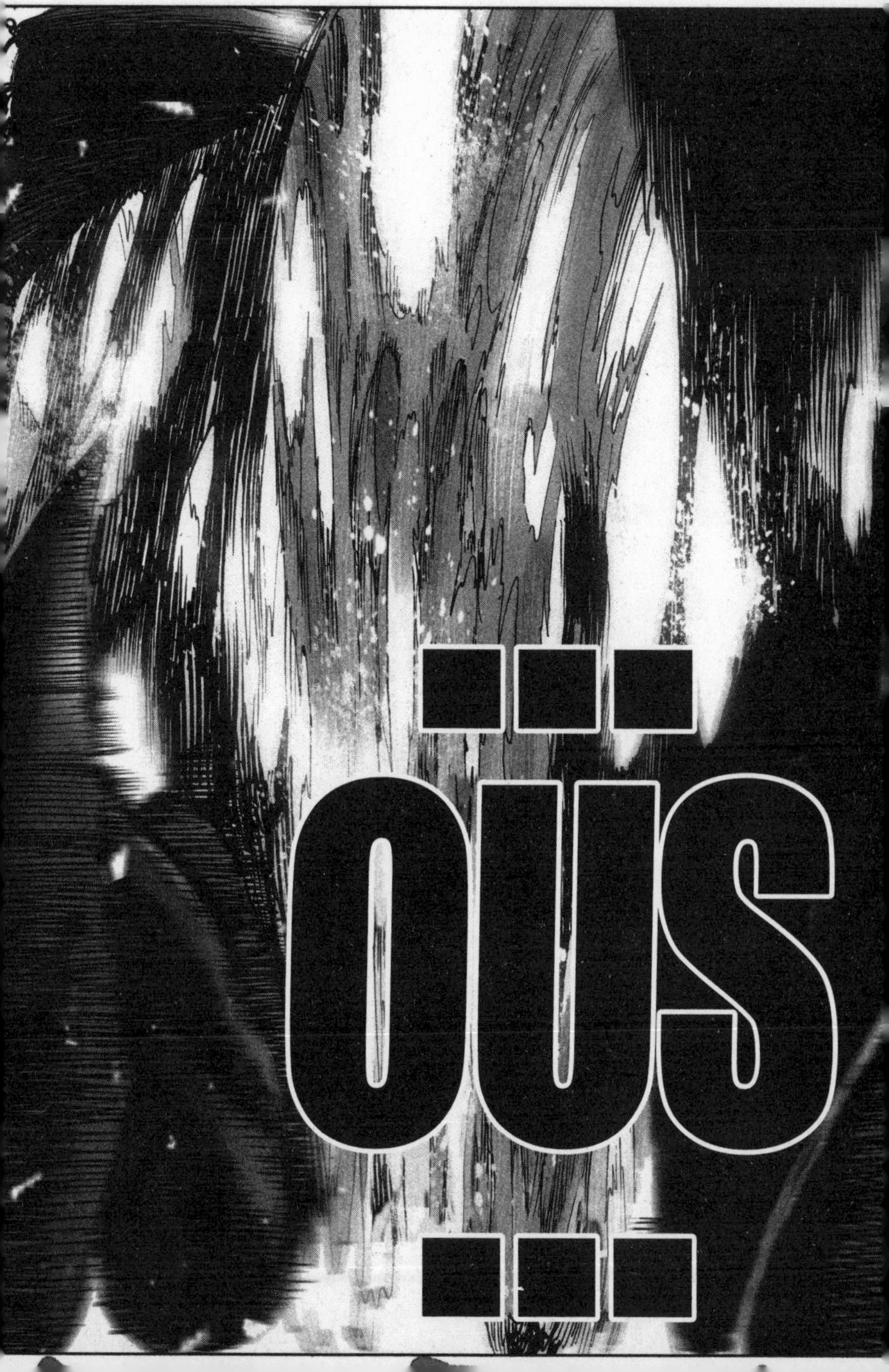
...
OUS
...

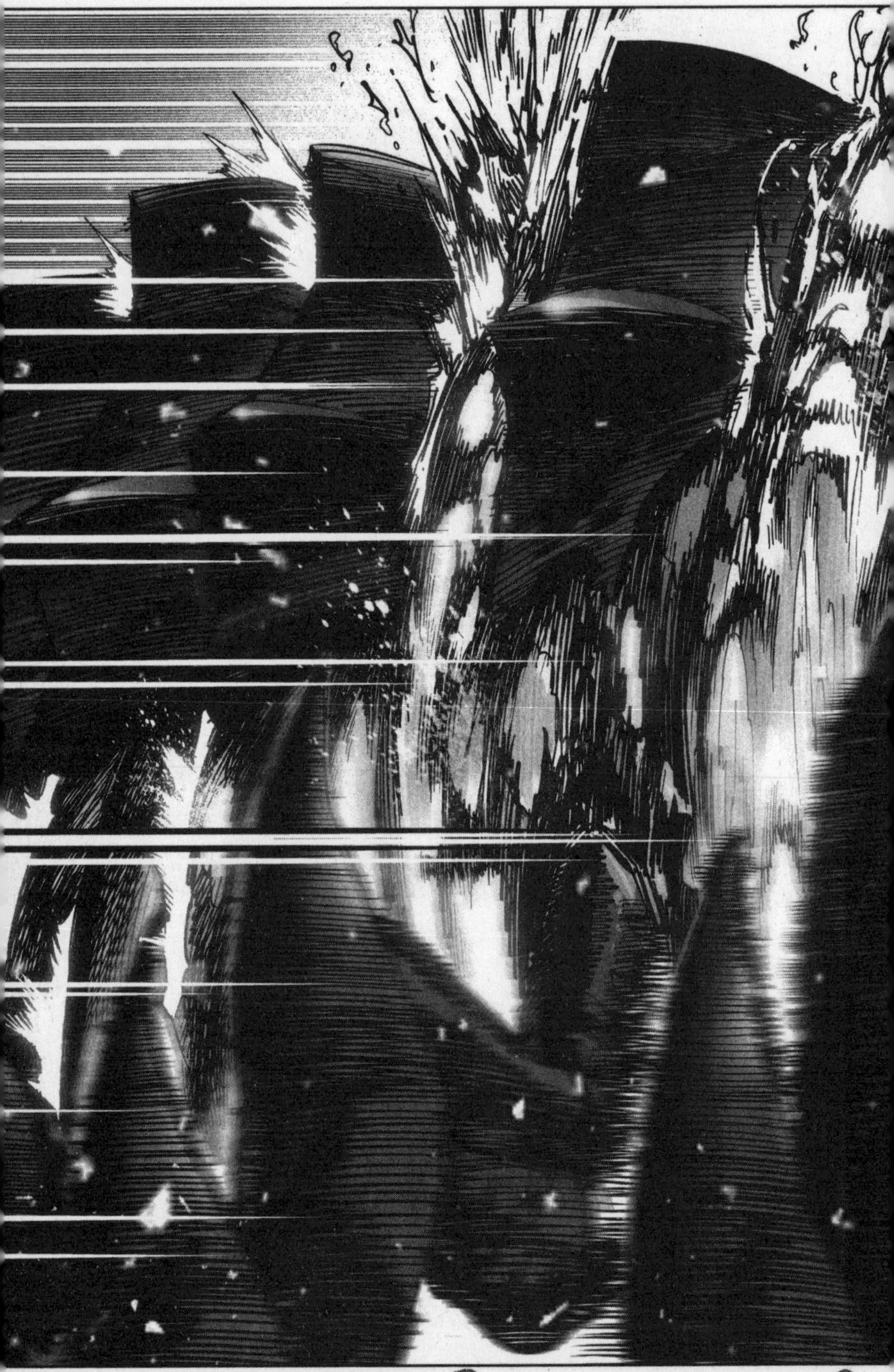

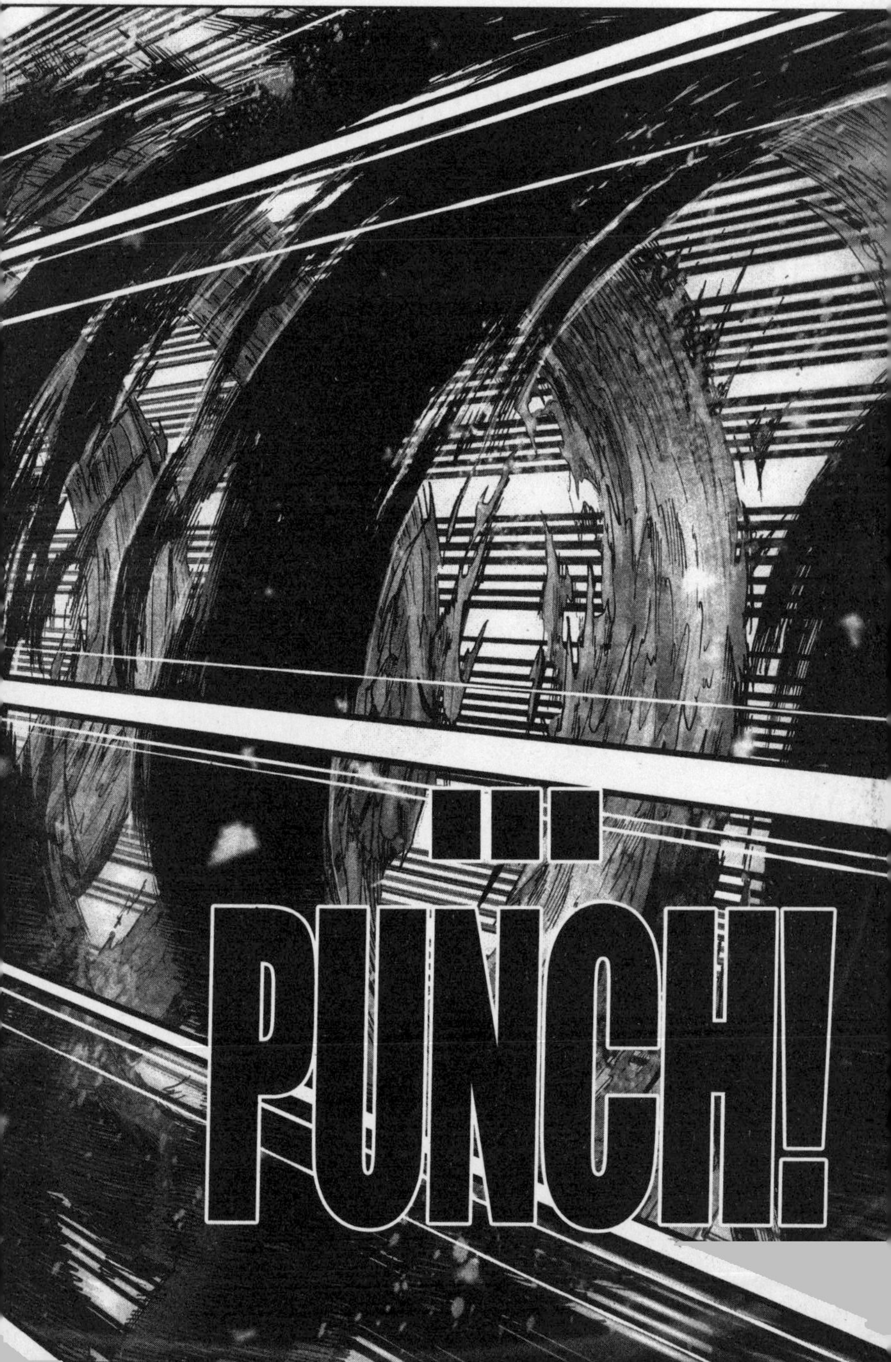
...
PUNCH!

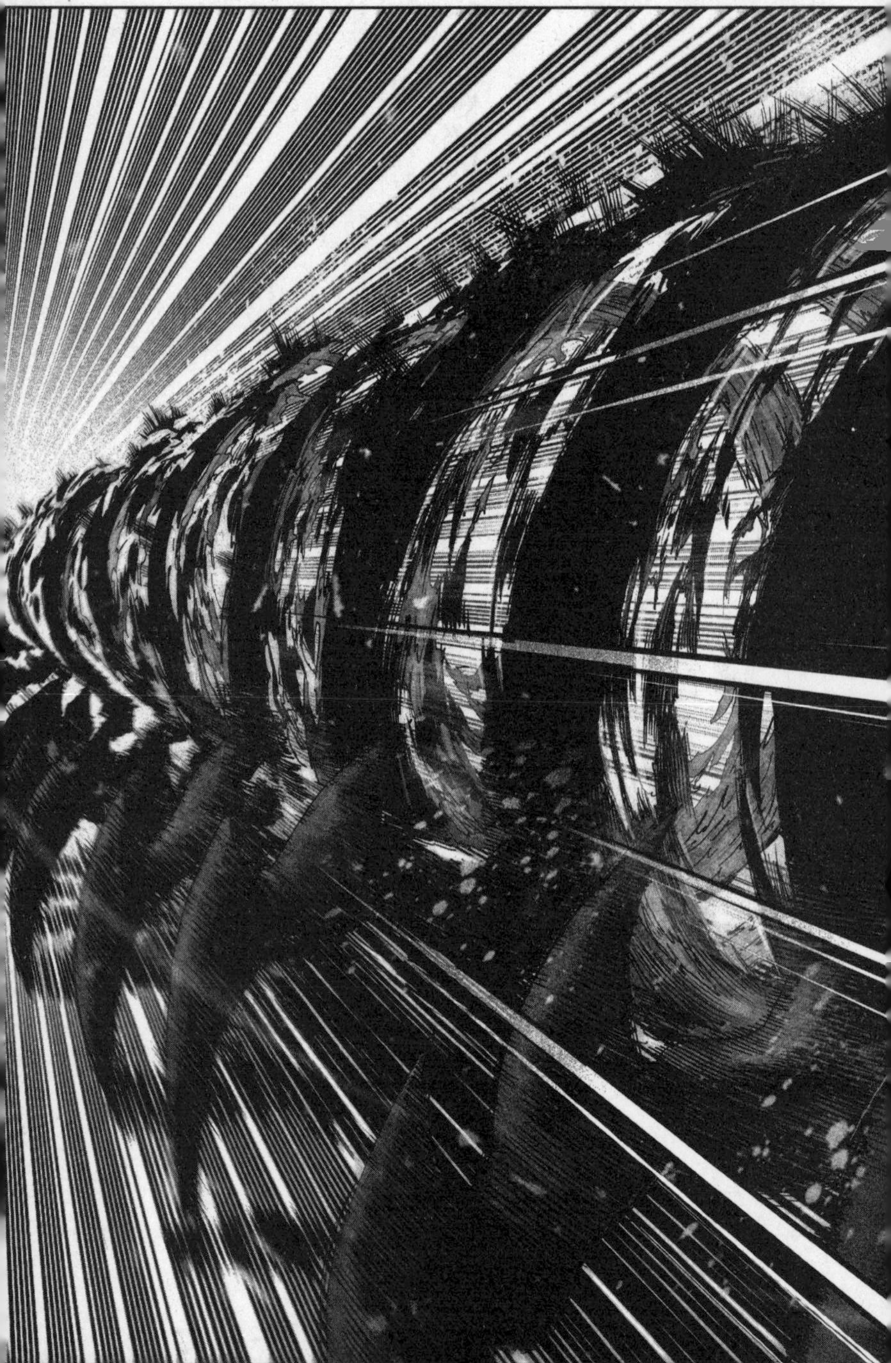

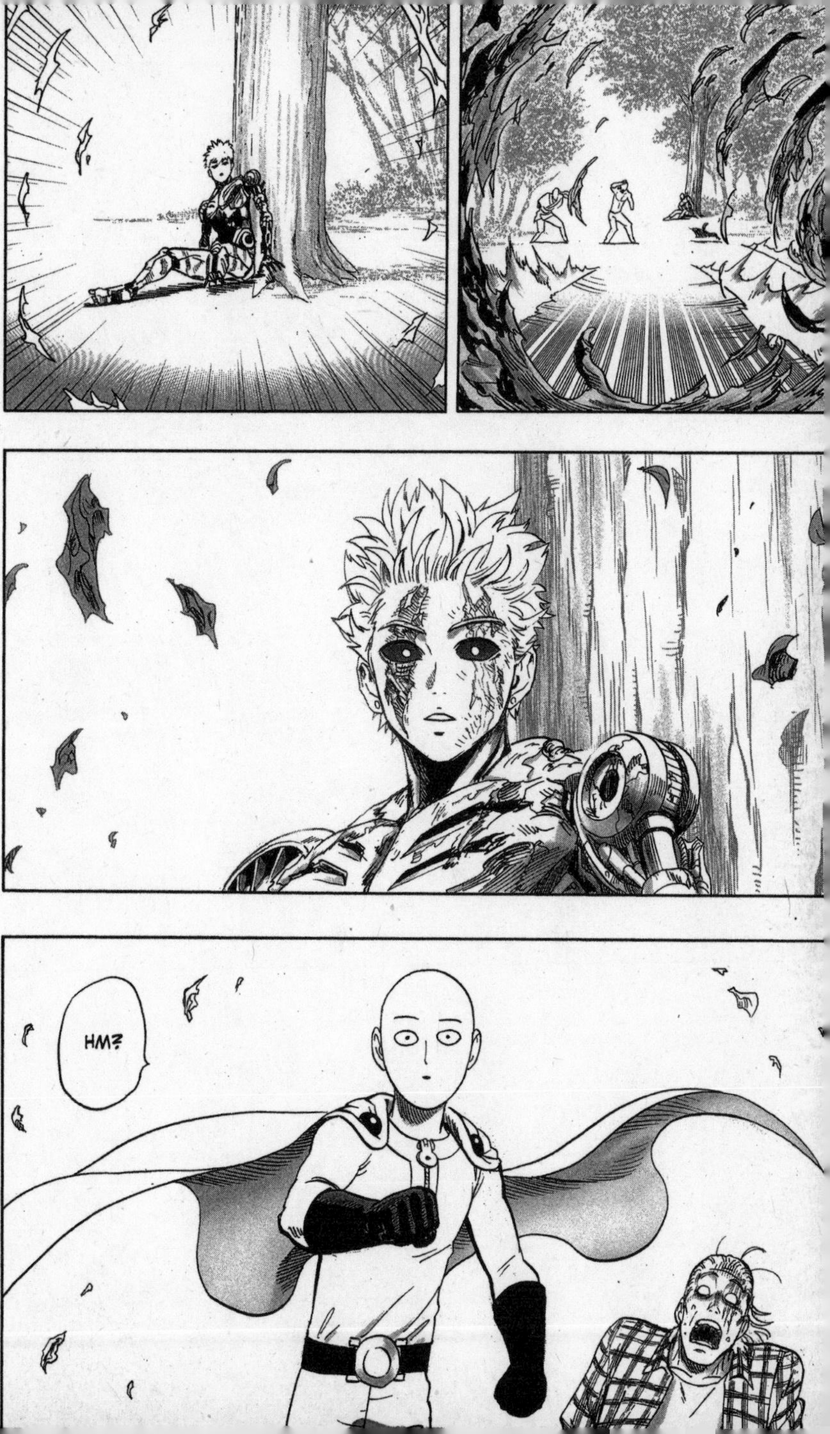
HM?

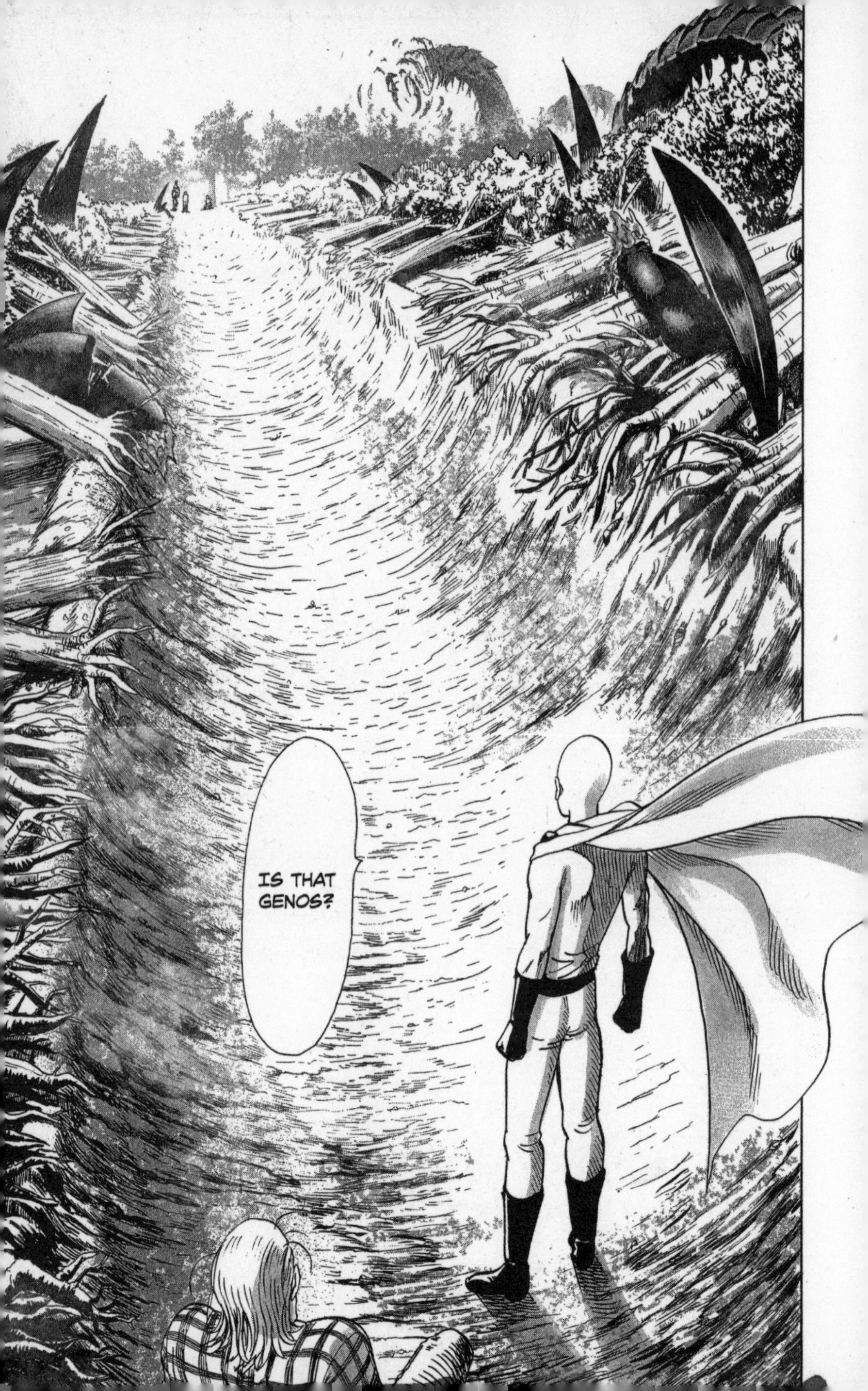
IS THAT GENOS?

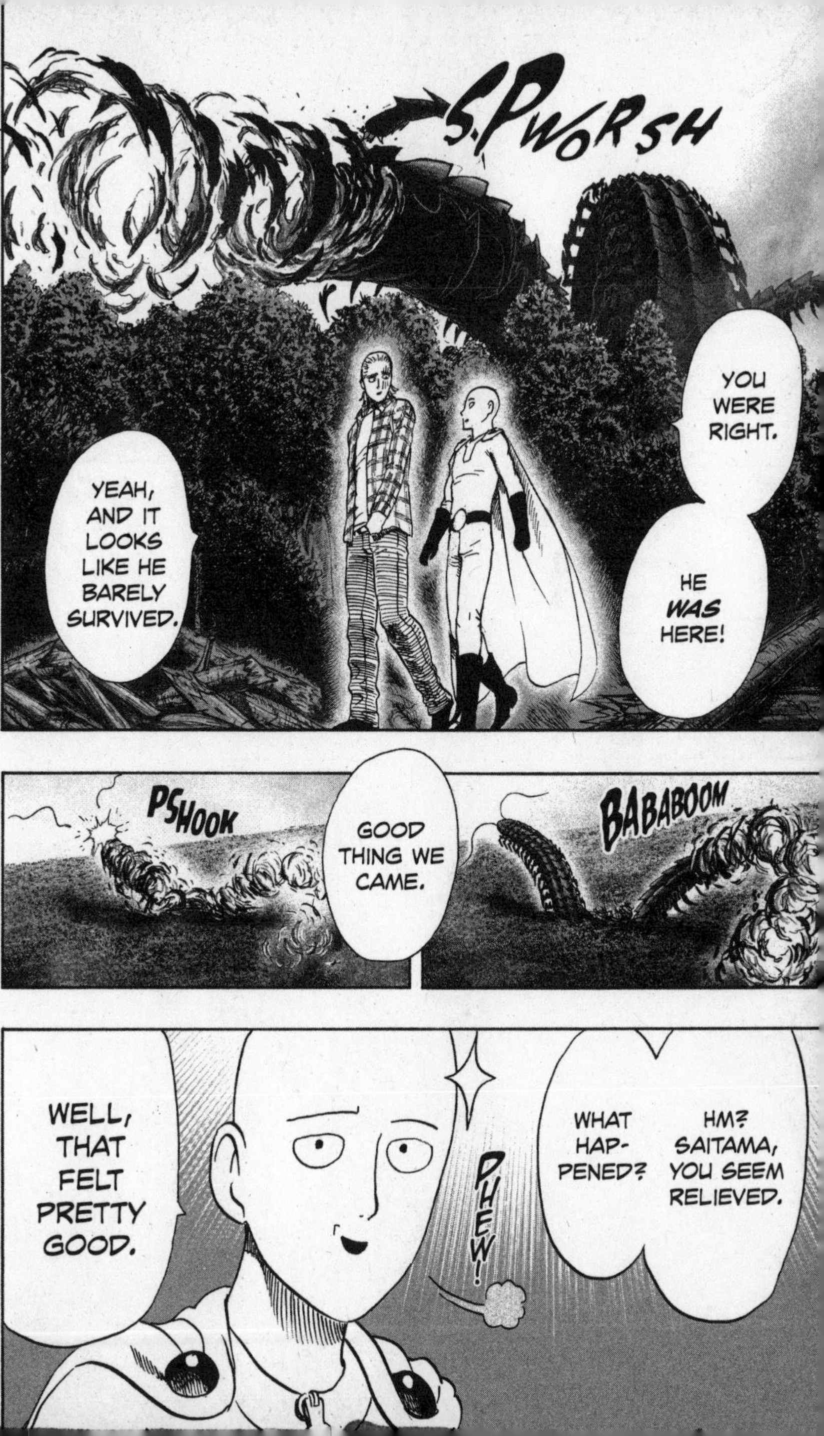
SPWORSH
YOU WERE RIGHT.
HE WAS HERE!
YEAH, AND IT LOOKS LIKE HE BARELY SURVIVED.
BABABOOM
GOOD THING WE CAME.
PSHOOK
HM? SAITAMA, YOU SEEM RELIEVED.
WHAT HAP-PENED?
PHEW!
WELL, THAT FELT PRETTY GOOD.

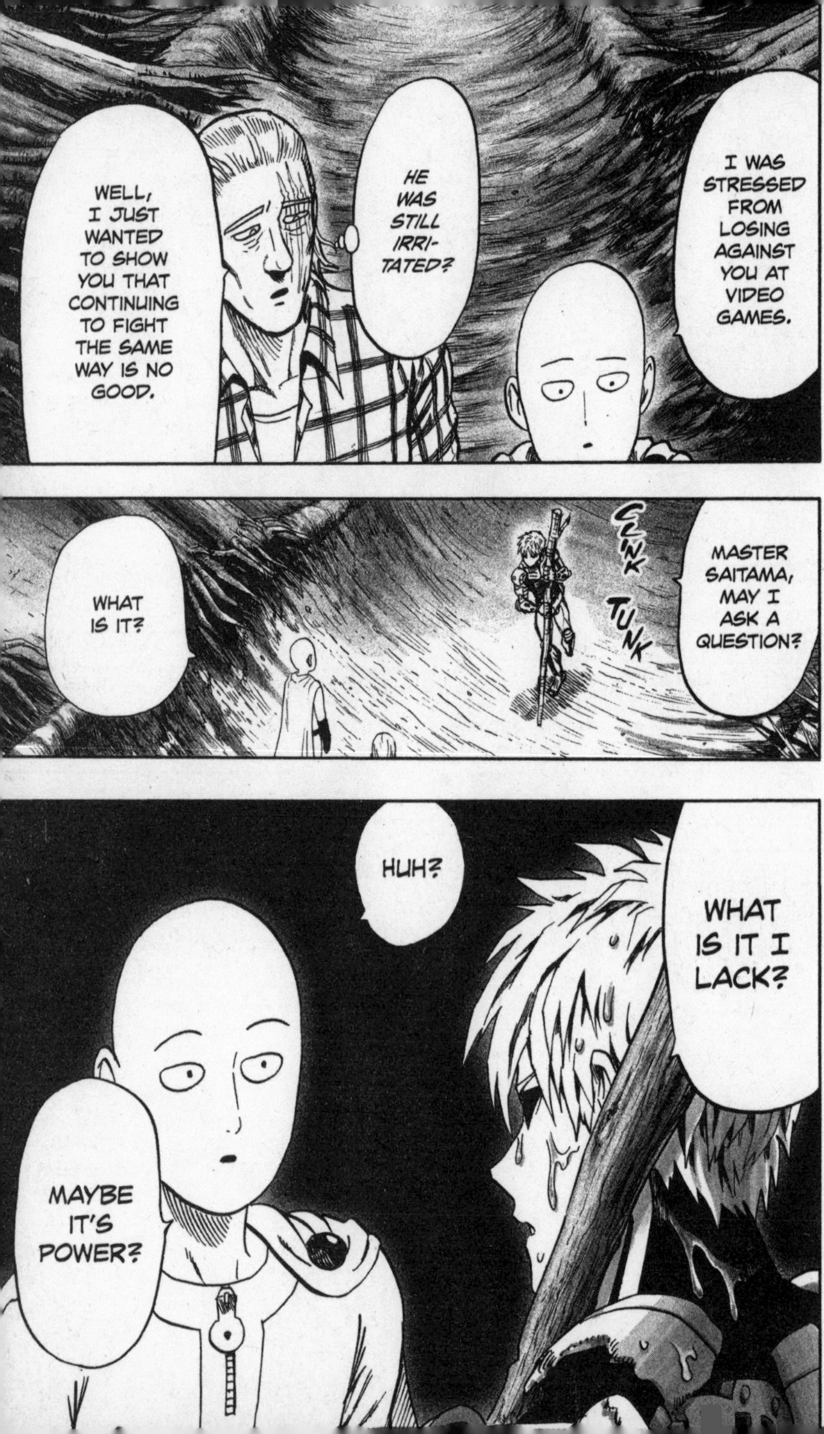
I WAS STRESSED FROM LOSING AGAINST YOU AT VIDEO GAMES.
HE WAS STILL IRRITATED?
WELL, I JUST WANTED TO SHOW YOU THAT CONTINUING TO FIGHT THE SAME WAY IS NO GOOD.
MASTER SAITAMA, MAY I ASK A QUESTION?
CLINK
TUNK
WHAT IS IT?
WHAT IS IT I LACK?
HUH?
MAYBE IT'S POWER?

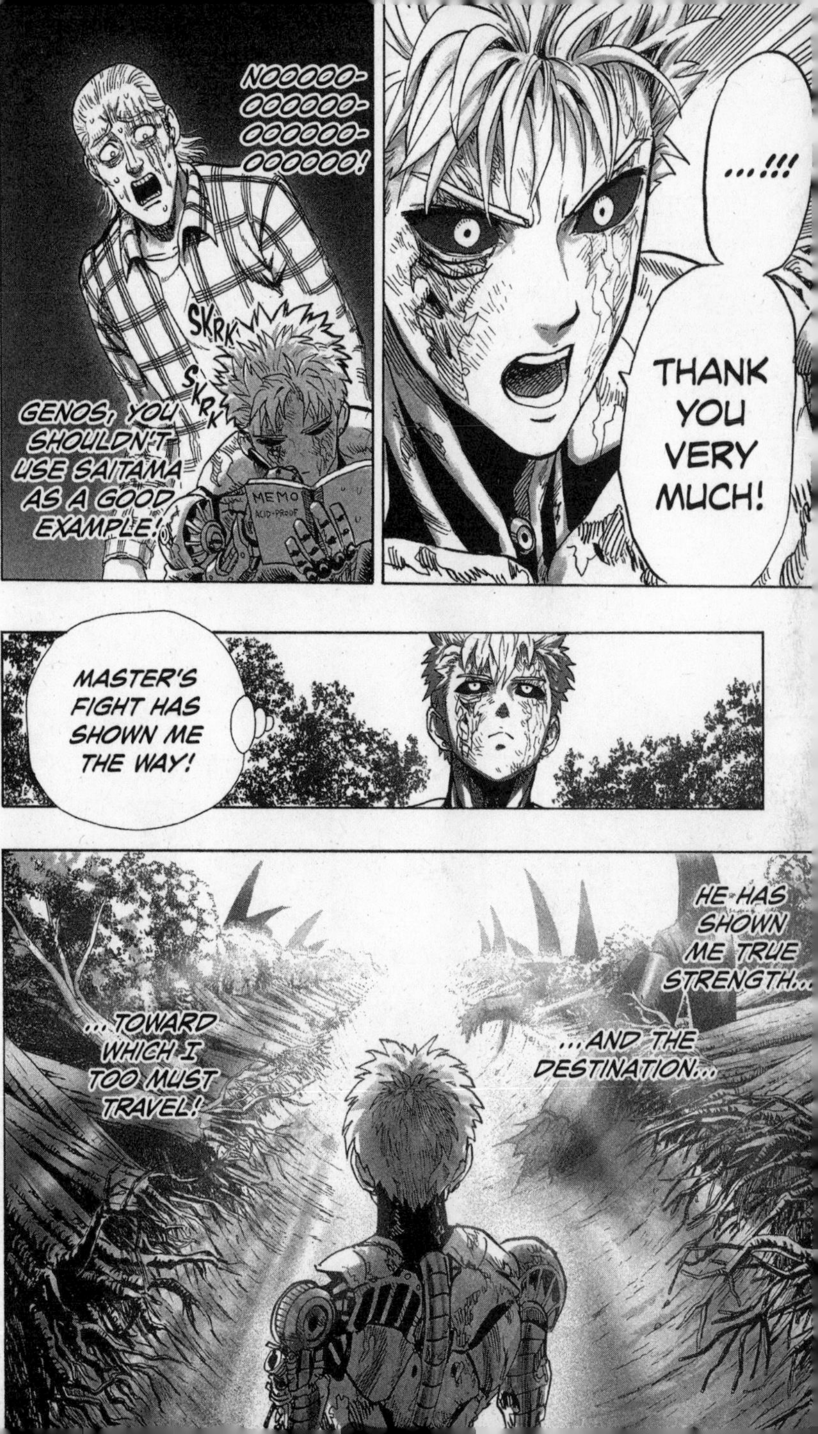
...!!!
THANK YOU VERY MUCH!
NOOOOO-OOOOOO-OOOOOO-OOOOOO!
SKRK SKRK SKRK
MEMO ACID-PROOF
GENOS, YOU SHOULDN'T USE SAITAMA AS A GOOD EXAMPLE!
MASTER'S FIGHT HAS SHOWN ME THE WAY!
HE HAS SHOWN ME TRUE STRENGTH...
...AND THE DESTINATION...
...TOWARD WHICH I TOO MUST TRAVEL!

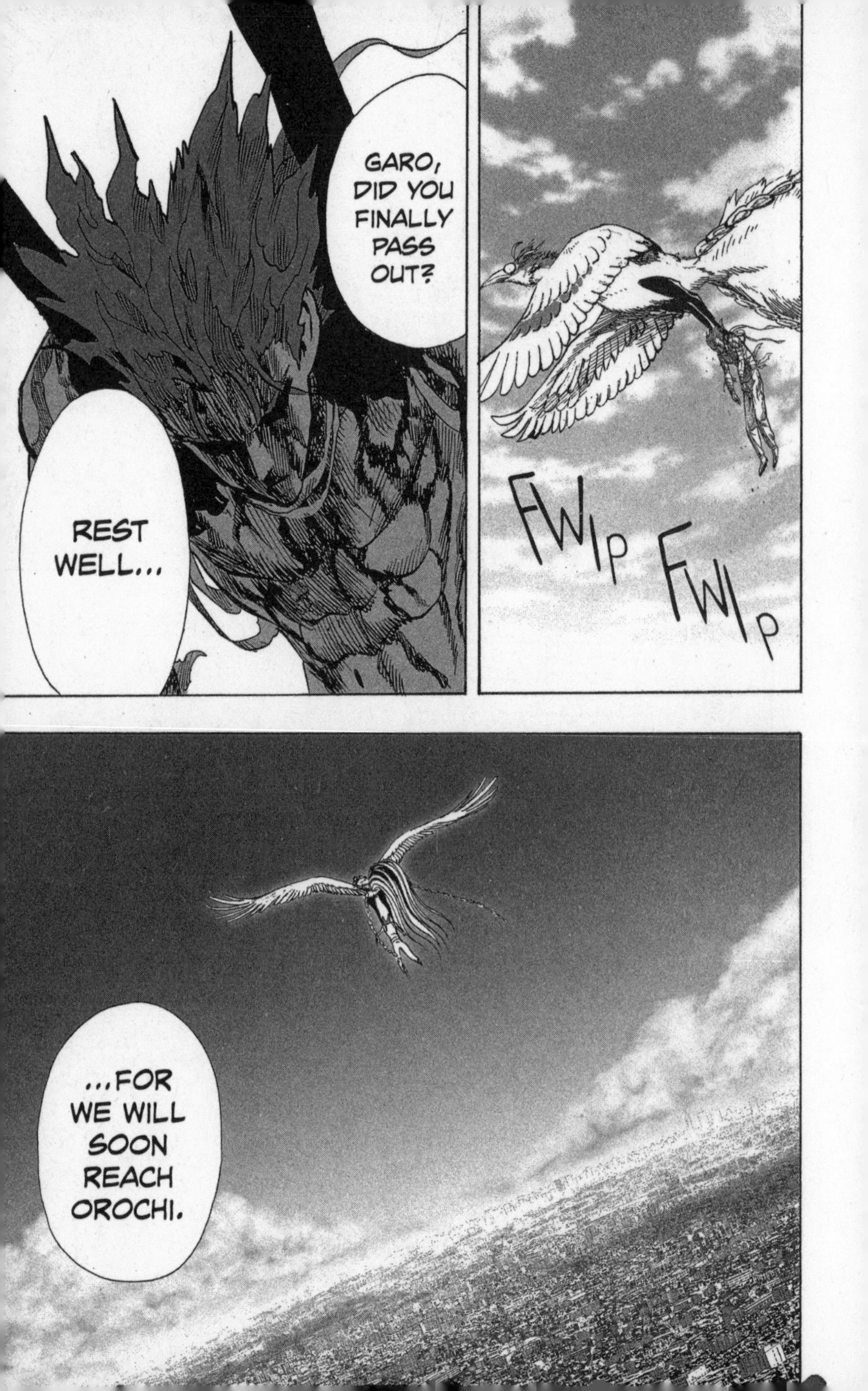
FWIP FWIP
GARO, DID YOU FINALLY PASS OUT?
REST WELL...
...FOR WE WILL SOON REACH OROCHI.

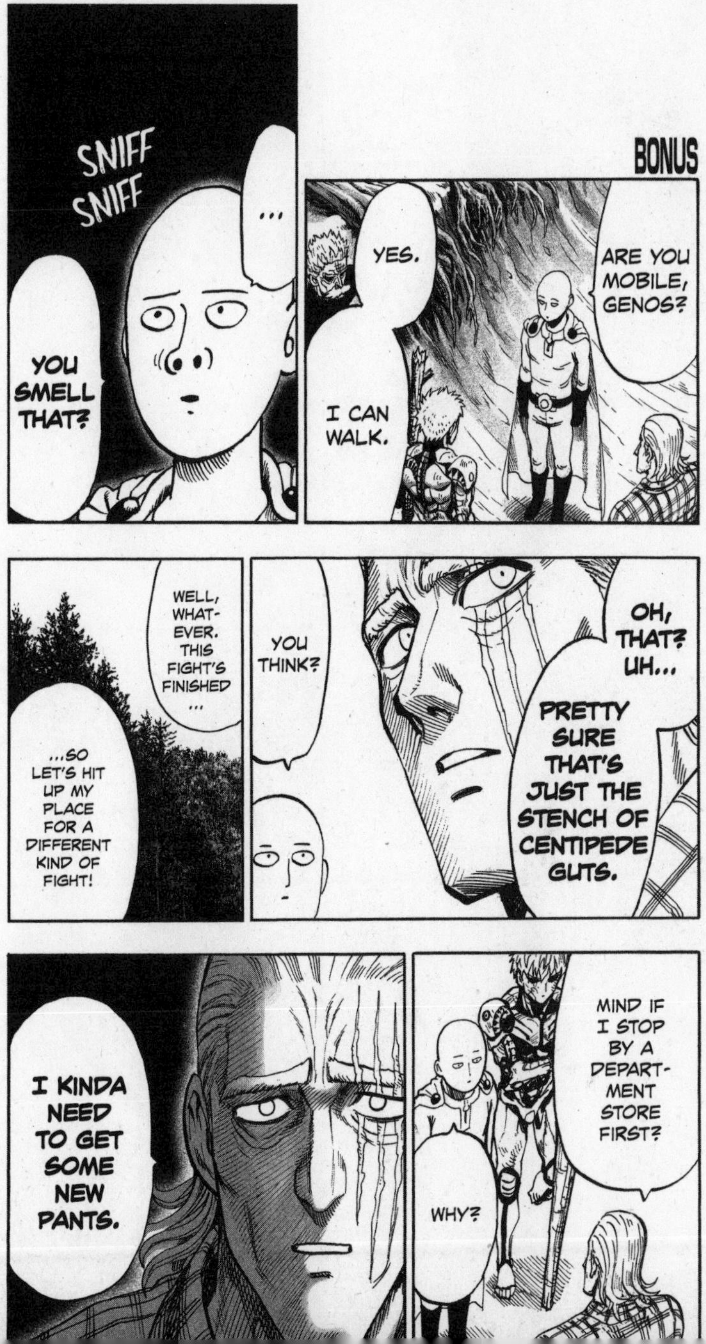
BONUS
ARE YOU MOBILE, GENOS?
YES.
I CAN WALK.
...
SNIFF SNIFF
YOU SMELL THAT?
OH, THAT? UH...
PRETTY SURE THAT'S JUST THE STENCH OF CENTIPEDE GUTS.
YOU THINK?
WELL, WHATEVER. THIS FIGHT'S FINISHED...
...SO LET'S HIT UP MY PLACE FOR A DIFFERENT KIND OF FIGHT!
MIND IF I STOP BY A DEPARTMENT STORE FIRST?
WHY?
I KINDA NEED TO GET SOME NEW PANTS.

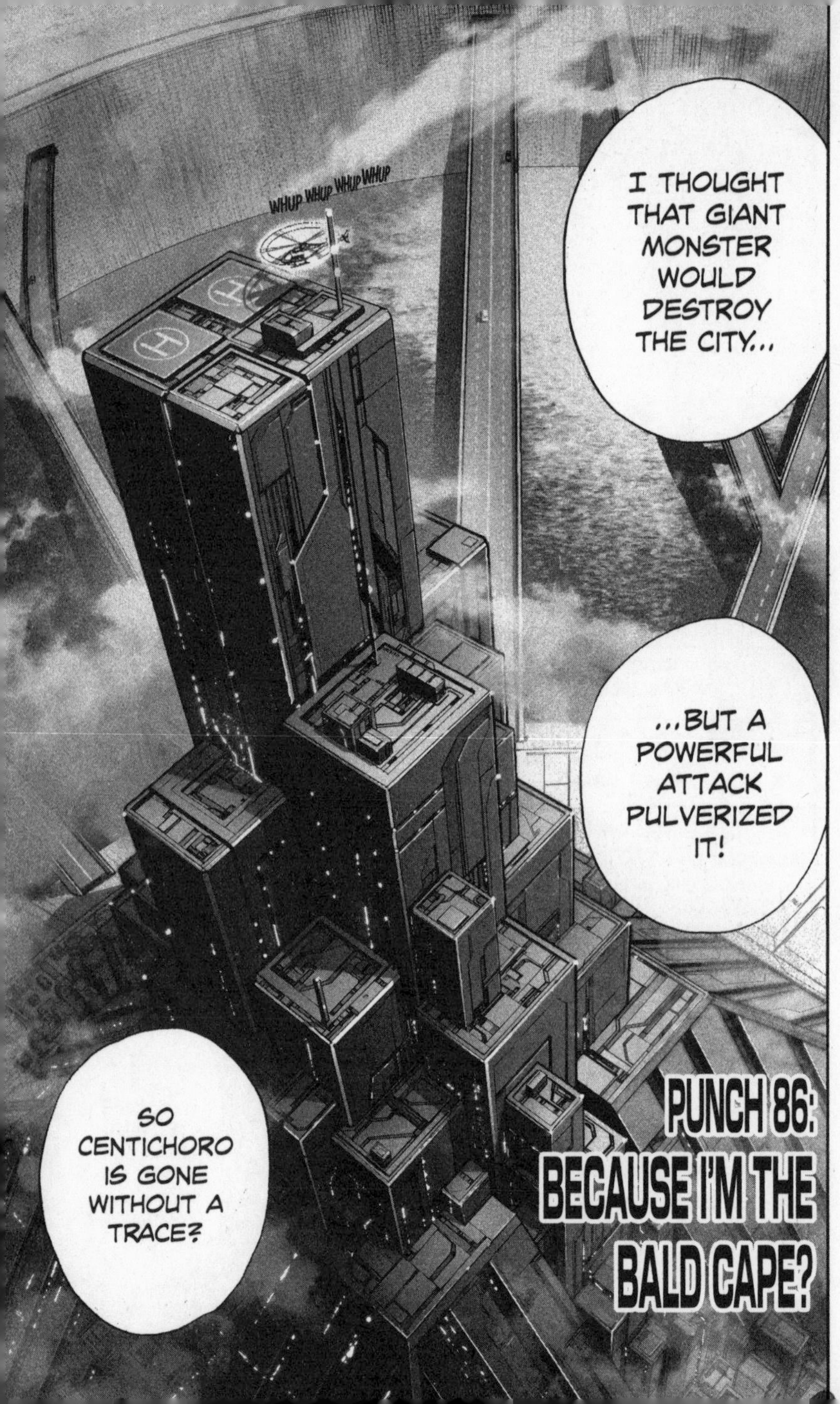
WHUP WHUP WHUP WHUP
I THOUGHT THAT GIANT MONSTER WOULD DESTROY THE CITY...
...BUT A POWERFUL ATTACK PULVERIZED IT!
PUNCH 86: BECAUSE I'M THE BALD CAPE?
SO CENTICHORO IS GONE WITHOUT A TRACE?

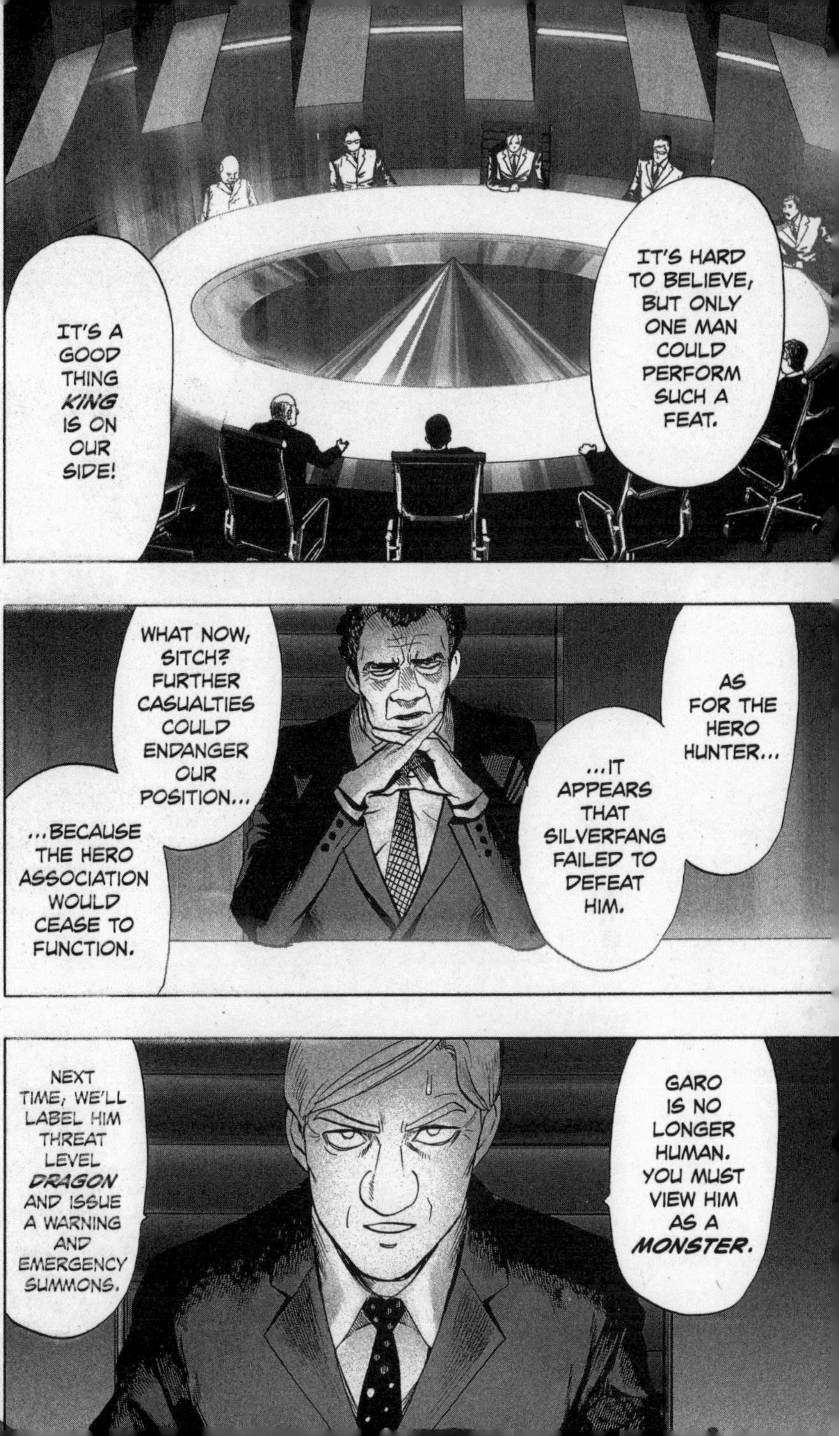
IT'S HARD TO BELIEVE, BUT ONLY ONE MAN COULD PERFORM SUCH A FEAT.
IT'S A GOOD THING KING IS ON OUR SIDE!
AS FOR THE HERO HUNTER...
...IT APPEARS THAT SILVERFANG FAILED TO DEFEAT HIM.
WHAT NOW, SITCH? FURTHER CASUALTIES COULD ENDANGER OUR POSITION...
...BECAUSE THE HERO ASSOCIATION WOULD CEASE TO FUNCTION.
GARO IS NO LONGER HUMAN. YOU MUST VIEW HIM AS A MONSTER.
NEXT TIME, WE'LL LABEL HIM THREAT LEVEL DRAGON AND ISSUE A WARNING AND EMERGENCY SUMMONS.

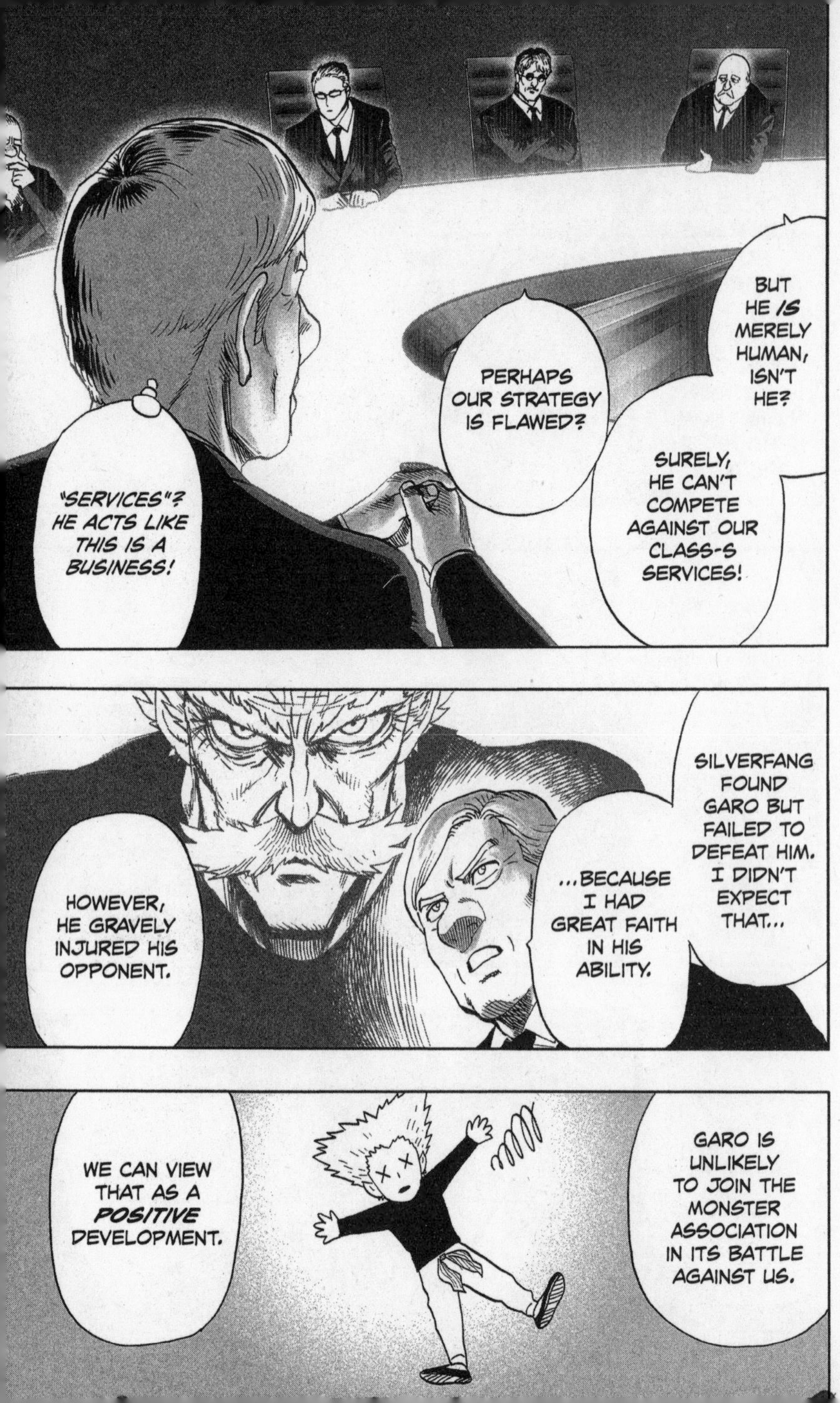
BUT HE IS MERELY HUMAN, ISN'T HE?
SURELY, HE CAN'T COMPETE AGAINST OUR CLASS-S SERVICES!
PERHAPS OUR STRATEGY IS FLAWED?
"SERVICES"? HE ACTS LIKE THIS IS A BUSINESS!
SILVERFANG FOUND GARO BUT FAILED TO DEFEAT HIM. I DIDN'T EXPECT THAT...
...BECAUSE I HAD GREAT FAITH IN HIS ABILITY.
HOWEVER, HE GRAVELY INJURED HIS OPPONENT.
GARO IS UNLIKELY TO JOIN THE MONSTER ASSOCIATION IN ITS BATTLE AGAINST US.
WE CAN VIEW THAT AS A POSITIVE DEVELOPMENT.

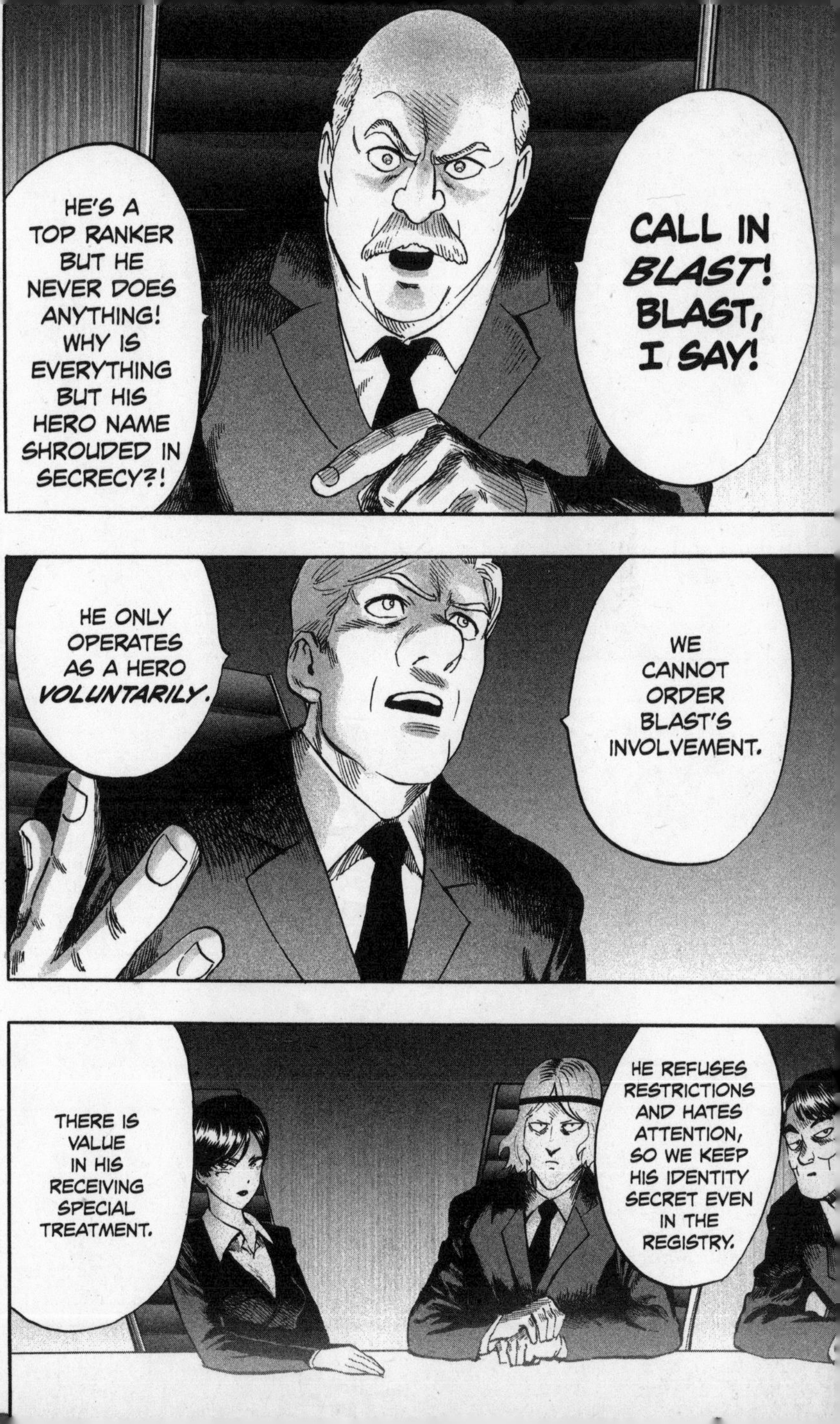
CALL IN *BLAST*! BLAST, I SAY!
HE'S A TOP RANKER BUT HE NEVER DOES ANYTHING! WHY IS EVERYTHING BUT HIS HERO NAME SHROUDED IN SECRECY?!
WE CANNOT ORDER BLAST'S INVOLVEMENT.
HE ONLY OPERATES AS A HERO *VOLUNTARILY*.
HE REFUSES RESTRICTIONS AND HATES ATTENTION, SO WE KEEP HIS IDENTITY SECRET EVEN IN THE REGISTRY.
THERE IS VALUE IN HIS RECEIVING SPECIAL TREATMENT.

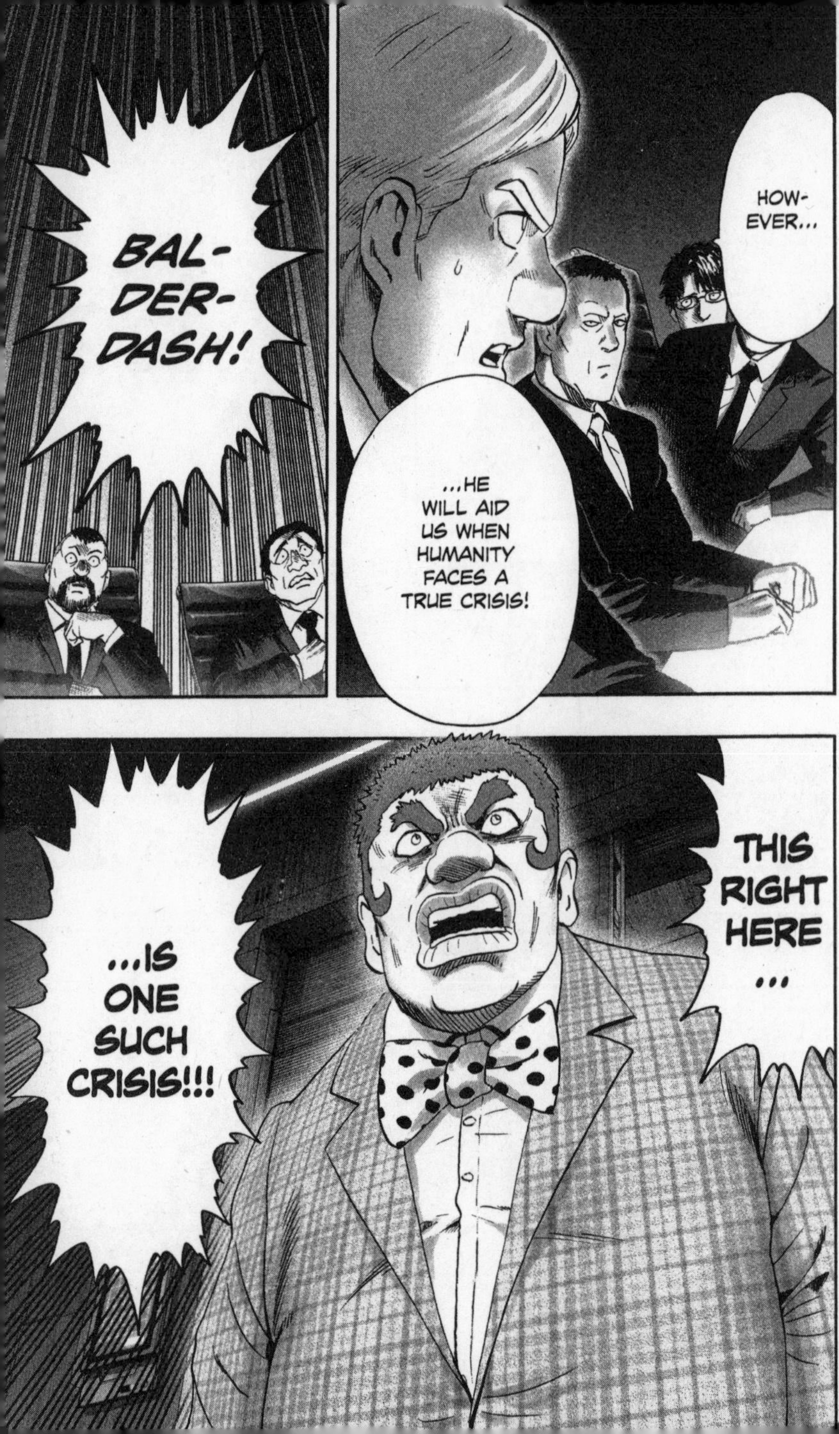
HOW-EVER...
...HE WILL AID US WHEN HUMANITY FACES A TRUE CRISIS!
BAL-DER-DASH!
THIS RIGHT HERE...
...IS ONE SUCH CRISIS!!!

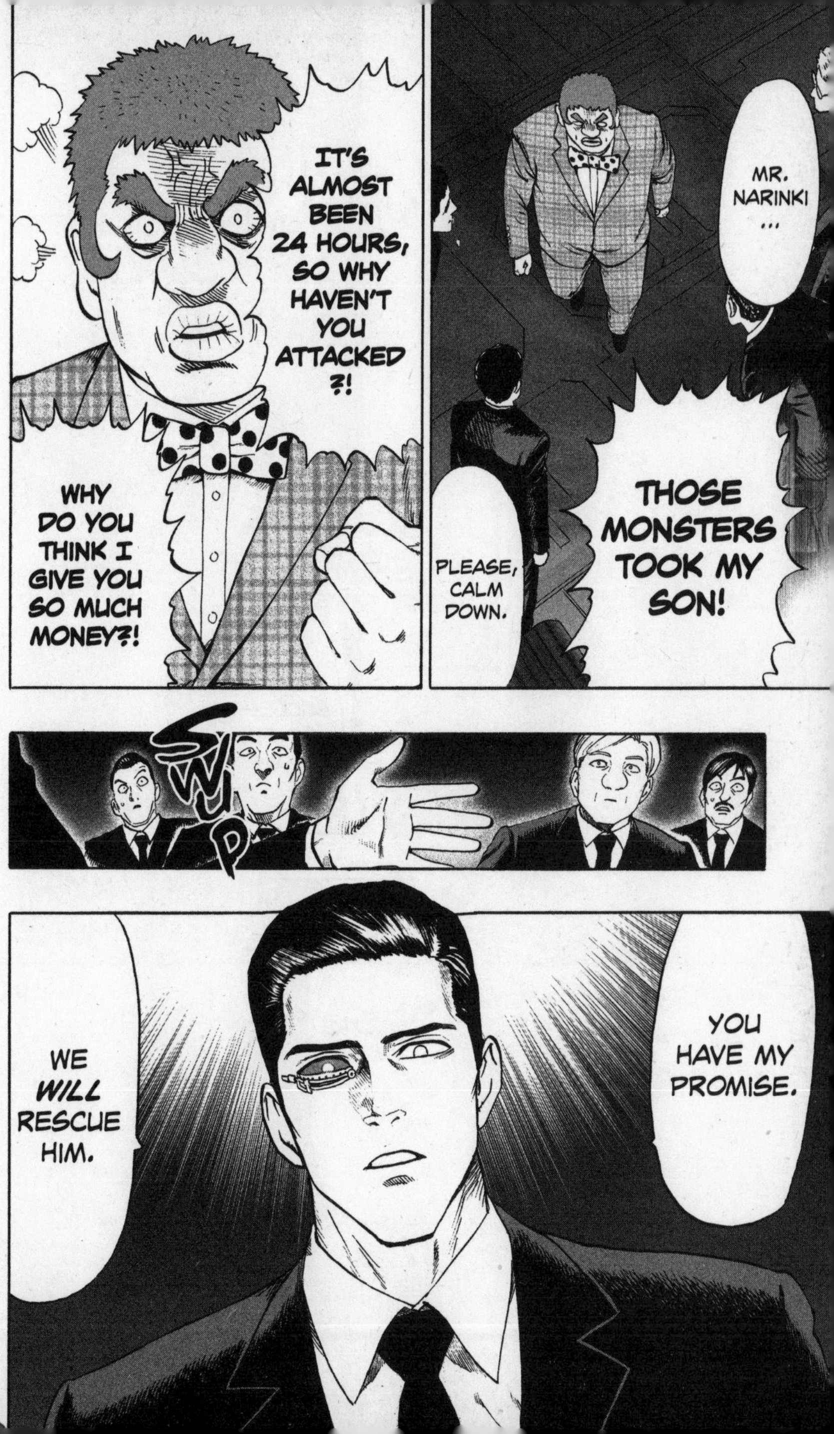
MR. NARINKI ...
THOSE MONSTERS TOOK MY SON!
PLEASE, CALM DOWN.
IT'S ALMOST BEEN 24 HOURS, SO WHY HAVEN'T YOU ATTACKED?!
WHY DO YOU THINK I GIVE YOU SO MUCH MONEY?!
SWUP
YOU HAVE MY PROMISE.
WE *WILL* RESCUE HIM.

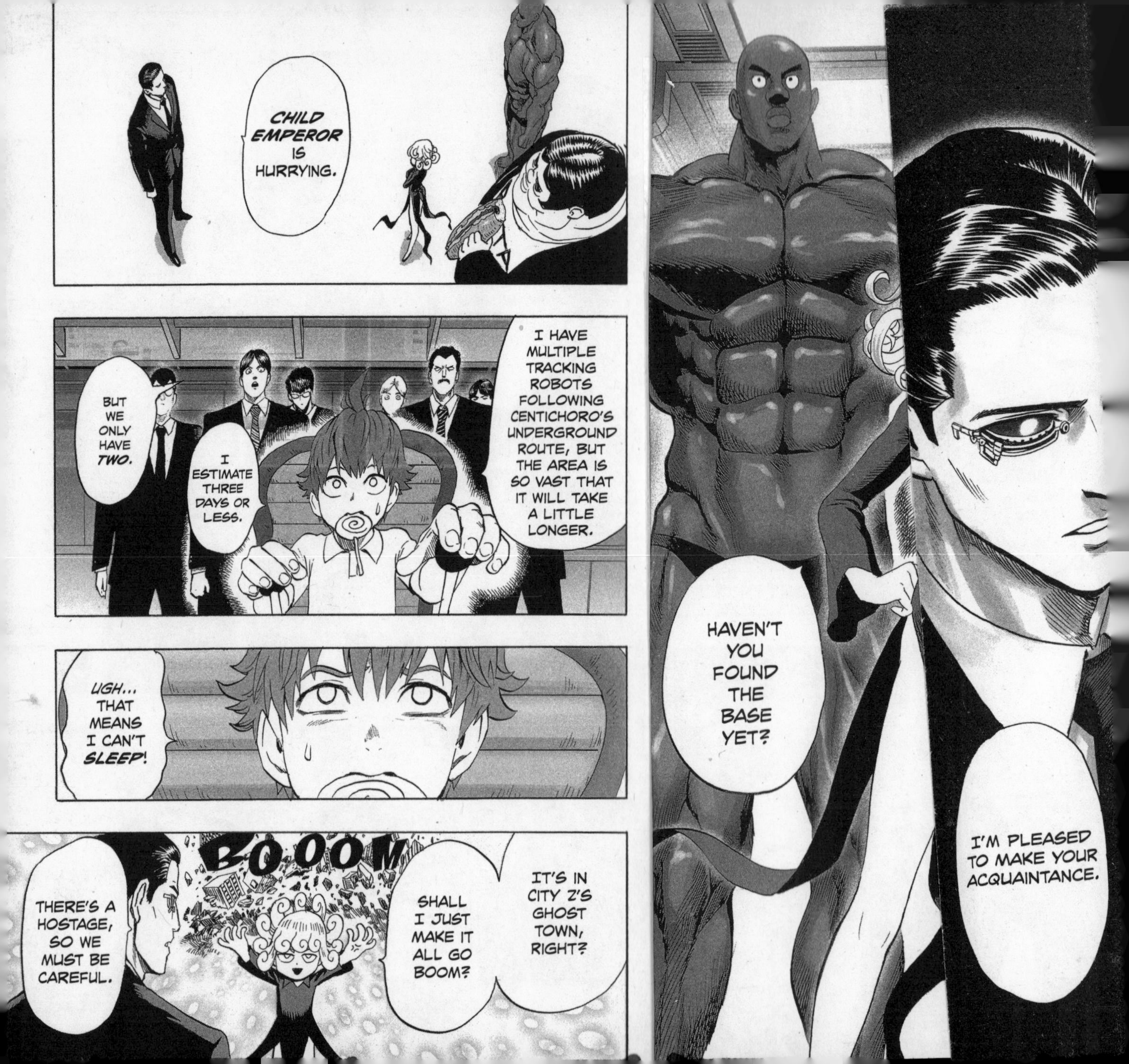
I'M PLEASED TO MAKE YOUR ACQUAINTANCE.
HAVEN'T YOU FOUND THE BASE YET?
CHILD EMPEROR IS HURRYING.
I HAVE MULTIPLE TRACKING ROBOTS FOLLOWING CENTICHORO'S UNDERGROUND ROUTE, BUT THE AREA IS SO VAST THAT IT WILL TAKE A LITTLE LONGER.
I ESTIMATE THREE DAYS OR LESS.
BUT WE ONLY HAVE *TWO.*
UGH... THAT MEANS I CAN'T *SLEEP*!
IT'S IN CITY Z'S GHOST TOWN, RIGHT?
SHALL I JUST MAKE IT ALL GO BOOM?
BOOOM
THERE'S A HOSTAGE, SO WE MUST BE CAREFUL.

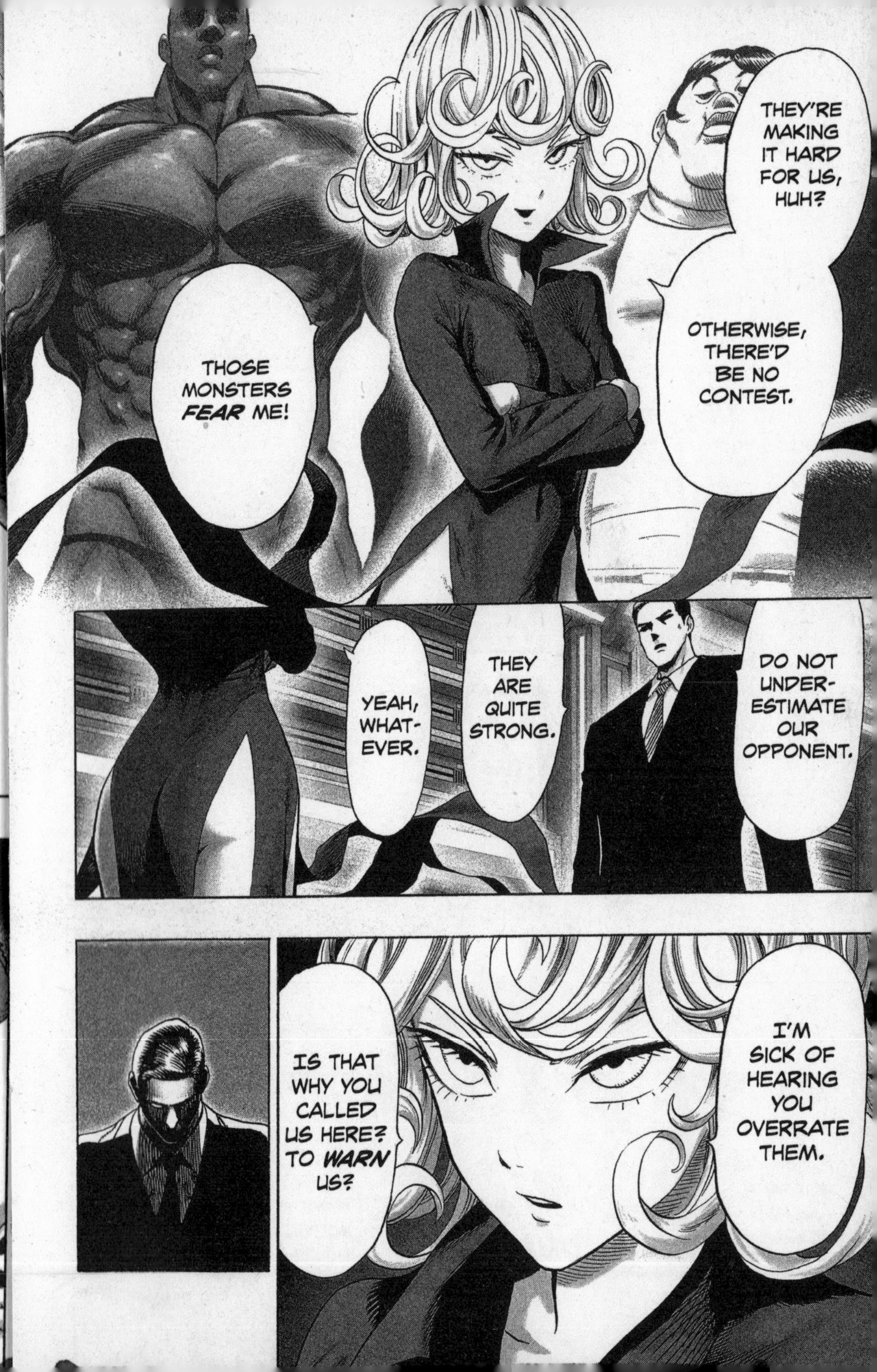
THEY'RE MAKING IT HARD FOR US, HUH?
OTHERWISE, THERE'D BE NO CONTEST.
THOSE MONSTERS *FEAR* ME!
DO NOT UNDER-ESTIMATE OUR OPPONENT.
THEY ARE QUITE STRONG.
YEAH, WHAT-EVER.
I'M SICK OF HEARING YOU OVERRATE THEM.
IS THAT WHY YOU CALLED US HERE? TO *WARN* US?
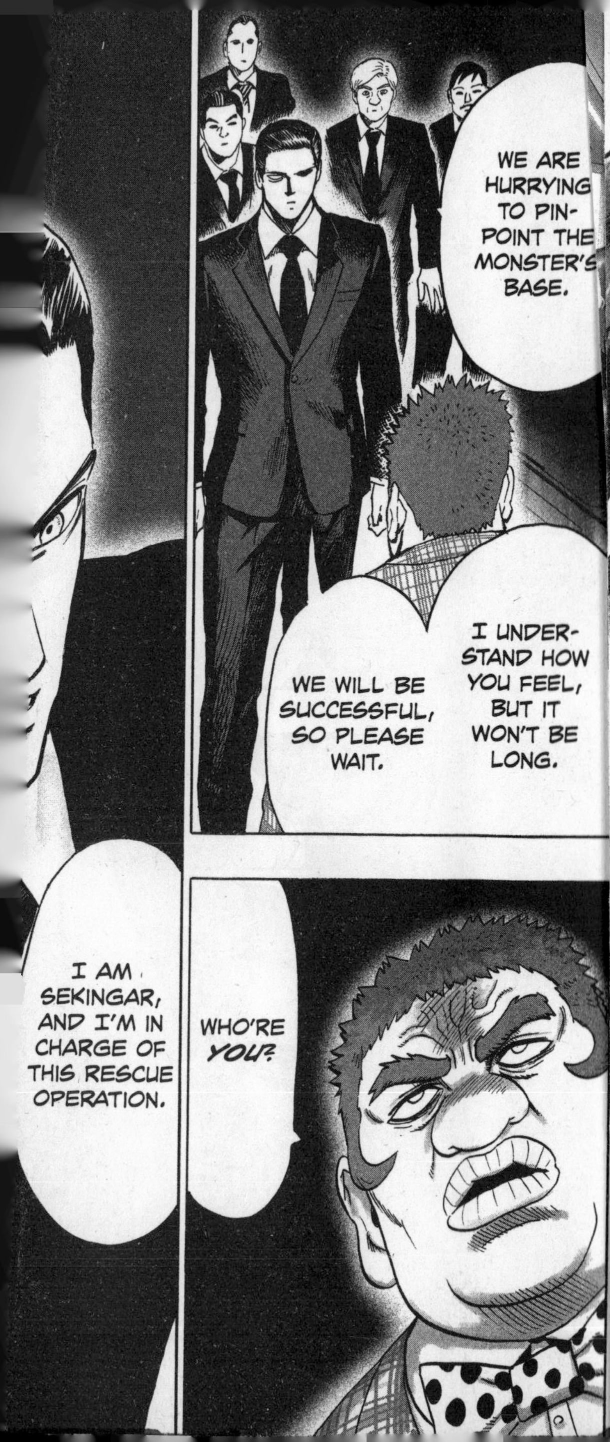
WE ARE HURRYING TO PIN-POINT THE MONSTER'S BASE.
I UNDER-STAND HOW YOU FEEL, BUT IT WON'T BE LONG.
WE WILL BE SUCCESSFUL, SO PLEASE WAIT.
WHO'RE *YOU*?
I AM SEKINGAR, AND I'M IN CHARGE OF THIS RESCUE OPERATION.

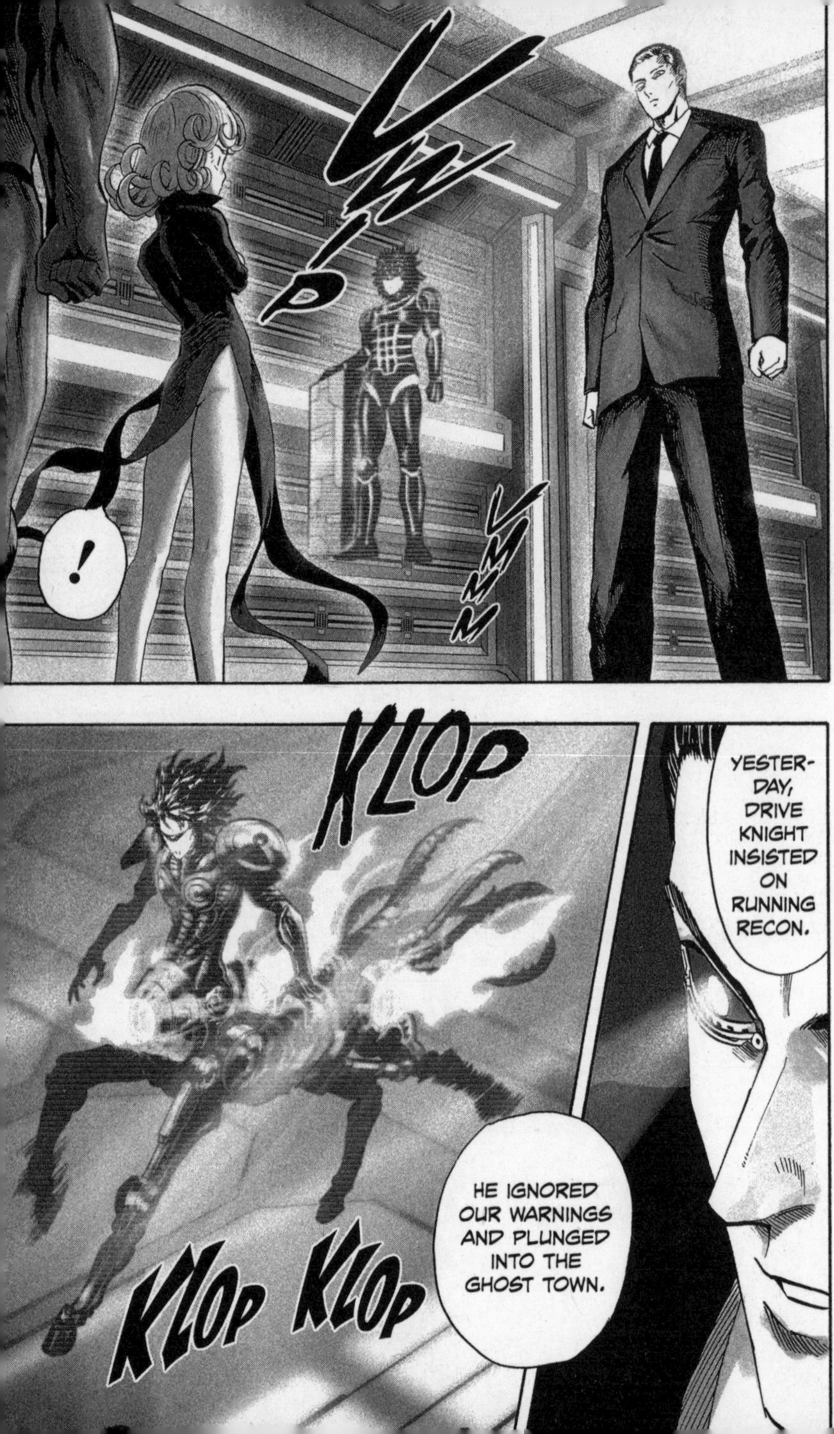
VWIP
VMMMM
!
YESTER-DAY, DRIVE KNIGHT INSISTED ON RUNNING RECON.
HE IGNORED OUR WARNINGS AND PLUNGED INTO THE GHOST TOWN.
KLOP
KLOP KLOP

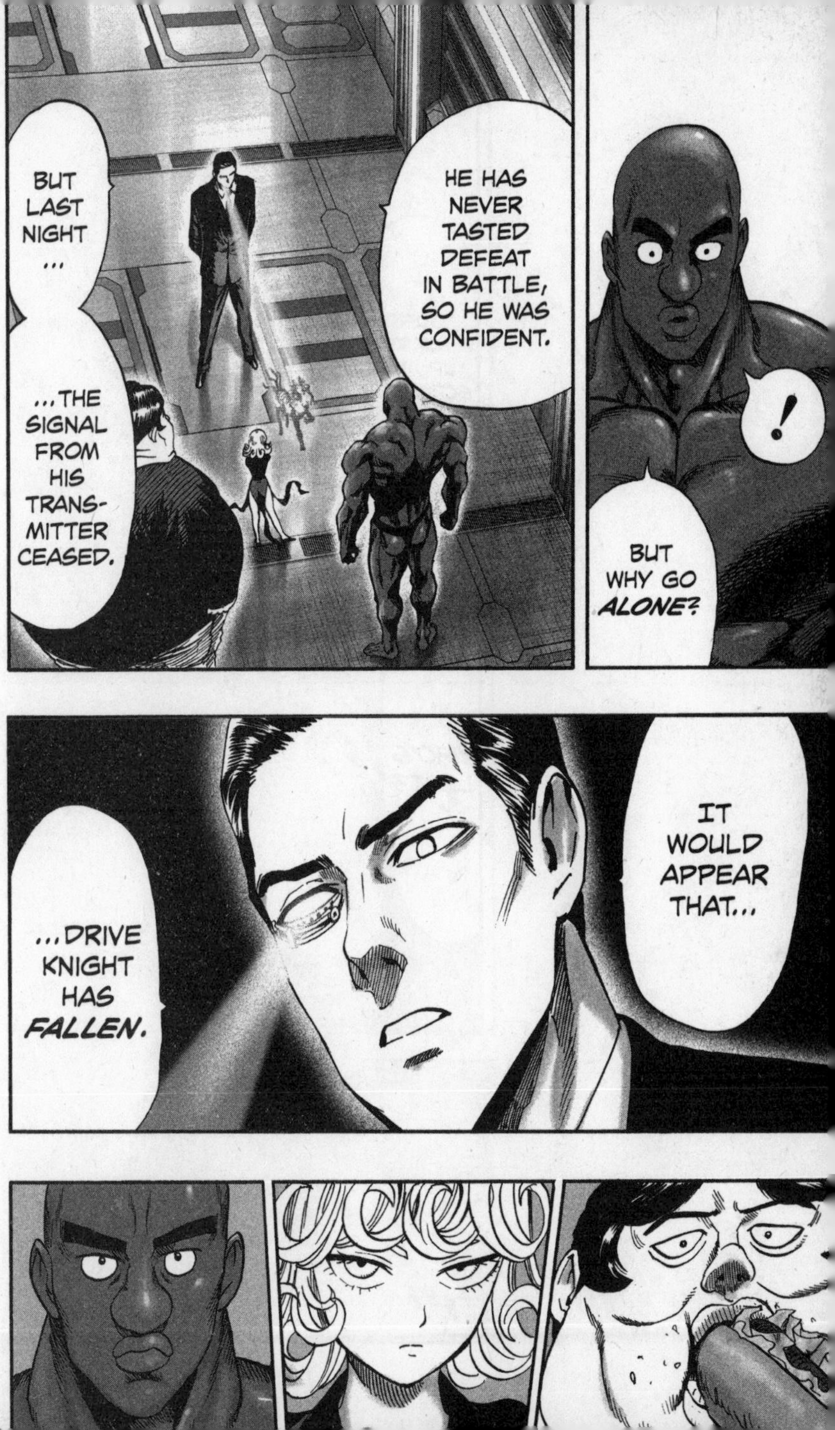
!
BUT WHY GO ALONE?
HE HAS NEVER TASTED DEFEAT IN BATTLE, SO HE WAS CONFIDENT.
BUT LAST NIGHT ...
...THE SIGNAL FROM HIS TRANS-MITTER CEASED.
IT WOULD APPEAR THAT...
...DRIVE KNIGHT HAS FALLEN.

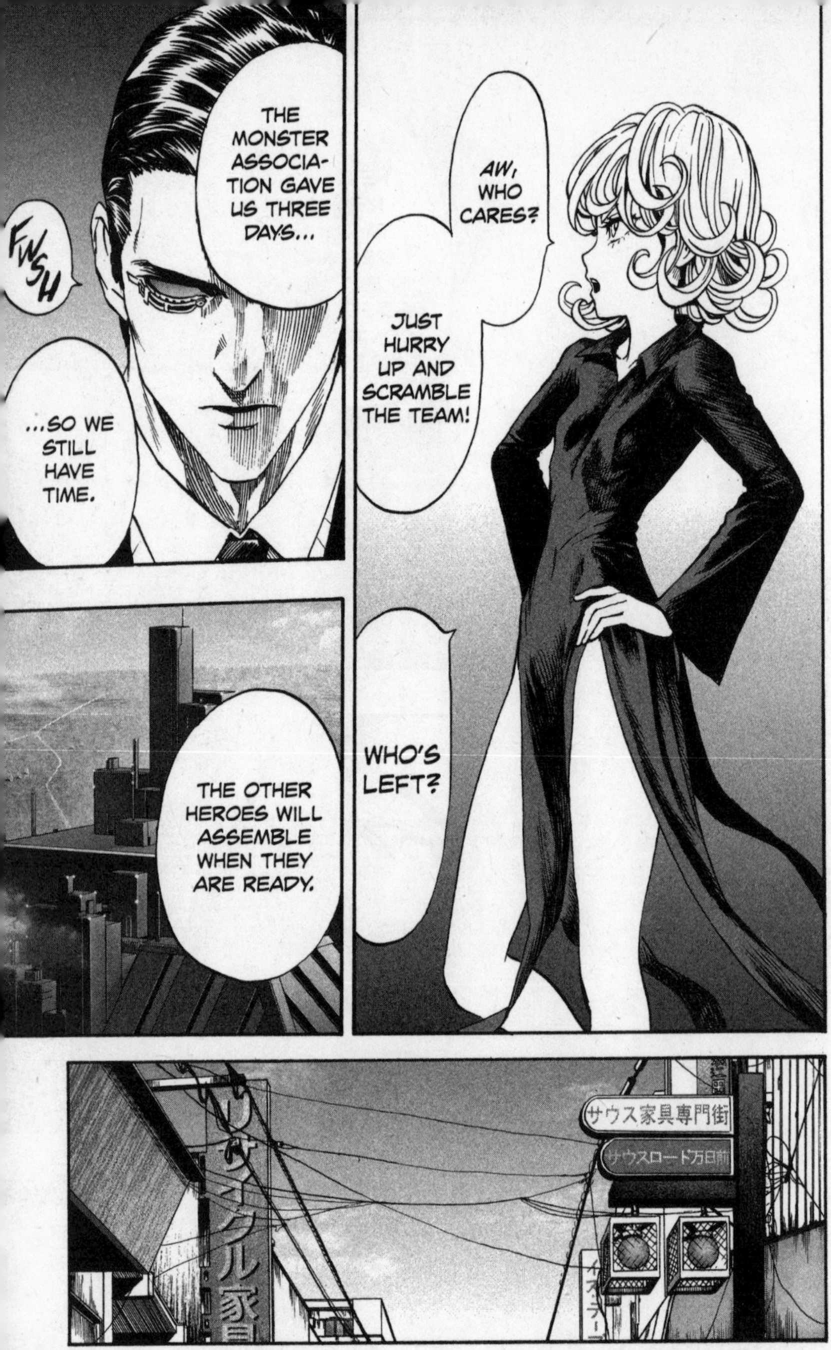
AW, WHO CARES?
JUST HURRY UP AND SCRAMBLE THE TEAM!
WHO'S LEFT?
THE MONSTER ASSOCIATION GAVE US THREE DAYS...
FWSH
...SO WE STILL HAVE TIME.
THE OTHER HEROES WILL ASSEMBLE WHEN THEY ARE READY.
サウス家具専門街
サウスロード万日前

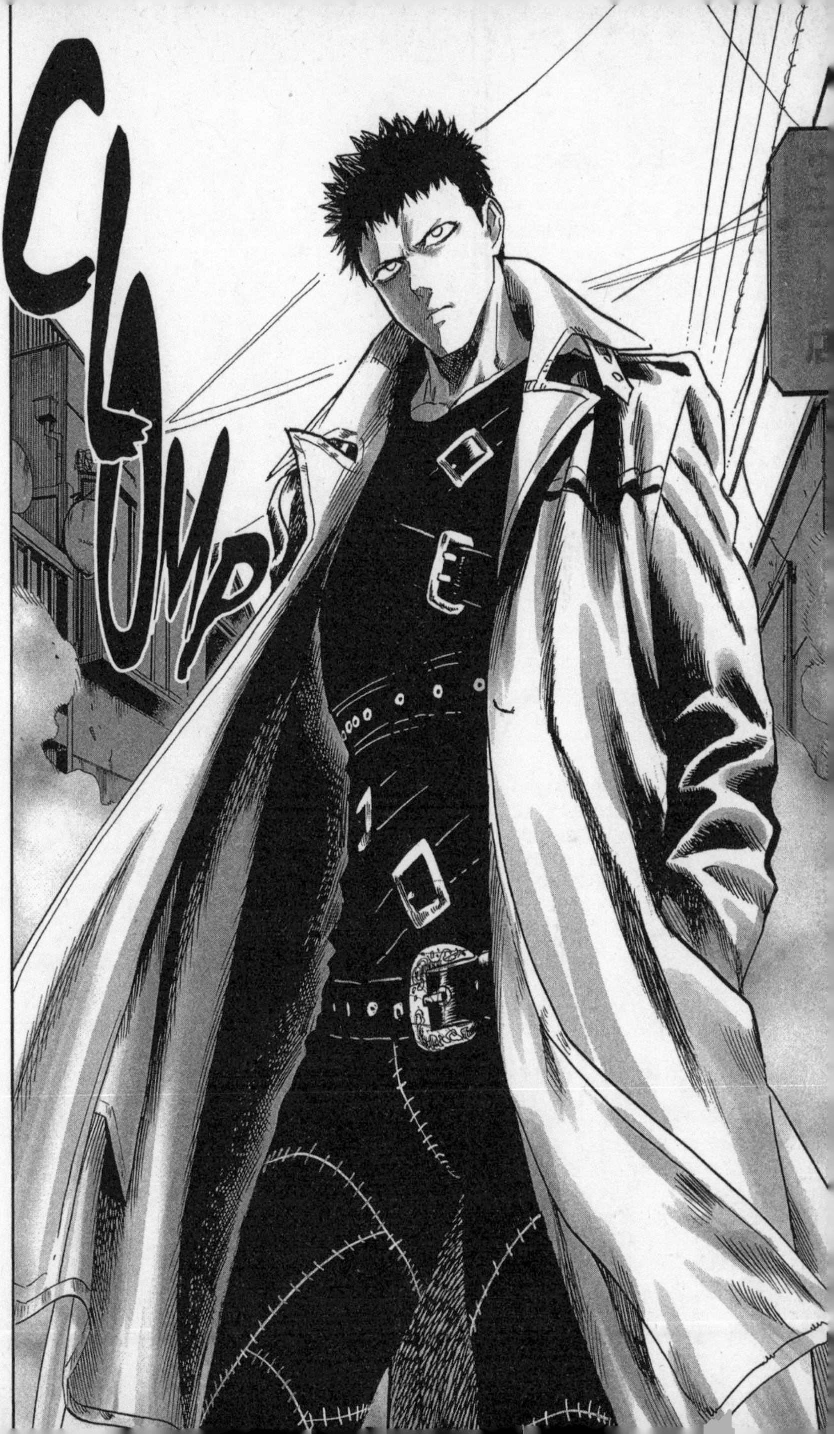
CLUMP

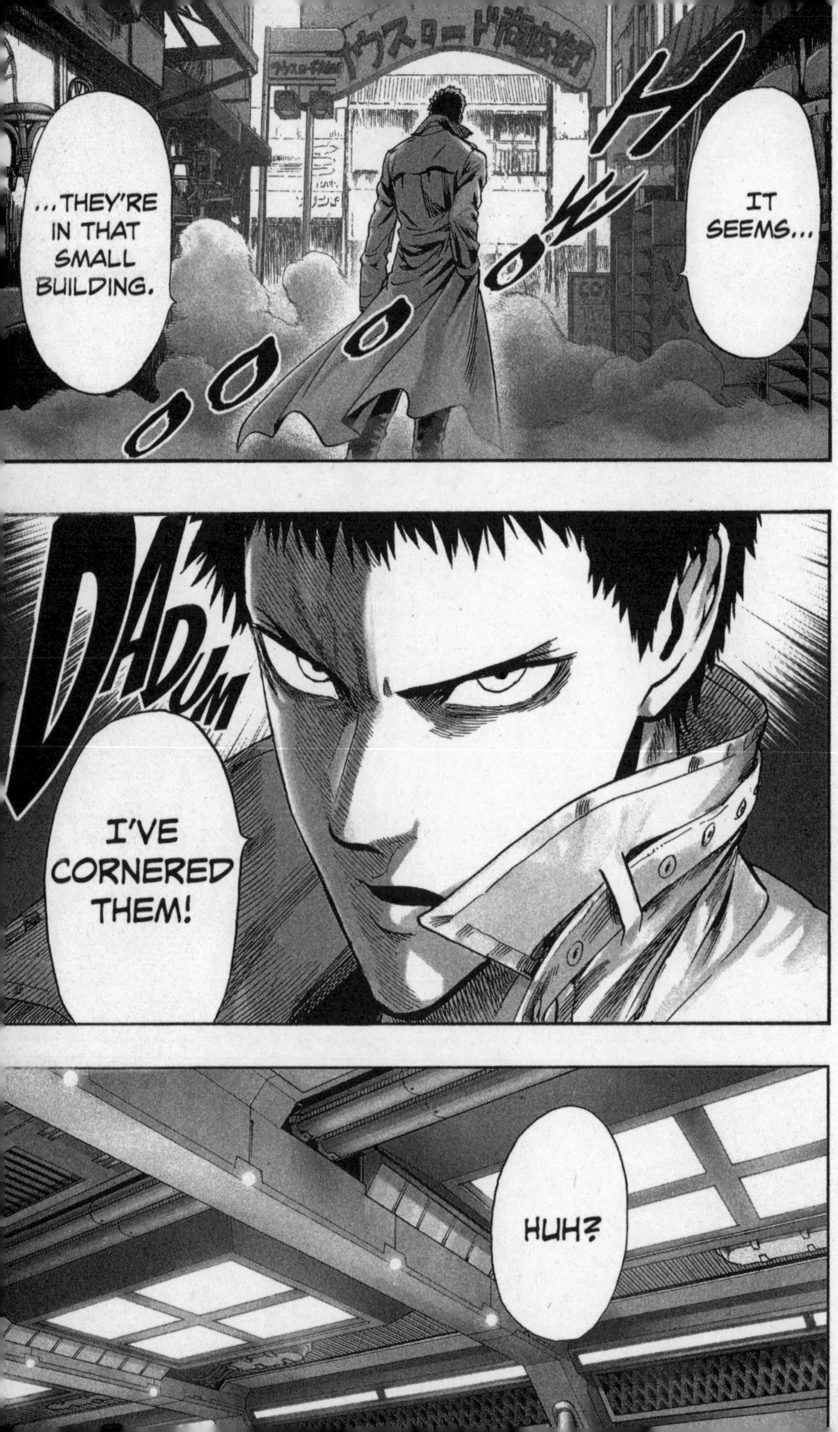
HWOOOOOO
IT SEEMS...
...THEY'RE IN THAT SMALL BUILDING.
DADUM
I'VE CORNERED THEM!
HUH?

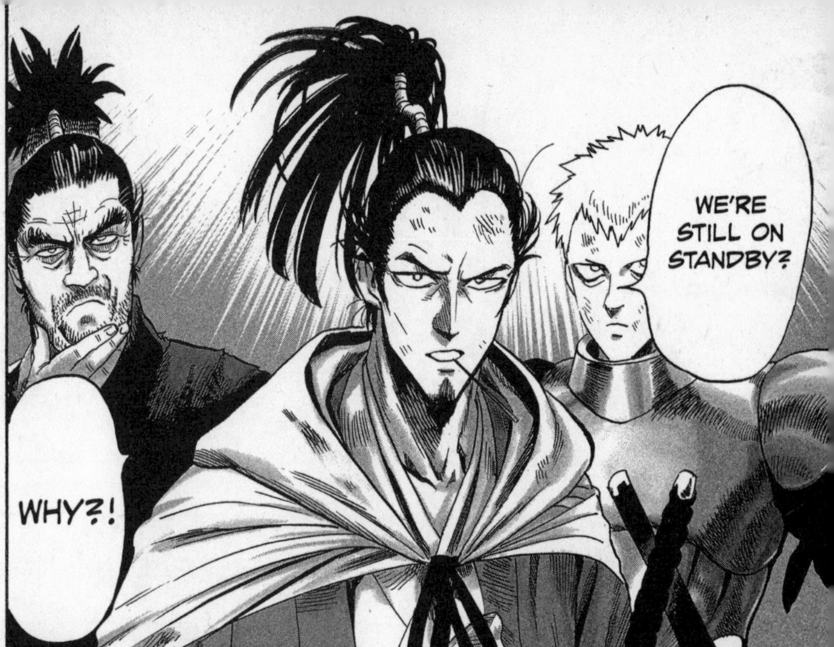
WE'RE STILL ON STANDBY?
WHY?!
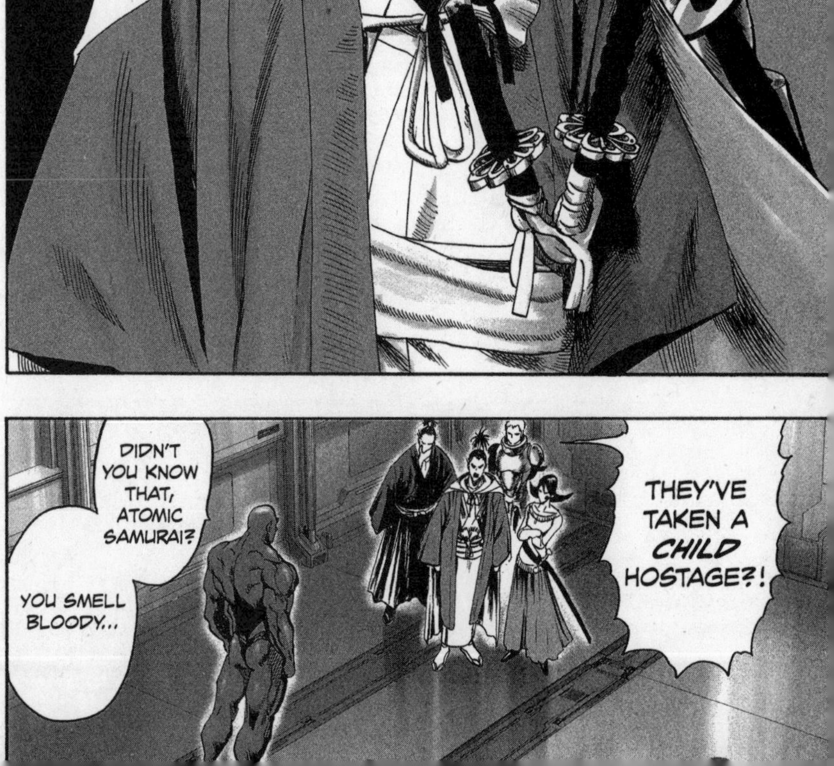
THEY'VE TAKEN A *CHILD* HOSTAGE?!
DIDN'T YOU KNOW THAT, ATOMIC SAMURAI?
YOU SMELL BLOODY...

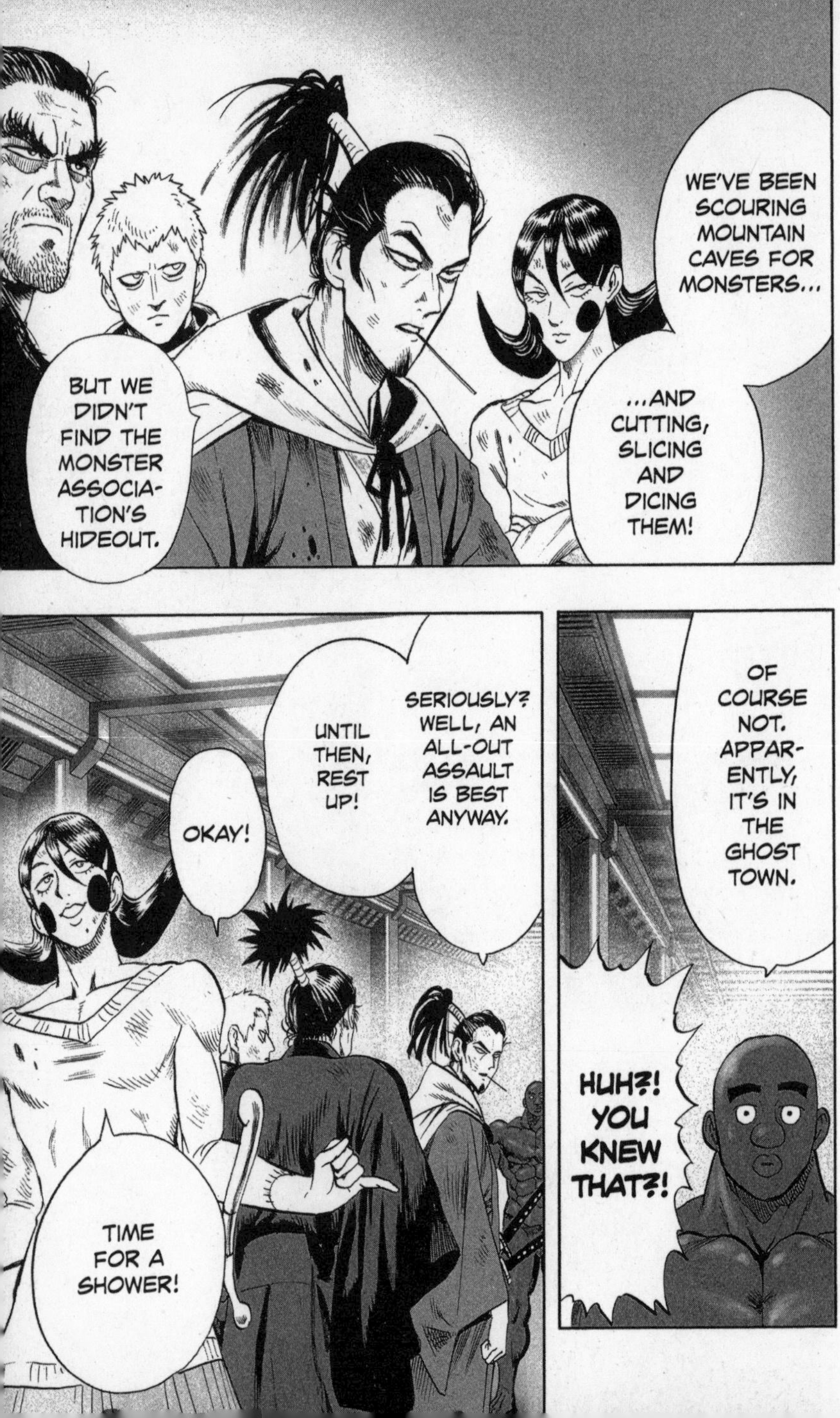
WE'VE BEEN SCOURING MOUNTAIN CAVES FOR MONSTERS...
...AND CUTTING, SLICING AND DICING THEM!
BUT WE DIDN'T FIND THE MONSTER ASSOCIA-TION'S HIDEOUT.
OF COURSE NOT. APPAR-ENTLY, IT'S IN THE GHOST TOWN.
HUH?! YOU KNEW THAT?!
SERIOUSLY? WELL, AN ALL-OUT ASSAULT IS BEST ANYWAY.
UNTIL THEN, REST UP!
OKAY!
TIME FOR A SHOWER!

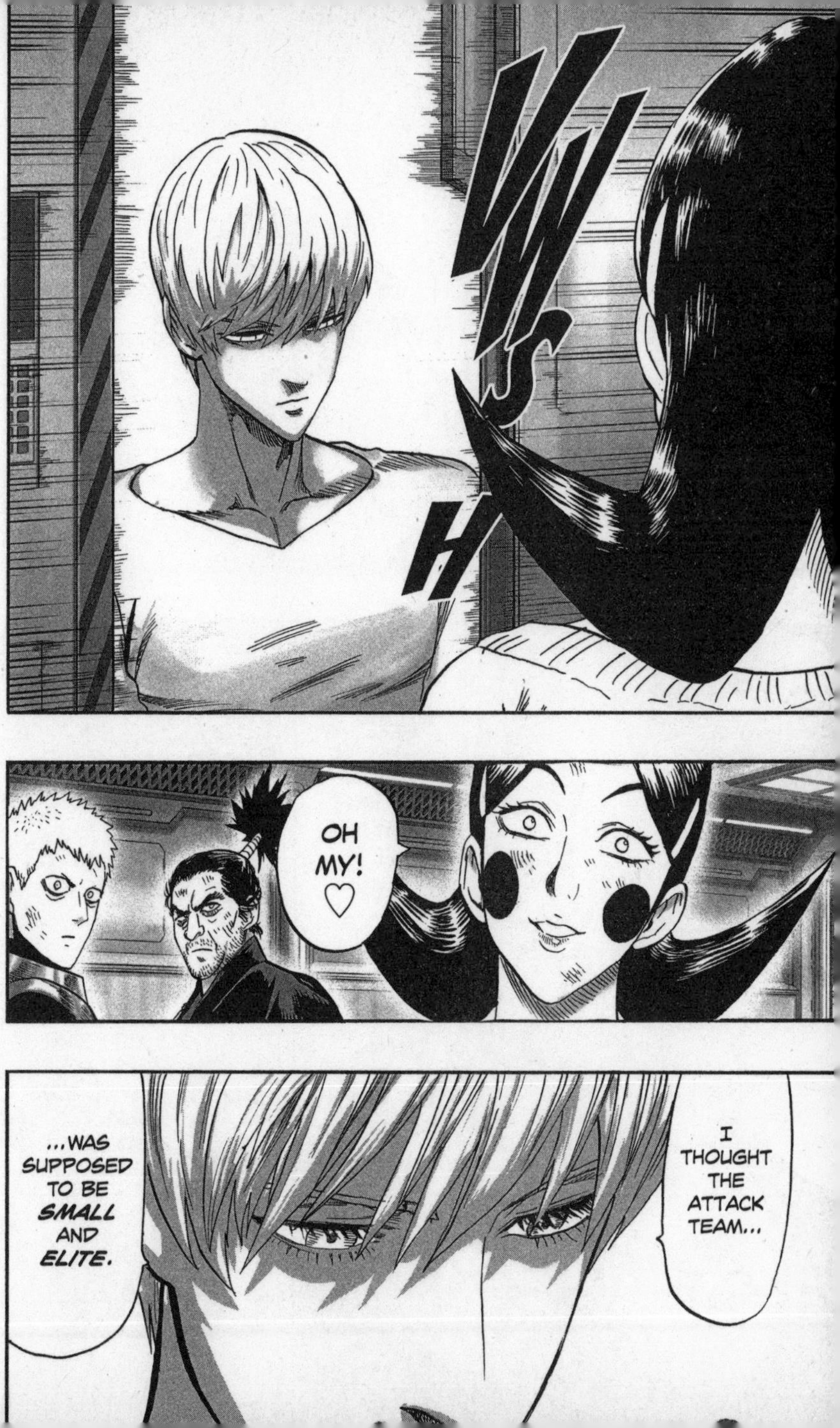

OH MY! ♡
I THOUGHT THE ATTACK TEAM...
...WAS SUPPOSED TO BE *SMALL* AND *ELITE*.

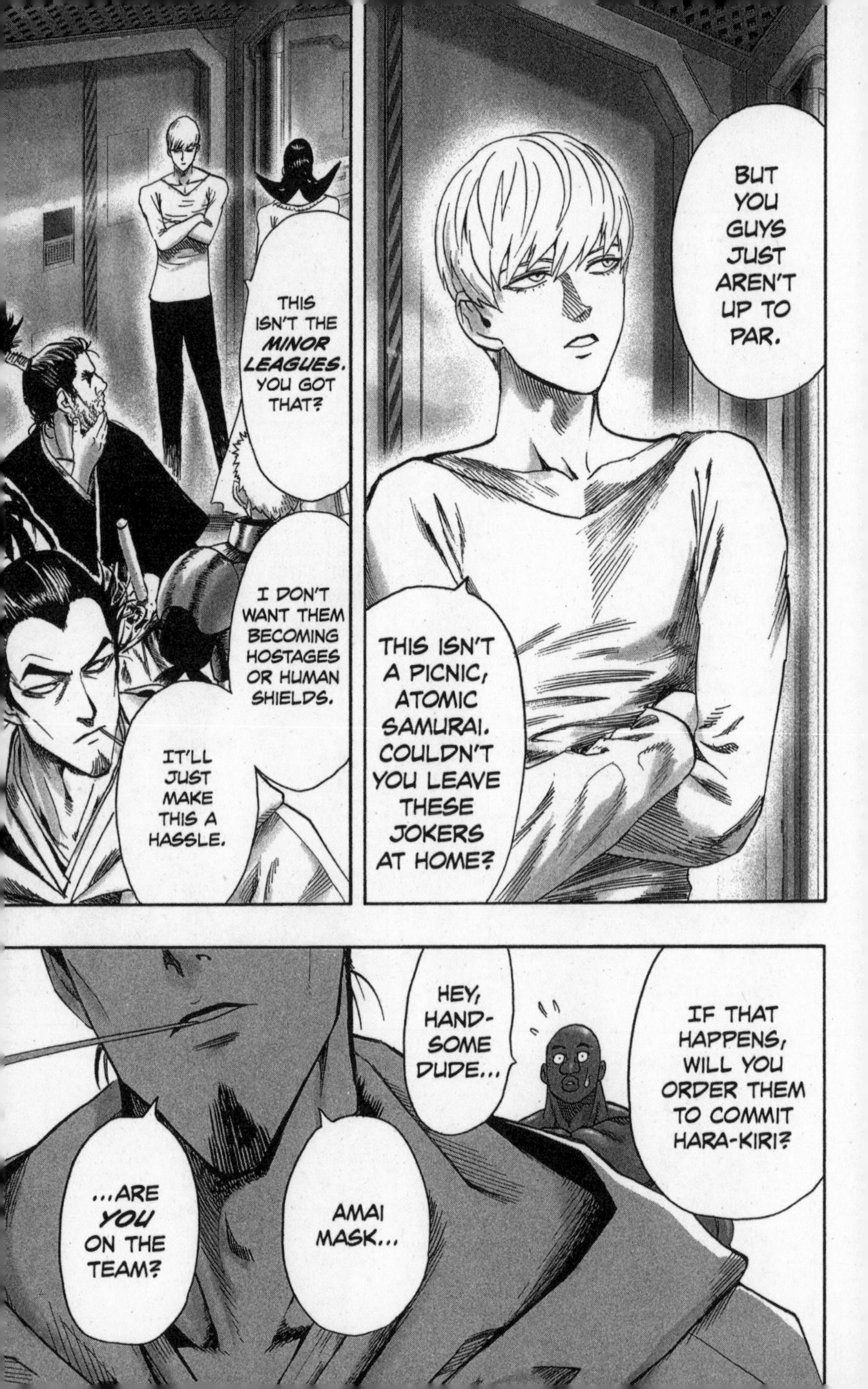
BUT YOU GUYS JUST AREN'T UP TO PAR.
THIS ISN'T A PICNIC, ATOMIC SAMURAI. COULDN'T YOU LEAVE THESE JOKERS AT HOME?
THIS ISN'T THE *MINOR LEAGUES*. YOU GOT THAT?
I DON'T WANT THEM BECOMING HOSTAGES OR HUMAN SHIELDS.
IT'LL JUST MAKE THIS A HASSLE.
IF THAT HAPPENS, WILL YOU ORDER THEM TO COMMIT HARA-KIRI?
HEY, HAND-SOME DUDE...
AMAI MASK...
...ARE *YOU* ON THE TEAM?

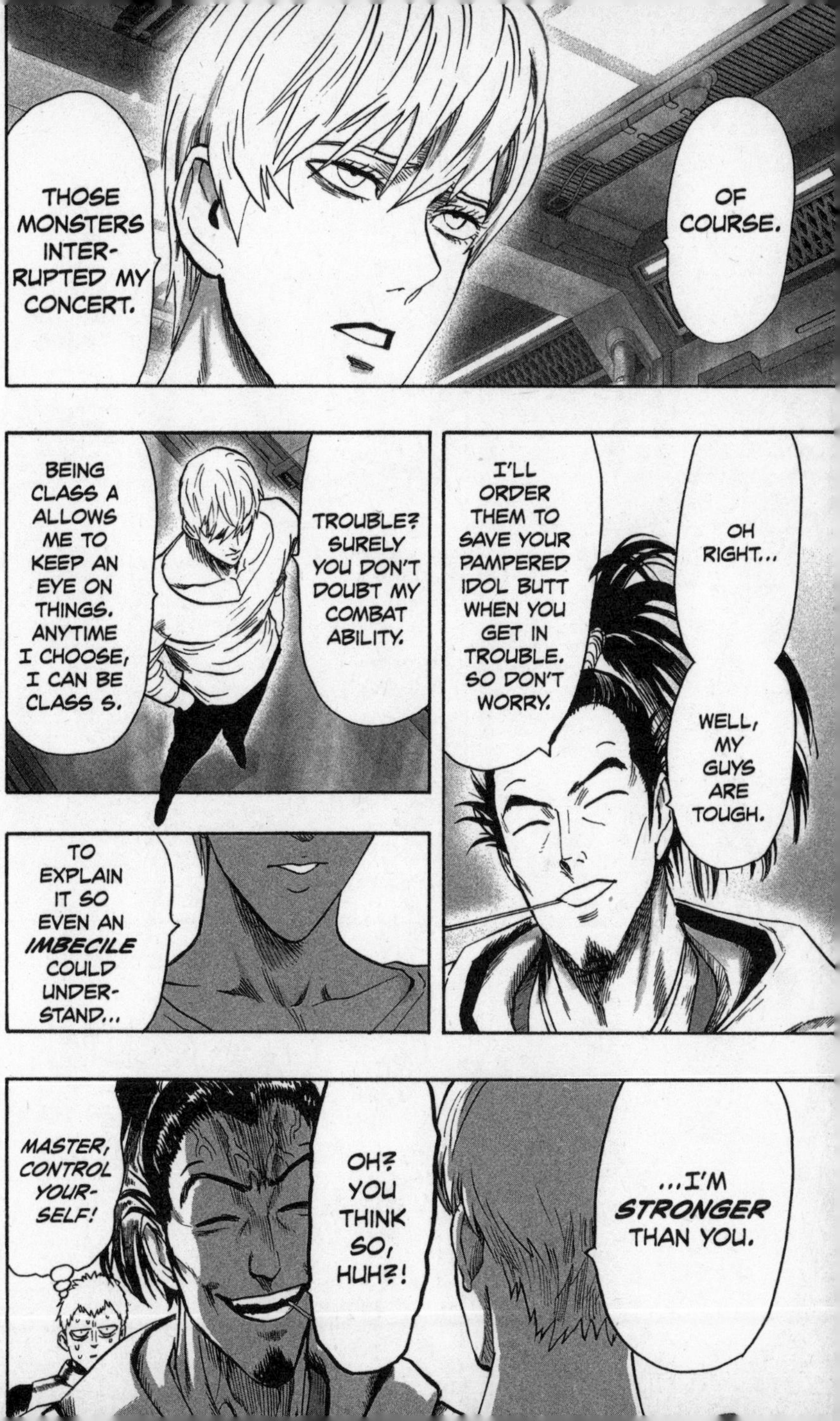

OF COURSE.
THOSE MONSTERS INTER-RUPTED MY CONCERT.
OH RIGHT...
I'LL ORDER THEM TO SAVE YOUR PAMPERED IDOL BUTT WHEN YOU GET IN TROUBLE. SO DON'T WORRY.
WELL, MY GUYS ARE TOUGH.
TROUBLE? SURELY YOU DON'T DOUBT MY COMBAT ABILITY.
BEING CLASS A ALLOWS ME TO KEEP AN EYE ON THINGS. ANYTIME I CHOOSE, I CAN BE CLASS S.
TO EXPLAIN IT SO EVEN AN *IMBECILE* COULD UNDER-STAND...
...I'M *STRONGER* THAN YOU.
OH? YOU THINK SO, HUH?!
MASTER, CONTROL YOUR-SELF!

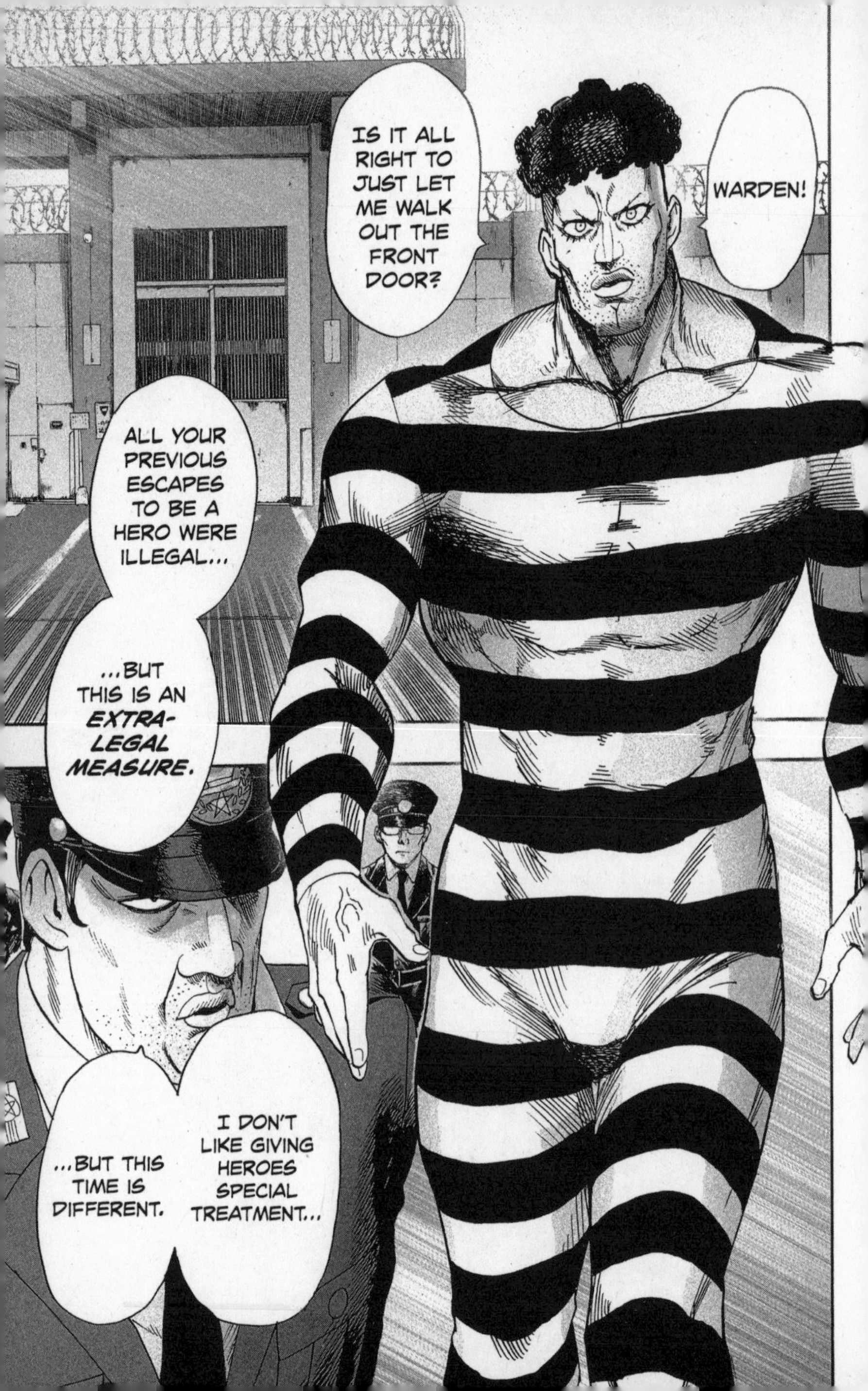
WARDEN!
IS IT ALL RIGHT TO JUST LET ME WALK OUT THE FRONT DOOR?
ALL YOUR PREVIOUS ESCAPES TO BE A HERO WERE ILLEGAL...
...BUT THIS IS AN *EXTRA-LEGAL MEASURE*.
I DON'T LIKE GIVING HEROES SPECIAL TREATMENT...
...BUT THIS TIME IS DIFFERENT.

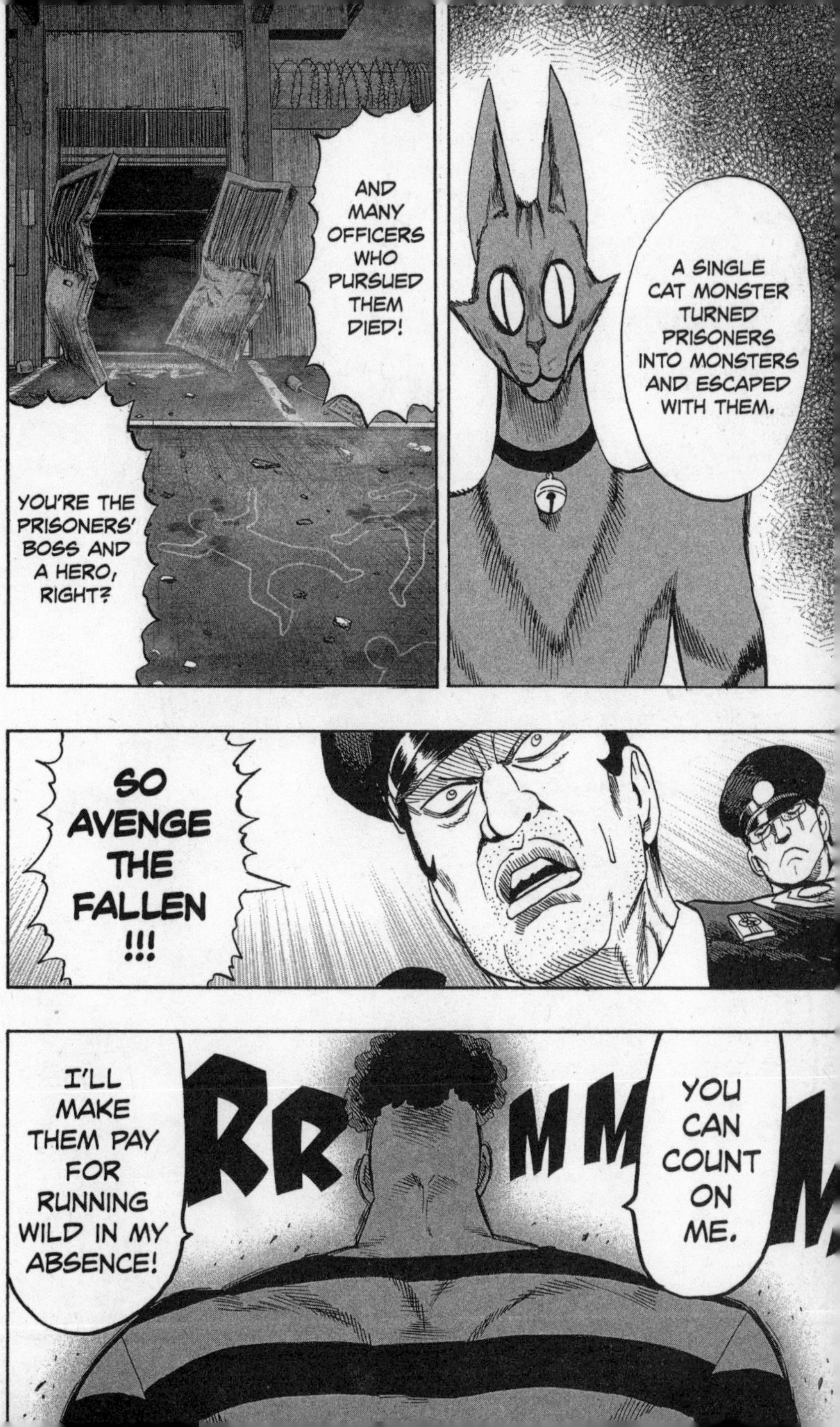
A SINGLE CAT MONSTER TURNED PRISONERS INTO MONSTERS AND ESCAPED WITH THEM.
AND MANY OFFICERS WHO PURSUED THEM DIED!
YOU'RE THE PRISONERS' BOSS AND A HERO, RIGHT?
SO AVENGE THE FALLEN!!!
YOU CAN COUNT ON ME.
RRMMM
I'LL MAKE THEM PAY FOR RUNNING WILD IN MY ABSENCE!

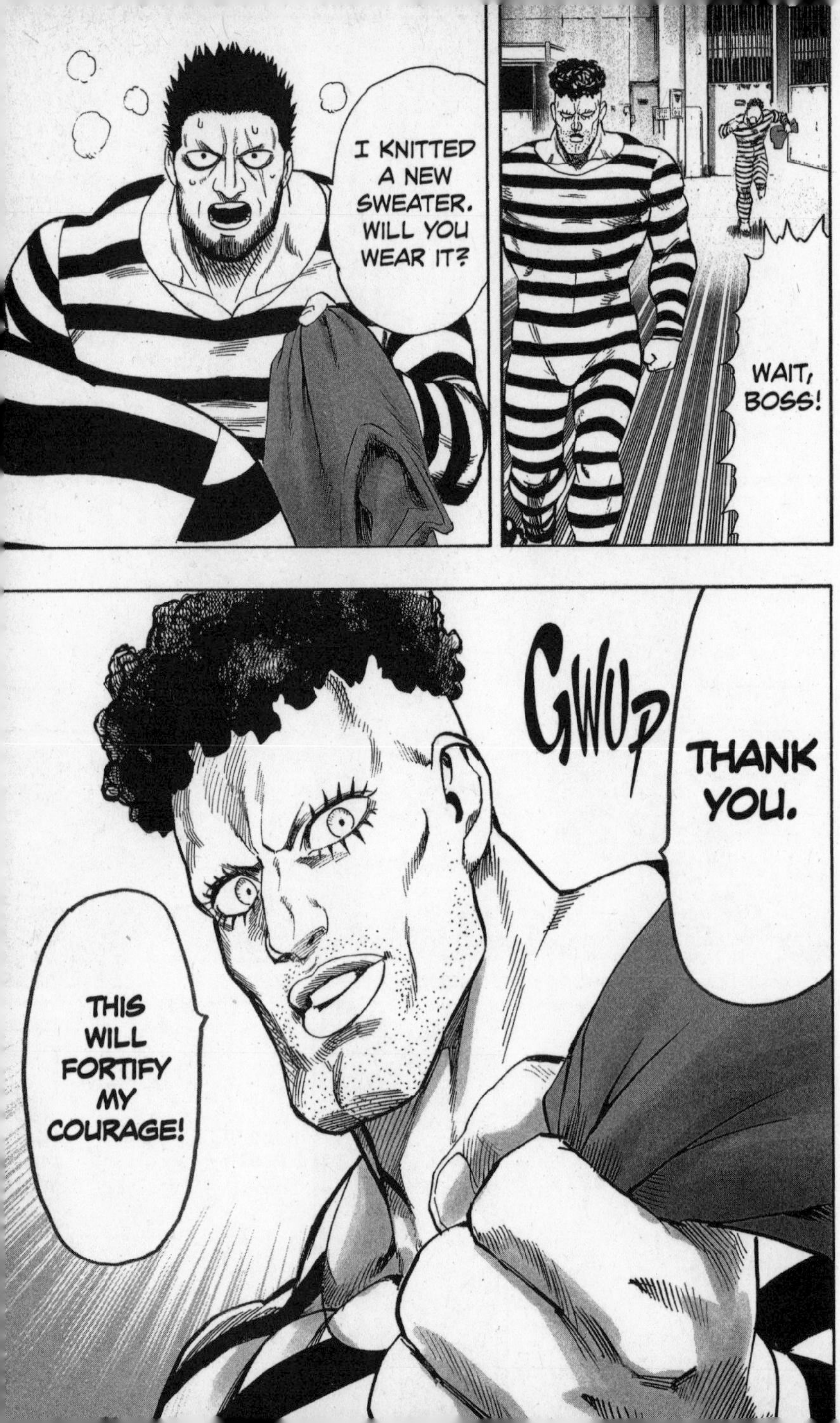
WAIT, BOSS!
I KNITTED A NEW SWEATER. WILL YOU WEAR IT?
GWUP
THANK YOU.
THIS WILL FORTIFY MY COURAGE!

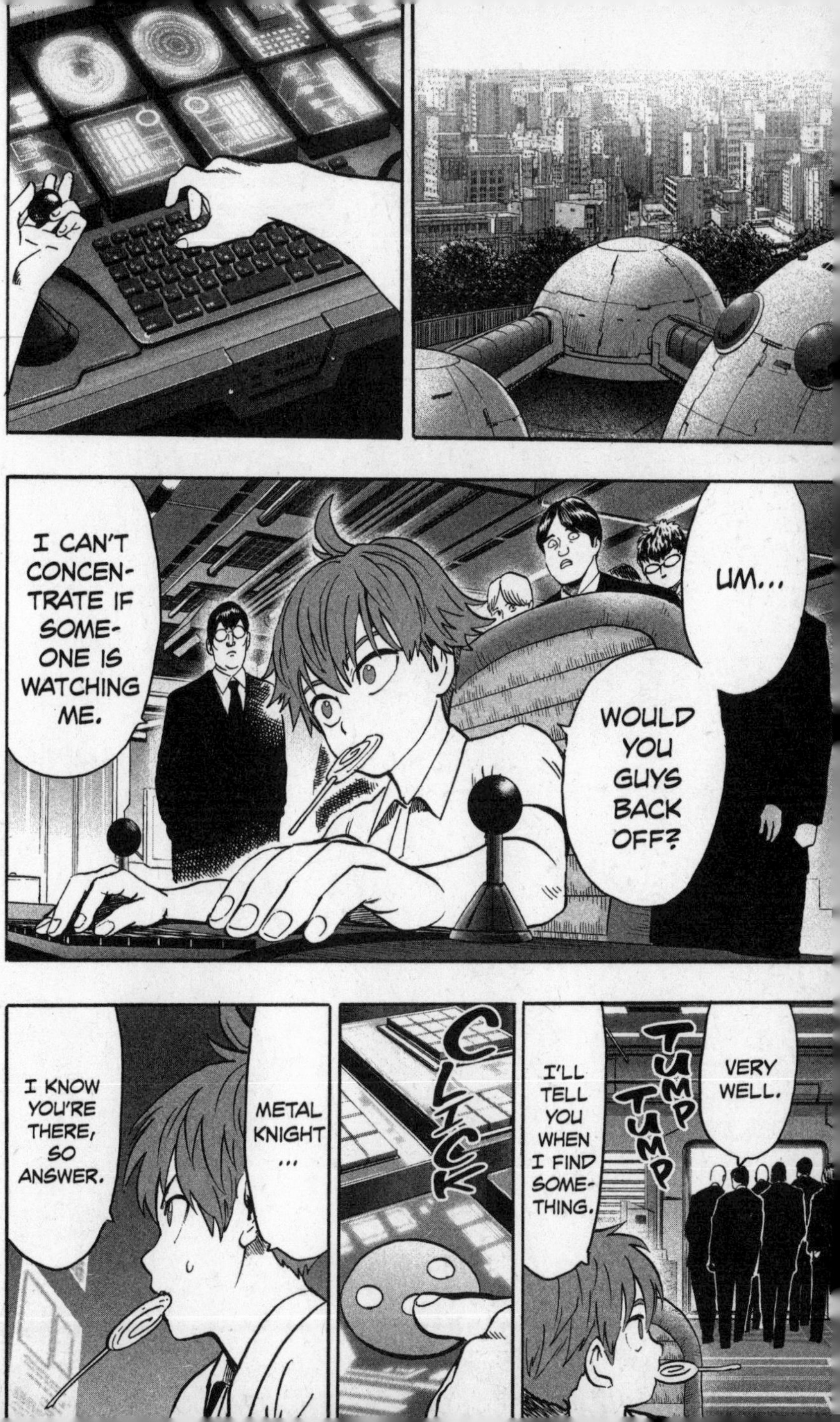
UM...
WOULD YOU GUYS BACK OFF?
I CAN'T CONCENTRATE IF SOMEONE IS WATCHING ME.
VERY WELL.
TUMP TUMP
I'LL TELL YOU WHEN I FIND SOMETHING.
CLICK
METAL KNIGHT...
I KNOW YOU'RE THERE, SO ANSWER.

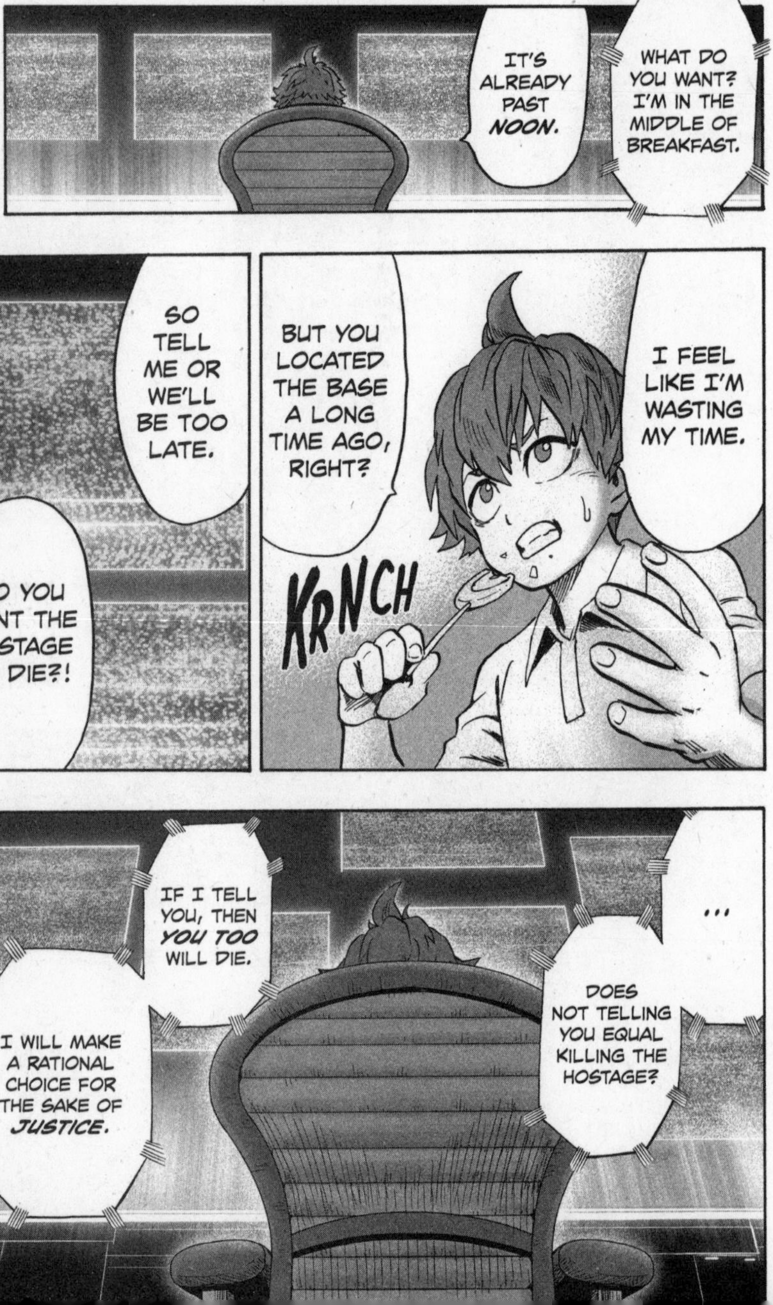
WHAT DO YOU WANT? I'M IN THE MIDDLE OF BREAKFAST.
IT'S ALREADY PAST NOON.
I FEEL LIKE I'M WASTING MY TIME.
BUT YOU LOCATED THE BASE A LONG TIME AGO, RIGHT?
KRNCH
SO TELL ME OR WE'LL BE TOO LATE.
DO YOU WANT THE HOSTAGE TO DIE?!
...
DOES NOT TELLING YOU EQUAL KILLING THE HOSTAGE?
IF I TELL YOU, THEN YOU TOO WILL DIE.
I WILL MAKE A RATIONAL CHOICE FOR THE SAKE OF JUSTICE.

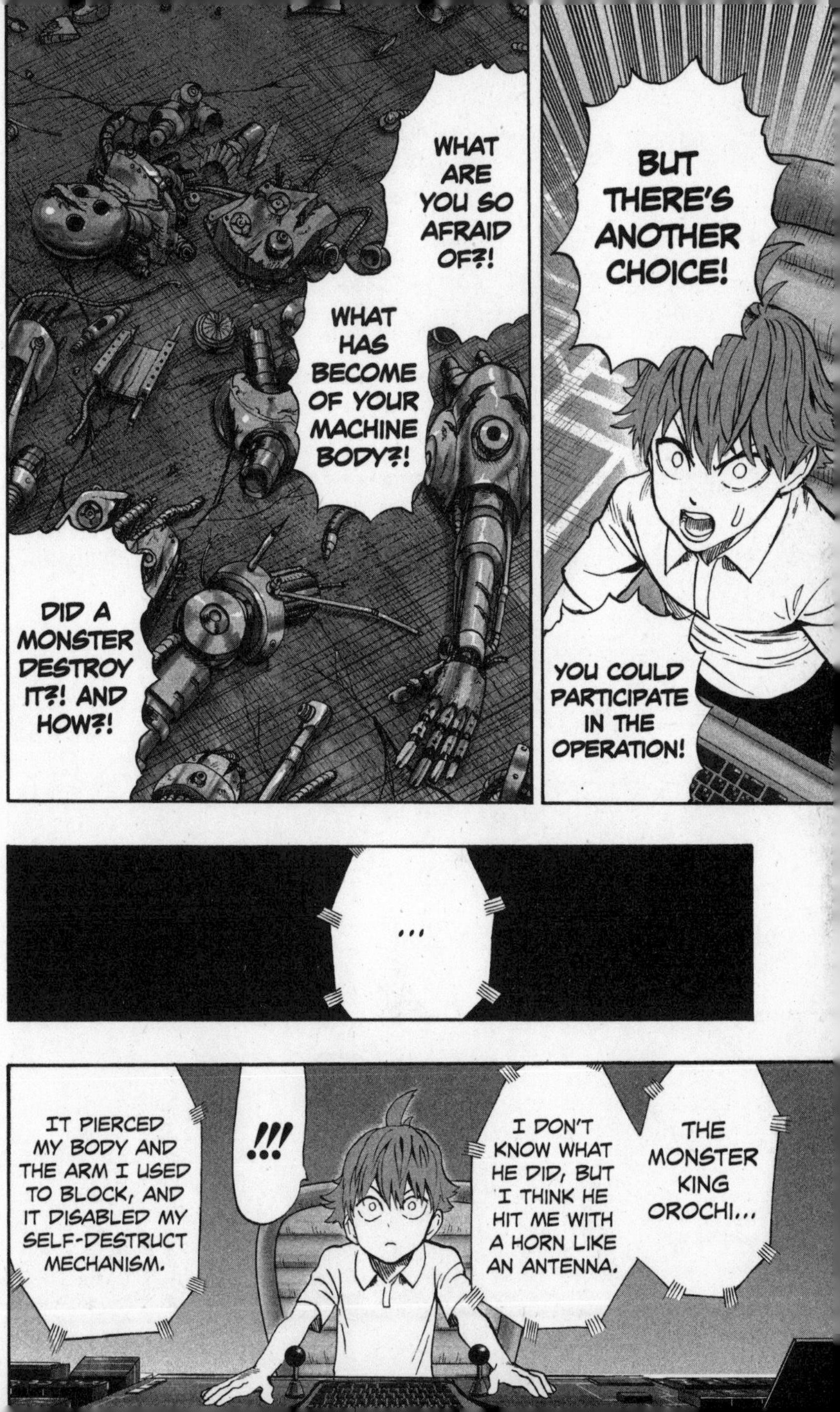
BUT THERE'S ANOTHER CHOICE!
YOU COULD PARTICIPATE IN THE OPERATION!
WHAT ARE YOU SO AFRAID OF?!
WHAT HAS BECOME OF YOUR MACHINE BODY?!
DID A MONSTER DESTROY IT?! AND HOW?!
...
THE MONSTER KING OROCHI...
I DON'T KNOW WHAT HE DID, BUT I THINK HE HIT ME WITH A HORN LIKE AN ANTENNA.
!!!
IT PIERCED MY BODY AND THE ARM I USED TO BLOCK, AND IT DISABLED MY SELF-DESTRUCT MECHANISM.

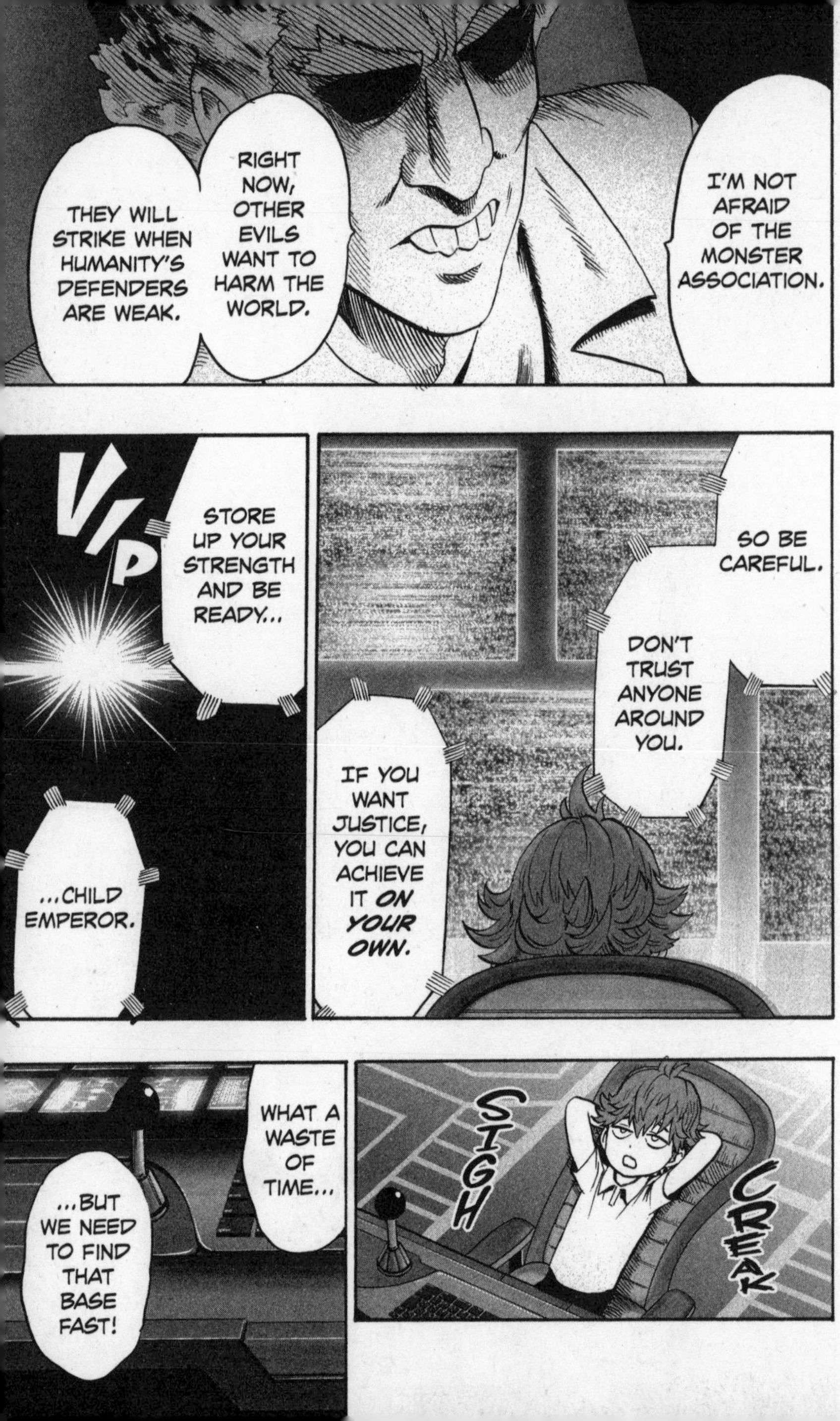
I'M NOT AFRAID OF THE MONSTER ASSOCIATION.
RIGHT NOW, OTHER EVILS WANT TO HARM THE WORLD.
THEY WILL STRIKE WHEN HUMANITY'S DEFENDERS ARE WEAK.
SO BE CAREFUL.
DON'T TRUST ANYONE AROUND YOU.
IF YOU WANT JUSTICE, YOU CAN ACHIEVE IT *ON YOUR OWN*.
STORE UP YOUR STRENGTH AND BE READY...
VIP
...CHILD EMPEROR.
SIGH
CREAK
WHAT A WASTE OF TIME...
...BUT WE NEED TO FIND THAT BASE FAST!

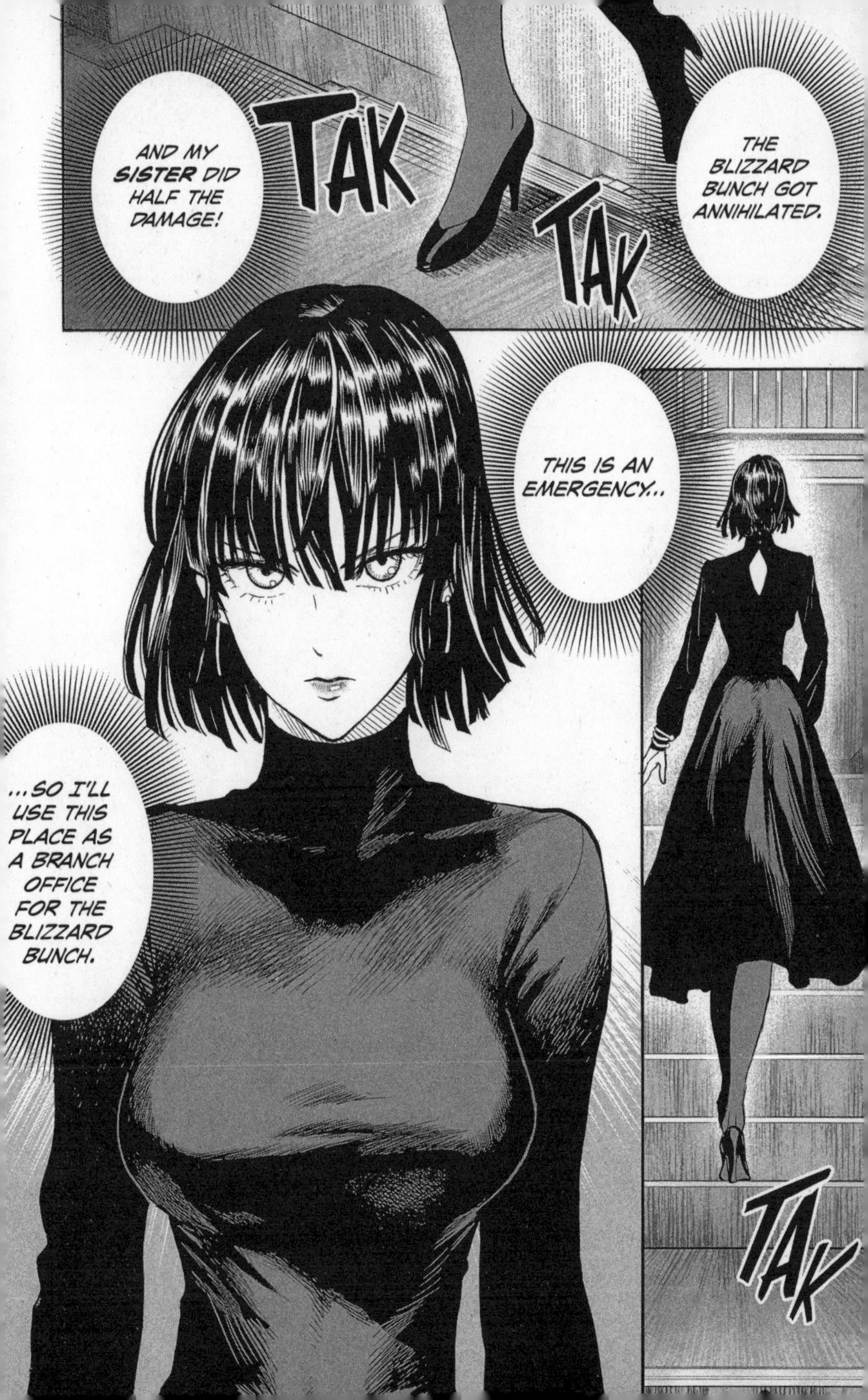
THE BLIZZARD BUNCH GOT ANNIHILATED.
TAK
TAK
AND MY SISTER DID HALF THE DAMAGE!
TAK
THIS IS AN EMERGENCY...
...SO I'LL USE THIS PLACE AS A BRANCH OFFICE FOR THE BLIZZARD BUNCH.

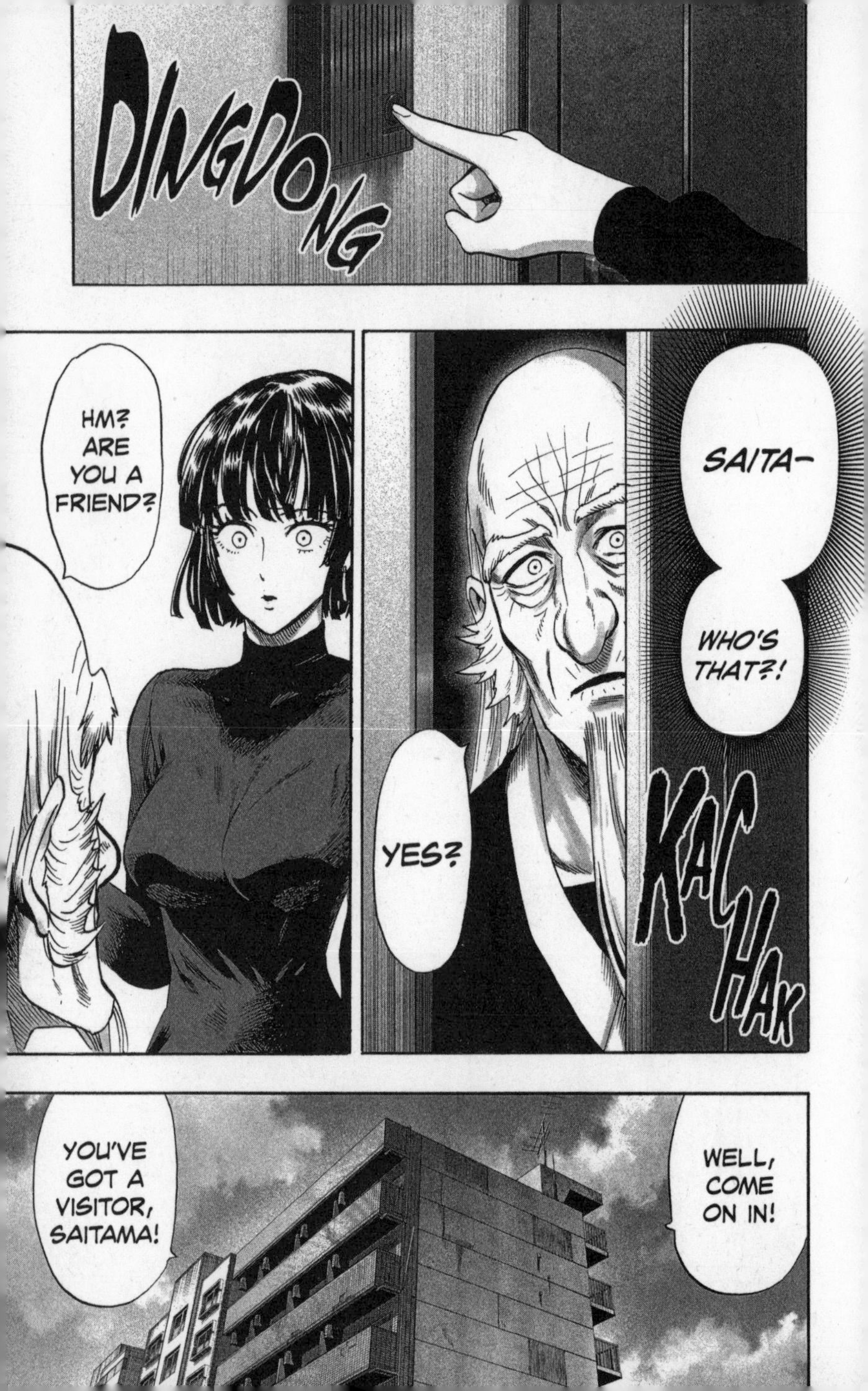
DINGDONG
SAITA-
WHO'S THAT?!
KACHAK
YES?
HM? ARE YOU A FRIEND?
WELL, COME ON IN!
YOU'VE GOT A VISITOR, SAITAMA!

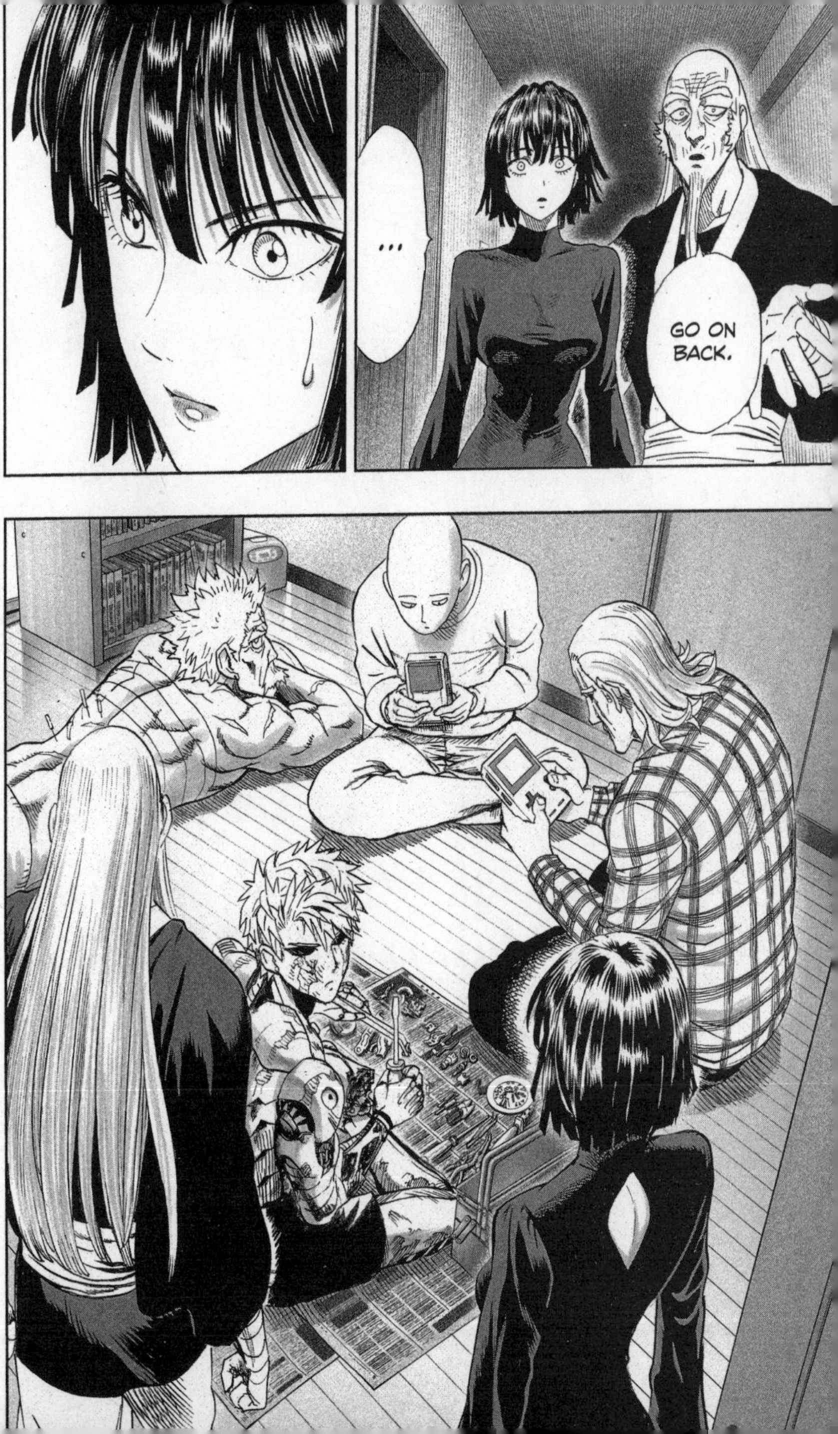
GO ON BACK.
...

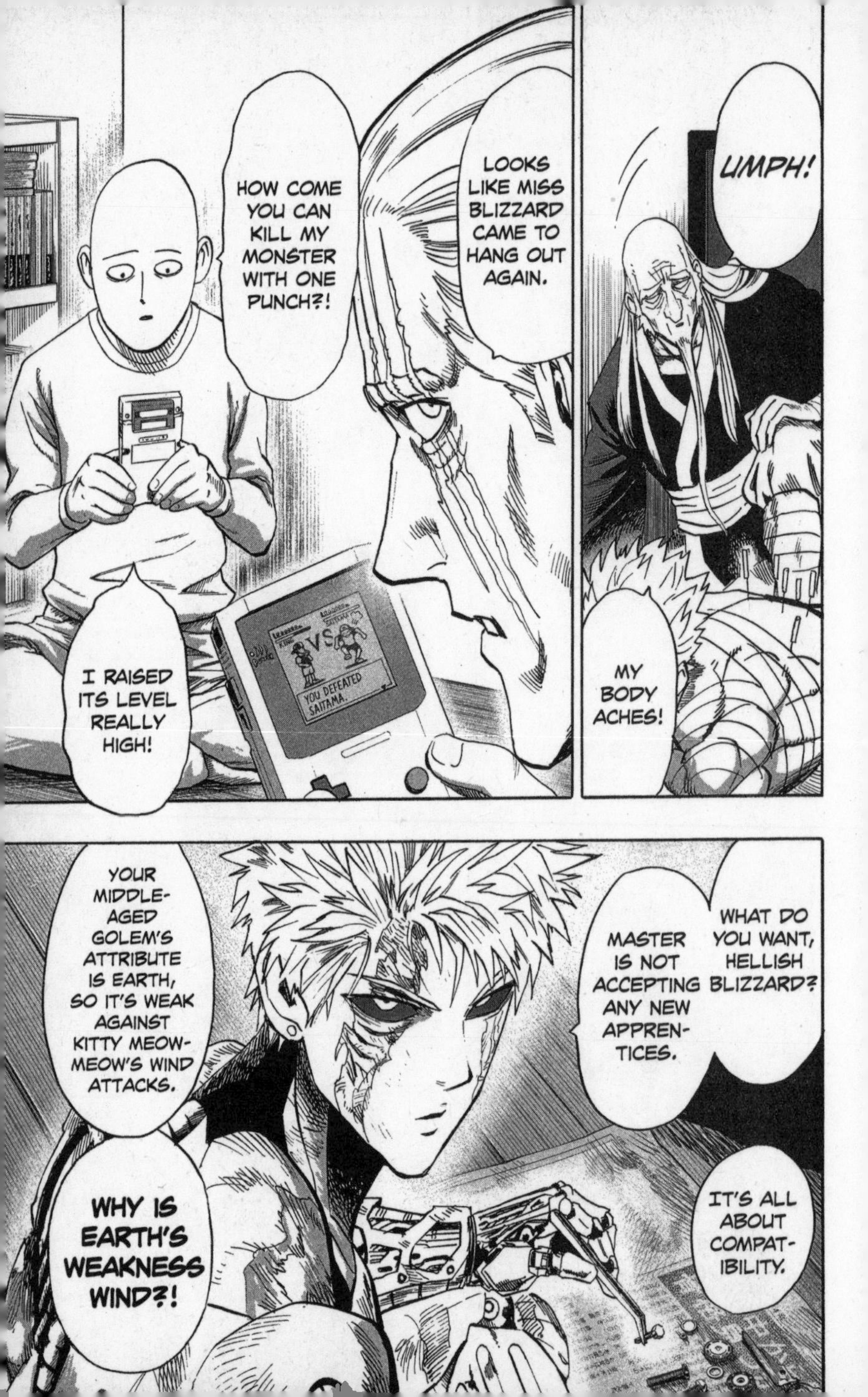
UMPH!
MY BODY ACHES!
LOOKS LIKE MISS BLIZZARD CAME TO HANG OUT AGAIN.
HOW COME YOU CAN KILL MY MONSTER WITH ONE PUNCH?!
YOU DEFEATED SAITAMA.
I RAISED ITS LEVEL REALLY HIGH!
WHAT DO YOU WANT, HELLISH BLIZZARD?
MASTER IS NOT ACCEPTING ANY NEW APPREN-TICES.
IT'S ALL ABOUT COMPAT-IBILITY.
YOUR MIDDLE-AGED GOLEM'S ATTRIBUTE IS EARTH, SO IT'S WEAK AGAINST KITTY MEOW-MEOW'S WIND ATTACKS.
WHY IS EARTH'S WEAKNESS WIND?!

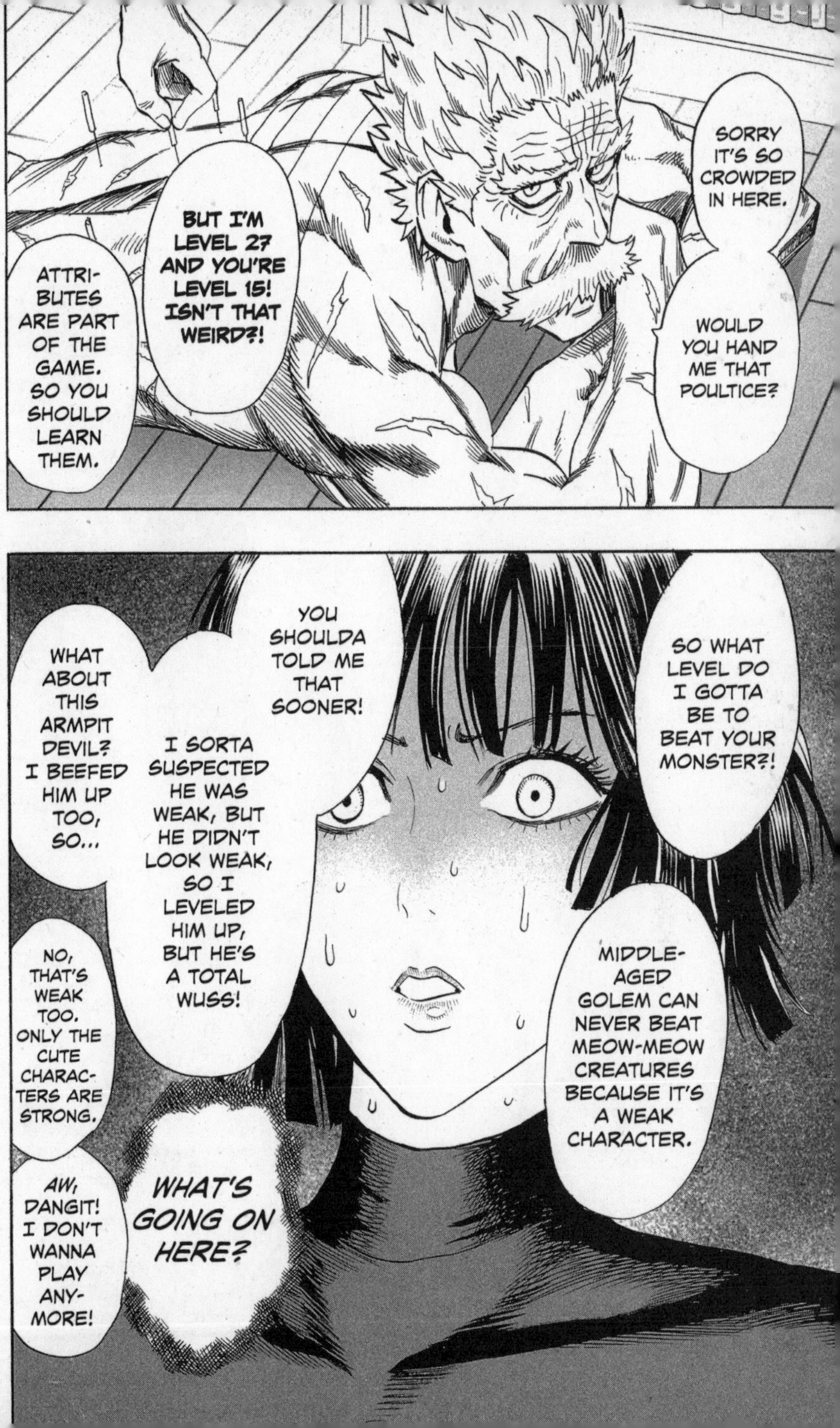
SORRY IT'S SO CROWDED IN HERE.
WOULD YOU HAND ME THAT POULTICE?
BUT I'M LEVEL 27 AND YOU'RE LEVEL 15! ISN'T THAT WEIRD?!
ATTRI-BUTES ARE PART OF THE GAME. SO YOU SHOULD LEARN THEM.
SO WHAT LEVEL DO I GOTTA BE TO BEAT YOUR MONSTER?!
MIDDLE-AGED GOLEM CAN NEVER BEAT MEOW-MEOW CREATURES BECAUSE IT'S A WEAK CHARACTER.
YOU SHOULDA TOLD ME THAT SOONER!
I SORTA SUSPECTED HE WAS WEAK, BUT HE DIDN'T LOOK WEAK, SO I LEVELED HIM UP, BUT HE'S A TOTAL WUSS!
WHAT ABOUT THIS ARMPIT DEVIL? I BEEFED HIM UP TOO, SO...
NO, THAT'S WEAK TOO. ONLY THE CUTE CHARAC-TERS ARE STRONG.
WHAT'S GOING ON HERE?
AW, DANGIT! I DON'T WANNA PLAY ANY-MORE!

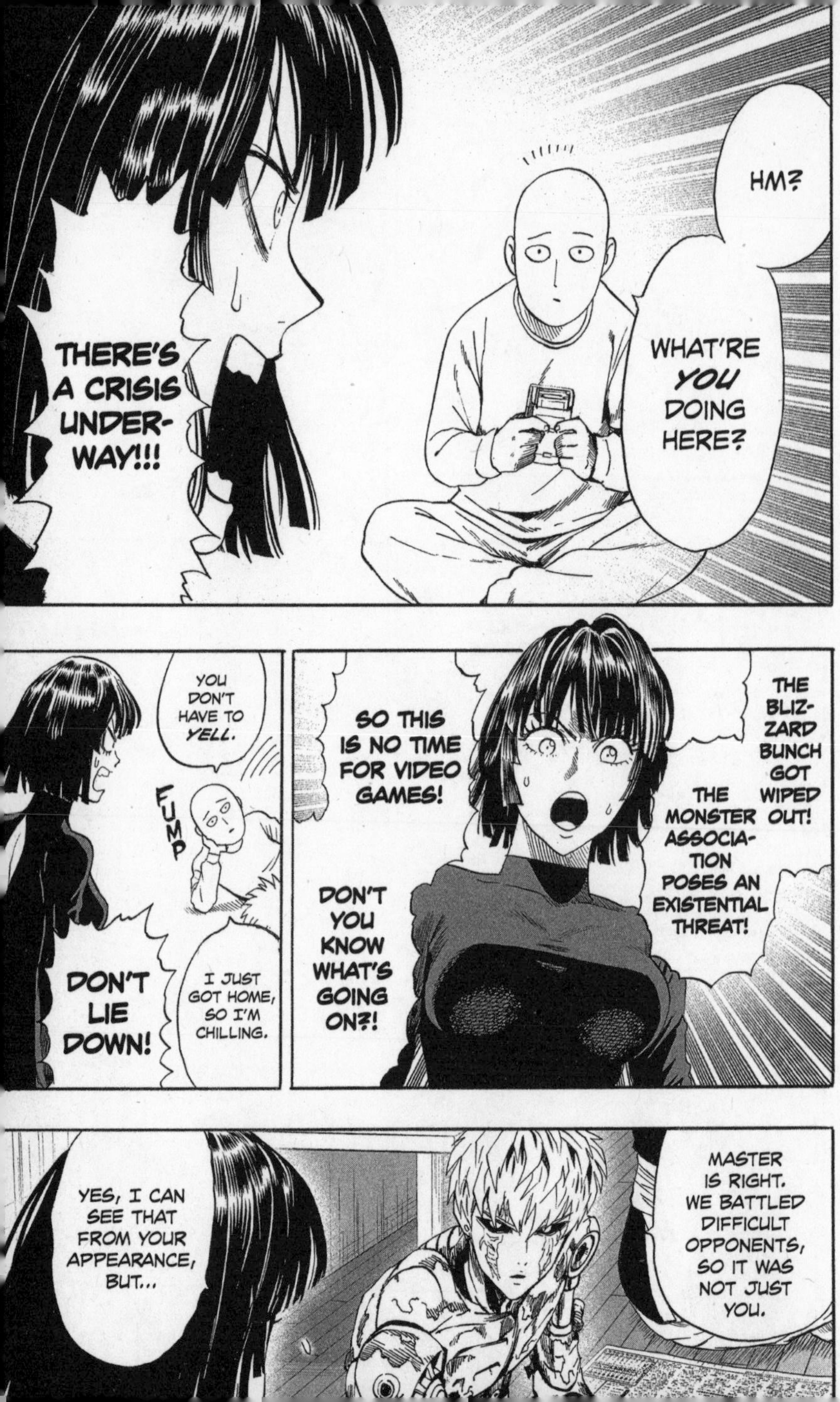
HM?
WHAT'RE *YOU* DOING HERE?
THERE'S A CRISIS UNDER-WAY!!!
THE BLIZ-ZARD BUNCH GOT WIPED OUT!
THE MONSTER ASSOCIA-TION POSES AN EXISTENTIAL THREAT!
SO THIS IS NO TIME FOR VIDEO GAMES!
DON'T YOU KNOW WHAT'S GOING ON?!
YOU DON'T HAVE TO *YELL*.
FUMP
I JUST GOT HOME, SO I'M CHILLING.
DON'T LIE DOWN!
MASTER IS RIGHT. WE BATTLED DIFFICULT OPPONENTS, SO IT WAS NOT JUST YOU.
YES, I CAN SEE THAT FROM YOUR APPEARANCE, BUT...

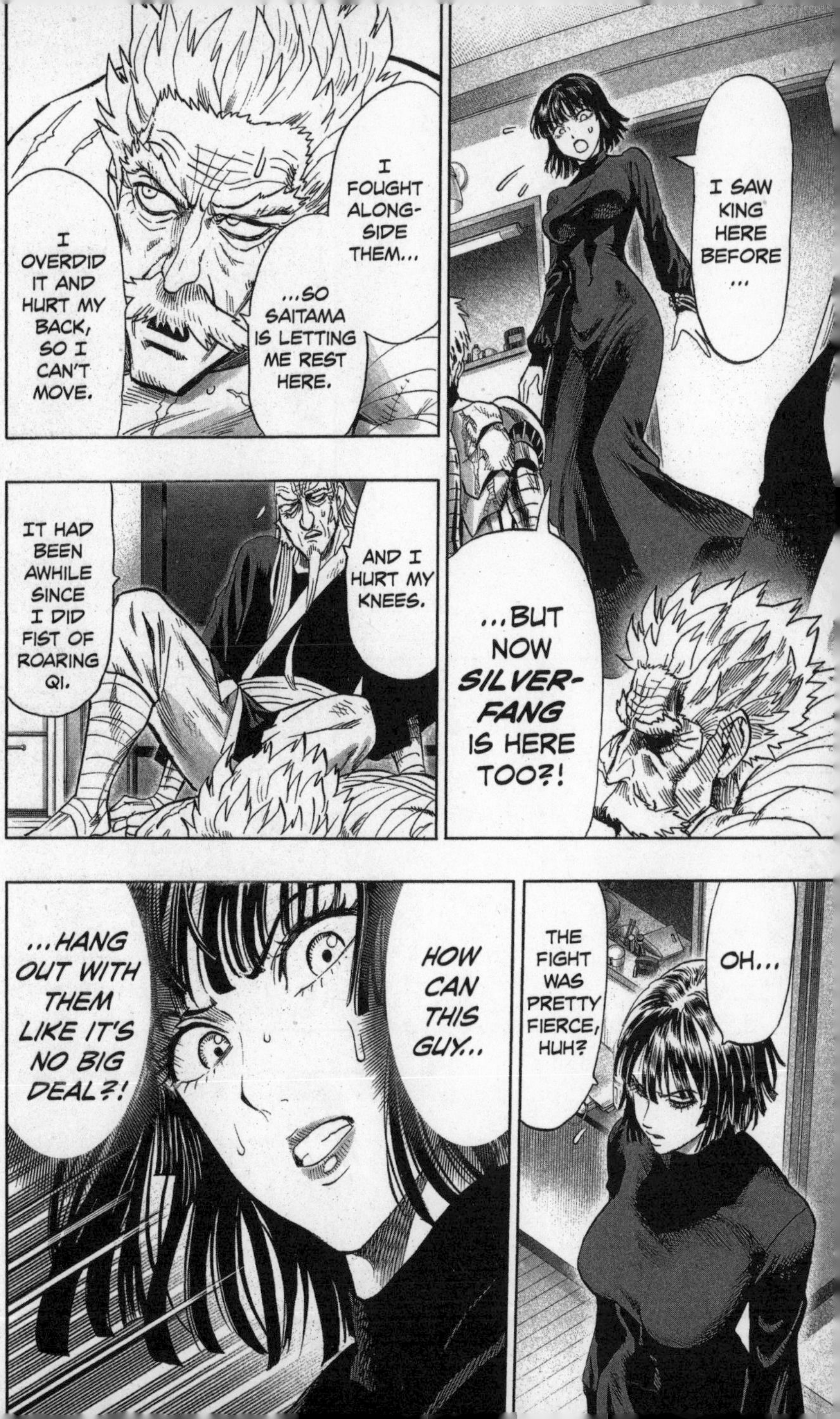
I SAW KING HERE BEFORE ...
...BUT NOW *SILVERFANG* IS HERE TOO?!
I FOUGHT ALONGSIDE THEM...
...SO SAITAMA IS LETTING ME REST HERE.
I OVERDID IT AND HURT MY BACK, SO I CAN'T MOVE.
AND I HURT MY KNEES.
IT HAD BEEN AWHILE SINCE I DID FIST OF ROARING QI.
OH...
THE FIGHT WAS PRETTY FIERCE, HUH?
HOW CAN THIS GUY...
...HANG OUT WITH THEM LIKE IT'S NO BIG DEAL?!

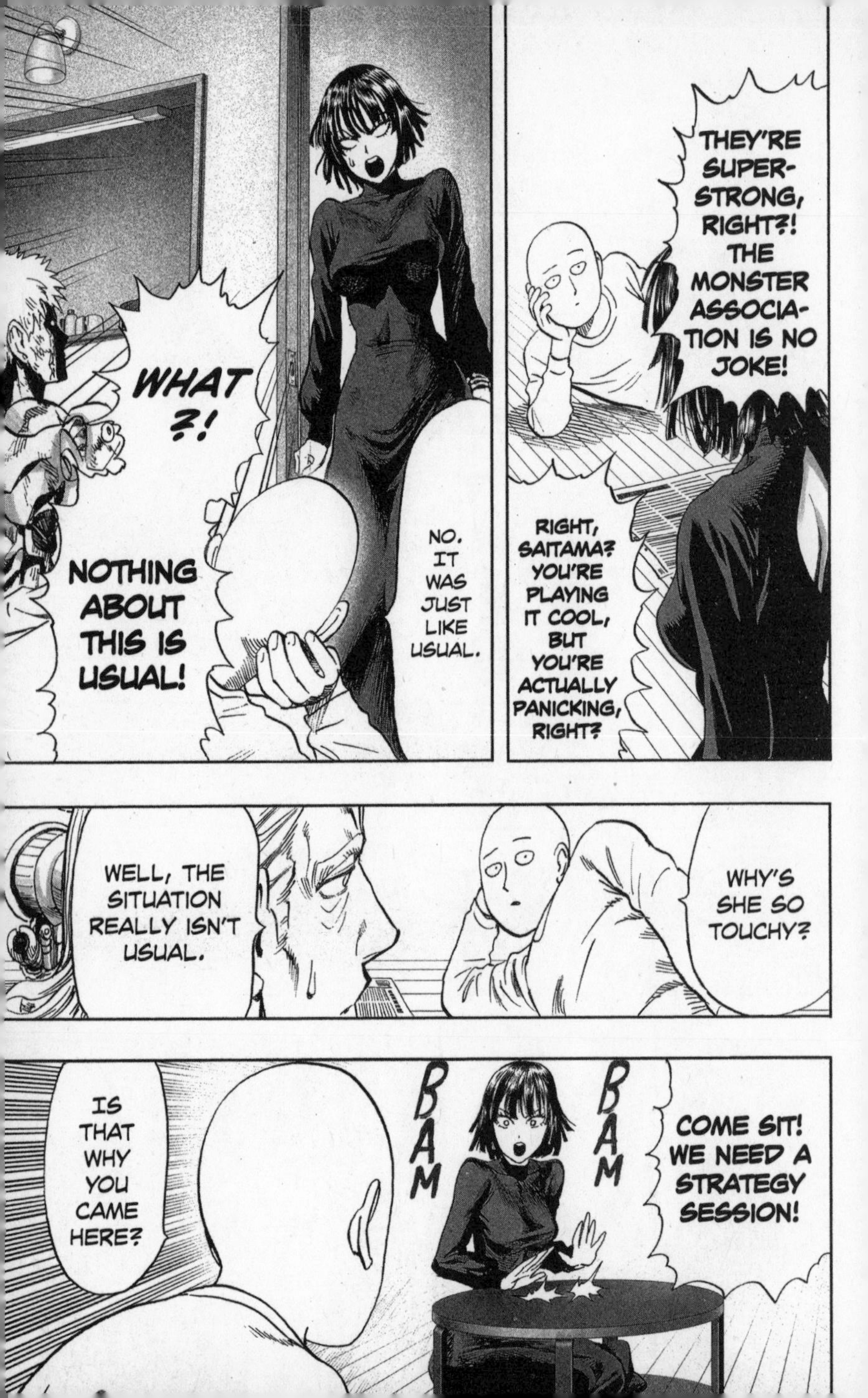
THEY'RE SUPER-STRONG, RIGHT?! THE MONSTER ASSOCIATION IS NO JOKE!
RIGHT, SAITAMA? YOU'RE PLAYING IT COOL, BUT YOU'RE ACTUALLY PANICKING, RIGHT?
NO. IT WAS JUST LIKE USUAL.
WHAT?!
NOTHING ABOUT THIS IS USUAL!
WHY'S SHE SO TOUCHY?
WELL, THE SITUATION REALLY ISN'T USUAL.
COME SIT! WE NEED A STRATEGY SESSION!
BAM
BAM
IS THAT WHY YOU CAME HERE?

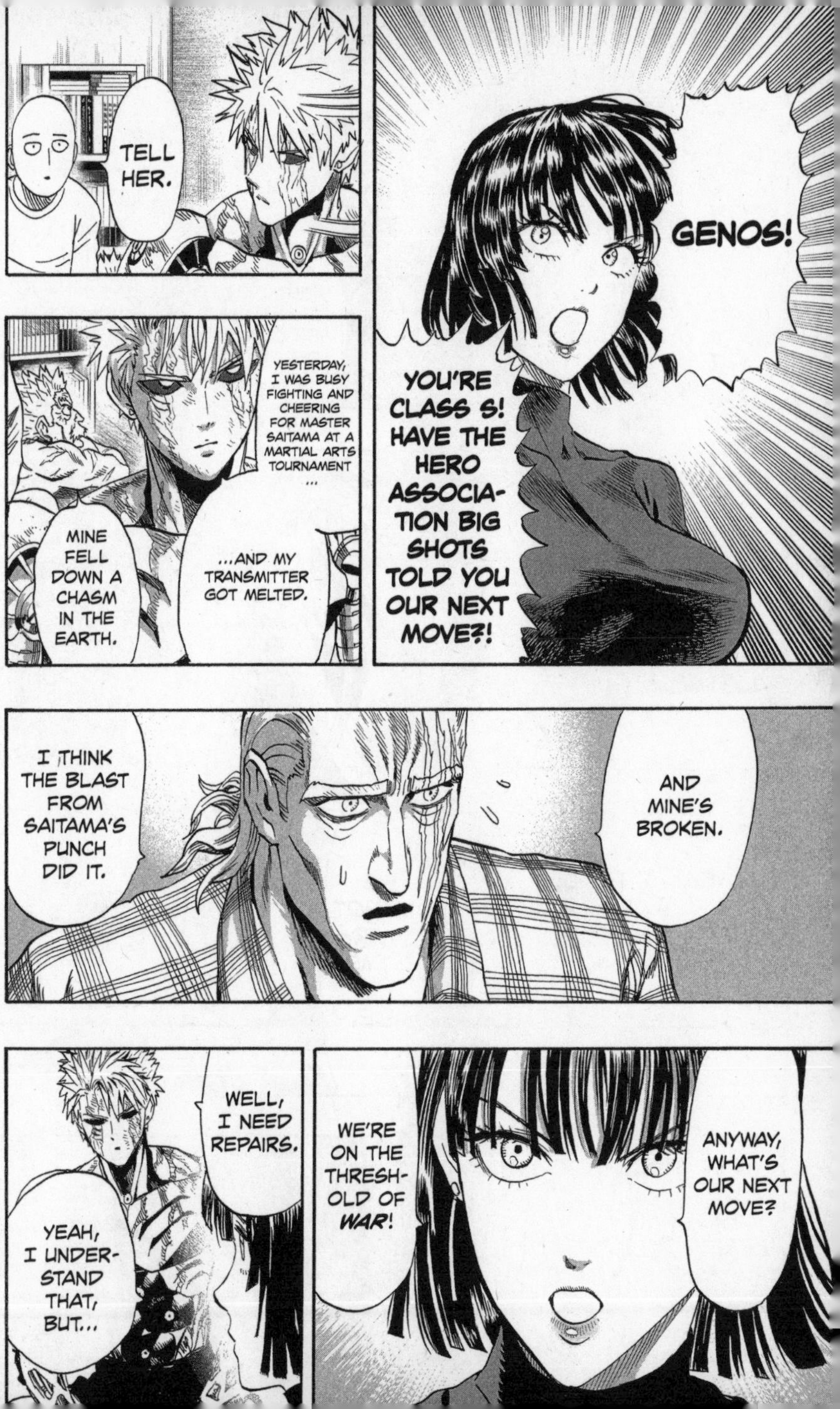
GENOS!
YOU'RE CLASS S! HAVE THE HERO ASSOCIATION BIG SHOTS TOLD YOU OUR NEXT MOVE?!
TELL HER.
YESTERDAY, I WAS BUSY FIGHTING AND CHEERING FOR MASTER SAITAMA AT A MARTIAL ARTS TOURNAMENT ...
...AND MY TRANSMITTER GOT MELTED.
MINE FELL DOWN A CHASM IN THE EARTH.
AND MINE'S BROKEN.
I THINK THE BLAST FROM SAITAMA'S PUNCH DID IT.
ANYWAY, WHAT'S OUR NEXT MOVE?
WE'RE ON THE THRESHOLD OF *WAR*!
WELL, I NEED REPAIRS.
YEAH, I UNDERSTAND THAT, BUT...

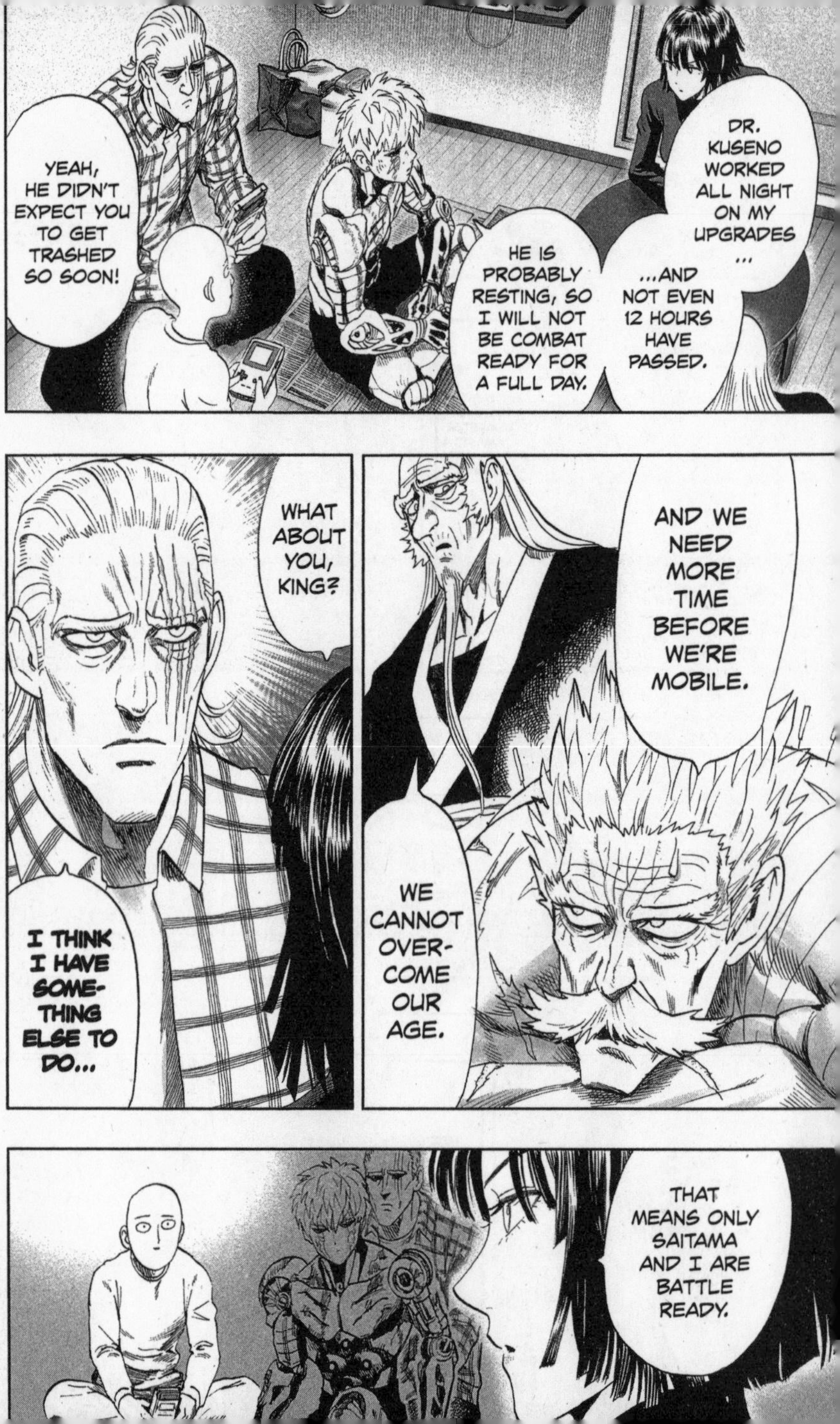
DR. KUSENO WORKED ALL NIGHT ON MY UPGRADES ...
...AND NOT EVEN 12 HOURS HAVE PASSED.
HE IS PROBABLY RESTING, SO I WILL NOT BE COMBAT READY FOR A FULL DAY.
YEAH, HE DIDN'T EXPECT YOU TO GET TRASHED SO SOON!
AND WE NEED MORE TIME BEFORE WE'RE MOBILE.
WE CANNOT OVERCOME OUR AGE.
WHAT ABOUT YOU, KING?
I THINK I HAVE SOMETHING ELSE TO DO...
THAT MEANS ONLY SAITAMA AND I ARE BATTLE READY.

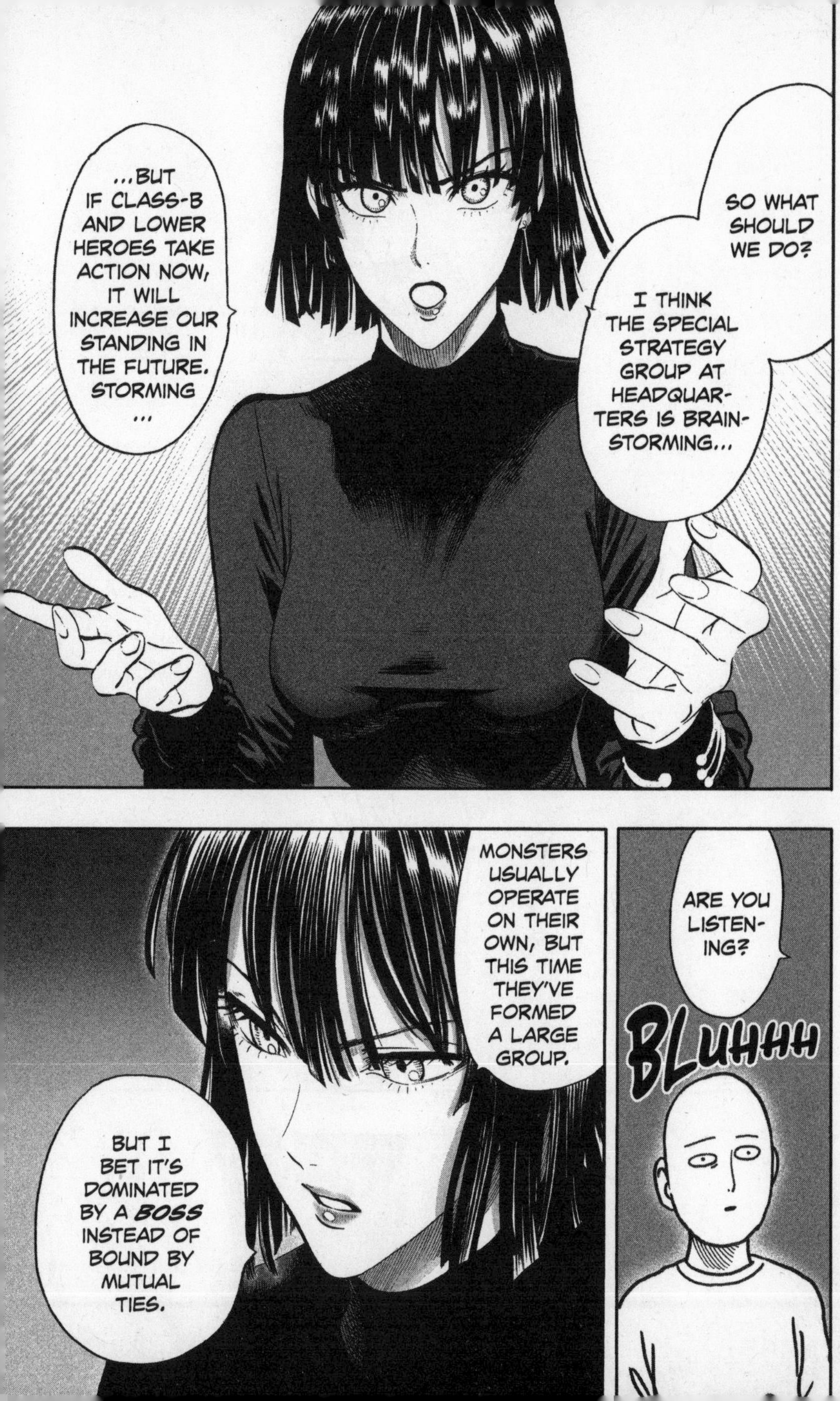
SO WHAT SHOULD WE DO?
I THINK THE SPECIAL STRATEGY GROUP AT HEADQUAR-TERS IS BRAIN-STORMING...
...BUT IF CLASS-B AND LOWER HEROES TAKE ACTION NOW, IT WILL INCREASE OUR STANDING IN THE FUTURE. STORMING ...
ARE YOU LISTEN-ING?
BLUHHH
MONSTERS USUALLY OPERATE ON THEIR OWN, BUT THIS TIME THEY'VE FORMED A LARGE GROUP.
BUT I BET IT'S DOMINATED BY A *BOSS* INSTEAD OF BOUND BY MUTUAL TIES.

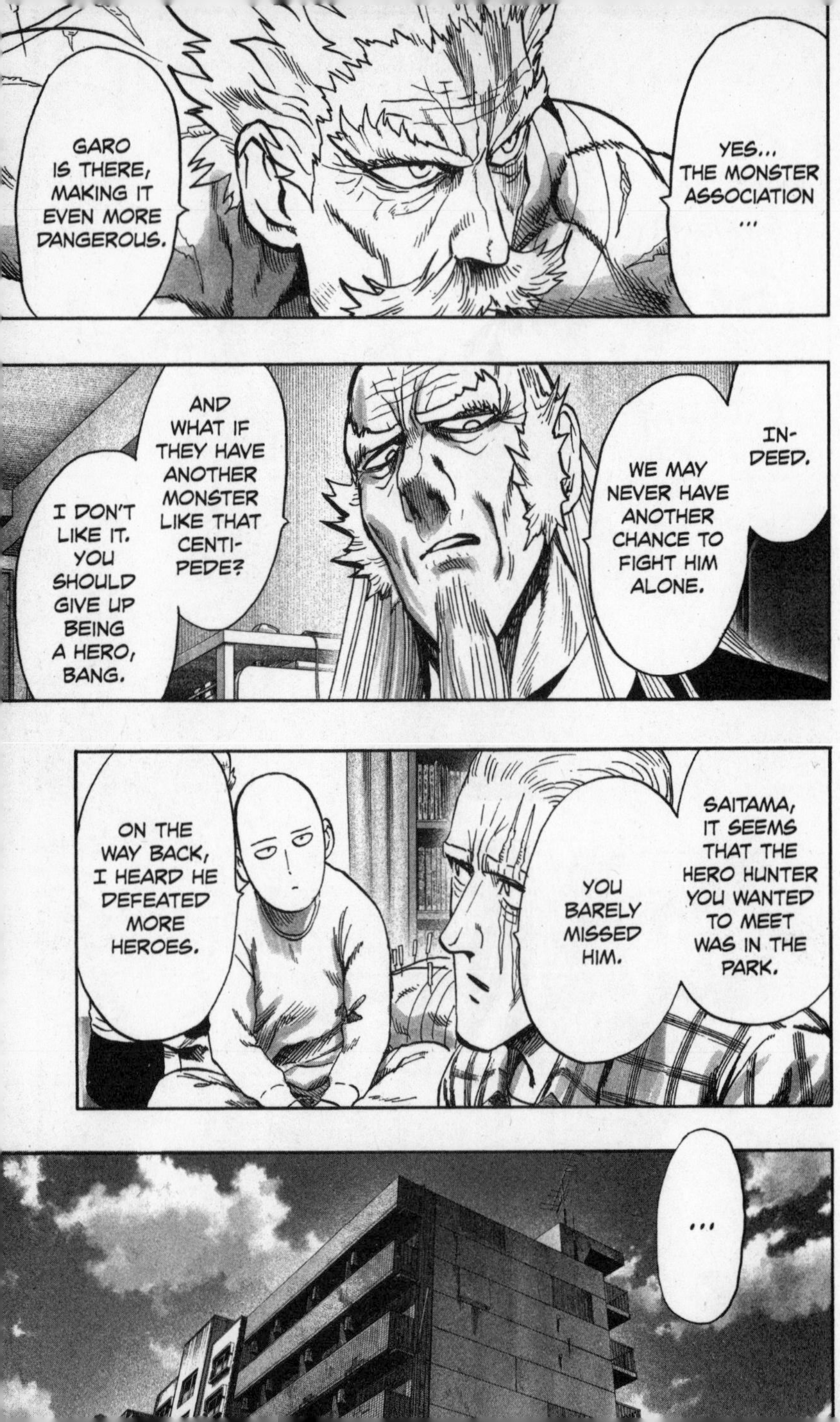
YES... THE MONSTER ASSOCIATION ...
GARO IS THERE, MAKING IT EVEN MORE DANGEROUS.
IN-DEED.
WE MAY NEVER HAVE ANOTHER CHANCE TO FIGHT HIM ALONE.
AND WHAT IF THEY HAVE ANOTHER MONSTER LIKE THAT CENTI-PEDE?
I DON'T LIKE IT. YOU SHOULD GIVE UP BEING A HERO, BANG.
SAITAMA, IT SEEMS THAT THE HERO HUNTER YOU WANTED TO MEET WAS IN THE PARK.
YOU BARELY MISSED HIM.
ON THE WAY BACK, I HEARD HE DEFEATED MORE HEROES.
...

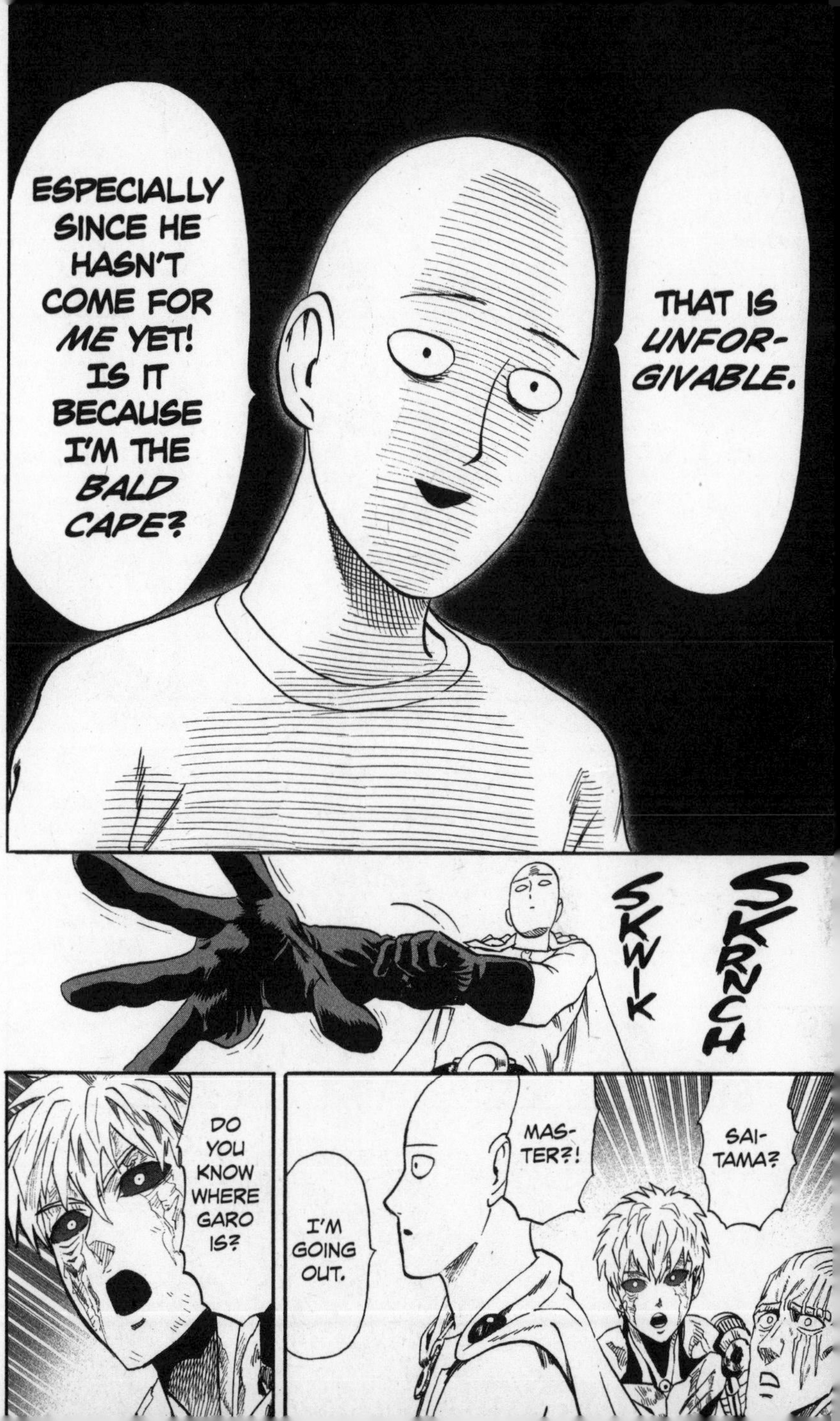
THAT IS UNFORGIVABLE.
ESPECIALLY SINCE HE HASN'T COME FOR ME YET! IS IT BECAUSE I'M THE BALD CAPE?
SKRNCH
SKWIK
SAI-TAMA?
MAS-TER?!
I'M GOING OUT.
DO YOU KNOW WHERE GARO IS?

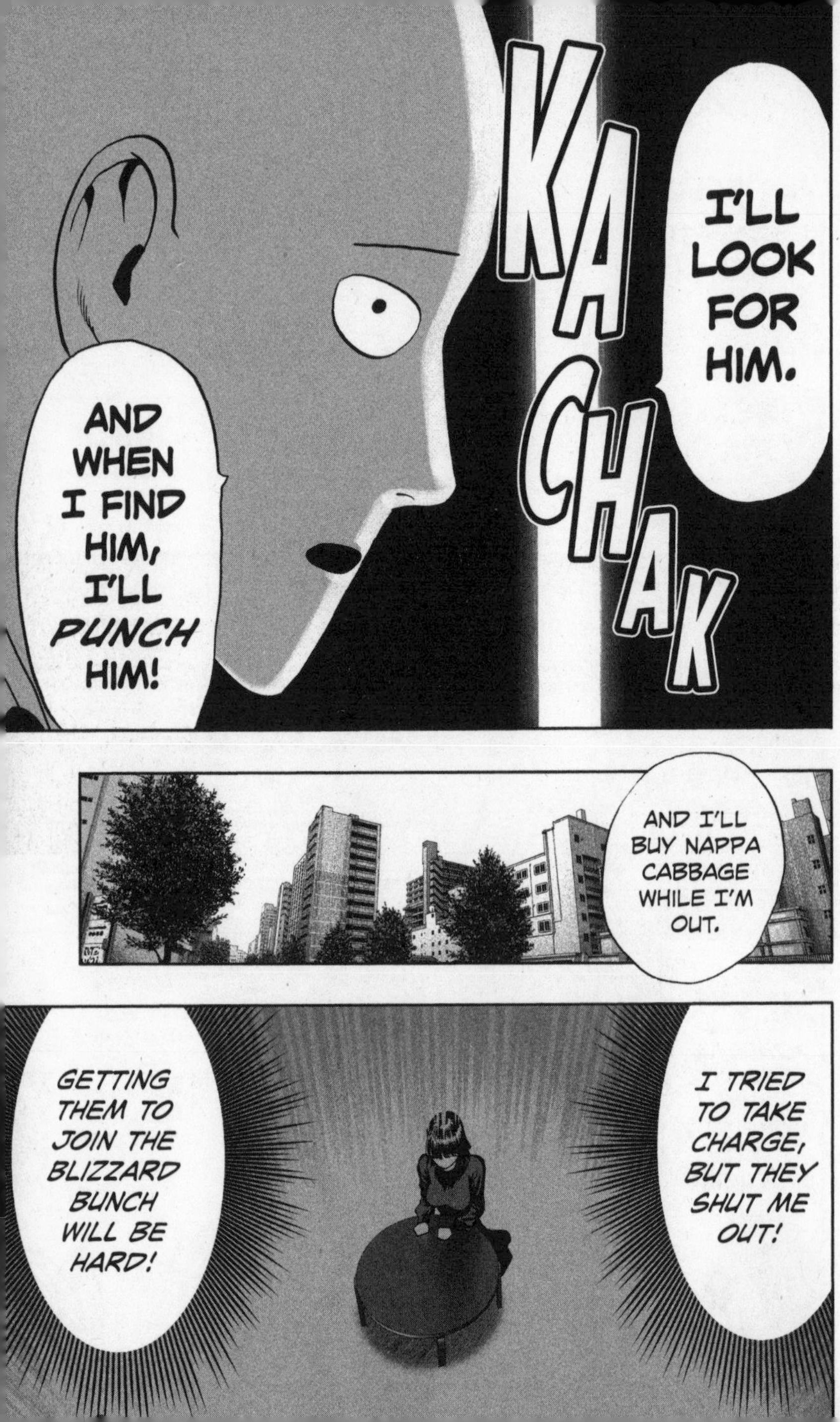
I'LL LOOK FOR HIM.
KACHAK
AND WHEN I FIND HIM, I'LL *PUNCH* HIM!
AND I'LL BUY NAPPA CABBAGE WHILE I'M OUT.
I TRIED TO TAKE CHARGE, BUT THEY SHUT ME OUT!
GETTING THEM TO JOIN THE BLIZZARD BUNCH WILL BE HARD!

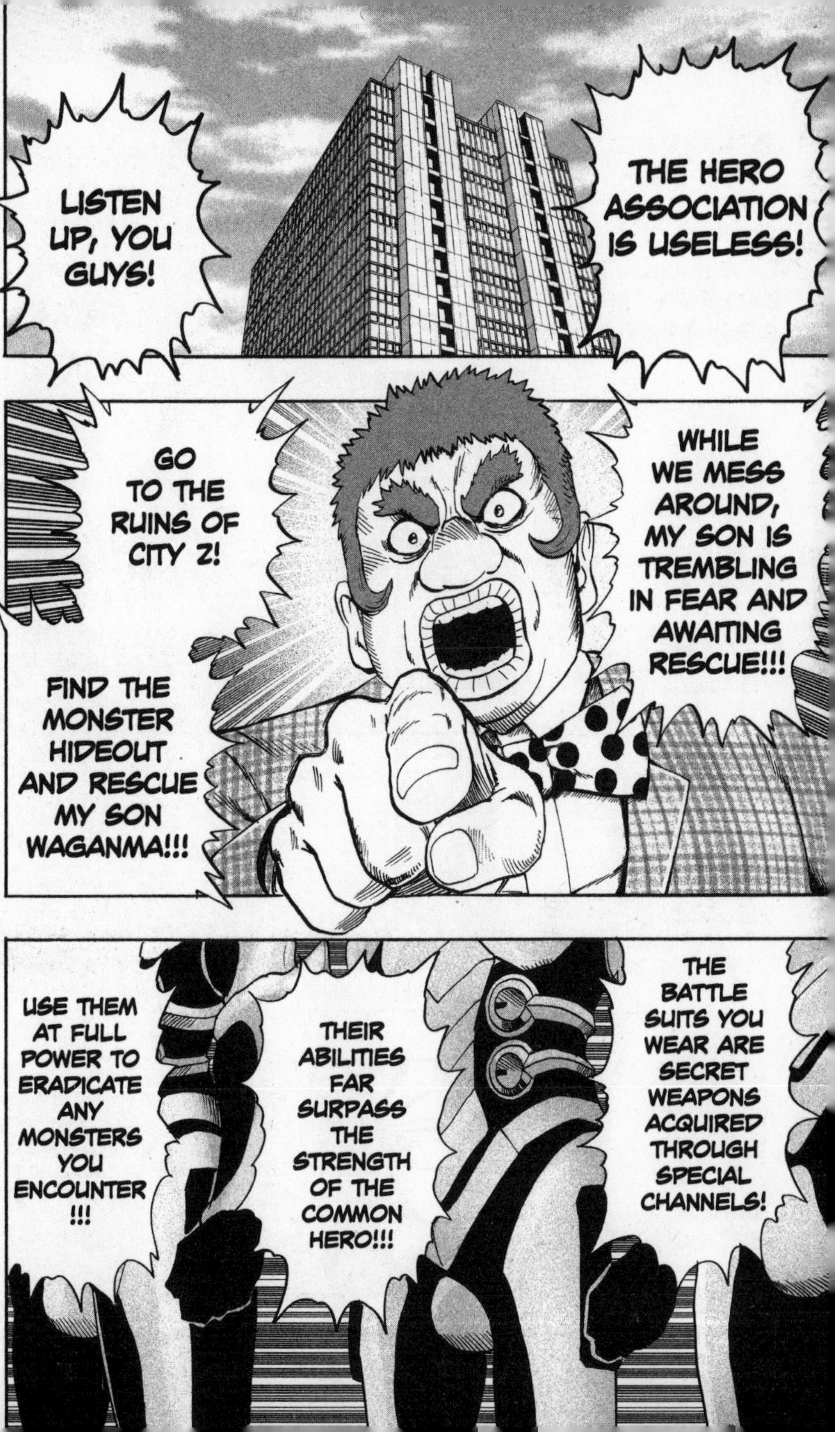
THE HERO ASSOCIATION IS USELESS!
LISTEN UP, YOU GUYS!
WHILE WE MESS AROUND, MY SON IS TREMBLING IN FEAR AND AWAITING RESCUE!!!
GO TO THE RUINS OF CITY Z!
FIND THE MONSTER HIDEOUT AND RESCUE MY SON WAGANMA!!!
THE BATTLE SUITS YOU WEAR ARE SECRET WEAPONS ACQUIRED THROUGH SPECIAL CHANNELS!
THEIR ABILITIES FAR SURPASS THE STRENGTH OF THE COMMON HERO!!!
USE THEM AT FULL POWER TO ERADICATE ANY MONSTERS YOU ENCOUNTER!!!

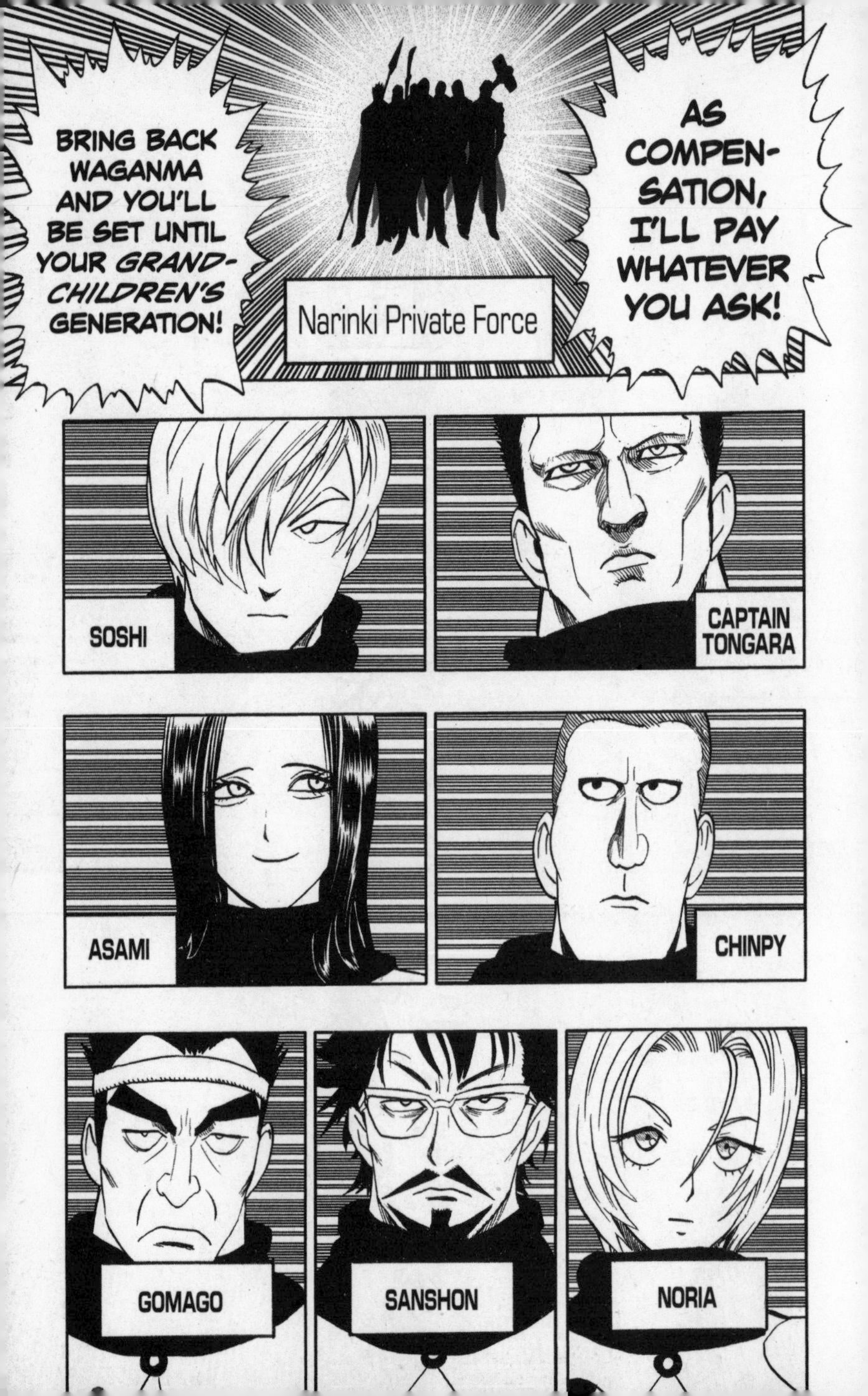
AS COMPEN-SATION, I'LL PAY WHATEVER YOU ASK!
BRING BACK WAGANMA AND YOU'LL BE SET UNTIL YOUR *GRAND-CHILDREN'S* GENERATION!
Narinki Private Force
CAPTAIN TONGARA
SOSHI
CHINPY
ASAMI
NORIA
SANSHON
GOMAGO

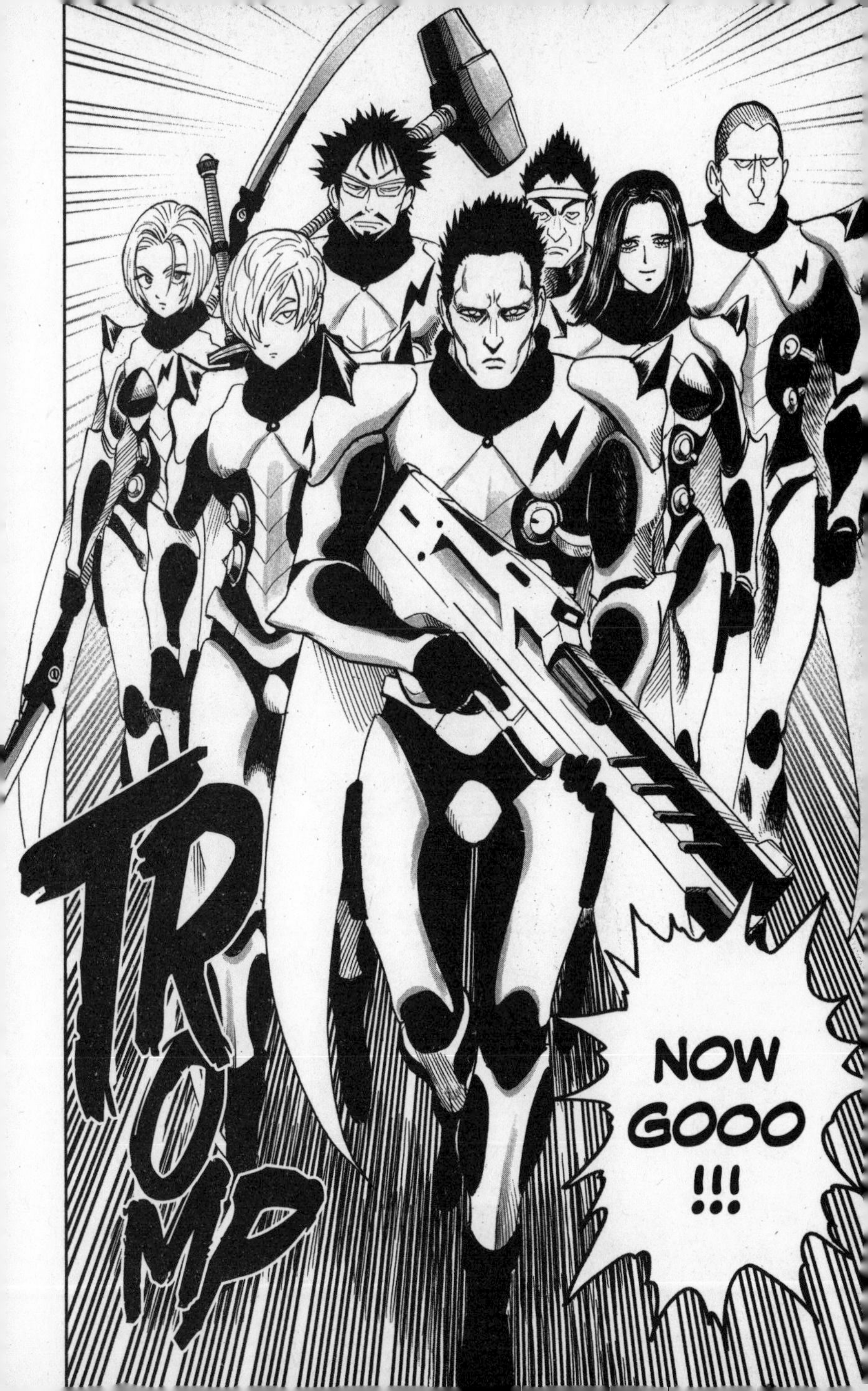
TROMP
NOW GOOO !!!

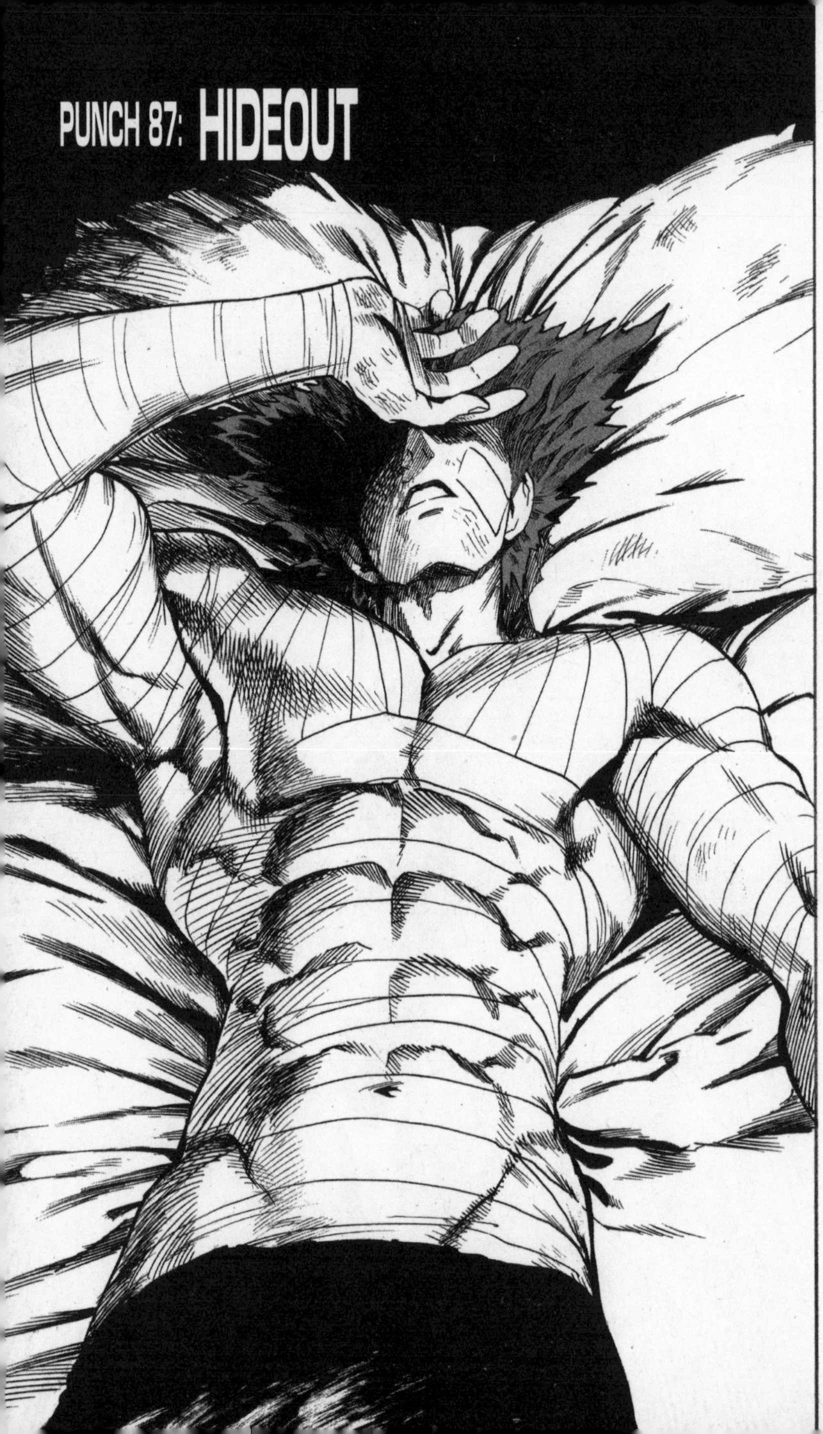
PUNCH 87: HIDEOUT

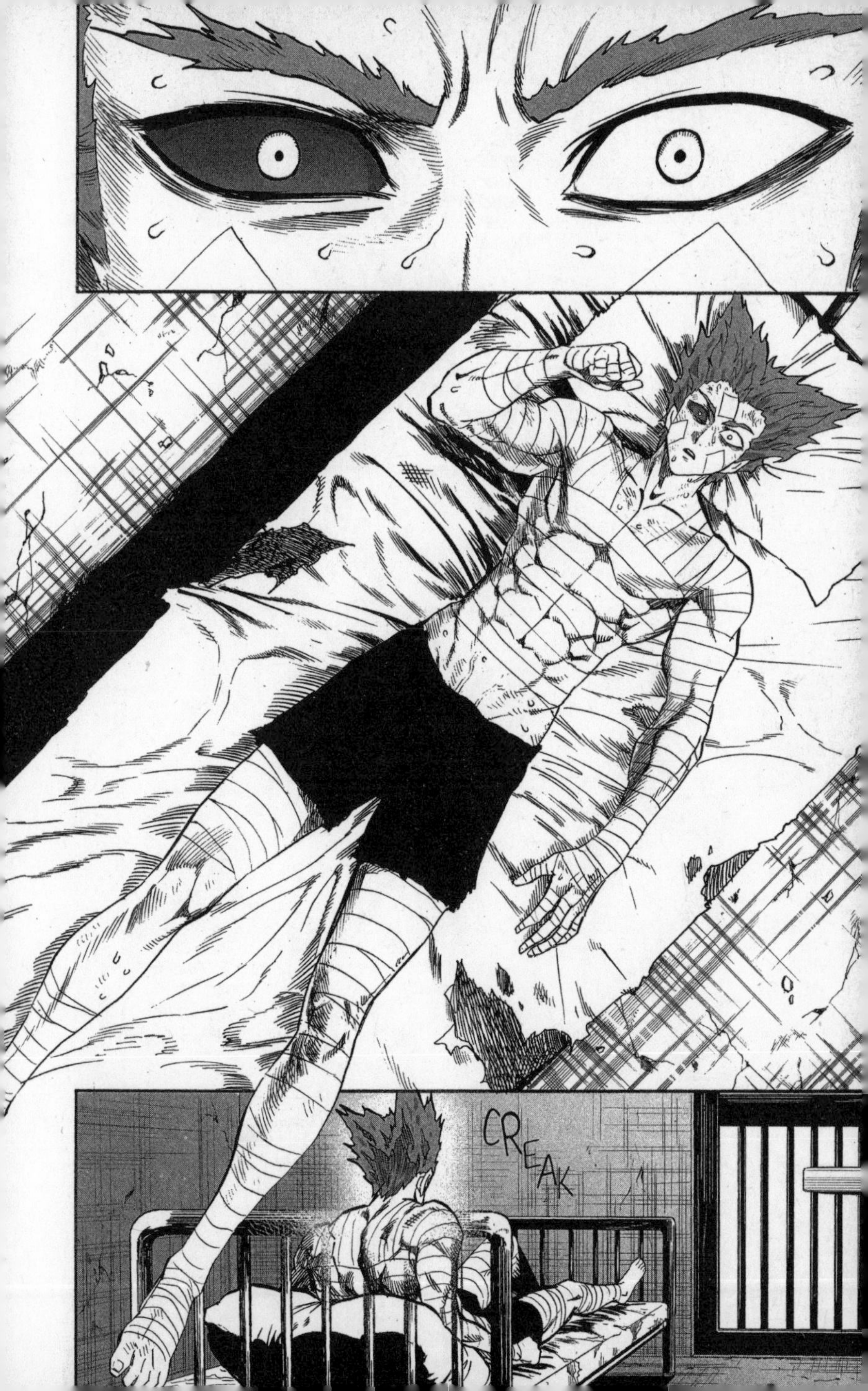
CREAK

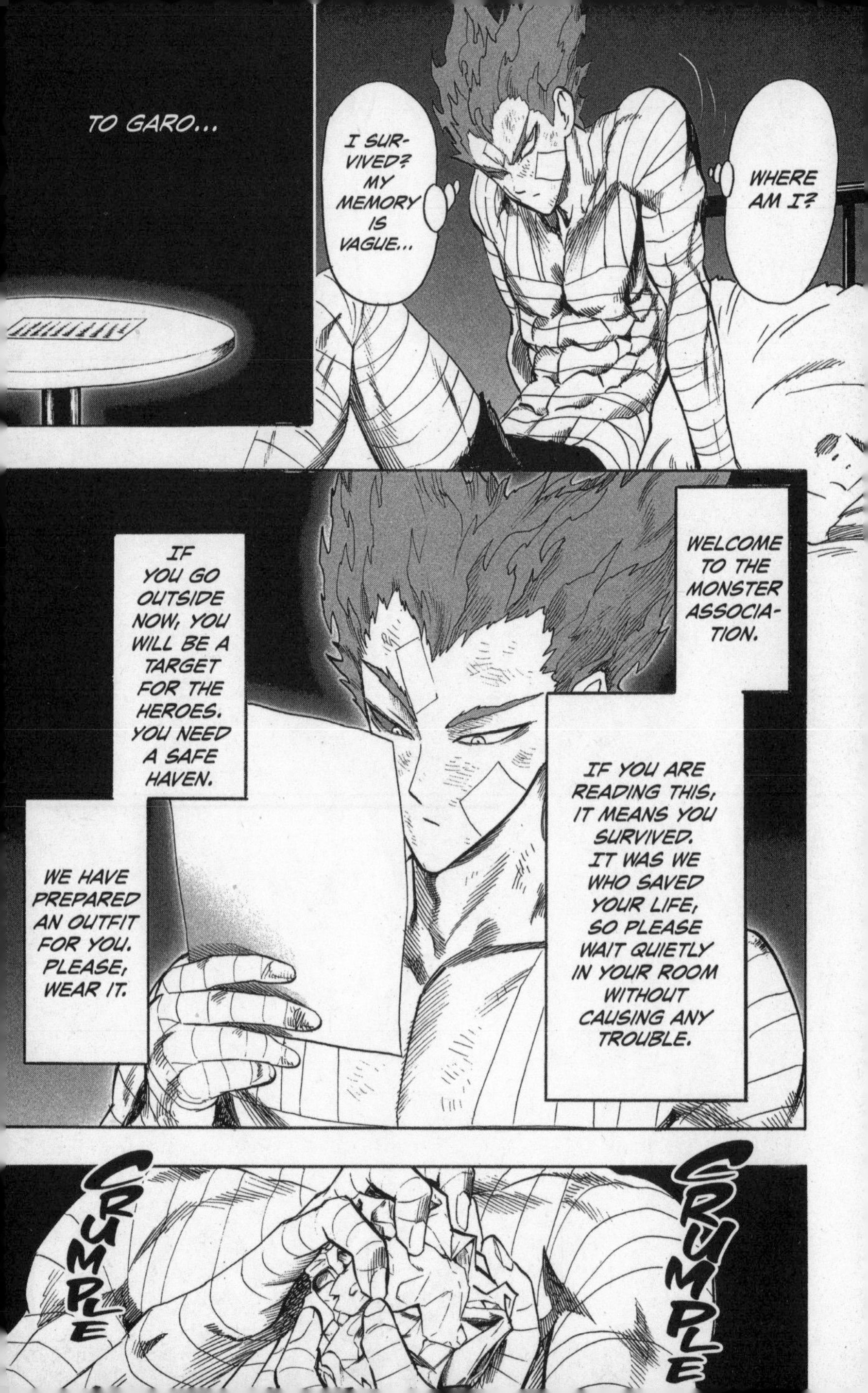

WHERE AM I?
I SURVIVED? MY MEMORY IS VAGUE...
TO GARO...
WELCOME TO THE MONSTER ASSOCIATION.
IF YOU GO OUTSIDE NOW, YOU WILL BE A TARGET FOR THE HEROES. YOU NEED A SAFE HAVEN.
IF YOU ARE READING THIS, IT MEANS YOU SURVIVED. IT WAS WE WHO SAVED YOUR LIFE, SO PLEASE WAIT QUIETLY IN YOUR ROOM WITHOUT CAUSING ANY TROUBLE.
WE HAVE PREPARED AN OUTFIT FOR YOU. PLEASE, WEAR IT.
CRUMPLE
CRUMPLE

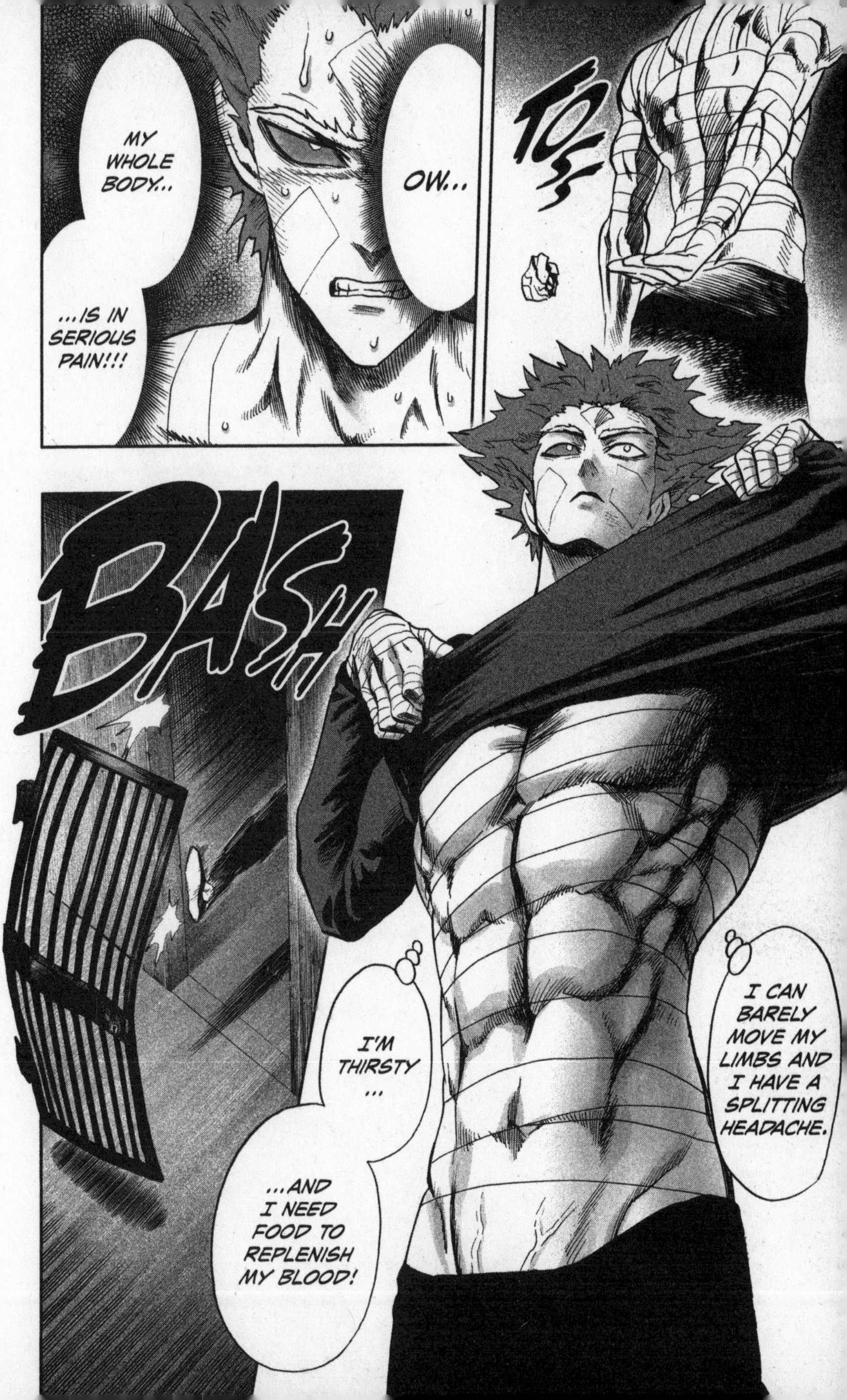
TOSS
OW...
MY WHOLE BODY...
...IS IN SERIOUS PAIN!!!
BASH
I CAN BARELY MOVE MY LIMBS AND I HAVE A SPLITTING HEADACHE.
I'M THIRSTY...
...AND I NEED FOOD TO REPLENISH MY BLOOD!

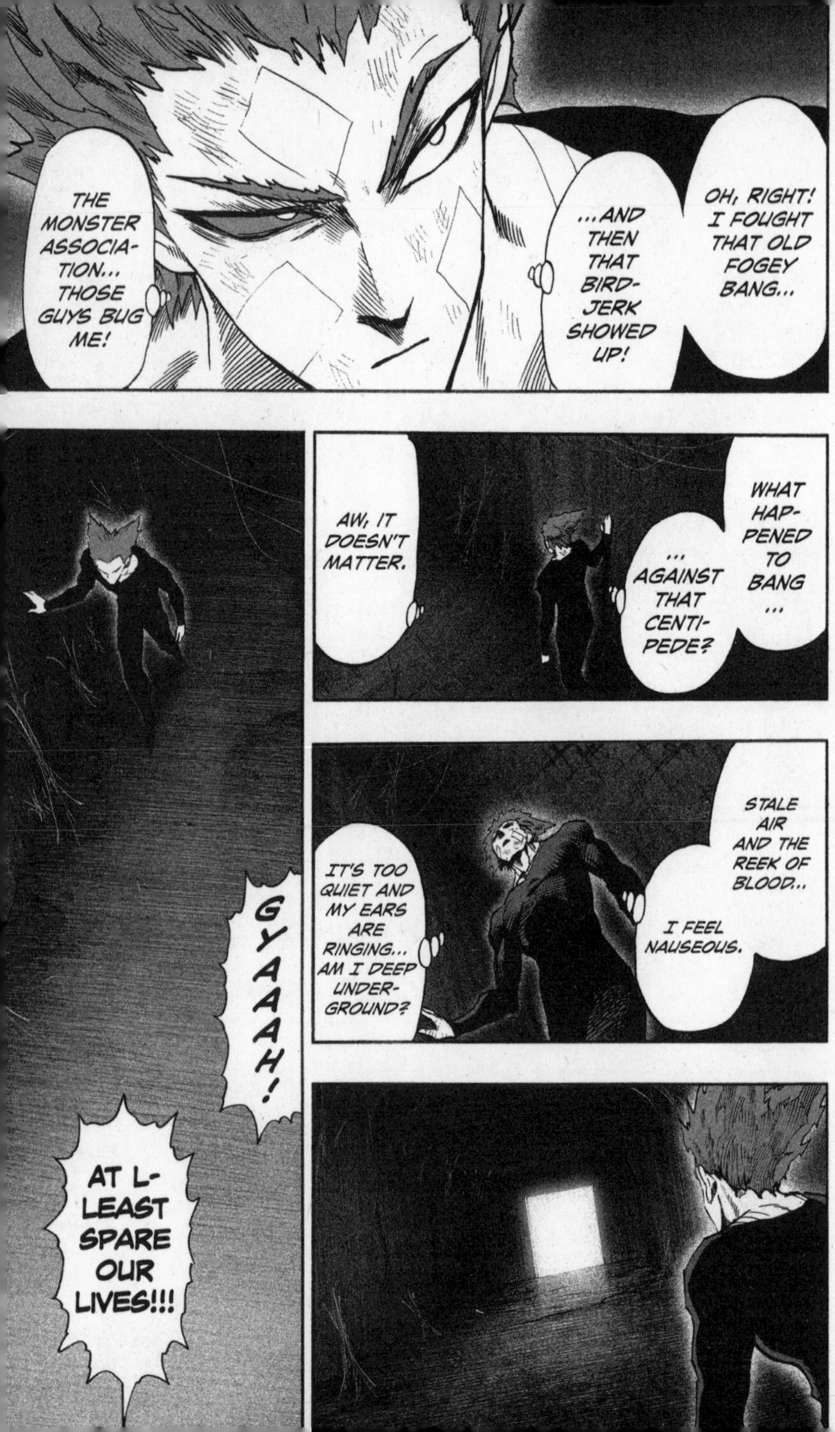
OH, RIGHT! I FOUGHT THAT OLD FOGEY BANG...
...AND THEN THAT BIRD-JERK SHOWED UP!
THE MONSTER ASSOCIA-TION... THOSE GUYS BUG ME!
WHAT HAP-PENED TO BANG ...
... AGAINST THAT CENTI-PEDE?
AW, IT DOESN'T MATTER.
STALE AIR AND THE REEK OF BLOOD...
I FEEL NAUSEOUS.
IT'S TOO QUIET AND MY EARS ARE RINGING... AM I DEEP UNDER-GROUND?
GYAAAH!
AT L-LEAST SPARE OUR LIVES!!!

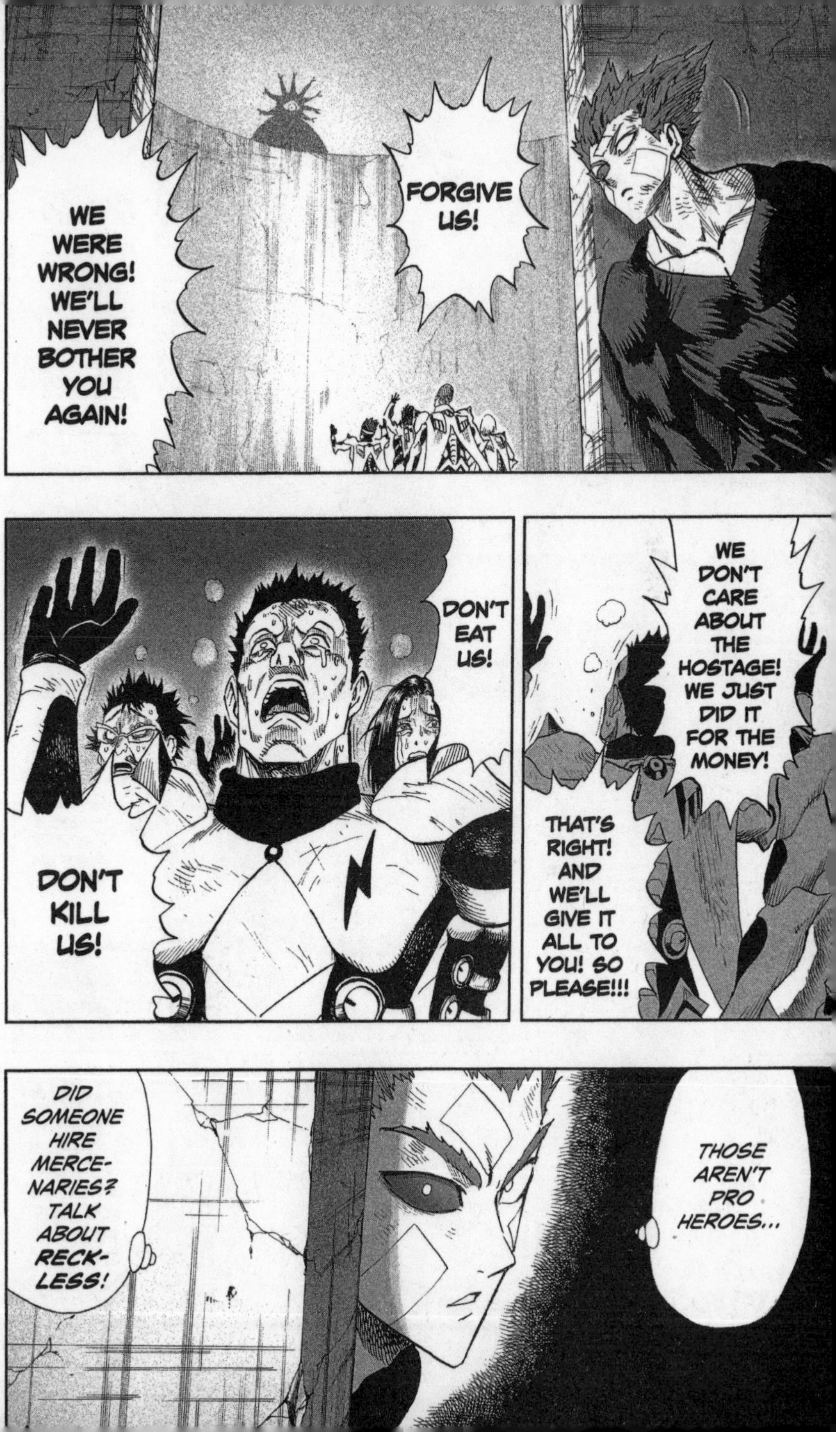
FORGIVE US!
WE WERE WRONG! WE'LL NEVER BOTHER YOU AGAIN!
WE DON'T CARE ABOUT THE HOSTAGE! WE JUST DID IT FOR THE MONEY!
THAT'S RIGHT! AND WE'LL GIVE IT ALL TO YOU! SO PLEASE!!!
DON'T EAT US!
DON'T KILL US!
THOSE AREN'T PRO HEROES...
DID SOMEONE HIRE MERCE-NARIES? TALK ABOUT RECK-LESS!

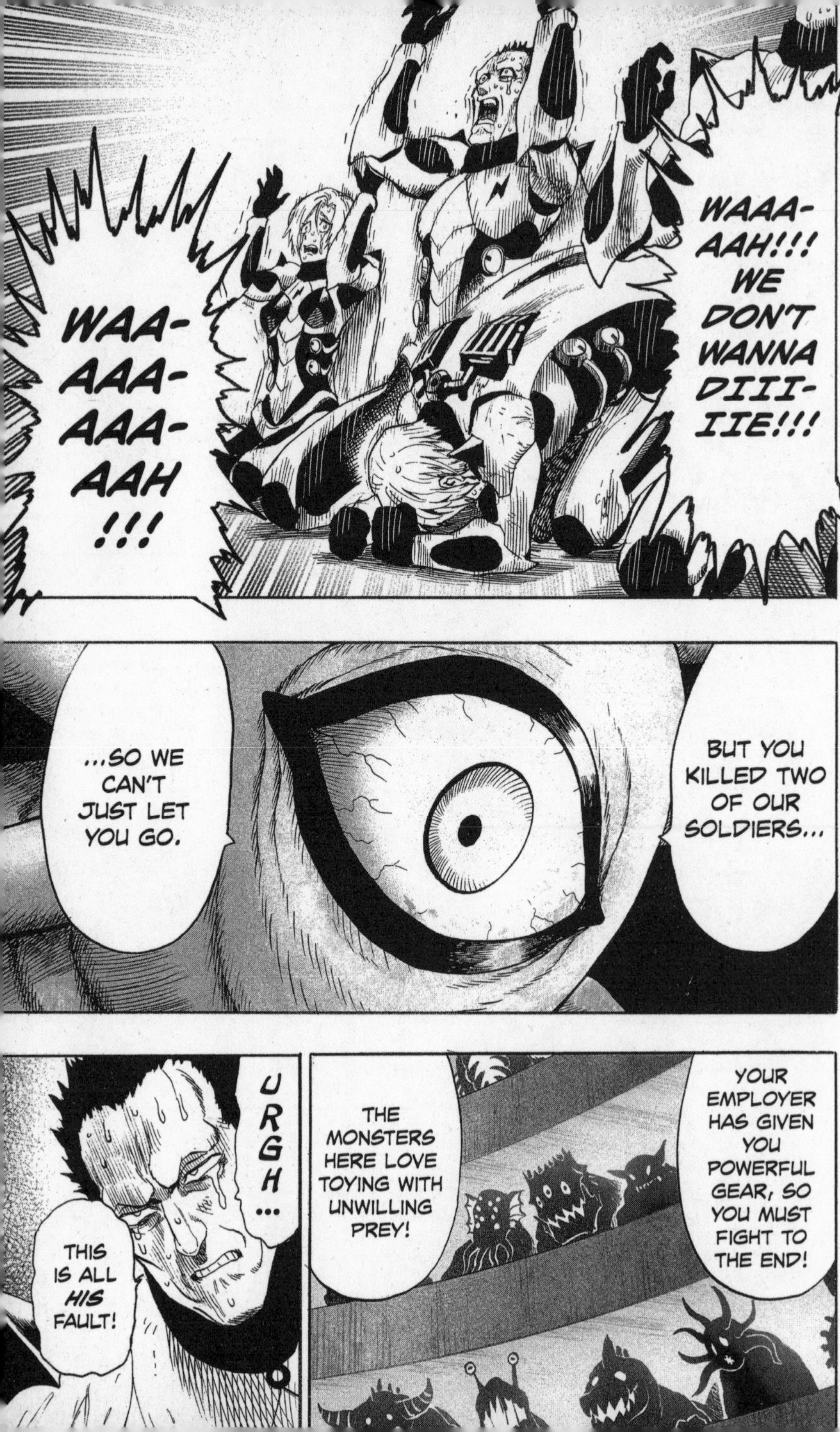
WAAAA-AAH!!! WE DON'T WANNA DIIII-IIE!!!
WAA-AAA-AAA-AAH!!!
BUT YOU KILLED TWO OF OUR SOLDIERS...
...SO WE CAN'T JUST LET YOU GO.
YOUR EMPLOYER HAS GIVEN YOU POWERFUL GEAR, SO YOU MUST FIGHT TO THE END!
THE MONSTERS HERE LOVE TOYING WITH UNWILLING PREY!
URGH...
THIS IS ALL *HIS* FAULT!

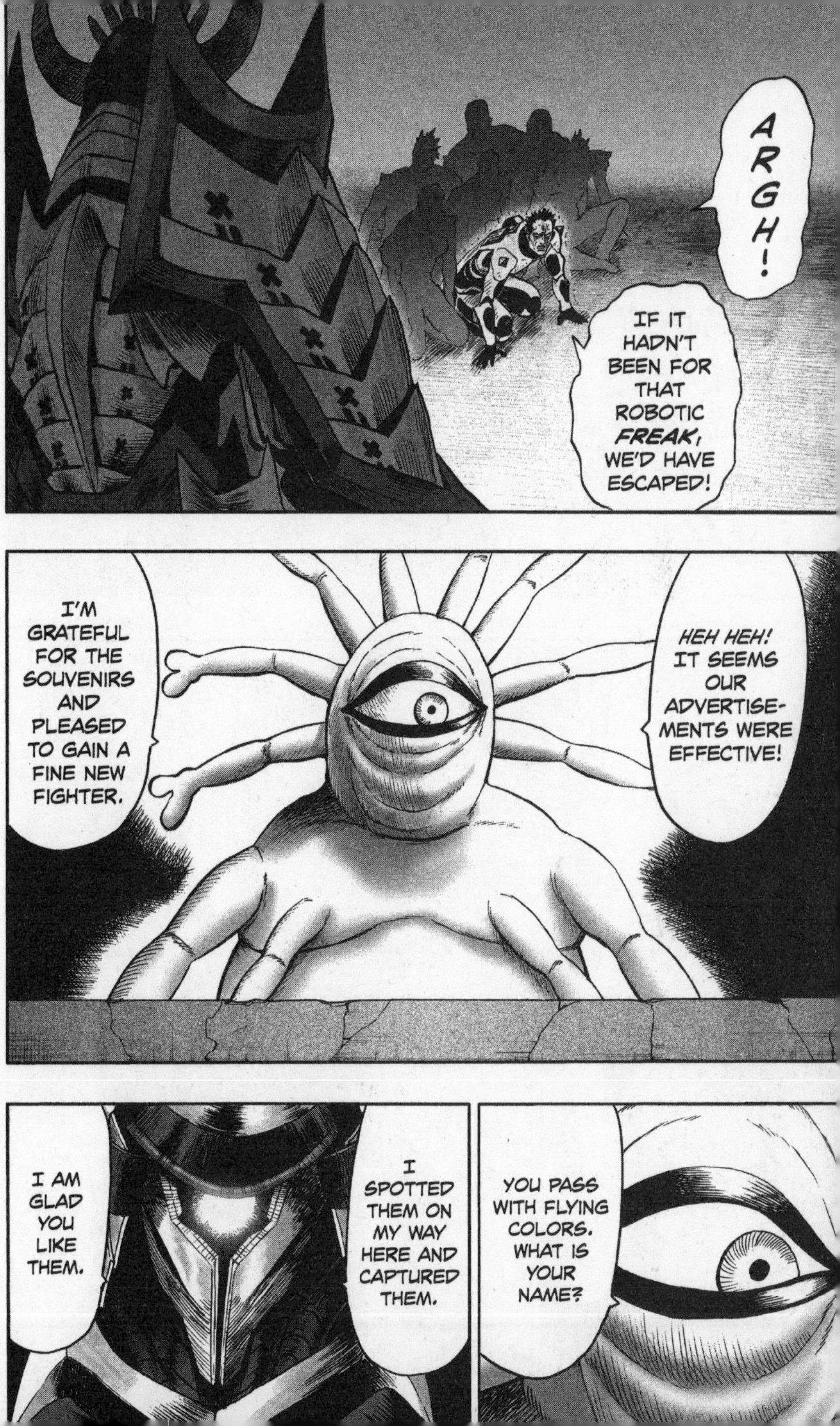
ARGH!
IF IT HADN'T BEEN FOR THAT ROBOTIC **FREAK**, WE'D HAVE ESCAPED!
HEH HEH! IT SEEMS OUR ADVERTISE-MENTS WERE EFFECTIVE!
I'M GRATEFUL FOR THE SOUVENIRS AND PLEASED TO GAIN A FINE NEW FIGHTER.
YOU PASS WITH FLYING COLORS. WHAT IS YOUR NAME?
I SPOTTED THEM ON MY WAY HERE AND CAPTURED THEM.
I AM GLAD YOU LIKE THEM.

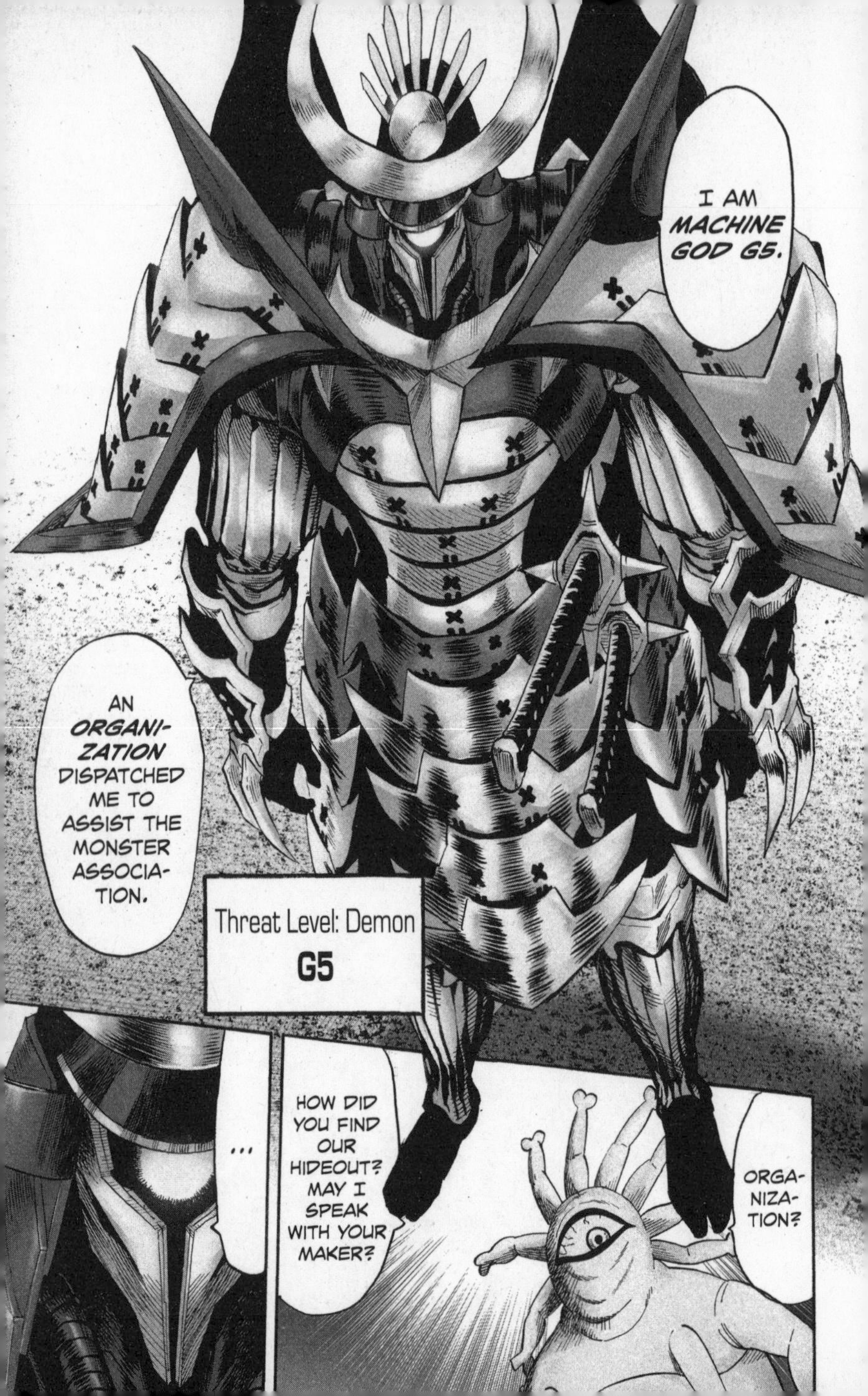
I AM MACHINE GOD G5.
AN ORGANIZATION DISPATCHED ME TO ASSIST THE MONSTER ASSOCIATION.
Threat Level: Demon
G5
ORGANIZATION?
HOW DID YOU FIND OUR HIDEOUT? MAY I SPEAK WITH YOUR MAKER?
...

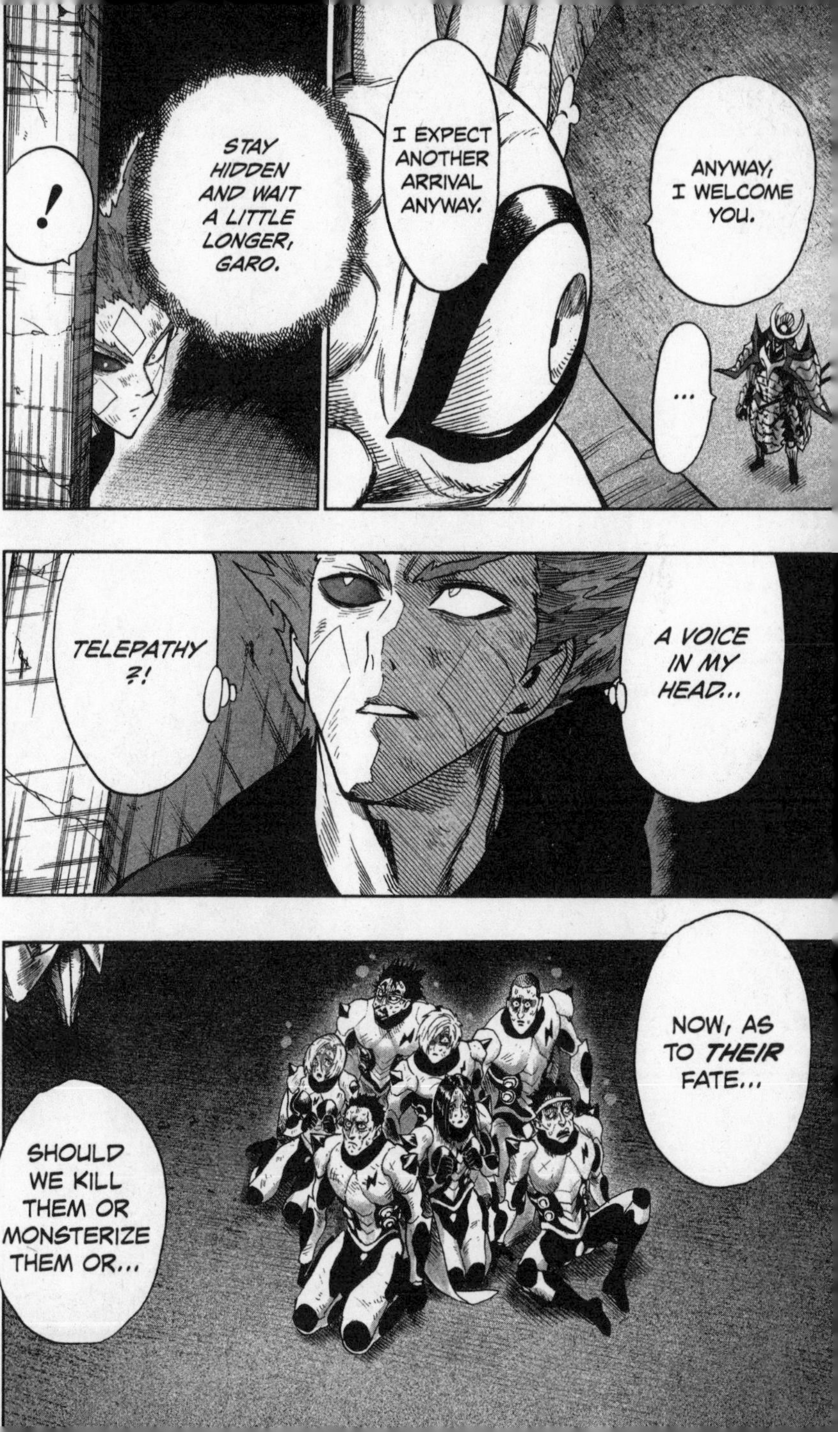
ANYWAY, I WELCOME YOU.
...
I EXPECT ANOTHER ARRIVAL ANYWAY.
STAY HIDDEN AND WAIT A LITTLE LONGER, GARO.
!
A VOICE IN MY HEAD...
TELEPATHY ?!
NOW, AS TO *THEIR* FATE...
SHOULD WE KILL THEM OR MONSTERIZE THEM OR...

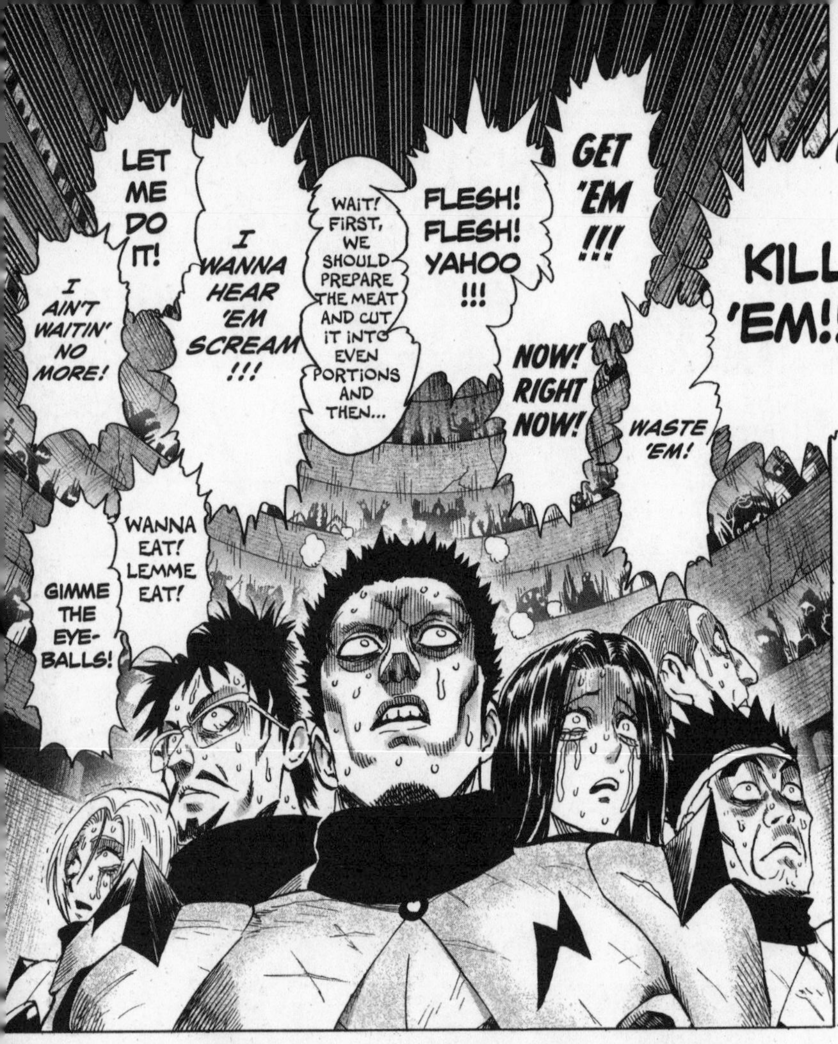
KILL 'EM!!!
GET 'EM!!!
FLESH! FLESH! YAHOO!!!
WAIT! FIRST, WE SHOULD PREPARE THE MEAT AND CUT IT INTO EVEN PORTIONS AND THEN...
I WANNA HEAR 'EM SCREAM!!!
LET ME DO IT!
I AIN'T WAITIN' NO MORE!
WASTE 'EM!
NOW! RIGHT NOW!
WANNA EAT! LEMME EAT!
GIMME THE EYEBALLS!
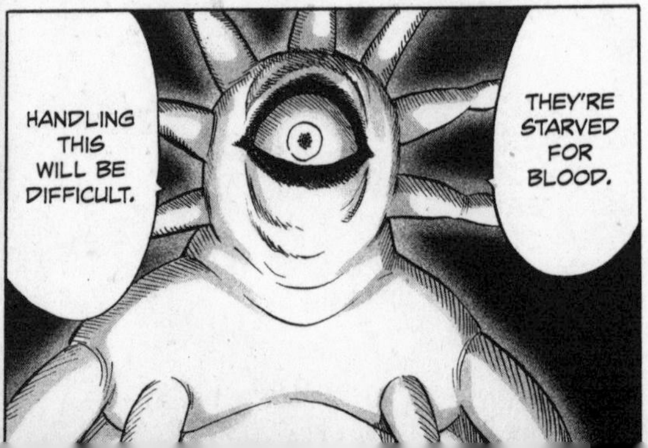
THEY'RE STARVED FOR BLOOD.
HANDLING THIS WILL BE DIFFICULT.
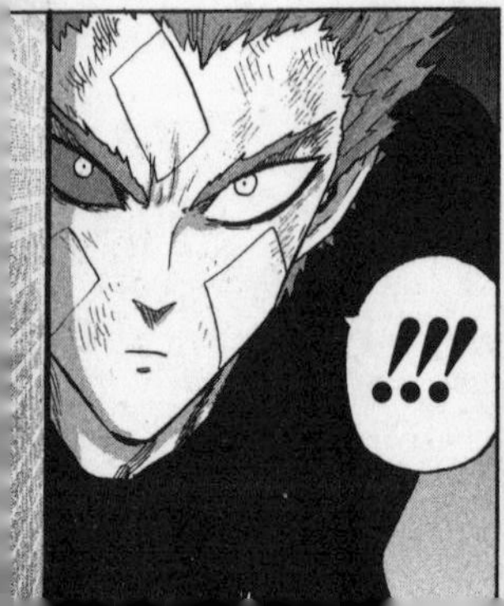
!!!

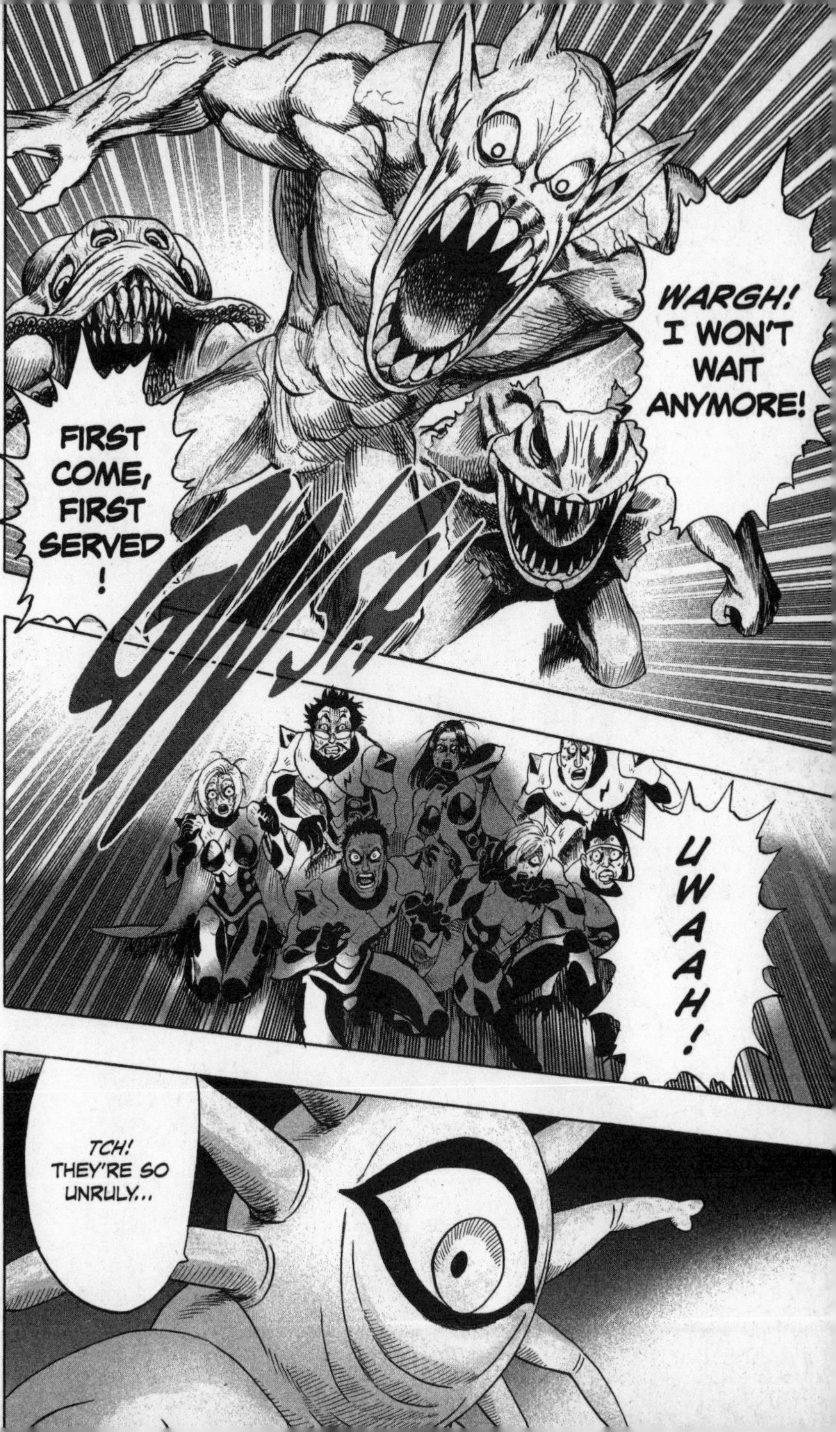
WARGH! I WON'T WAIT ANYMORE!
FIRST COME, FIRST SERVED!
UWAAH!
TCH! THEY'RE SO UNRULY...

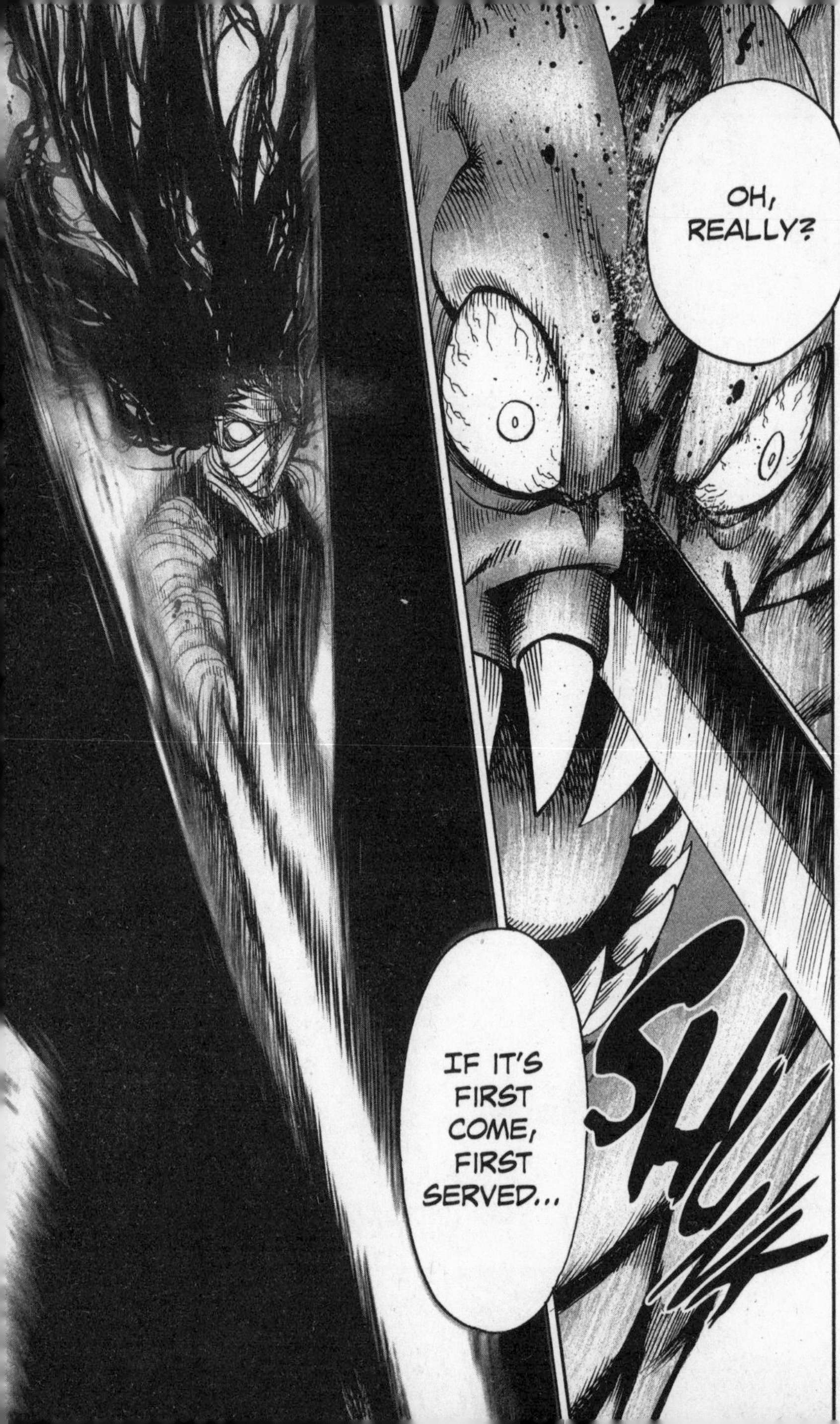
OH, REALLY?
IF IT'S FIRST COME, FIRST SERVED...
SHUK

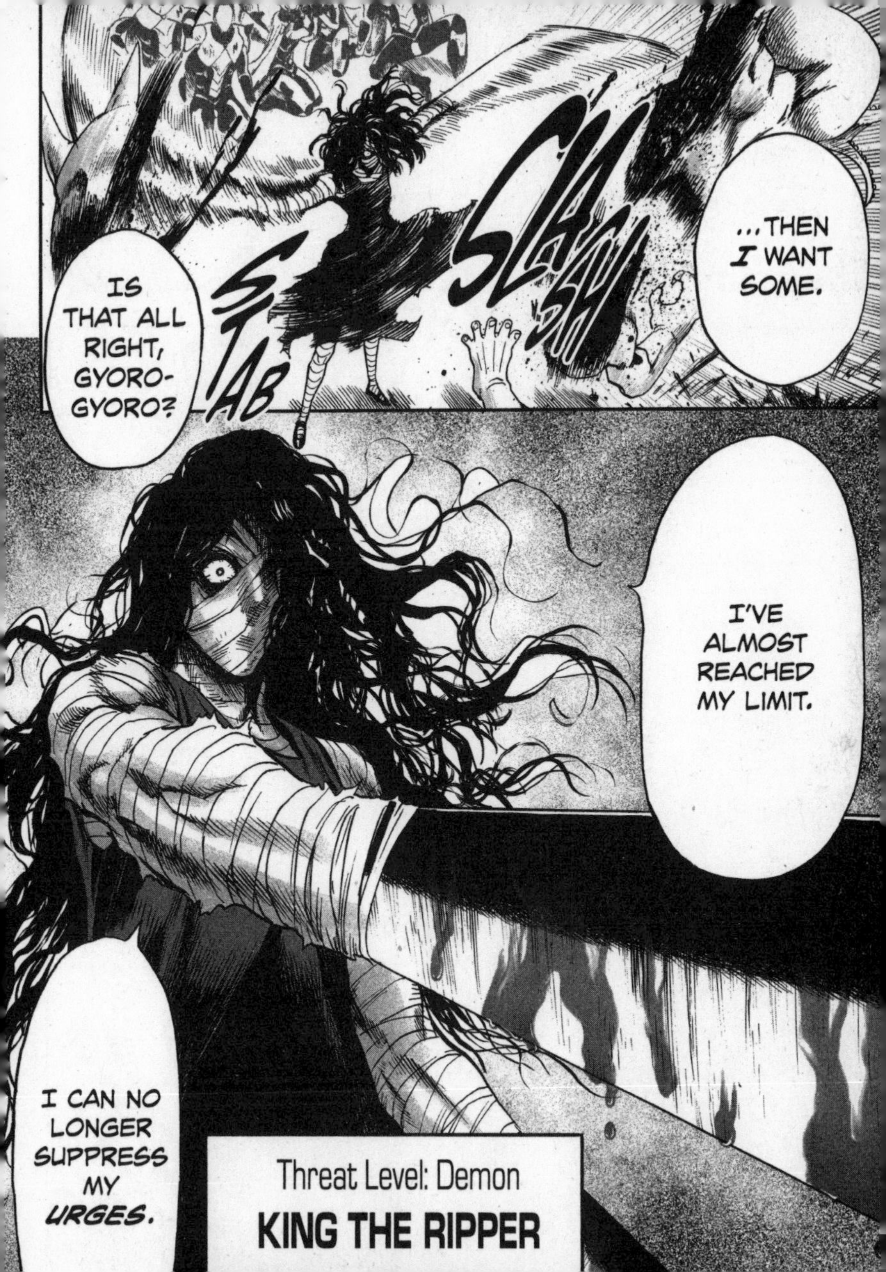
...THEN I WANT SOME.
STAB
IS THAT ALL RIGHT, GYORO-GYORO?
I'VE ALMOST REACHED MY LIMIT.
I CAN NO LONGER SUPPRESS MY URGES.
Threat Level: Demon
KING THE RIPPER

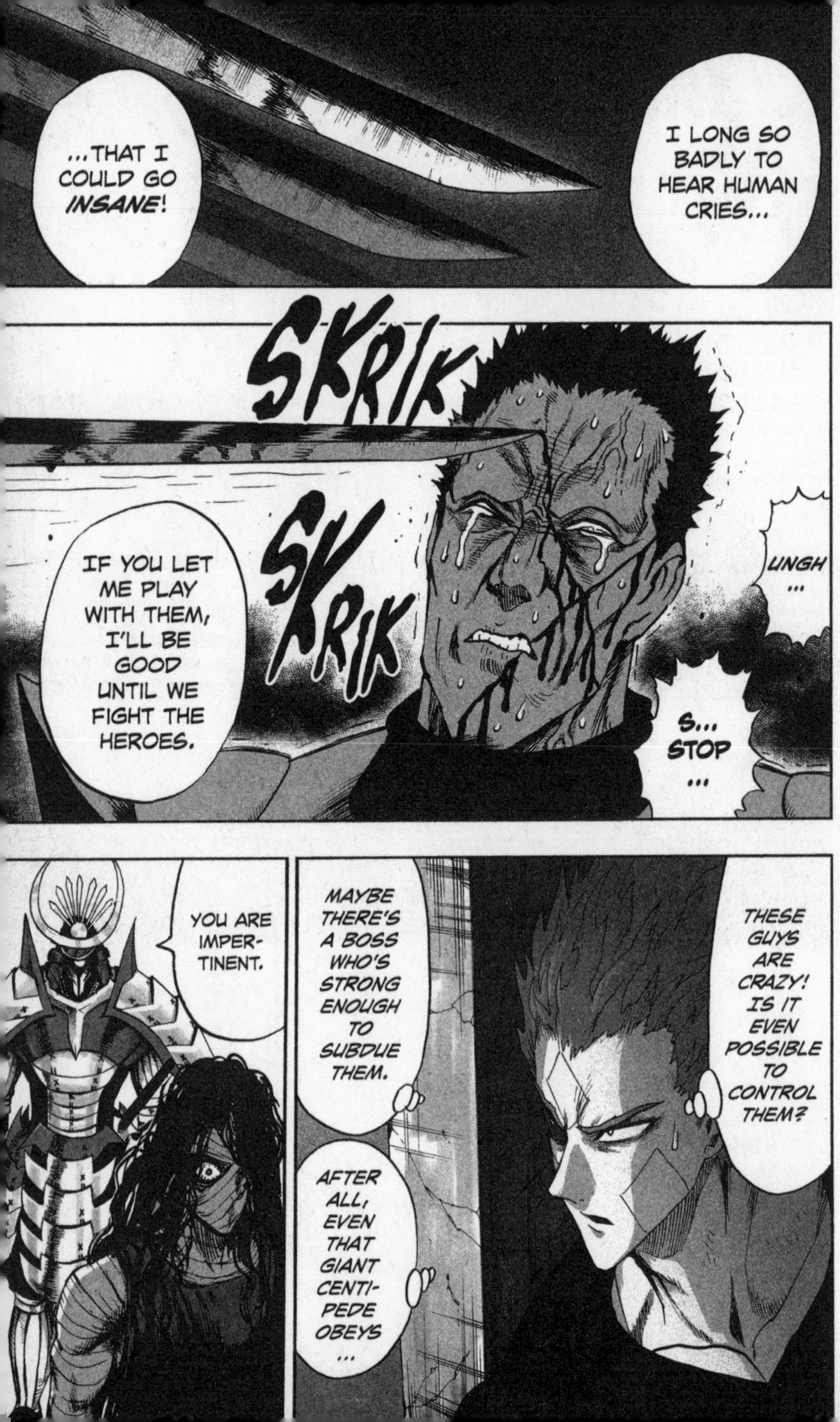
I LONG SO BADLY TO HEAR HUMAN CRIES...
...THAT I COULD GO *INSANE*!
SKRIK
UNGH...
SKRIK
S... STOP...
IF YOU LET ME PLAY WITH THEM, I'LL BE GOOD UNTIL WE FIGHT THE HEROES.
THESE GUYS ARE CRAZY! IS IT EVEN POSSIBLE TO CONTROL THEM?
MAYBE THERE'S A BOSS WHO'S STRONG ENOUGH TO SUBDUE THEM.
AFTER ALL, EVEN THAT GIANT CENTIPEDE OBEYS...
YOU ARE IMPERTINENT.

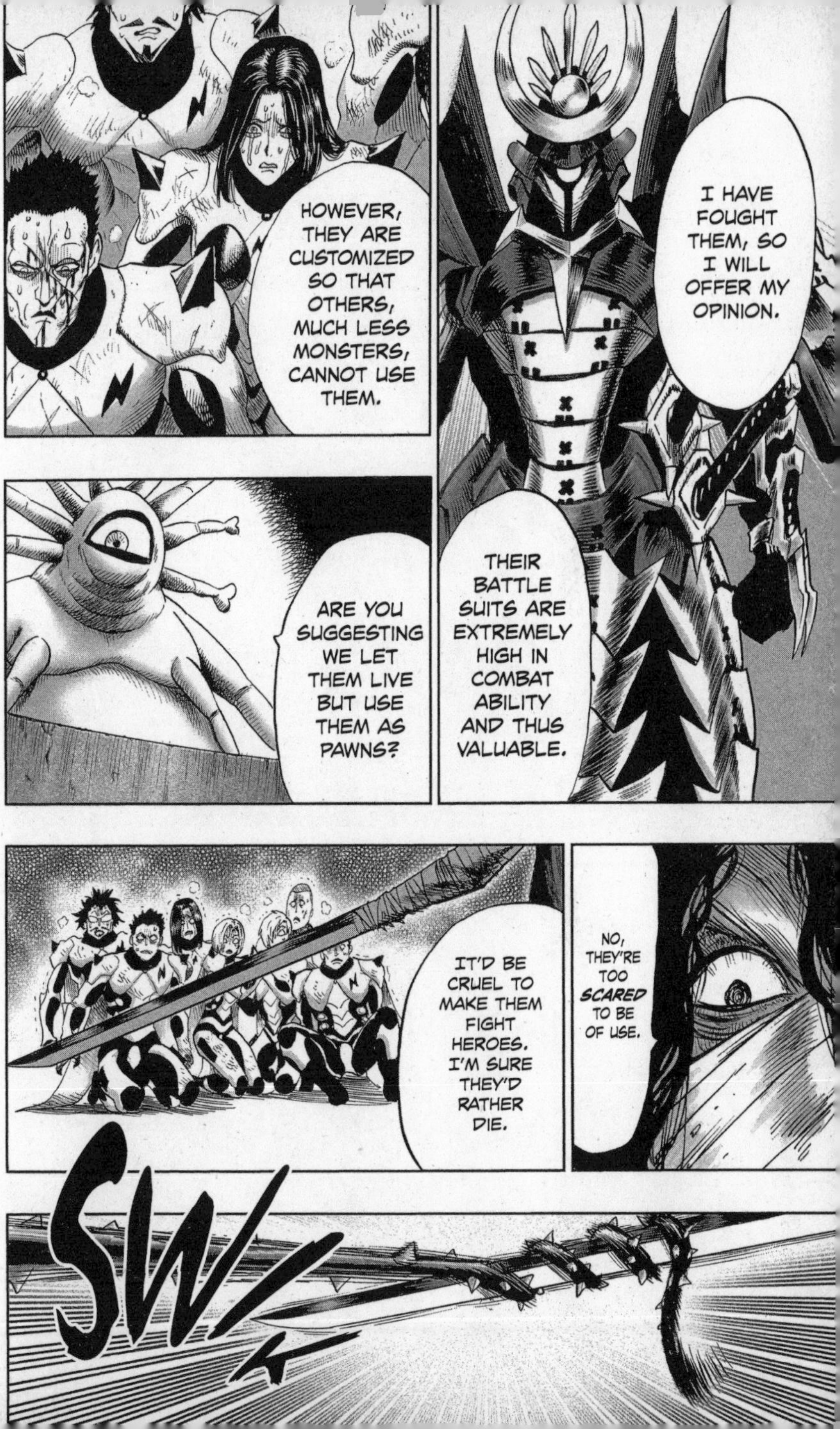
I HAVE FOUGHT THEM, SO I WILL OFFER MY OPINION.
THEIR BATTLE SUITS ARE EXTREMELY HIGH IN COMBAT ABILITY AND THUS VALUABLE.
HOWEVER, THEY ARE CUSTOMIZED SO THAT OTHERS, MUCH LESS MONSTERS, CANNOT USE THEM.
ARE YOU SUGGESTING WE LET THEM LIVE BUT USE THEM AS PAWNS?
NO, THEY'RE TOO *SCARED* TO BE OF USE.
IT'D BE CRUEL TO MAKE THEM FIGHT HEROES. I'M SURE THEY'D RATHER DIE.
SWI

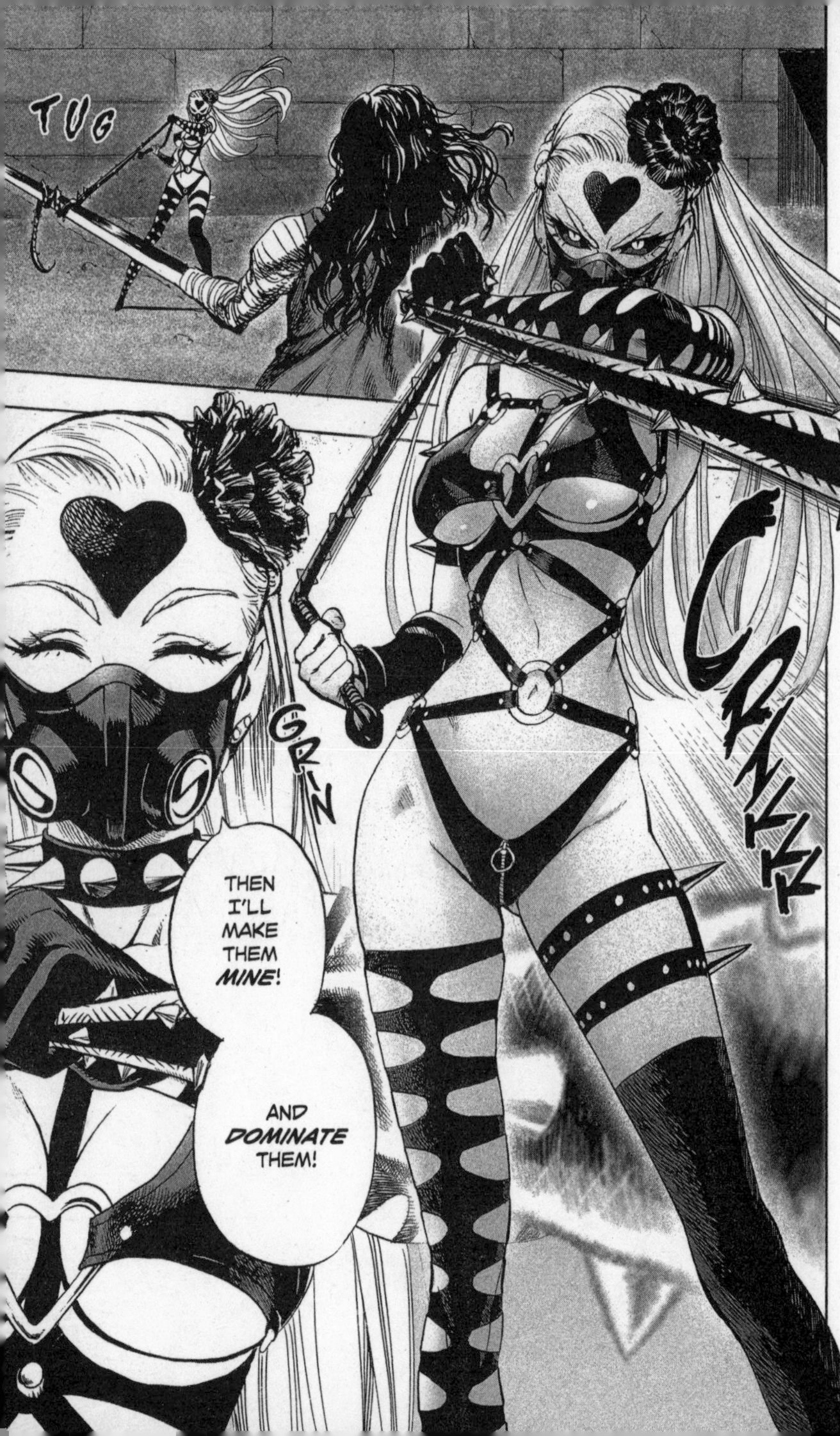
TUG
CRNKKK
GRIN
THEN I'LL MAKE THEM *MINE*!
AND *DOMINATE* THEM!

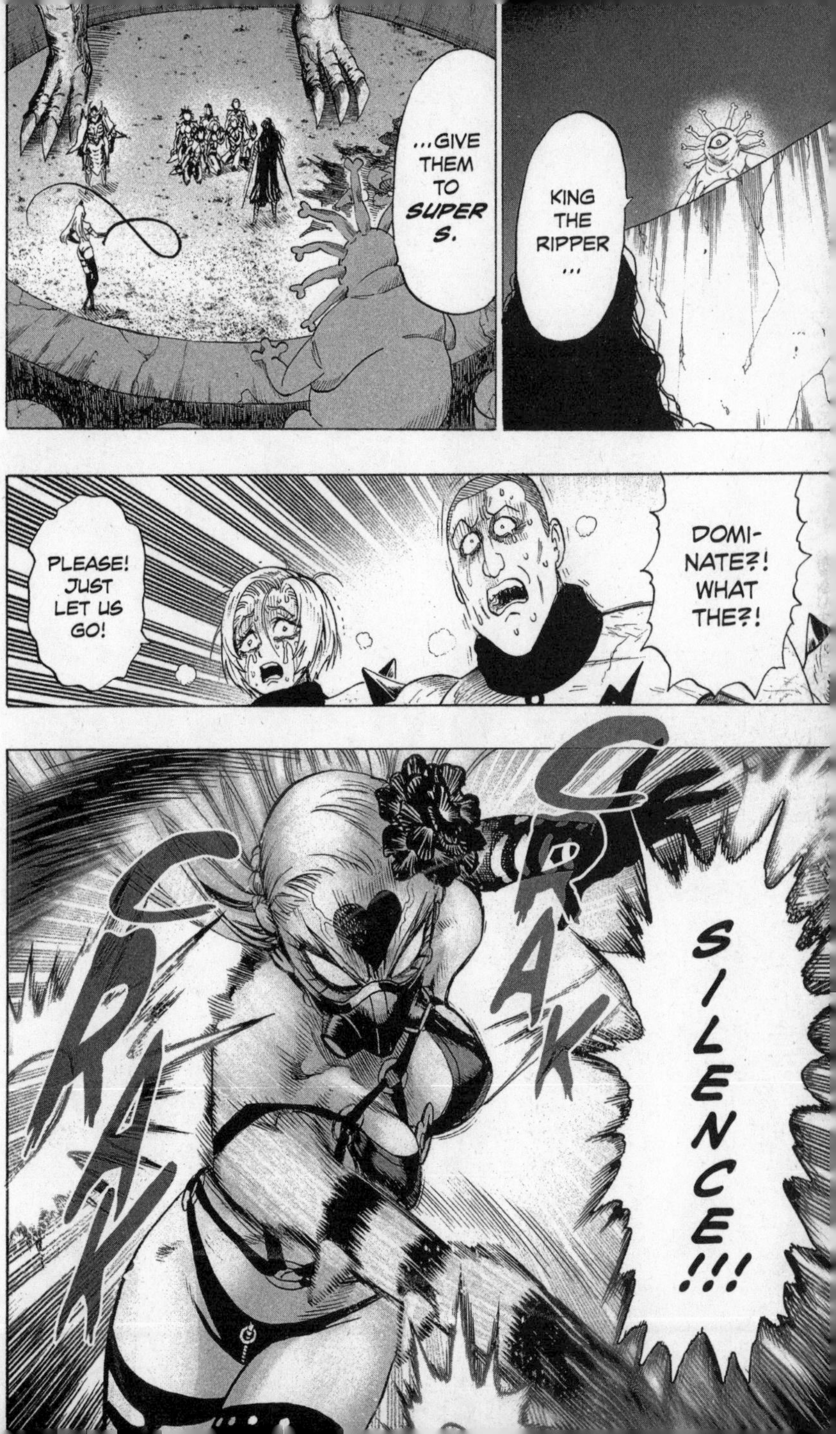
KING THE RIPPER ...
...GIVE THEM TO SUPER S.
DOMI-NATE?! WHAT THE?!
PLEASE! JUST LET US GO!
CRAK
SILENCE!!!
CRAK

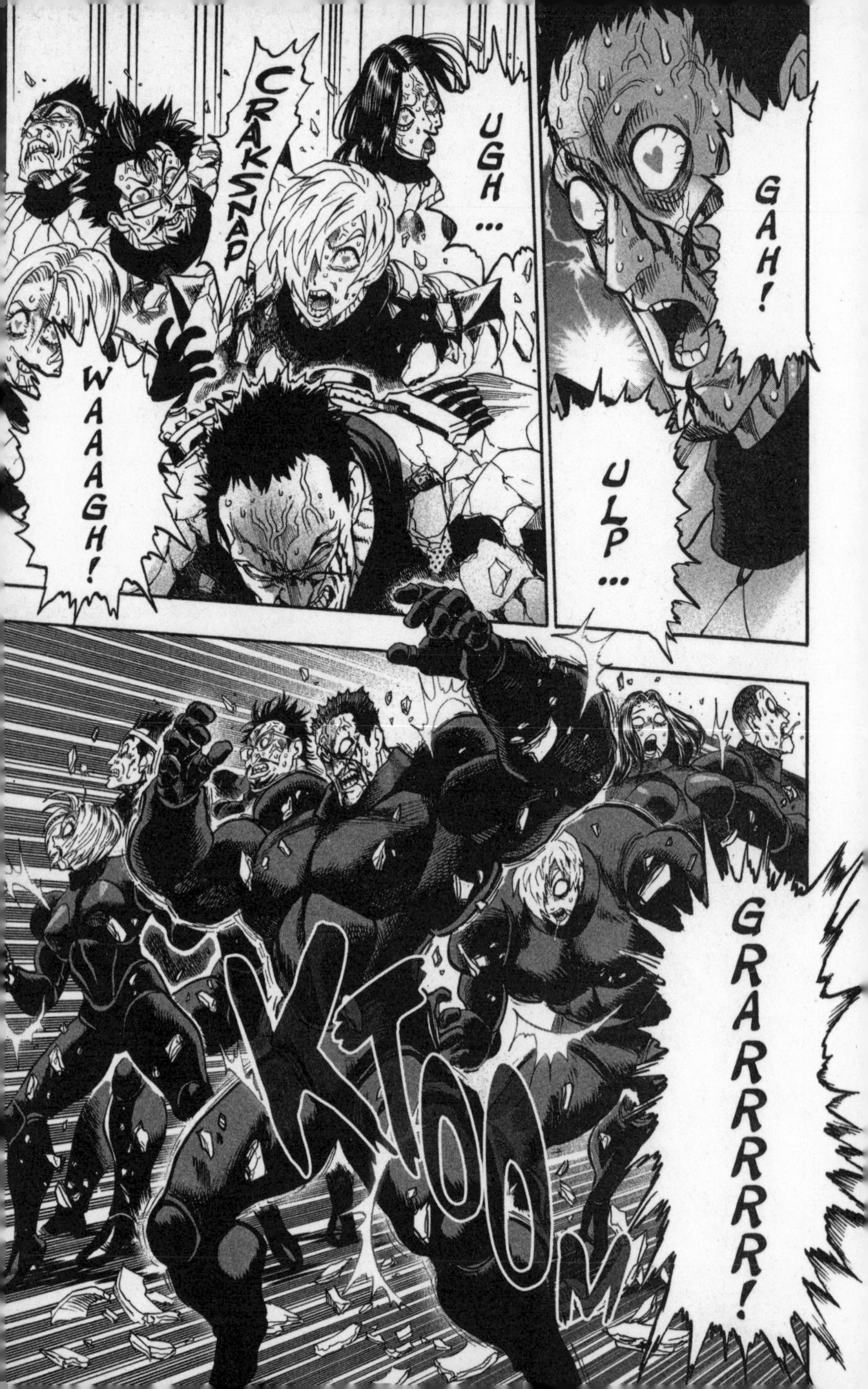
GAH!
ULP...
UGH...
CRAKSNAP
WAAAAGH!
GRARRRRR!
KTOOOM

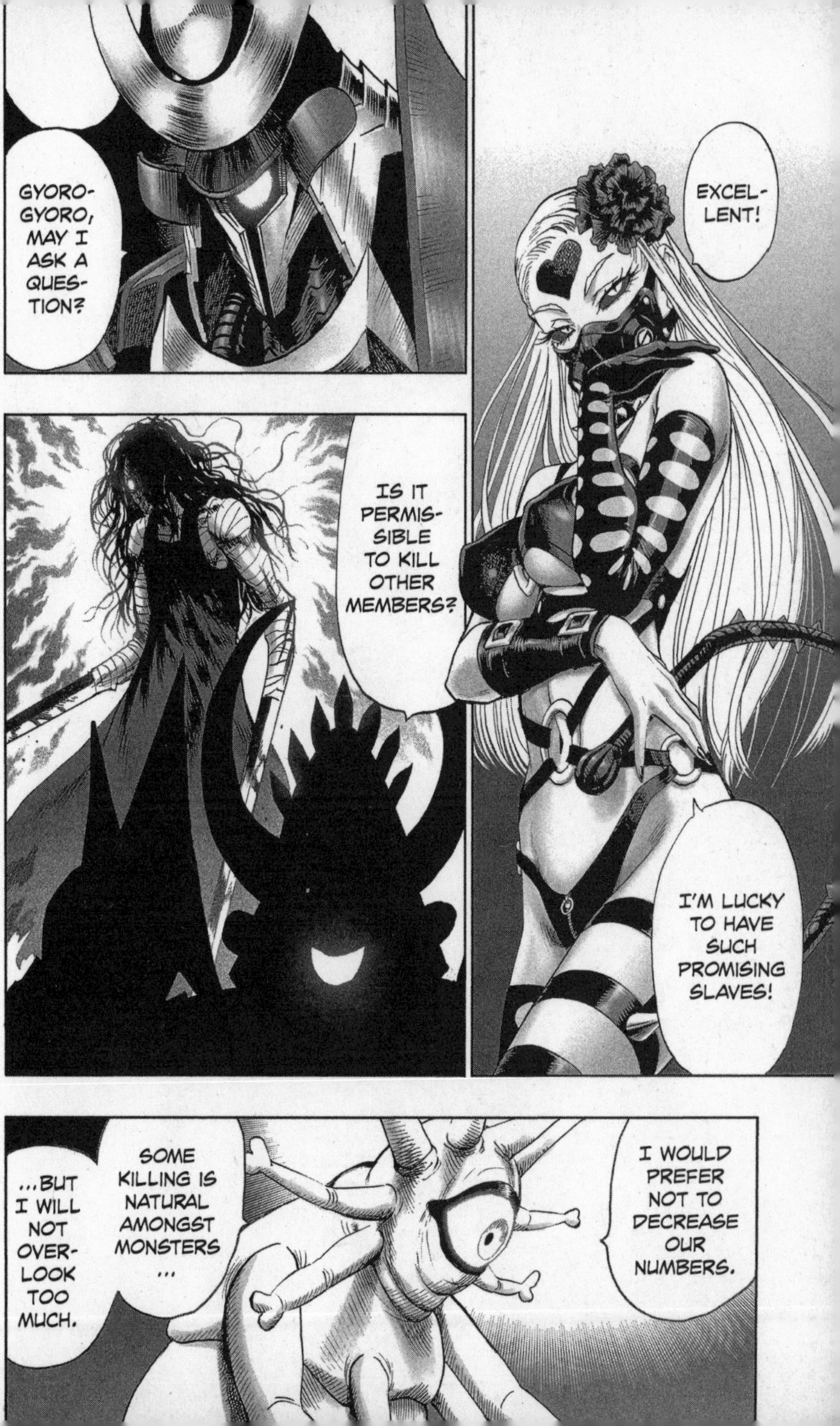
EXCEL-LENT!
I'M LUCKY TO HAVE SUCH PROMISING SLAVES!
GYORO-GYORO, MAY I ASK A QUES-TION?
IS IT PERMIS-SIBLE TO KILL OTHER MEMBERS?
I WOULD PREFER NOT TO DECREASE OUR NUMBERS.
SOME KILLING IS NATURAL AMONGST MONSTERS ...
...BUT I WILL NOT OVER-LOOK TOO MUCH.

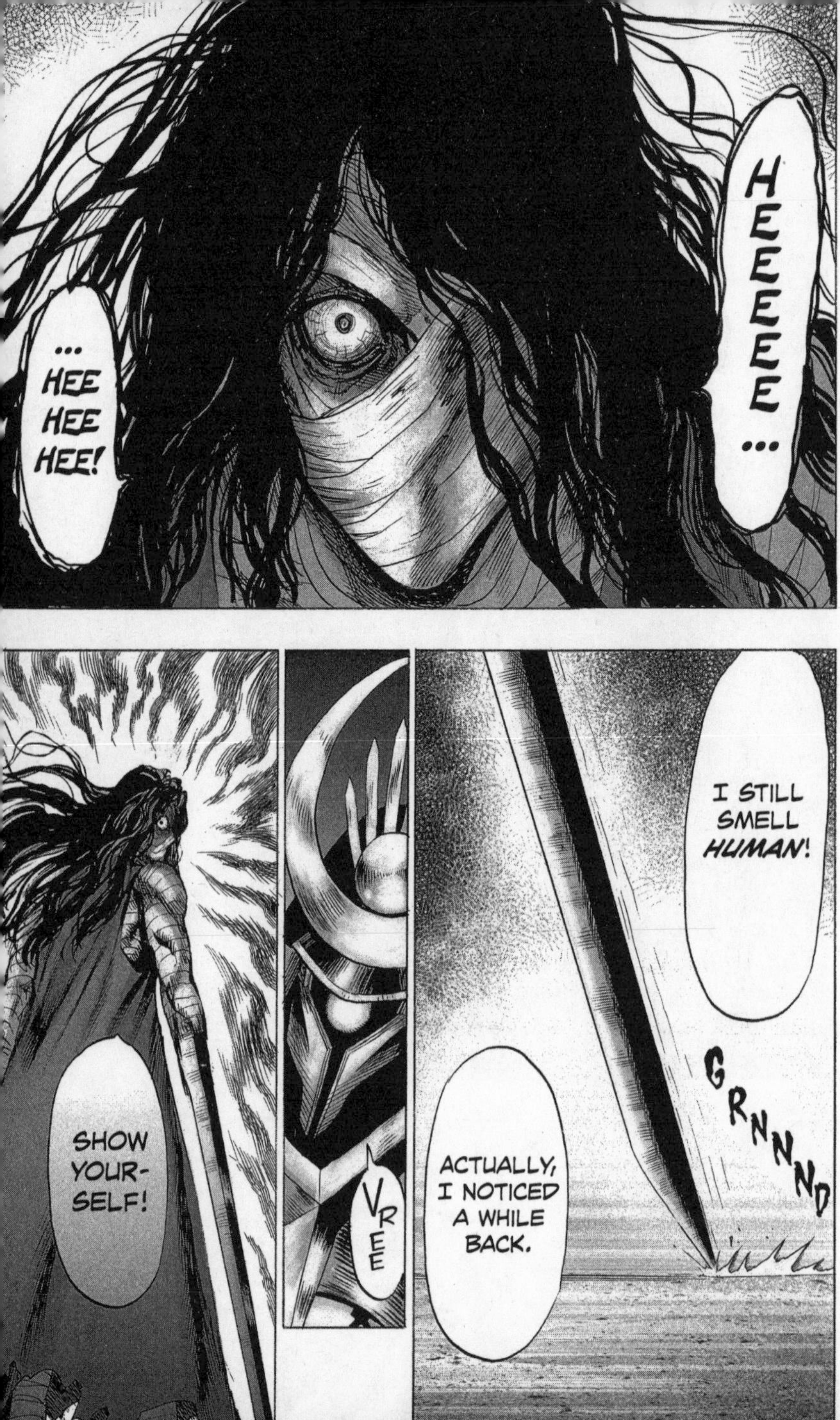
HEEEEE...
...HEE HEE HEE!
I STILL SMELL *HUMAN*!
GRNNND
ACTUALLY, I NOTICED A WHILE BACK.
VREE
SHOW YOURSELF!

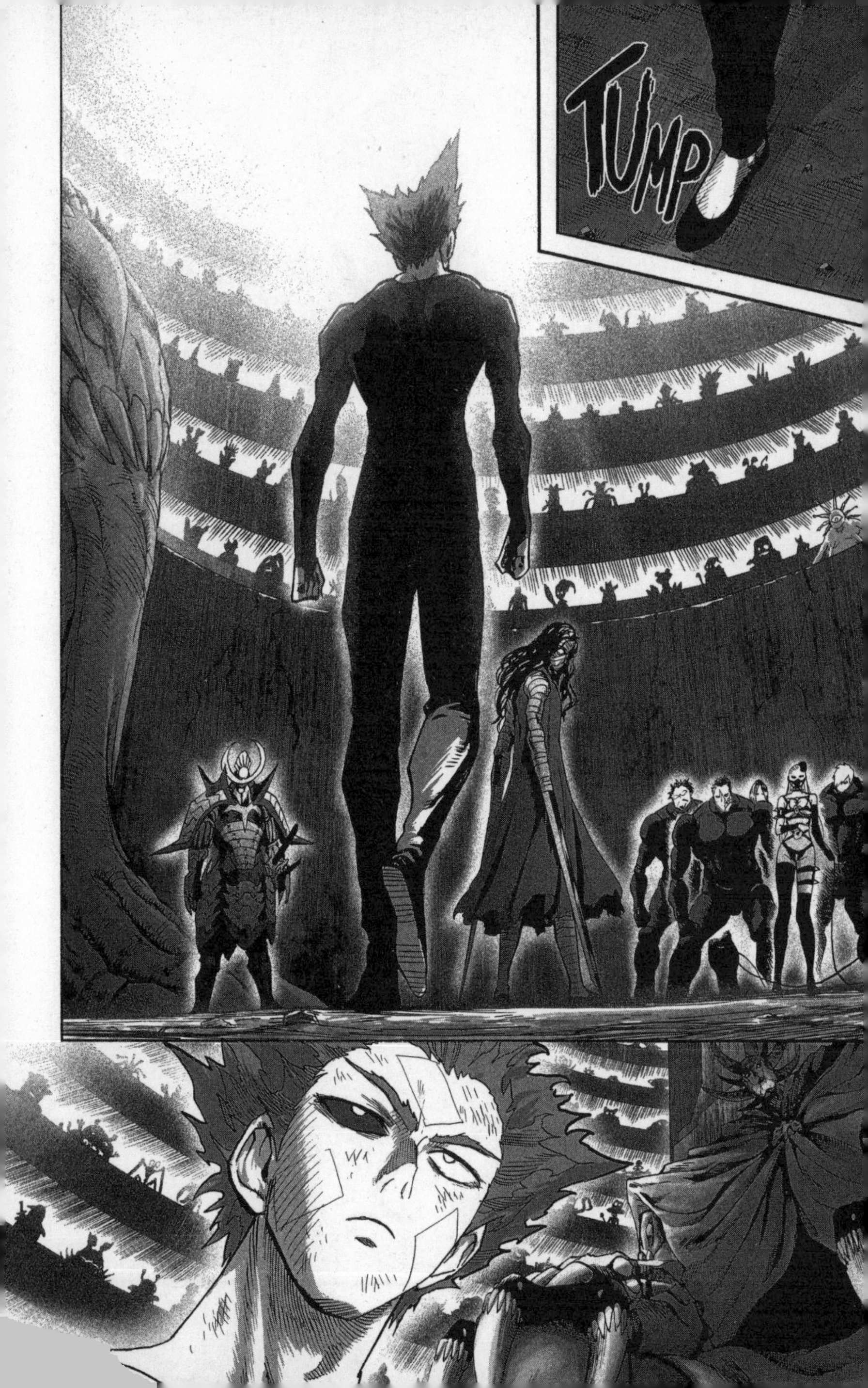
TUMP

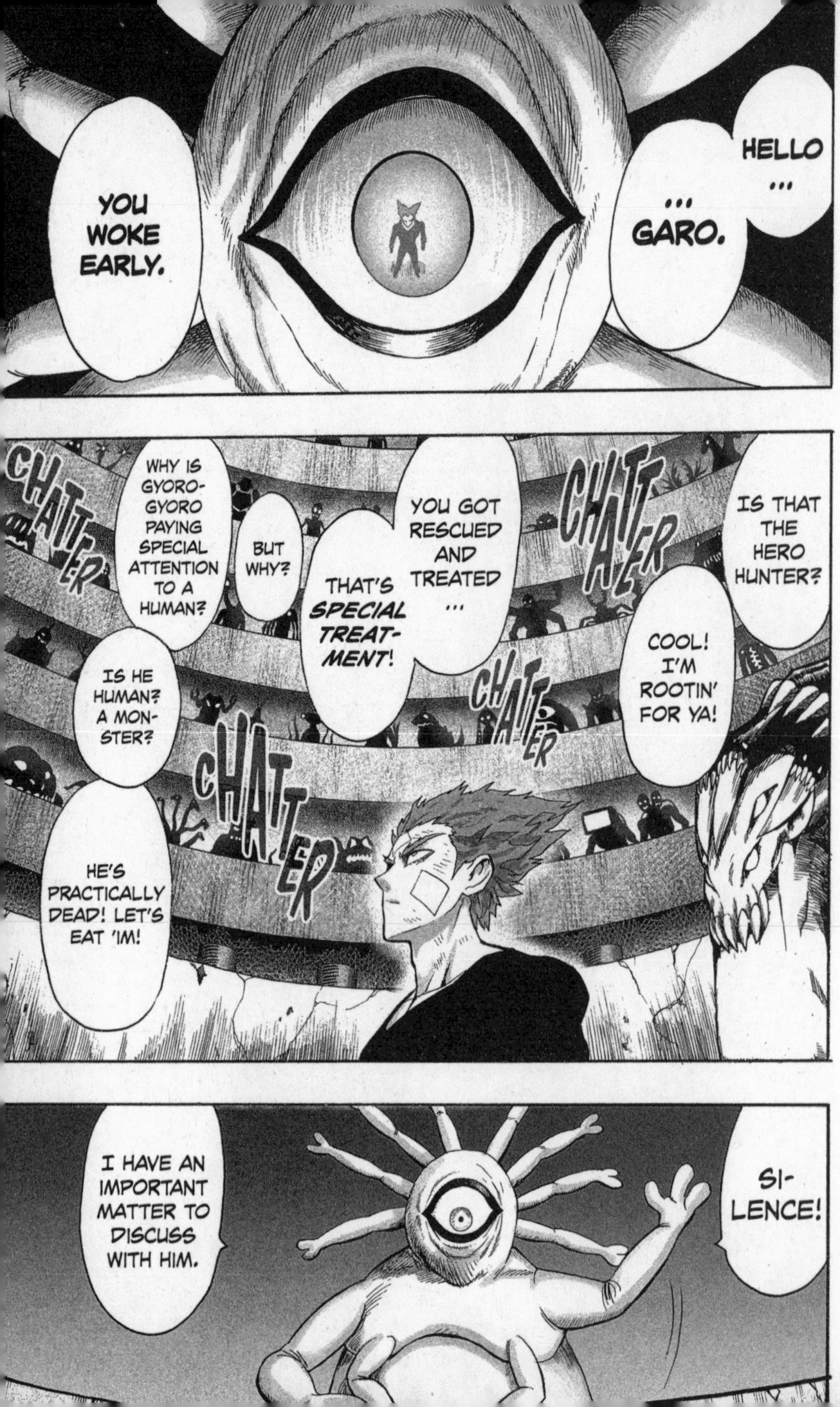
HELLO ... ... GARO.
YOU WOKE EARLY.
IS THAT THE HERO HUNTER?
CHATTER
COOL! I'M ROOTIN' FOR YA!
CHATTER
YOU GOT RESCUED AND TREATED ...
THAT'S SPECIAL TREATMENT!
BUT WHY?
WHY IS GYORO-GYORO PAYING SPECIAL ATTENTION TO A HUMAN?
CHATTER
CHATTER
IS HE HUMAN? A MONSTER?
HE'S PRACTICALLY DEAD! LET'S EAT 'IM!
SI-LENCE!
I HAVE AN IMPORTANT MATTER TO DISCUSS WITH HIM.

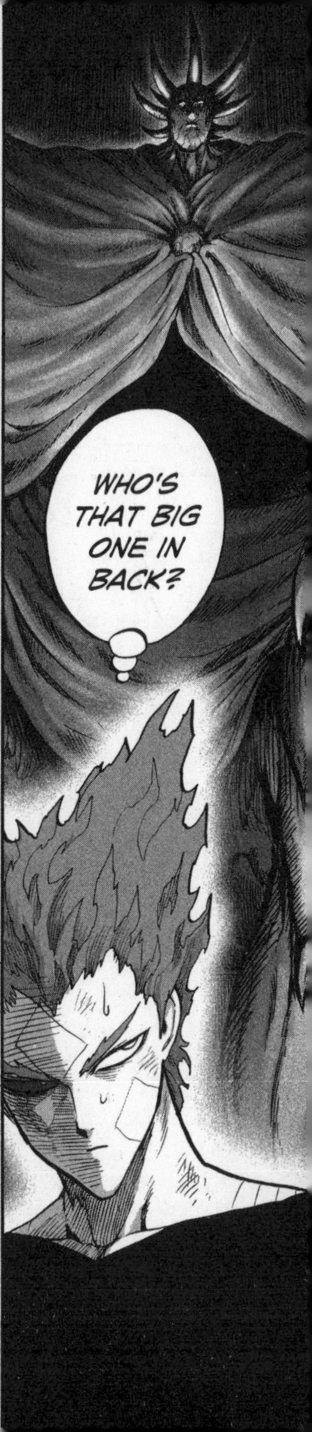
WHO'S THAT BIG ONE IN BACK?

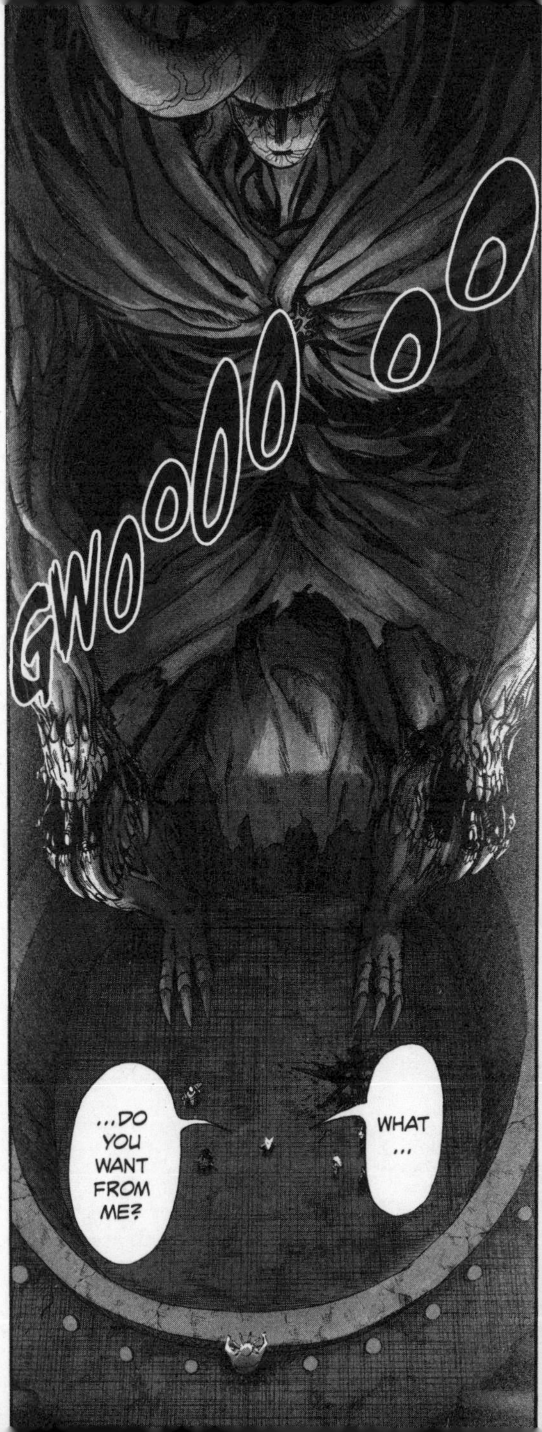
GWOOOOOOO
WHAT ...
...DO YOU WANT FROM ME?

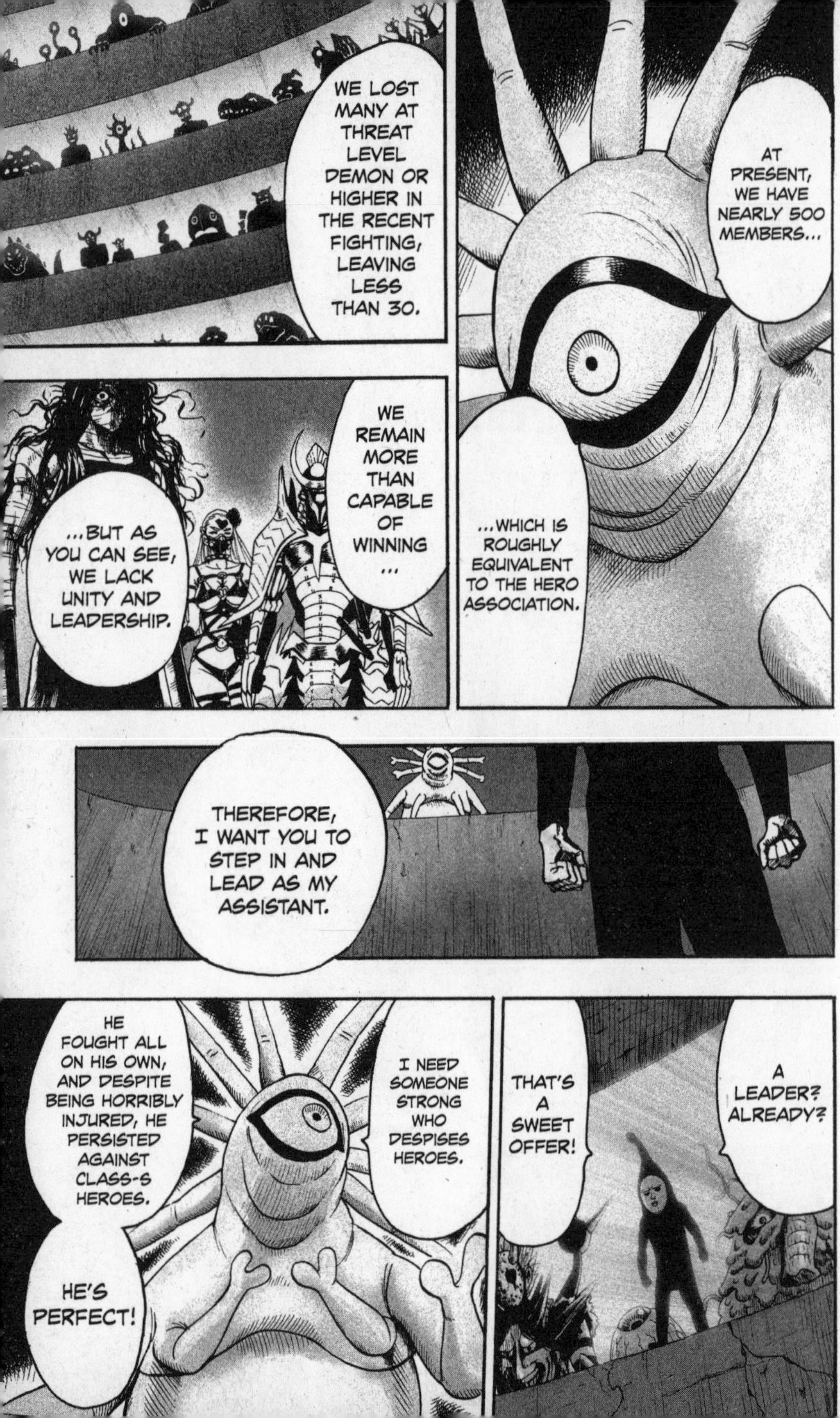
AT PRESENT, WE HAVE NEARLY 500 MEMBERS...
...WHICH IS ROUGHLY EQUIVALENT TO THE HERO ASSOCIATION.
WE LOST MANY AT THREAT LEVEL DEMON OR HIGHER IN THE RECENT FIGHTING, LEAVING LESS THAN 30.
WE REMAIN MORE THAN CAPABLE OF WINNING...
...BUT AS YOU CAN SEE, WE LACK UNITY AND LEADERSHIP.
THEREFORE, I WANT YOU TO STEP IN AND LEAD AS MY ASSISTANT.
A LEADER? ALREADY?
THAT'S A SWEET OFFER!
I NEED SOMEONE STRONG WHO DESPISES HEROES.
HE FOUGHT ALL ON HIS OWN, AND DESPITE BEING HORRIBLY INJURED, HE PERSISTED AGAINST CLASS-S HEROES.
HE'S PERFECT!

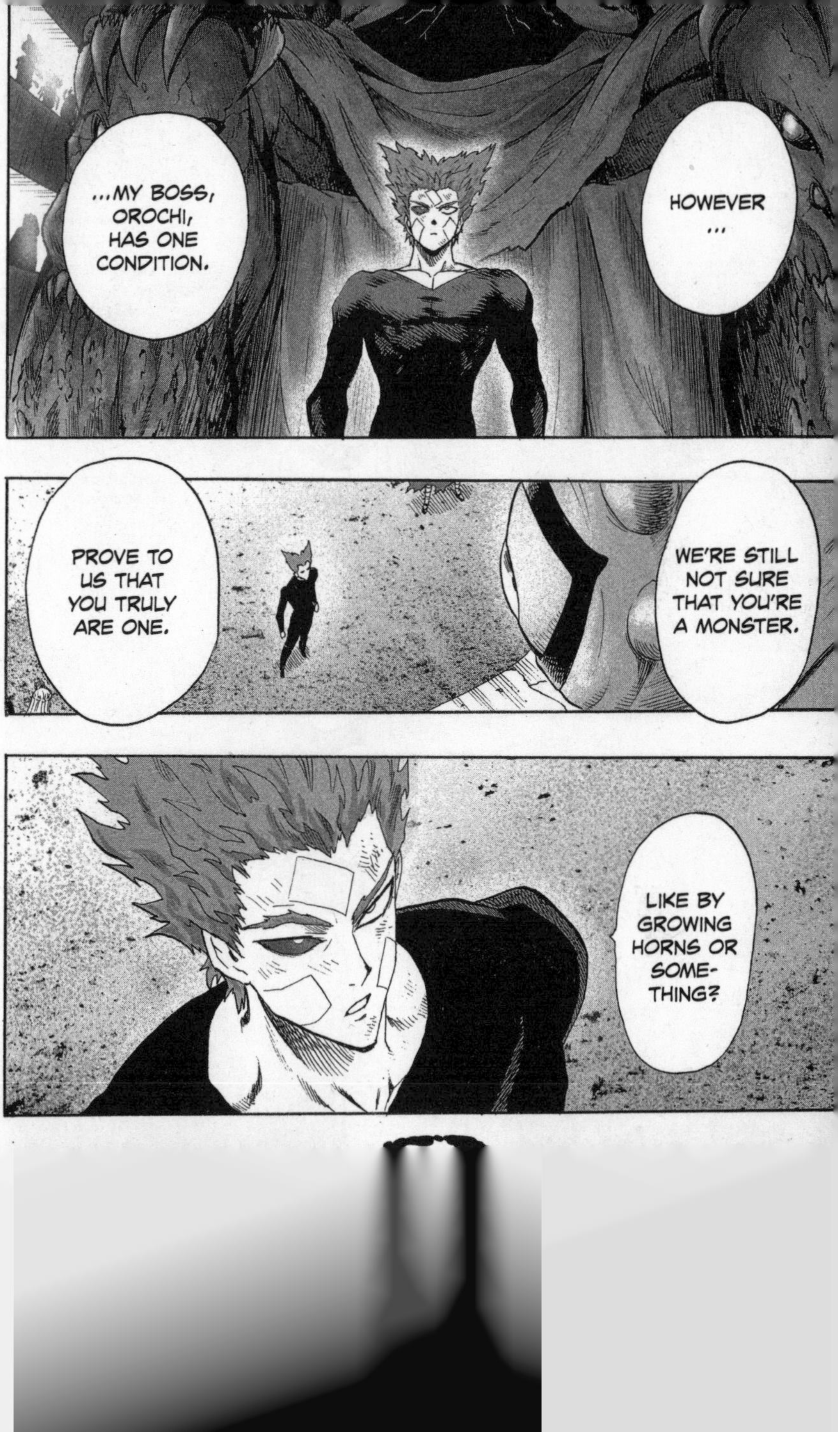
HOWEVER ...
...MY BOSS, OROCHI, HAS ONE CONDITION.
WE'RE STILL NOT SURE THAT YOU'RE A MONSTER.
PROVE TO US THAT YOU TRULY ARE ONE.
LIKE BY GROWING HORNS OR SOME-THING?

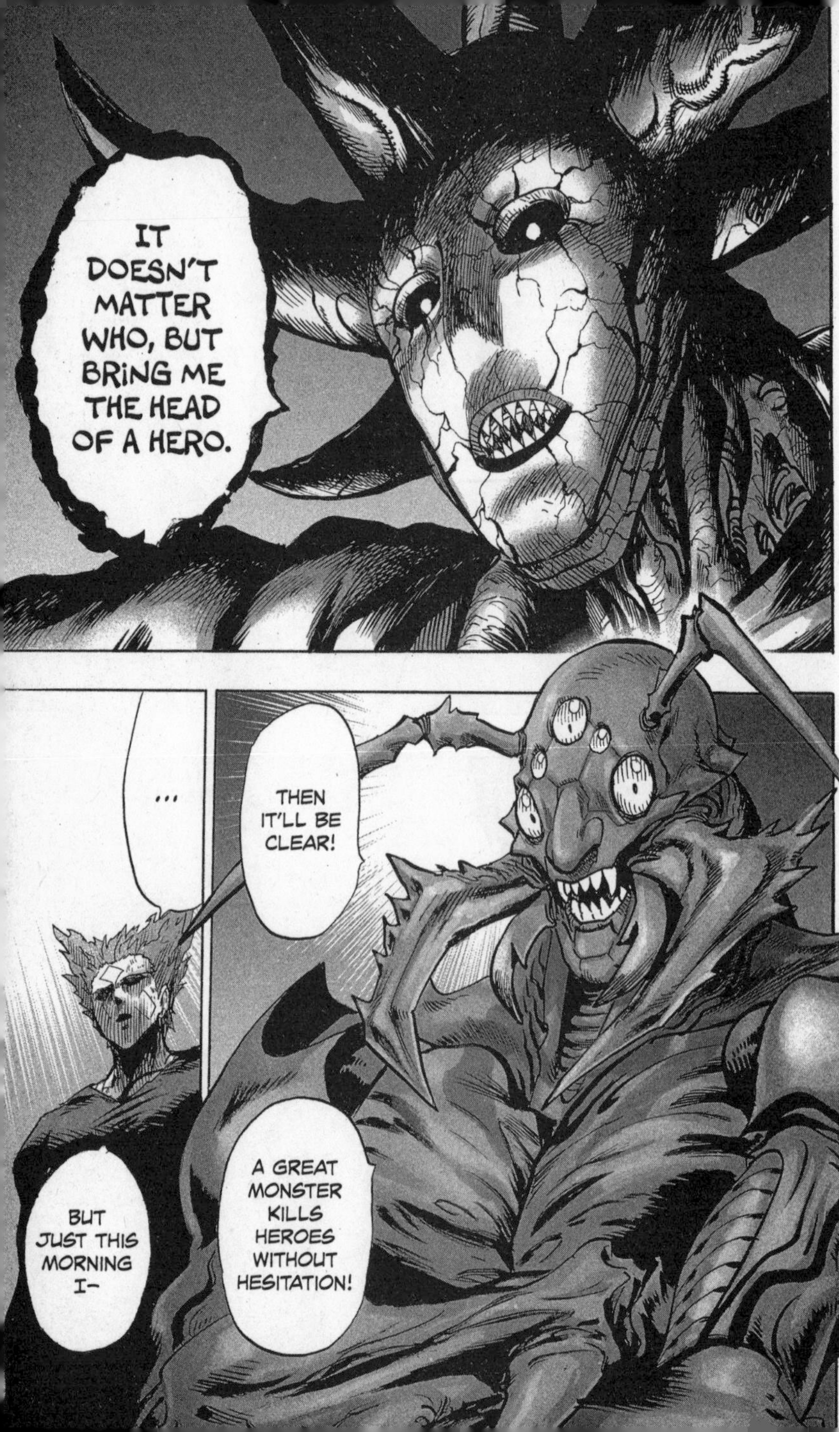
IT DOESN'T MATTER WHO, BUT BRING ME THE HEAD OF A HERO.
THEN IT'LL BE CLEAR!
A GREAT MONSTER KILLS HEROES WITHOUT HESITATION!
...
BUT JUST THIS MORNING I—

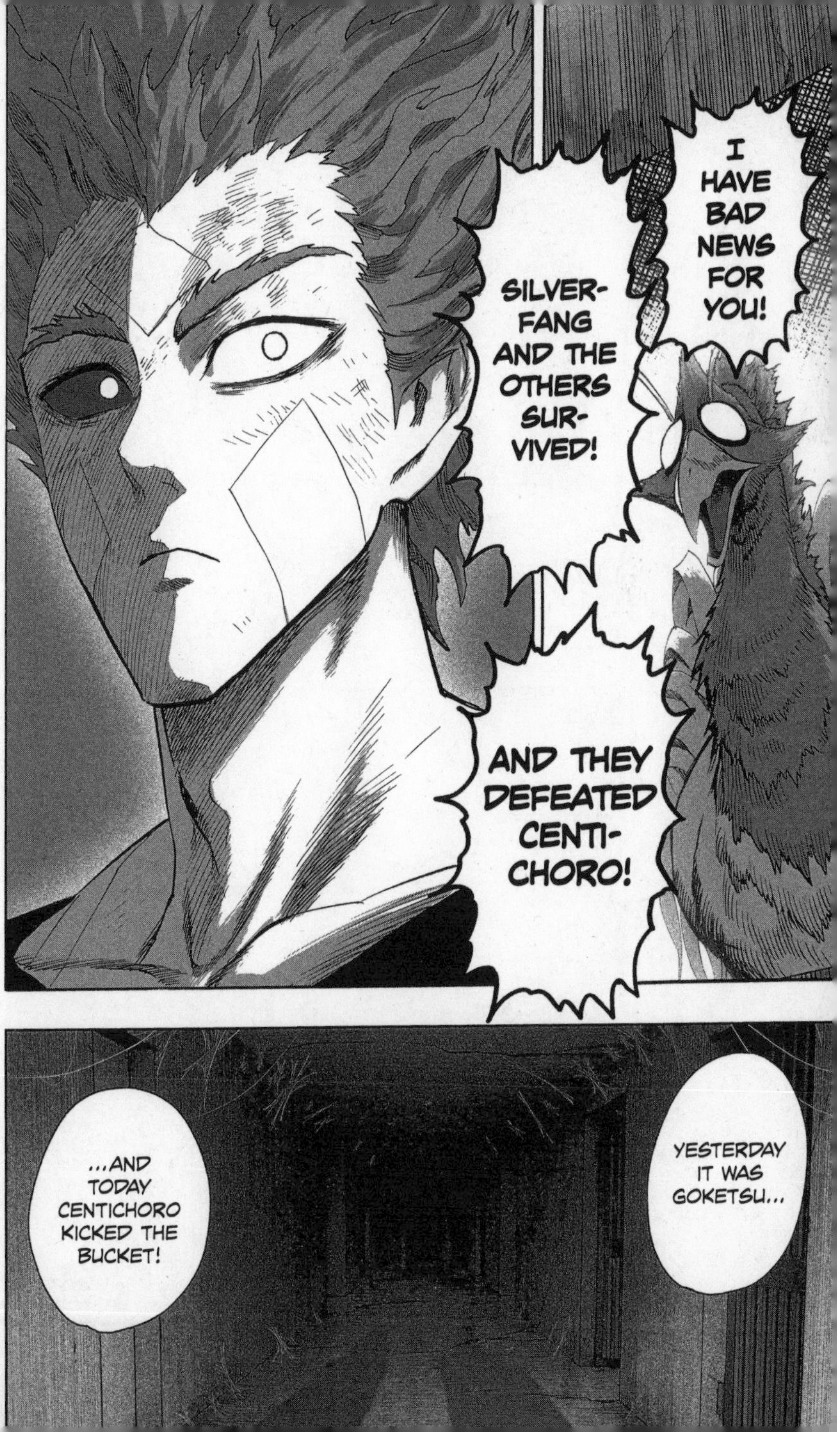
I HAVE BAD NEWS FOR YOU!
SILVER-FANG AND THE OTHERS SUR-VIVED!
AND THEY DEFEATED CENTI-CHORO!
YESTERDAY IT WAS GOKETSU...
...AND TODAY CENTICHORO KICKED THE BUCKET!

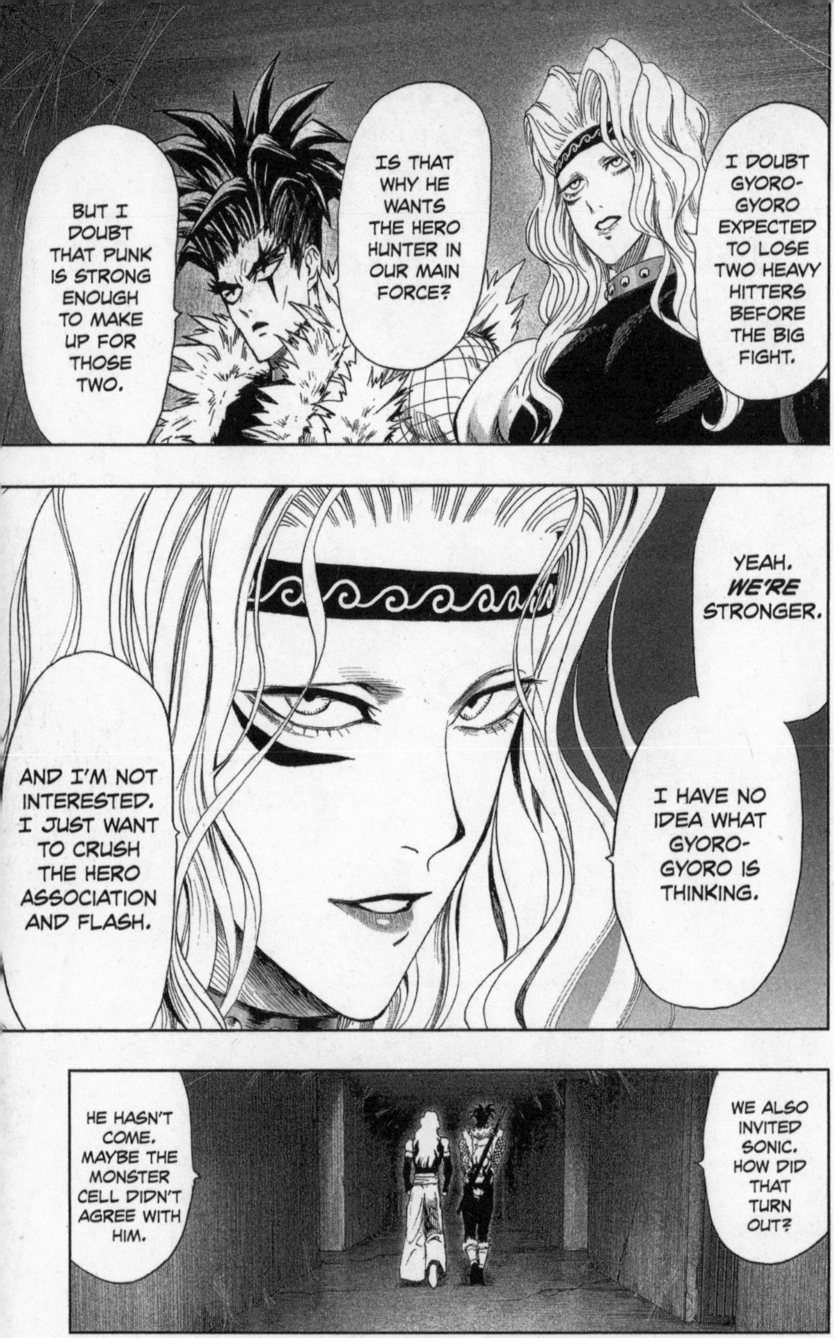
I DOUBT GYORO-GYORO EXPECTED TO LOSE TWO HEAVY HITTERS BEFORE THE BIG FIGHT.
IS THAT WHY HE WANTS THE HERO HUNTER IN OUR MAIN FORCE?
BUT I DOUBT THAT PUNK IS STRONG ENOUGH TO MAKE UP FOR THOSE TWO.
YEAH. *WE'RE* STRONGER.
I HAVE NO IDEA WHAT GYORO-GYORO IS THINKING.
AND I'M NOT INTERESTED. I JUST WANT TO CRUSH THE HERO ASSOCIATION AND FLASH.
WE ALSO INVITED SONIC. HOW DID THAT TURN OUT?
HE HASN'T COME. MAYBE THE MONSTER CELL DIDN'T AGREE WITH HIM.

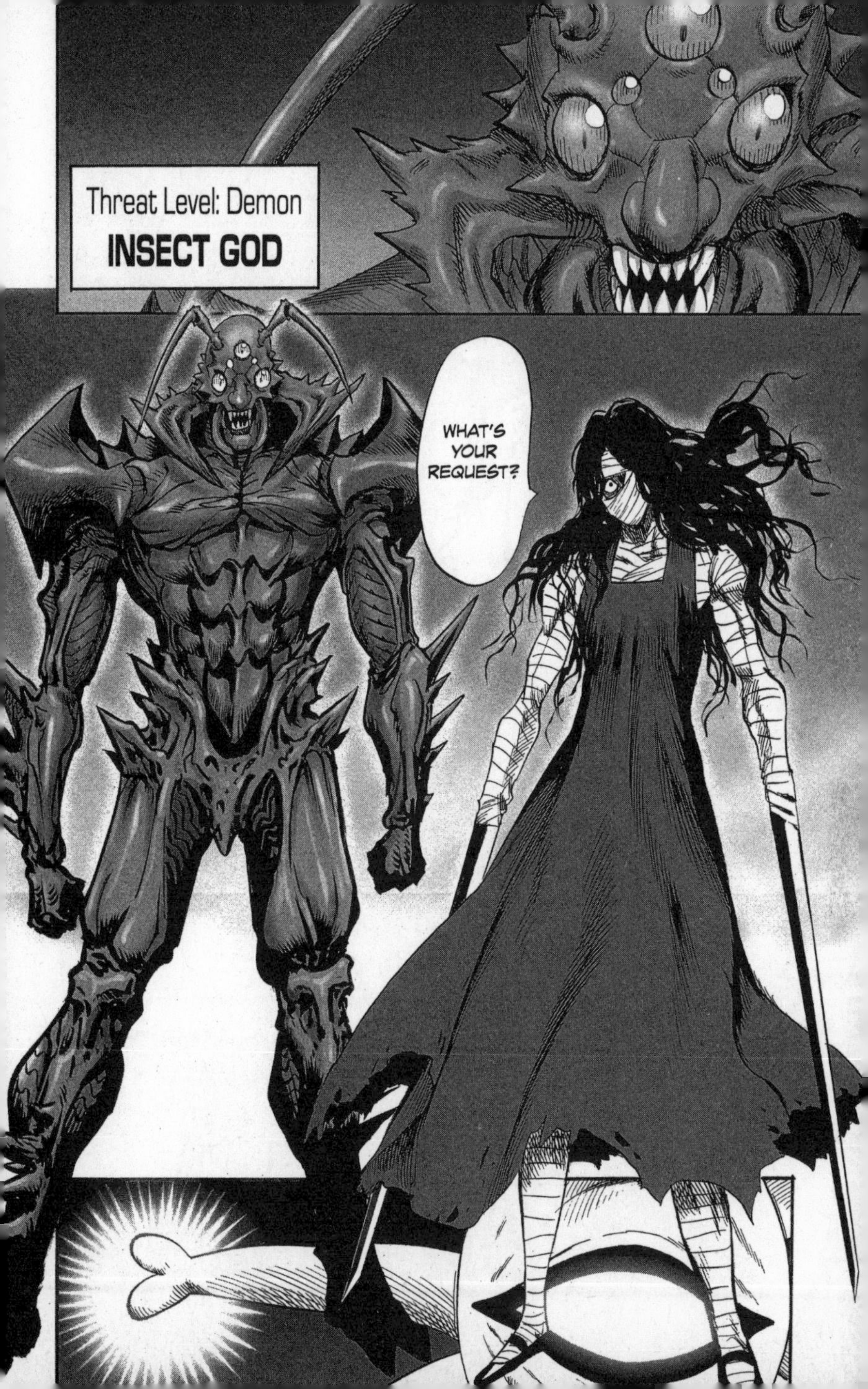
Threat Level: Demon
INSECT GOD
WHAT'S YOUR REQUEST?

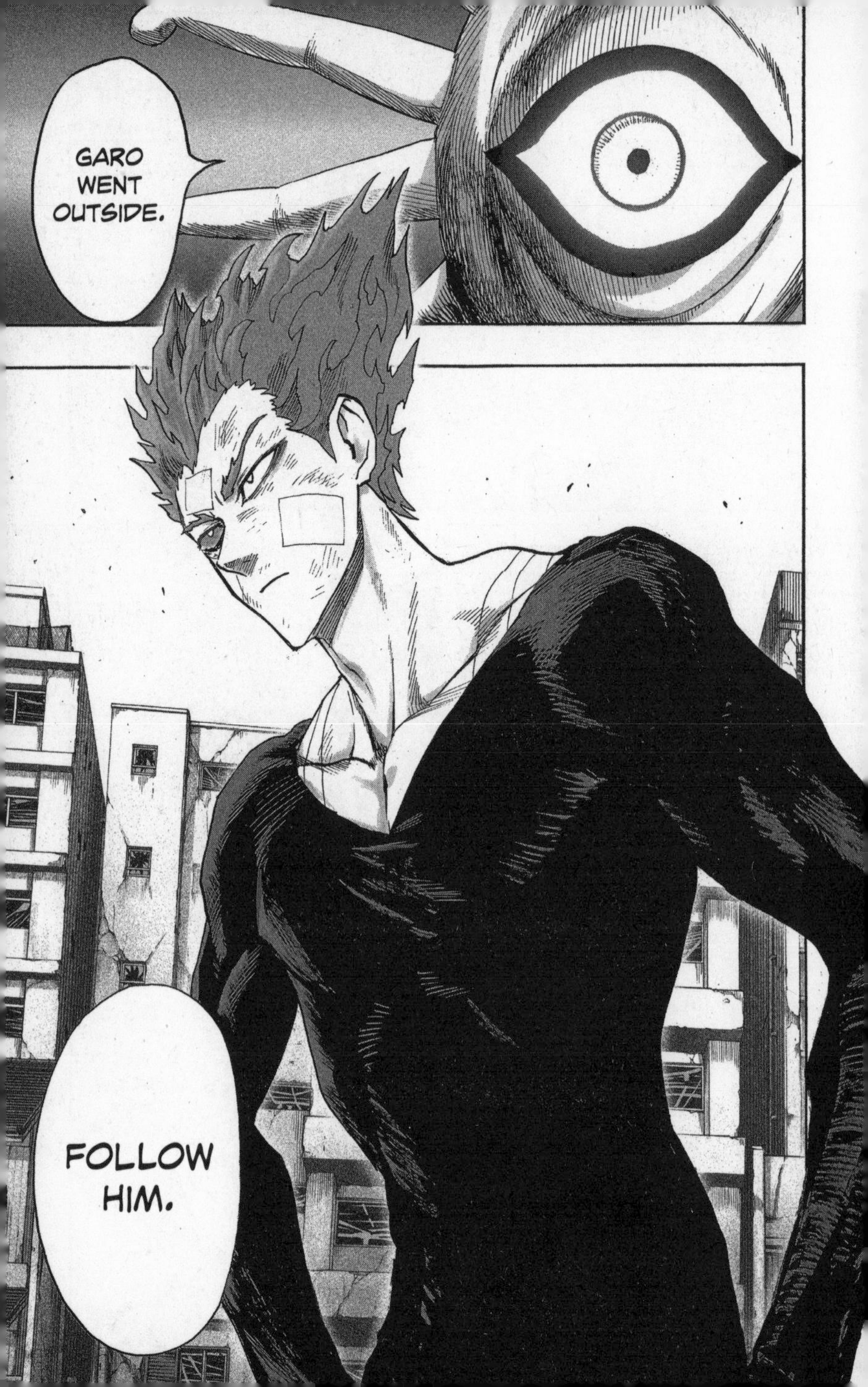
GARO WENT OUTSIDE.
FOLLOW HIM.

BONUS MANGA: CONFIDENCE

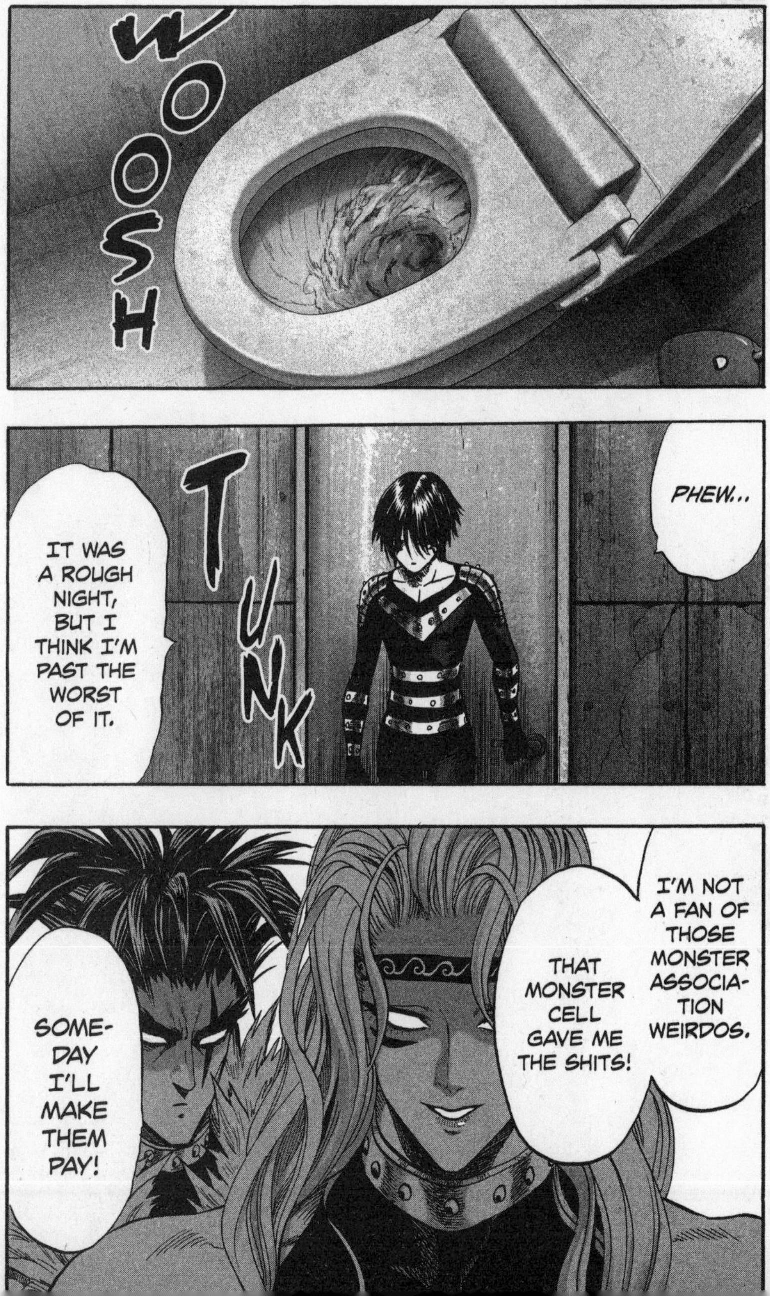
WOOSH
PHEW...
TUNK
IT WAS A ROUGH NIGHT, BUT I THINK I'M PAST THE WORST OF IT.
I'M NOT A FAN OF THOSE MONSTER ASSOCIA-TION WEIRDOS.
THAT MONSTER CELL GAVE ME THE SHITS!
SOME-DAY I'LL MAKE THEM PAY!

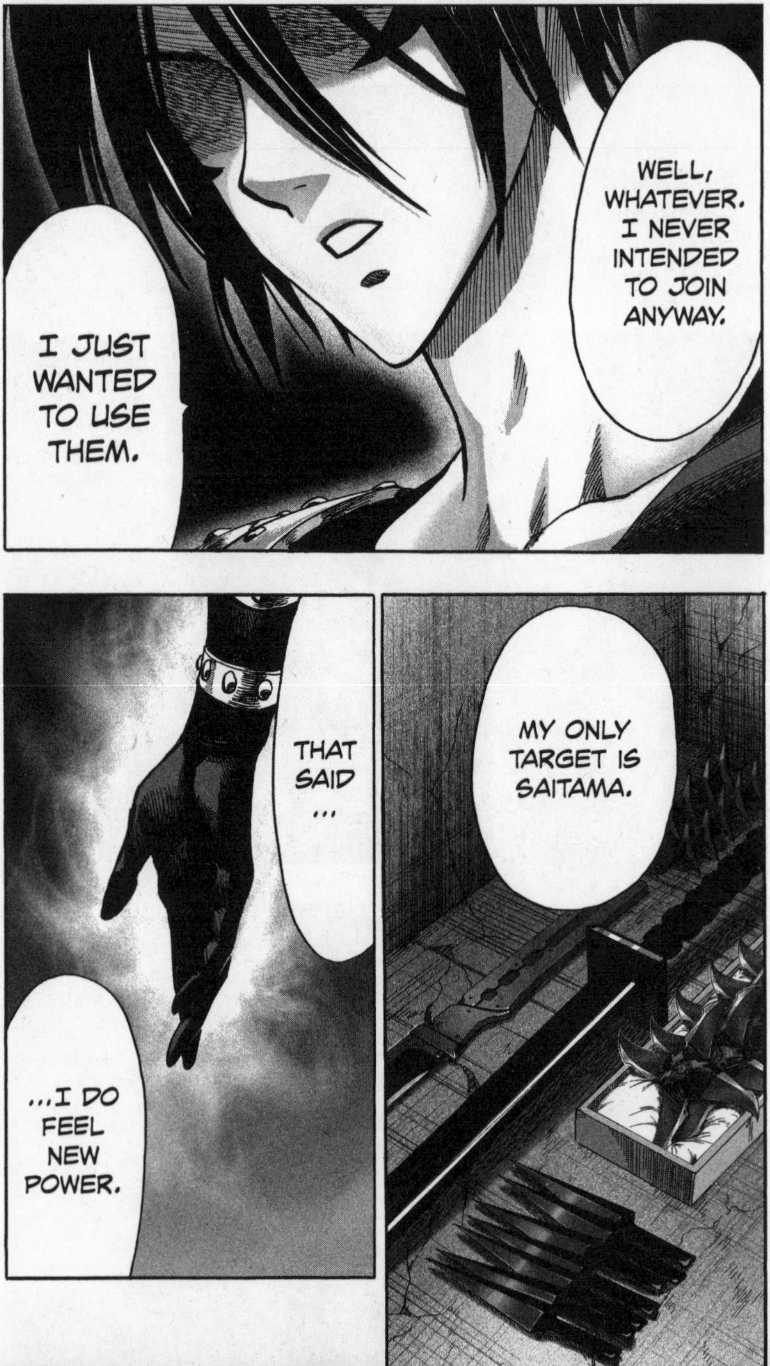
WELL, WHATEVER. I NEVER INTENDED TO JOIN ANYWAY.
I JUST WANTED TO USE THEM.
MY ONLY TARGET IS SAITAMA.
THAT SAID ...
...I DO FEEL NEW POWER.

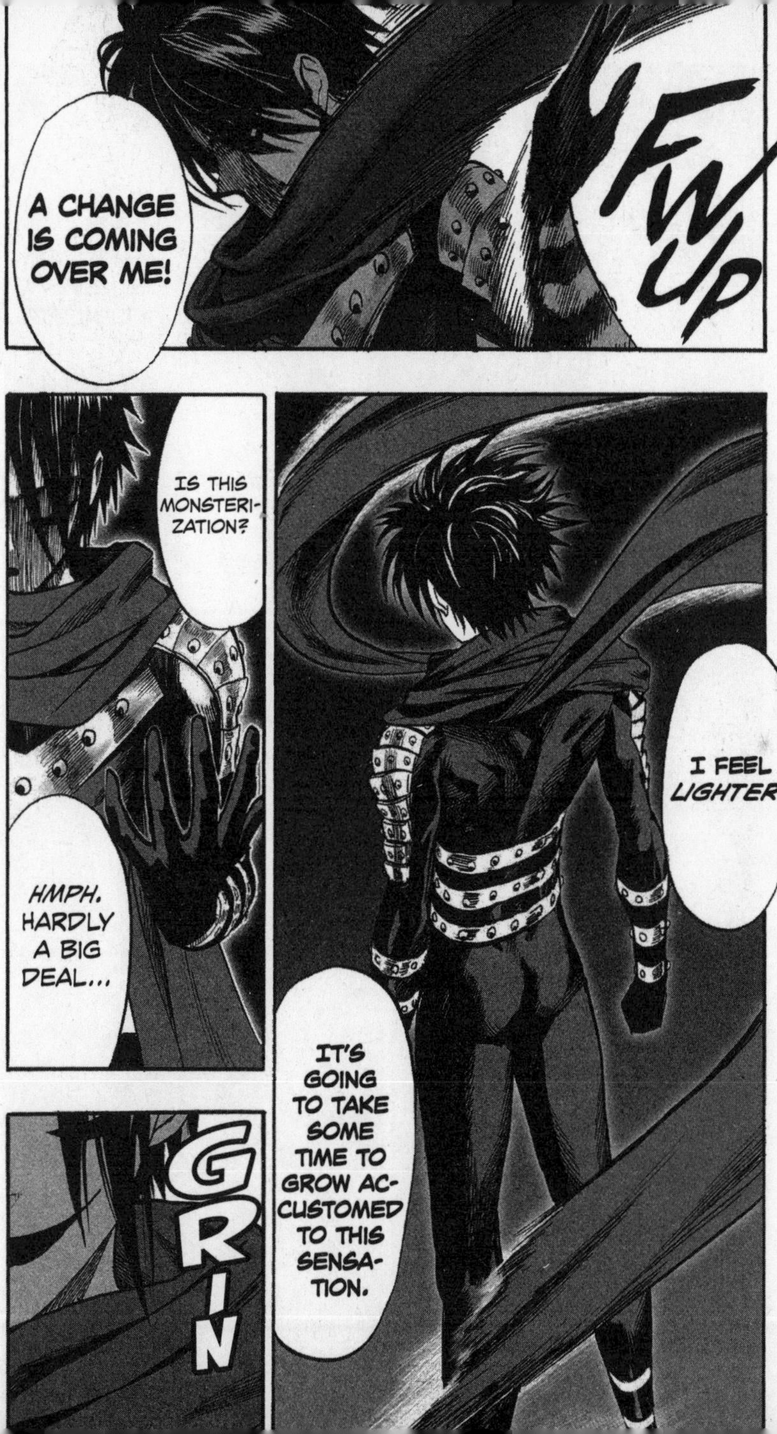
FWUP
A CHANGE IS COMING OVER ME!
I FEEL LIGHTER!
IT'S GOING TO TAKE SOME TIME TO GROW ACCUSTOMED TO THIS SENSATION.
IS THIS MONSTERIZATION?
HMPH. HARDLY A BIG DEAL...
GRIN

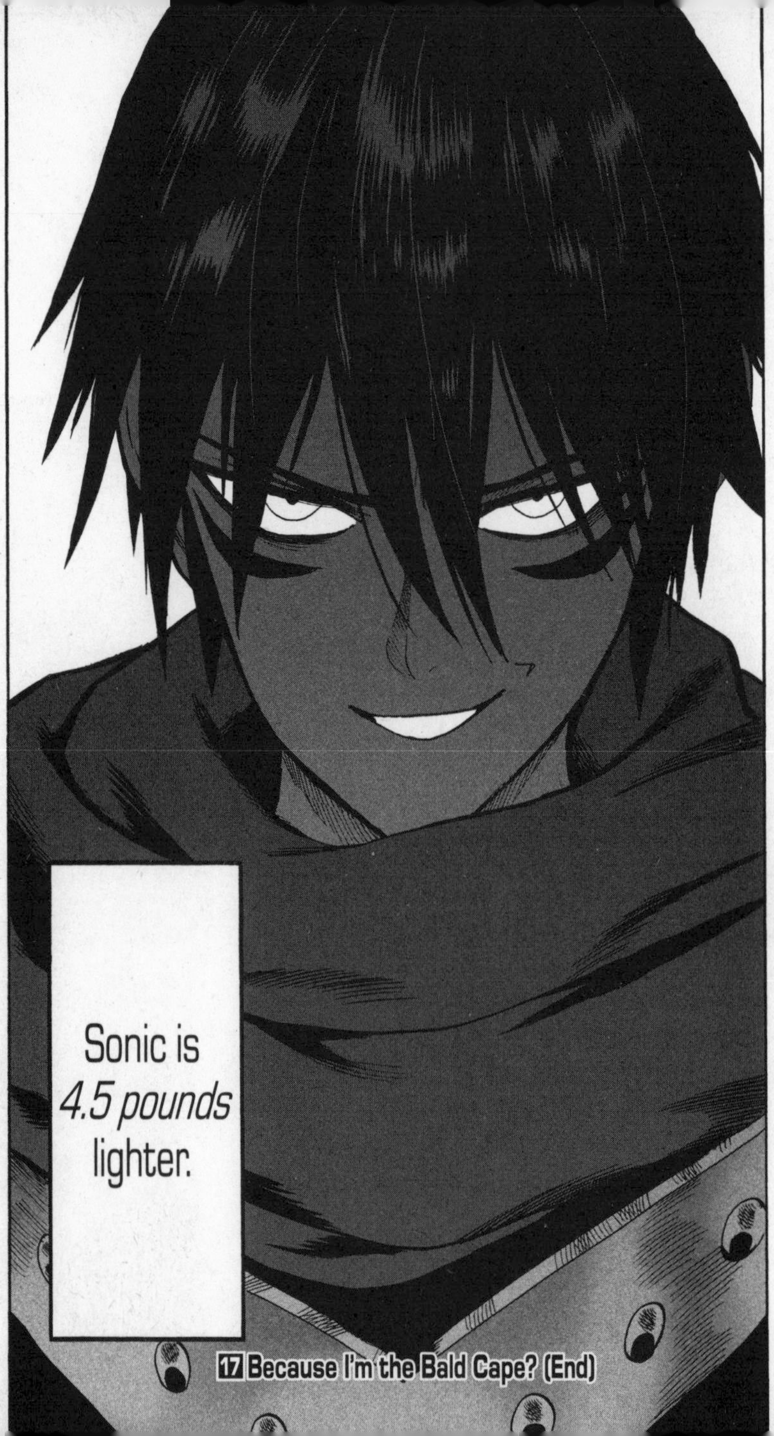
Sonic is *4.5 pounds* lighter.
17 Because I'm the Bald Cape? (End)

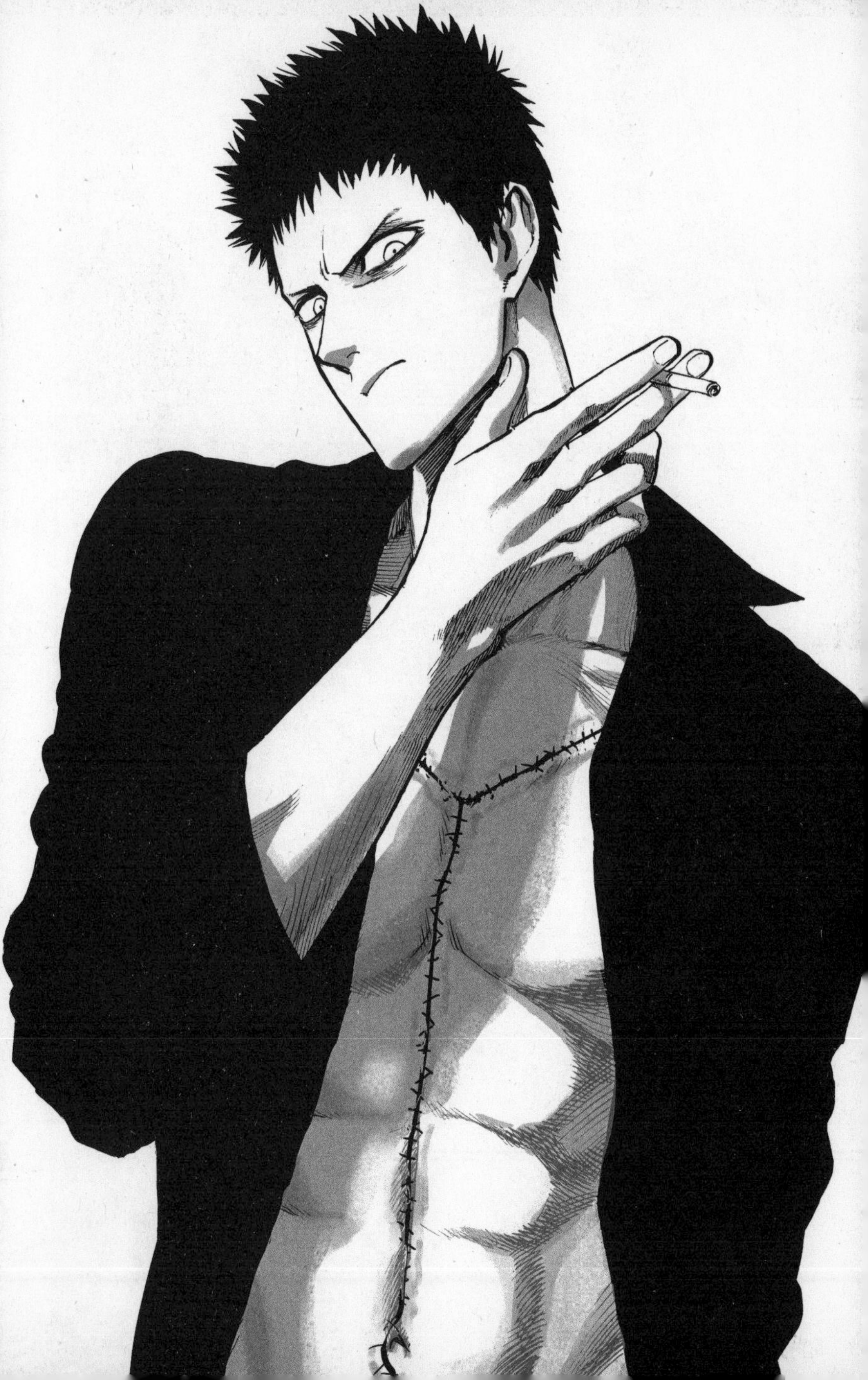